Useful Cinema

D1739274

USEFUL CINEMA

CHARLES R. ACLAND &
HAIDEE WASSON, EDITORS

DUKE UNIVERSITY PRESS Durham & London 2011

© 2011 Duke University Press
All rights reserved.

Printed in the United States of America on acid-free paper ∞
Designed by Jennifer Hill
Typeset in Arno Pro by Tseng Information Systems, Inc.

Library of Congress Cataloging-in-Publication Data appear
on the last printed page of this book.

For Lillian Ava and Stella Lucy

CONTENTS

ix Acknowledgments

1 Introduction: Utility and Cinema
Haidee Wasson and Charles R. Acland

1 CELLULOID CLASSROOMS

17 "What a Power for Education!":
The Cinema and Sites of Learning in the 1930s
Eric Smoodin

34 "We Can See Ourselves as Others See Us":
Women Workers and Western Union's Training
Films in the 1920s
Stephen Groening

59 Hollywood's Educators:
Mark May and Teaching Film Custodians
Charles R. Acland

81 UNESCO, Film, and Education:
Mediating Postwar Paradigms of Communication
Zoë Druick

103   Health Films, Cold War, and the Production
      of Patriotic Audiences: *The Body Fights Bacteria* (1948)
      Kirsten Ostherr

2   CIVIC CIRCUITS

125   Projecting the Promise of 16mm, 1935–45
      Gregory A. Waller
149   A History Long Overdue: The Public Library and Motion Pictures
      Jennifer Horne
178   Big, Fast Museums / Small, Slow Movies:
      Film, Scale, and the Art Museum
      Haidee Wasson
205   Pastoral Exhibition: The YMCA Motion Picture Bureau
      and the Transition to 16mm, 1928–39
      Ronald Walter Greene
230   "A Moving Picture of the Heavens":
      The Planetarium Space Show as Useful Cinema
      Alison Griffiths

3   MAKING USEFUL FILMS

263   Double Vision: World War II, Racial Uplift, and the
      All-American Newsreel's Pedagogical Address
      Joseph Clark
289   Mechanical Craftsmanship: Amateurs Making Practical Films
      Charles Tepperman
315   Experimental Film as Useless Cinema
      Michael Zryd

337   Filmography
343   Bibliography
365   About the Contributors
369   Index

ACKNOWLEDGMENTS

This book grew from a workshop on functional uses of cinema, held at Concordia University, Montreal, in August 2006. It was a lively event, and all participants helped us formulate the organization and structure of the book that followed. We would especially like to recognize the contributions of William Boddy, Lee Grieveson, Barbara Klinger, Mark Langer, Anna McCarthy, Janine Marchessault, Christine Ramsay, and Pierre Véronneau. Thanks are also due to Bill Buxton, Bruno Cornellier, Amelie Hastie, Jonathan Kahana, Martin Lefebvre, and Carrie Rentschler.

We have been fortunate in having extraordinary research and editorial assistance during the production of this book. In this respect, we owe much gratitude to Peter Lester, Zoë Constantinides, Matthew Ogonoski, and Heather Macdougall.

Duke University Press provided determined support from beginning to end. We are grateful to our anonymous readers who offered detailed and probing questions, as well as astute commentary. This project also benefited from assistance and encouragement supplied by Duke's expert editorial and production team, including Ken Wissoker, Fred Kameny, and Leigh Barnwell.

Financial aid came from the Social Science and Humanities Research Council of Canada (Standard Research Grant and Scholarly Workshop Grant programs), the Concordia University Research Chair in Communication Studies Fund, and the Advanced Research Team in the History and Epistemology of Moving Image Studies, funded by Quebec's Fonds de recherche sur la société et la culture.

Haidee Wasson and Charles R. Acland

M ovies seem to appear everywhere: the palm of the
hand, the top of a desk, the façade of a building. No
longer an evening's entertainment — the reigning definition
of cinema for the better part of the twentieth century —
movies are now common modes of personal expression,
diversified global business strategies, and grand architectural monuments. From iPhone to Imax, from blog inserts
to Jumbotrons, moving images serve an expanding range
of corporate, governmental, rhetorical, and aesthetic functions. More than this, they are integral to our experience
of institutional and everyday life. While we knowingly and
unknowingly, happily and critically, live with this current
common sense, recorded motion and sound was not always
this ubiquitous. Clearly, we know too little about the formative precursors to this current situation of saturation and
ubiquity. What might those antecedents tell us about our
present context? How did moving images become a foundational building block for the way so much of the post-
industrial world looks and operates?

    To explore these questions, we must begin by acknowledging that, far from unique to our age of technological excess, moving images circulated widely, serving multiple functions from the earliest years of the twentieth century. Within this dispersed technological, aesthetic, and cultural phenomena cinema has played an important role. Movies have long operated as mobile and flexible cultural materials, making and remaking the concrete and seemingly immaterial worlds we inhabit. Film technologies—screens, projectors, and cameras—were long ago integrated into a surprising range of spaces and situations, shaping the aesthetics as well as the display of and engagement with motion pictures. And these places, beyond conventionally defined movie theaters, included classrooms, factories, museums, community halls, and modes of transportation like trains, planes, and ships; each has been a key site for the formation and reformation of cinema itself. In such screening contexts, people encountered particular genres including industrial, educational, training, advertising, adult, and home movies, as well as Hollywood, foreign, and art films. And in those settings, people found a convergence of film gauges, projectors, and screens, as well as other media, including radio, newspapers, magazines, and photographs. Varied spaces, particular film types, and hybrid technological forms together created a very different view to the forms and functions of what we call cinema.

To be sure, the world of public commercial entertainment has long had an important place as a ritualized part of popular commune and the naturalization of moving images in modern life. But there was this other cinema, one defined by film's ability to transform unlikely spaces, convey ideas, convince individuals, and produce subjects in the service of public and private aims. This functional understanding of and investment in motion pictures helped to shape a certain common sense about cinema's place in a variety of cultural mandates, inestimably contributing to the status of moving images as both banal and extraordinary elements of everyday life and work. Indeed, whether measured in terms of numbers of films, size of audience, penetration of technologies, or amount of economic activity, the often-termed non-theatrical sector was substantial enough to be an enduring and stable parallel industry to the more spectacular realm of what we commonly think of as commercial film. The essays assembled for this volume ask how we conceptualize and assess the impact of this *other* cinema.

While extant scholarship on film generally focuses on its relationship to modern concepts of art and mass entertainment, this volume asserts that cinema has also been *useful*, at times involved more with functionality than with beauty, to employ the familiar Kantian dichotomy. As such, cinema has long been implicated in a broad range of cultural and institutional functions, from transforming mass education to fortifying suburban domestic ideals. Schools, businesses, and public agencies invested in celluloid and its diverse family of technologies in order to instruct, to sell, and to make or remake citizens. In other words, cameras, films, and projectors have been taken up and deployed variously—beyond questions of art and entertainment—in order to satisfy organizational demands and objectives, that is, *to do something* in particular. Accordingly, cinema has been influential upon a modern understanding of culture's utility or what Tony Bennett calls "useful culture."[1] For Bennett, following certain strains of Michel Foucault's work, culture is productively conceptualized as an institutional tool, and as a set of relations and things whose appearance is intimately linked, and perhaps secondary, to their function. Building on this insight, critical policy studies have advanced analyses of the governmental management of culture.[2] Culture, in this respect, shapes debates, moves populations, directs capital, furthers authority, and ordains the self. Beginning with the concept of culture as "useful," this volume explores the history of cinema as one element of a more generalized useful culture. More specifically, our authors conceptualize useful cinema as a body of films and technologies that perform tasks and serve as instruments in an ongoing struggle for aesthetic, social, and political capital.

Though still marginal in cinema studies, a growing body of research serves as the foundation for the examinations of the useful assembled in this volume. Important book-length studies have tilled this ground, including Vinzenz Hediger's and Patrick Vonderau's edited volume *Films That Work: Industrial Film and the Productivity of Media*, a book that focuses on industrial uses of media in Europe, and Peter Bloom's *French Colonial Documentary: Myths of Humanitarianism*, which offers exemplary research on colonialist agendas employing non-fiction film. Leading the way, documentary studies have kept our focus on the socio-institutional articulation and multiple impacts of the rhetoric of the image for years.[3] This book builds on the arguments made in these works, particularly Hediger's and Vonderau's emphasis on the specificities of context, examining films as constellations of "media, technology, forms of knowledge, discourse and social organization."[4] Where many works tend to root themselves in genre categories, ours contributes a broad theorization of the relations among film form, audiovisual technologies, and a range of institutional mandates and spaces.

We offer useful cinema as a provocative paradigm that is meant to be neither theoretically nor ideologically unidimensional. The concept of the useful frames a dispersed body of texts, contexts, and practices. It overlaps with, but is not equivalent to, similar terms such as "functional film," "educational film," "non-fictional film," and "non-theatrical film." We define useful cinema to include experimental films and a variety of didactic films that are fictional as well as non-fictional, narrative as well as non-narrative. The concept of useful cinema does not so much name a mode of production, a genre, or an exhibition venue as it identifies a disposition, an outlook, and an approach toward a medium on the part of institutions and institutional agents. In this way, useful cinema has as much to do with the maintenance and longevity of institutions seemingly unrelated to cinema as it does with cinema per se. For instance, the library's adoption of film was about building the better library and not building the better film, though a discourse of film betterment did, and does, exist. Even as institutions may extol the virtues of technological innovation and progressive change, at one level such actions help preserve and reproduce that institution. Film has long been used in this seemingly paradoxical sense: to both promote change and to resist it.

It is our contention that the expression "useful cinema" productively captures a dominant feature of cinema, one that has not figured prominently in the historiography of moving images to date. The category allows us to open up previously underexplored areas of inquiry that converge under the broader and established rubrics of non-theatrical exhibition, mobile technologies, and the long middle period of film history (roughly from the 1910s to the early 1980s). Using these intersecting rubrics in the organization of its material, our book has several objectives. First, with its focus on American case studies, the book expands directly the dominant understanding of American film history during these years. It does so by augmenting the standard narrative of Hollywood's rise and fall during the so-called classical period with a parallel narrative detailing robust expansion and growth.[5] The authors of the chapters in this book identify a film culture that coexisted with Hollywood during these years, and yet was sufficiently distinct from it to warrant very different production, distribution, and exhibition dynamics. Second, the book shows that concepts such as mobility, hybridity, and malleability are central and continuous throughout film history; they are not only germane to periods of instability or what are often termed the early and late periods of film history.[6] For instance, at mid-century, film technologies were taken for granted and broadly exploited as a mobile technological apparatus. Small-gauge projectors, to take one example, were specifically designed and sold to be highly adaptable to a range of spaces and compatible with a range of other audiovisual gadgets. This helped ensure their enduring place in diverse settings and their use in a range of applications beyond main street's movie theater. Lastly, this book is equally shaped by the recent surge of interest in neglected genres of cinema, including orphan, industrial, and educational films. In this area, the tireless agenda-setting enterprise of Rick Prelinger and Dan Streible to make precious materials available and to provide contexts for scholarly discussion warrants special acknowledgment. A core concern of this collection builds on this interest in primary and obscure film objects, linking them to the vast history of small and incidental movie theaters, specialized audiences, and subcultural formations. The book explores these films and their contexts, presuming strategies to influence minds, shape taste, and affect behaviors. All genres of cinema, including neglected ones such as the orphan or ephemeral film, are most fully revealed when subject to methods of analysis that consider institutional location and deployment, in addition to aesthetic and formal analysis.

Understanding the diverse and varied pockets of moving images and cultures has not been well-assisted by film studies itself, an academic discipline that initially marshaled ideas germane to literary study, art history, and linguistics to better understand film as a distinct and distinguished aesthetic phenomenon. Yet, partly in response to the dramatic and recent changes in moving-image culture over the last two decades, scholarly investigation of previously marginal forms of cinema has invigorated the discipline. With the ascendance of digital technologies and the proliferation of distribution and display modes, the object of film inquiry has been subject to lively debate. Augmenting film scholarship with insights from cultural and media studies, the field now addresses all manners of moving-image texts and contexts, from DVD box-sets of entire television seasons to fans of industrial film clips from the early twentieth century. Modes of analysis have thus also multiplied. Many studies of cinema now rely on the assertion that cultural texts should be more broadly conceived as phenomena intertwined with the politics of public life and modern institutions; matters concerning gender, class, race, sexuality, and social conduct are also brought to the fore.[7] These insights are actively employed throughout this volume. Scholars who have shown that cinema was deployed early on across a range of technologies and urban spaces, rife with polyglot possibility for all varieties of change, have been particularly influential. The work of Vanessa Schwartz, Rick Altman, Tom Gunning, Lee Grieveson, and Anne Friedberg have provided key signposts for us with their resounding push to conceptualize cinema as a kind of expansive yet negotiated technology, integral to a range of homeostatic as well as dynamic social and intellectual paradigms.[8]

Our book builds on studies that have destabilized dominant conventions and practices of cinema history, many of them focused on early cinema. It expands previous insights, applying them to that loosely defined middle period of American film history. The essays here challenge the assumption that this period involved merely a stabilization of the cinematic apparatus, demonstrating that our still dominant definition of cinema as a theatrical mode has long coexisted with multiple and widespread manifestations of moving-image culture.[9] In this respect, among the many gauges (such as 28mm, 9.5mm, and 8mm) relevant for understanding cinema beyond the commercial movie theater, 16mm, introduced in 1923, held a particularly important place in American culture.[10] Thus, given the years and geography most prominently treated here, 16mm and celluloid figure strongly in this volume, although our authors are mindful of the fact that their studies run parallel to other developments in film and related media, including television. Indeed, collectively our contributors show a remarkable diversification and splintering of the technologies, spaces, and uses of moving images, ones that precede the VCR, the World Wide Web, and the digital revolution. In the end, this book demonstrates that useful cinema became an integral element of everyday life throughout mid-century continuing into the present day.

Historiographically, this book participates in several ongoing debates. It rejects the strain of current work heralding the revolutionary aspects of new media as producing transformed bodies, spaces, and aesthetic practice in unprecedented ways. Our authors approach the history of emergent technology and culture to assess the manners in which the new and the old are intimate consorts.[11] As important as the aforementioned dispersal of moving images has been for some recent film historiography and for this book—identifying new audiences and new functions of cinema—it is equally important, our authors claim, to identify cinema's reconsolidation in identifiable institutions that sought to multiply film publics but also often to assert authority over these publics and their own image. The chapters here demonstrate therefore that cinema has been actively used to refigure select spaces as both a respite from and an encounter with public and private mandates. This has entailed crafting cinema into a tool that is useful, a tool that makes, persuades, instructs, demonstrates, and *does* something. Such functions include creating the captive audiences and compulsory spectatorship of classroom and training venues, and also the voluntary and edifying gatherings of museums, planetariums, and public libraries.[12]

This book assembles research grounded in specific institutions, focused on their relation to wider debates about vision, aesthetics, power, and modernity. This is not a speculative or metaphoric work on the idea of history or representations of functionality. Included here is materialist historical research that identifies concrete examples, supports claims with original archival research, and problematizes core theoretical concepts based upon findings. Authors demonstrate and explore how cultural technologies are complex systems and ways of knowing that have specificity in history and across social contexts. Significantly, this research treats a wide spectrum of institutions, from local libraries to the United Nations Educational, Scientific and Cultural Organization (UNESCO), from amateur film clubs to industrial film producers, and from public schools to labor training programs.

The chapters in part I, "Celluloid Classrooms," investigate the appropriation of film for educational programs. Eric Smoodin studies the use of both popular Hollywood and educational films in schools during the 1930s. He situates these films and their pedagogical use carefully within a range of phenomena: theories and practices of learning, new ideas about the child, the growth of visual and media education, the active role of the film industry, highly varied local experiments, and the growth of national networks. Smoodin demonstrates that classroom film use was seen as a phase in modernizing the American classroom, equipping classrooms with new technologies and tapping the wide appeal of leisure activities to enhance learning. In practice, watching films was harnessed to many activities (discussion, reenactment, sewing, arts, and crafts) and to many organizations inside and outside of schools (film clubs, movie theaters, and community groups). Notably, he argues, the lessons were as often about operating within bureaucratic structures and modern business procedure, as they were about aesthetics, morality, or character education.

Using Western Union as a case study, Stephen Groening examines the industrial uses to which films were put primarily during the 1920s. In keeping with Taylorist strategies of worker management and efficiency, many modern corporations throughout this period both made films and showed films to their employees. Such plans took on a particularly gendered tone at Western Union, reflecting a changing workforce and an influx of women into somewhat rote but nonetheless white collar jobs. These films set out to train workers in basic company procedures, and also to shape their attitudes toward work in general. Western Union showed films to its women workers that crafted analogies between domestic labor, domestic leisure, and their new jobs. Leisure operated as both an invitation to better work habits and as a metaphor for the mechanics of this new form of labor. As Groening reveals, a moral propriety pervaded the telegraphy company's film program that worked to educate, and ultimately to assimilate and manage, its new employees. Accordingly, many of its films also included strong anti-union sentiment.

Charles Acland begins by revisiting the formative Payne Fund Studies to reconsider their importance for film history. Long used to index widespread anxiety about the negative influence of cinema, the studies in fact produced a varied and often contradictory knowledge of cinema. Following from this, Acland recasts the Payne Fund researchers as part of a cadre of emerging media activists, educationalists, and experts who — among other things — willingly assumed positions of authority in matters of media influence, continuing to exert that influence decades after the initial studies. These researchers became particularly important to the establishment of the most basic assumptions about film and its role in educational reform, particularly in the postwar period. Acland demonstrates that the use of cinema to expand sites of learning was integral to more fundamental efforts to shape modern, mass-mediated publics. As such, his essay examines educational film by critically considering the ways in which social hierarchies were recreated through developments in cinematic pedagogy, including techniques such as group discussion, structured debate, and choreographed experiences. Acland grounds these insights in a case study: the career of the Payne Fund researcher Mark May and his educational film outfit, Teaching Film Custodians.

Zoë Druick investigates the film policies and programs of UNESCO during the early years of the cold war. The United Nations Educational, Scientific and Cultural Organization was the primary UN organ charged with implementing the organization's doctrine of the free flow of information, doing so by working to eliminate illiteracy and supplying lessons in modernization. Druick shows us that while UNESCO instrumentalized cinema for these humanitarian ends, it equally cooperated with American geopolitical maneuvering. And yet, Druick argues that UNESCO's use of film supports a contradictory family of policies and practices, and offers a compelling case for thinking about the unpredictability of the utility of cinema and culture more generally. She tends to the regionally varied strategies invoked to offer alternatives to American cinema's international dominance, and to mobilize, literally, cinema in underdeveloped areas. These enterprises helped to build a technological infrastructure that ultimately contributed to the fomentation of resistance to American and Western hegemony.

Pursuing the genre of the educational film, and seeking to understand the politics of films that expressly try to teach and persuade, Kirsten Ostherr focuses on the postwar production of health films. Many of these films borrowed from documentary and propaganda film techniques developed during the war, espousing civic virtue while also furthering the interests of the insurance, dental, and medical establishments. Ostherr considers the unique qualities of these films as compared to their Hollywood counterparts, identifying the properties that constitute the genre and the viewing conditions that made these films meaningful. She discusses the 1948 film *The Body Fights Bacteria* in detail, supplementing her analysis with a study of the medical institution as it incorporated cinema into its operations and interfaced with other actors in the film world, including George Eastman and Will Hays. This sets the stage for an analysis of the governmental, medical, and educational forces that affected the shift toward educational films in the postwar period. In the end, Ostherr considers the unique form of spectatorship inculcated by these films, asking what we can say about film viewing that is largely compulsory, patriotic, and pedagogical.

Part II, "Civic Circuits," studies the deployments of film in a variety of public institutions, in an effort to build, guide, and direct the nature of life in mass democratic, and advanced industrial, contexts. Gregory Waller tracks the establishment of 16mm technologies as the dominant infrastructure for distributing and exhibiting films beyond conventional movie theaters throughout the 1930s and 1940s. He does this in two ways, first by using surveys produced by industry and government bodies on technology use, and second, by identifying the proliferation of discourses about 16mm promulgated in the trade press and related advertising material. Waller shows that, as with other media technologies, major equipment manufacturers such as DeVry, Bell & Howell, RCA, and Victor Animatograph forwarded 16mm as a powerful portable machine, offering the utopian ideal of transforming everyday life with moving images, linking viewers to an often nationalized world of global wonder.

Jennifer Horne argues that the public library should first and foremost be understood as an institution that brought the goals of self-improvement and social control closer together, enacting policies that were both pious and secular, instituting leisure as moral education. But the public library did not enact these principles by assembling and lending books alone. Indeed, the public library has long had an interest in a range of audio and visual technologies.

Photograph rooms, sound collections, and film holdings have each in their own way been corralled to serve the institution's mandates. Horne's interest specifically is in mapping the use of film by public libraries. Beginning in the 1910s and ending her focus in the late 1930s, Horne shows that librarians deployed cinema to help fortify the library as a site for respectable cultural engagement and civic responsibility. Studying the public library in its local specificities and national abstractions, we can see an institution that engaged with regulatory debates, industry groups, the better films and visual education movements, changing exhibition practices, and emergent cinema technologies. Horne argues that a distinct mode of spectatorship emerged, one that might be described as "civic spectatorship."

Haidee Wasson examines another institutionally specific manifestation of cinema's utility, namely films made by museum educators and shown at museums and elsewhere. Concerned to foreground questions of scale, temporality, and movement, Wasson focuses on the Metropolitan Museum of Art (New York) and its longstanding relationship to film, beginning in the 1920s. In such a large museum with such a deep historical reach and grand architectural style, what did it mean to augment its display techniques with modern film technology, composed of white screens, projected light, and moving images? Cinema came to this particular art museum largely as a pedagogical and display device charged with helping educators to display their art plainly and simply. Film helped visitors make sense of the overwhelming and often exhausting experience of the large, cavernous, and cluttered museum, which was long derided as essentially consisting of static spaces. Indeed, this period saw a proliferation of discussions pertaining to the challenge of putting the museum and its objects in motion. At the Met, films helped the museum to manage motion in its halls and galleries, working to direct the viewer's eye, to standardize the museum gaze, and to provide physical relief from the demanding nature of the museum stroll. Wasson's essay presents questions about the meeting of different modes of visuality and temporality, considering the management of perception by the modern institutions of cinema and the museum.

Ronald Greene addresses the implications of a changing technological infrastructure, namely 16mm projectors and films, for a nationally significant network of film distribution and exhibition. He asserts that the emergence of a formidable technological infrastructure in the 1920s and 1930s must be understood as more than an expansion of the film field, or as a democratic alternative to Hollywood's vertical management of the theatrical film field. While the growth of the 16mm gauge helped to standardize previous and multiple film

technologies used outside of movie theaters, the gauge also helped to reconfigure corporate, political, moral, and educational interests during this period.
Greene demonstrates this thesis by examining the Motion Picture Bureau of
the YMCA, from 1928 to 1939, one of the largest non-theatrical film distributors in the country. For Greene, film was made useful at the YMCA as a form
of "pastoral power," assembling an audience of people, and then, with a Y secretary acting as animator, providing a kind of secular but highly moral instruction in civic-industrial order, inspired by the undergirding logics of religion
and governance.

Alison Griffiths examines the modern planetarium, a cultural form that
borrowed heavily from popular film genres and amusements to forward a new
kind of spectatorship that asserted a spectacular link between the terrestrial
and the extraterrestrial. For Griffiths, the planetarium is a physical site as well
as an index for larger sociopolitical currents. She discusses the long history
of looking at the stars and the historically specific conditions that catalyzed
the planetarium's twentieth-century incarnation. She focuses on the planetarium's popularity during the 1950s, linking this to postwar cultural dynamics
such as suburbanization, the cold war, nuclear anxieties, and the popularity
of science fiction films. Its relevance for cinema rests in the ways in which
the cinematic apparatus is signified in the planetarium, especially through the
use of large-scale moving images and amplified sounds. Griffiths shows that
cinematic discourses have long shaped the public presentation of planetarium
shows: advertisements, public discussion, and even audience reactions frequently invoke cinematic language. Yet, planetariums have achieved this by
relying on other media as well (literature, theaters, radio, television, popular
music, video games, and liturgy), suggesting that definitions and experiences
of cinema are themselves often constituted in relation to other media forms.

With part III, "Making Useful Films," we close the volume with research
that considers the making of useful films, with a special emphasis on nontraditional modes of production. Joseph Clark investigates the relationships
between one independently produced African American newsreel outfit that
ran during World War II, All-American Newsreel, and the larger debates that
surrounded it. For all its uniqueness, the series was marginal for several reasons. Its content put it at odds with the dominant industry practice of portraying black Americans in exclusively racist and stereotypical roles. As a result, All-American's business model required distribution to minor theatrical
and non-theatrical screens, where positive images of self-reliant black men
and women performing exemplary acts of patriotism and citizenship could be

presented. Clark documents how the newsreels got made and where they got shown, demonstrating that the films linked segregated theaters in the south to primarily black theaters in the north, and also to African American college campuses and to military camps. He then examines the complicated mode of address invoked by these films, connecting the topics and stories to film style, mode of production, and wider debates about racial identity, cinema, and patriotism. Clark's chapter is a case study in useful cinema that shows the importance of conventional as well as alternative distribution and exhibition modes for non-fiction subjects, and the related efforts to forward and contest racialized identities in wartime America.

Focusing on the 1930s, Charles Tepperman discusses the development of amateur filmmaking. Using cinema to negotiate between a modern, industrial world and that of the individual craftsman, Tepperman argues that amateur filmmakers used cameras and projectors alike to forge a unique encounter with technology in general and film in particular. By examining the history of the Amateur Cinema League, founded in 1926, and analyzing a whole range of films made and seen by amateurs, Tepperman targets "the practical film," a genre that was both personal and engaged with subjects of social concern. These films demonstrate, according to Tepperman, a certain utopian aspiration as they employed aesthetic experimentation with the goals of self- and social improvement. Moreover, they were made with an eye to an expanded context of distribution and exhibition, one that extended far beyond the main street theater. In other words, Tepperman suggests that amateur filmmakers creatively endeavored to use cinema to remake their everyday lives, making and showing films as methods for re-imagining their private, public, and working lives.

And in our concluding chapter, Michael Zryd tackles the relationship between avant-garde film practice and institutional pedagogies. He asks how it is that an experimental film could be purposefully difficult to understand, dogmatically anti-institutional, and resistant to dominant ideas about cinema's utility—it does not entertain, make money, or tell a story—and yet also be simultaneously crucial to a longstanding practice of teaching and learning in university classrooms. Building on the basic necessity of universities for the health of avant-garde filmmakers, Zryd pursues this seeming paradox by tracing the history of avant-garde filmmakers and films that were directly inspired by the desire to teach. He pays special attention to institutional experiments at the State University of New York at Binghamton and the State University of New York at Buffalo in the late 1960s and early 1970s. Zryd asserts that the commonly assumed chasm between the dynamics of avant-garde film and the homeostatic model of institutional learning has long been blurred by a sizable group of filmmaker-teachers who openly immersed themselves in the complicated nature of learning and literacy through their experimental film practice made possible by university support.

At heart, the scholars whose work appears here advance several core insights: 1) the longstanding and diversified nature of cinema despite the seeming monopoly of Hollywood and the dominance of the feature film; 2) the flexible technologies of cinema, consisting of portable projectors, mobile screens, and lightweight cameras, rather than the often-presumed simple, uniform, and professionalized apparatus; and 3) the integration of moving-image culture into a fuller spectrum of historical analysis to reveal the intricate relations among films, institutions, and exhibition locations. The research included here helps us begin to understand the American cinema we so often casually castigate and define as the opposite of Hollywood, that is, as "nontheatrical," "minor," and "marginal." Using the model of useful cinema, film's role as a functional device and range of practices is foregrounded, thus highlighting the crucial ways in which cinema has transformed everyday spaces and was adapted to institutional directives, wielding influence outside of the multiplex and the art house. While our case studies here focus on the United States, we suggest that useful cinema and the lessons offered by our authors are by no means limited to this national context. Their insights will have applications to moving-image studies in other locations, though revisions will be necessary to account for specific social, political, national, and international valences.

This book addresses the range of uses to which individual films and film technologies have been put beyond the movie theater. The following chapters treat the concept of useful cinema as a multidimensional and flexible concept; each emphasizes a different aspect of the phenomenon. It is not our intention to introduce a newly fixed genre. Nor do we wish to diminish the value of ongoing work on the function of fiction features, that is, studies of entertainment's utility, whether for ideological purposes or otherwise. Instead, the description of cinema as useful should provoke a reorientation of the kinds of questions we ask of our film and media history, ideally directing us to institutional dimensions of cultural life that have tended to fall by the wayside in our received historical narratives. With this book we contribute to the project of taking account of the ways film as an adaptable mobile medium shaped our understanding of visual culture, new technology, and everyday life throughout the twentieth century and beyond.

NOTES

1. Bennett, "Useful Culture."
2. See for example Lewis and Miller, *Critical Cultural Policy Studies*.
3. Hediger and Vonderau, *Films That Work*; Bloom, *French Colonial Documentary*; Gaines and Renov, *Collecting Visible Evidence*; Waldman and Walker, *Feminism and Documentary*; and Kahana, *Intelligence Works*.
4. Hediger and Vonderau, *Films That Work*, 11.
5. Bordwell, Thompson, and Staiger, *The Classical Hollywood Cinema*.
6. Early cinema generally refers to the period of film history before the rise of the nickelodeon in 1905. Late cinema usually refers to the period after the rise of the VCR. For one of the more influential essays that link these two periods see Hansen, "Early Cinema, Late Cinema."
7. H. Jenkins, *Convergence Culture*; Klinger, *Beyond the Multiplex* and "Cinema's Shadow"; Manovich, *The Language of New Media*; Marchessault and Lord, *Fluid Screens, Expanded Cinema*; Thorburn and Jenkins, *Rethinking Media Change*.
8. Friedberg, *Window Shopping* and *The Virtual Window*; Gunning, "An Aesthetic of Astonishment" and "The Cinema of Attractions"; Hansen, *Babel and Babylon*; Sobchack, *The Persistence of History*; Charney and Schwartz, *Cinema and the Invention of Modern Life*; Rabinovitz, *For the Love of Pleasure*; Ruoff, *Virtual Voyages*; Altman, *Silent Film Sound*.
9. Other works that expand our understanding of film history during this period include important works such as Morey, *Hollywood Outsiders*; Schaefer, *"Bold! Daring! Shocking! True!"*; Smoodin, *Regarding Frank Capra*; Wasson, *Museum Movies*; Zimmermann, *Reel Families*; and Ishikuza and Zimmermann, *Mining the Home Movie*.
10. For other work that demonstrates the role of 16mm see Brown, "Coming Soon to a Hall Near You"; R. Greene, "Y Movies"; Hendershot, "In Focus: 16mm"; Lester, "The Perilous Gauge"; Schaefer, "Gauging a Revolution"; Waller, "Free Talking Picture"; Wasson, "Electric Homes! Automatic Movies! Efficient Entertainment!"; Rossi-Snook, "Persistence of Vision."
11. Acland, *Residual Media*; Gitelman and Pingree, *New Media, 1740–1915*.
12. Acland, "Classrooms, Clubs and Community Circuits"; Boule, "Hot Rods, Shy Guys, and Sex Kittens"; Fagelson, "Fighting Films"; Horníček, "The Institutionalization of Classroom Films in Czechoslovakia between the Wars"; Masson, "Celluloid Teaching Tools"; Streible, Orgeron, and Orgeron, *Learning with the Lights Off*.

1   CELLULOID CLASSROOMS

"WHAT A POWER FOR EDUCATION!"
THE CINEMA AND SITES OF LEARNING
IN THE 1930S

Eric Smoodin

A moment of film viewing first made me aware that film education had an extended history, and that it was, indeed, more common many years ago than I may have thought. I remember watching *A Tale of Two Cities* on late-night TV with my mother and my sister, and while the movie came out in 1935, the viewing I am talking about took place in the mid-1960s, when I was twelve or thirteen years old. After we had all been properly moved by Sidney Carton's selfless death and heroic last words ("It's a far, far better thing I do . . .") my mother mentioned, somewhat offhandedly, that she recalled seeing the film when she was in public high school in Chicago in the mid-1930s, because it had been part of a classroom assignment. She had read the book in her English class, and then her teacher had told the students to go see the movie, so that they could discuss the novel and film together. I cannot remember asking my mother much more about this, but I was struck by this apparently natural link between the movies and the classroom, and by how popular motion pictures had had a place in the curriculum at a time that seemed so distant to me.

In fact, as the work of a number of film scholars over the last fifteen years has shown, the cinema had a central role in various educational settings in the 1930s, and the decade marked something of a golden era in film education in the United States. Hollywood films were studied in grammar school, junior high, and high school classrooms as well as at the university; educational films were produced for classroom use; and other settings became the sites of viewing these films and of studying the cinema generally. Some of these sites beyond the classroom seem perfectly logical to us now — the library, for instance. Some might seem surprising — the prison, and even the department store, as in the case in 1934 when Macy's announced that the entire department store chain would begin showing *The Story of a Country Doctor* to its customers, with the film documenting the renowned surgical practices of a famous doctor.[1] In these places during the period, we have both the study of Hollywood film as an aesthetic and industrial object, and the study of other subjects through film.

There was, as well, a vast body of literature produced about motion picture pedagogy and film-related educational activities. These materials ranged from textbooks to scholarly essays to an ongoing journal dedicated to the field, *Educational Screen*. The sheer volume of scholarly articles from the 1930s about film education in grammar and secondary schools, in such journals as the *English Journal*, the *Journal of Educational Sociology*, and the *Elementary School Journal*, demonstrates a broad humanities and social science interest in the subject. The titles of some of these articles, such as "Testing Some Objectives of Motion-Picture Appreciation," "Relative Importance of Placement of Motion Pictures in Class-Room Instruction," and "Can Youth's Appreciation of Motion Pictures Be Improved," show the possibilities of a precise science of film education in which results can be quantified and categorized. Other articles, like Mark A. May's "Educational Possibilities of Motion Pictures," from 1937, hint at the belief in the utopian pedagogy that movies provided.[2]

In an article about film studies at New York University (NYU) published in February 1934, *Educational Screen*, the monthly journal devoted to film pedagogy, expressed some of the excitement that Depression-era educators felt about motion pictures. Citing Dr. Frederic M. Thrasher, who helped to institute the serious study of film at NYU, the article claimed that "the enormous influence of the popular motion picture [has] forced the public schools and the colleges and universities to recognize the permanence of this great educational instrument and its potentialities in all educational fields." The editorial continued with "education can no longer neglect the motion picture," and then went on with practically an admonition to teachers: "It must be studied."[3] Just a month later, in an editorial, *Educational Screen* sounded something of an alarm, as if the fast and widespread acceptance of film education in public schools had already produced a crisis. With the place of film education in schools no longer questioned, the editorial said, "we incline to wonder if those concerned really know what it's about," and asked, further, "are they sure in how far the theatre is part of the school's job," and even, "do they know whether they are contributing to or complicating the educational problem?"[4]

Both the enthusiasm for and concern with motion picture pedagogy situate the film education movement in the center of some of the era's significant debates about elementary and secondary schools. Of course, the dominant philosophical movement among educators at this time was that of progressive education, developed primarily by John Dewey, but also indebted to the work of G. Stanley Hall and George Counts, among others. The progressive education movement can be difficult to pin down because it was practiced so differently by so many different people in a number of different areas, but it typically dealt with the perception of a central problem in American education. Progressive educators, whether they came from the leftist-socialist wing of the movement or from the center, believed that, as noted by the education historian Mustafa Emirbayer, "in the midst of massive socioeconomic and political changes, a new generation was coming of age that was woefully lacking in the citizenship skills needed to sustain a true democracy."[5]

Thus it was the project of the American school to make fundamental changes both in pedagogical practice and in American society. Educational reforms ranged from the space of the classroom—chairs that were not bolted to the floor—to an extension of educational space well beyond the school, and an insistence that "the everyday life of the community must furnish the main content of education."[6] This brief description hardly does the movement justice, but we can begin to see the place of cinema in the educational practices of the period. The cinema was itself viewed as one of the agents of modernity, of the vast social and technological changes that had so affected the population. Appearing first in the 1890s, the cinema developed alongside the increasing implementation among states and localities of compulsory education, with the theater and the classroom thereby becoming two of the central sites of childhood and adolescent activity. The cinema also functioned as one of those communal spaces beyond the classroom that were seen as so important to the progressives, and that also, if young people could only learn to use the cinema properly, might become a space of educational and intellectual work, a prospect attractive to a new generation of educators who typically rejected traditional notions of homework.[7]

But the cinema was not simply a utopian space of promise and democracy. It also posed dangers, dangers examined by many connected to a broad progressive movement in the United States, such as Jane Addams in *The Spirit of Youth and the City Streets* (1909). Much later, at the same time as the flourishing film education movement, we can see similar concerns posed by the Payne Fund Studies, which were indebted to Dewey but also on the periphery of the progressive movement. Those scientific analyses of the effects of movies upon children adopted G. Stanley Hall's notion of children as "fragile, innocent creatures," and so assumed the dangers that movies posed to the intellectual, moral, and emotional development of young people, and even to their physical well-being, as in the studies' concern with such things as the effects of movies upon sleeping habits.[8] Indeed, as I will discuss, much of the film education movement depended on a belief in the child as an incipient adult, able to make adult judgments, which may well have separated 1930s-style motion picture study from the progressive ideal.

The Payne Fund Studies, moreover, show the breadth of film studies during the period, and the broad range of educators connected to the movement. Many of the studies embrace the liberal mission of the social sciences from the period, the belief that viewers could be measured and quantified, and the effects of cinema perfectly understood. From the apparent mathematical precision of the studies came the hope that movies would be used to produce consumers who were anti-racist and anti-nationalist, who understood the social causes of crime and poverty, and who realized the necessity of Prohibition and measures designed to eliminate gambling. *All Quiet on the Western Front* (1930) demonstrably fostered the belief that war was always futile, according to the studies, just as *The Criminal Code* (1931) became a tract on the link between social practices and crime, and a film unknown today, *Son of the Gods* (1930), produced more favorable attitudes among white students toward the Chinese.[9]

This liberal impulse manifested in so many of the studies was both complemented by and contrasted with the goals of cultural improvement in such elite institutions as the Museum of Modern Art (MOMA) and NYU, and also, often, in the American high school. In these locations, film studies was as much a humanities discipline as a social science one, and so was clearly marked by aesthetic instruction, by issues of camerawork, national style, and realism.

The institutional locations of film studies also give evidence of the breadth of the program, and also, of course, of possible internal conflicts. Instruction and leadership came from those elite institutions, including the University of Chicago, Harvard, Columbia, and the University of Southern California in addition to MOMA and NYU. But Edgar Dale, who became the main prophet of film education during the era, taught at Ohio State University. Sarah McLean Mullen, who published a film studies textbook in 1935 and frequently contributed to *The Motion Picture and the Family*, a tabloid-style publication that rated films and gave suggestions for classroom instruction, taught at Abraham Lincoln High School in Los Angeles. That leaders of film studies came from "lesser" locations—the state university, the high school—as well as elite ones gives a sense of the grass-roots nature of the movement during the 1930s, as well as its dependence on the prestige of the Ivy League or the major urban museum.[10]

The methodologies of film studies ranged from L. L. Thurstone's psychometrics—the science, so important to the Payne Fund Studies, of measuring intelligence and the effects on attitudes of various social and cultural stimuli—to the more literary and art historical approaches of Robert Gessner, who taught film appreciation and history at NYU during the period. Thus we have a movement united by a field of study—the cinema—but marked also by the conflicts between the humanities and social sciences, by methodological differences, by the needs of teachers in varying educational locations, and often by a conviction in either the political or aesthetic benefits of studying film.

There were other reasons for bringing film to the classroom that had far less to do with pedagogical philosophy and much more to do with the daily difficulties of education in the 1930s. Educators at the time realized that the high school population had increased dramatically over the course of the century, and that there were now, during the period, millions and millions of kids in secondary school who had no interest in scholarship or in college, and so film seemed like the best way to reach these disinterested masses. Further, as was the case with my mother and *A Tale of Two Cities*, films might make students into better readers of books. Teachers also seemed to have the sense, regardless of their philosophical commitments, that education needed to change profoundly to serve a mass clientele, and that the cinema would be the instrument of this change. According to Edgar Dale, "everyone recognizes that we are going to live in a new kind of world, in which increased meaning, enriched experience and enjoyment are to be the heritage of everyone."[11] In other words, early twentieth-century modernity was marked by the near-universal availability of leisure time, and the activities of that leisure — viewing films, for instance — could be tapped by various institutions to educate the masses who participated in them so avidly.

Thus Dale and many other educators recognized the possibility of using the school to effect positive changes in leisure. Dale wrote that more and more educators were concerned with "how youth [are] to be trained, first of all, in the wise selection of motion picture entertainment," with the role of film education that of making children and adolescents better consumers of film, and thereby forcing Hollywood to make better movies.[12] Along with this link between the site of education and the movie theater, there was also a connection between the educational institution and that other great site of agitation about film quality during the period, the church. According to an editorial in *Educational Screen* in 1934, "there should be a school movement, synchronized and articulated with" church programs for better films, a school movement that "could stand worthily beside the church plan as the schools share in the great effort."[13] Here, then, we have the two significant programs for better films, a liberal, progressive one, for want of better terms, and a more reactionary one. Scholars have with endless elaboration examined the censorship movement spearheaded by the church, the one that led, however circuitously, to the more rigorous Motion Picture Production Code of 1934. But there was also an anti-censorship movement, engaged in largely by progressive educators, to improve films not by mandating content and representation, but by producing better consumers of film.[14]

In this chapter I am interested in the classrooms and libraries that were the spaces of film education during the 1930s, and also in the fluidity between the film industry and the "normal" theatrical sites of film exhibition, and those sites that we may not immediately think of as having a connection to film. I also want to expand the notion of cinema in these apparently nontraditional locations, and examine not just films, but also film culture more broadly. Thus, in addition to the screenings of films, we can discuss the uses of film stills in the classroom, film conferences that would take place in educational settings, and the activities of film clubs.

Local and national efforts from the period demonstrate the links between schools and the film industry, and also the practices of film education in schools and in the film industry. In an instance of film education in a specific place, New Haven, Connecticut, served as one of the testing grounds for the movement, having become "movie conscious," in the words of a 1937 issue of the *Journal of Educational Sociology*, in 1933. When the National Council of Teachers of English "appointed a committee to begin experimenting with the motion picture as a part of the English curriculum" in high schools, the New Haven school system eagerly joined the program.[15]

The project in New Haven required an extensive film studies bureaucracy. The city's effort was aimed at high school students, but the school board realized that for high school students to become movie conscious, much younger students needed to be targeted. As a result, "Motion Picture Councils were established in every eighth-grade, junior high, and high school in the city."[16] These councils themselves were highly regulated, with a governing student council, an overseeing faculty council, and then two New Haven teachers overseeing all of that. The councils left little up to the individual schools. They mandated that, in the fall of 1935, all high school English classes needed to devote "at least ten lessons . . . to the study of photoplay appreciation each year,"[17] although individual teachers could, apparently, shape these lessons according to their own interests. Most teachers used the same textbook: Edgar Dale's *How to Appreciate Motion Pictures*, which had first been published in 1933.

The smooth functioning of the program depended upon the cooperation of the film industry. The industry's trade association, the Motion Picture Producers and Distributors Association of America, provided movie posters and film stills, which schools displayed in libraries and other rooms, and even produced study guides for use in classrooms. Even more importantly, first-run theaters in the area gave reduced admission prices to "any group accompanied by a teacher," thus allowing "more valuable discussions" about films in classrooms "than would otherwise be possible."[18] Once a week, the school itself became a theater, with local exhibitors allowing the motion picture councils to preview coming films. Ideally combining educational practice with industrial assistance, the Board of Education "furnished the auditorium, lights, and power," while the projectionist "was supplied by the exhibitor booking the picture, and the film itself was loaned by the distributor."[19] Here the school became an extension of the theater, with the posters turning the library into something of a theater lobby and with the school auditorium showing movies. The first-run theaters also became educational spaces, as they acknowledged students and teachers as a special audience among the mass audience, a group of viewers whose attendance at the movies was the same as their attendance in a classroom. So the cultural artifacts of leisure — posters and movies, for instance — came to be at home within the culture of pedagogy — the classroom and the school auditorium — while the theater, the typical location of leisure, became the site for an extension of the relationship between students and teachers.

Film culture in New Haven education also connected different types of schools and different types of youth organizations, with the motion picture councils existing in private and public institutions, and also in such organizations as the Campfire Girls. The motion picture councils produced fifteen minute radio programs under the sponsorship of the New Haven Theatre Patrons, "an adult group devoted to the encouragement of better films and theatrical entertainment," with these programs ranging in tone from self-congratulatory ("The Origin and Purpose of the New Haven Junior Motion Picture Councils") to showcasing the discerning taste of the students ("Selecting the Twelve Best Movies of 1936" and "How to Judge Motion Pictures").[20] At least in New Haven, then, the film education movement had connections to a variety of media such as radio, and linked children and adolescents with adults in a broad-based movement for better films generally.

The apparent signs of the success of the New Haven program could be measured in several ways. First, the school year ended in a film symposium. In 1937, local exhibitors provided the space for the symposium, giving over New Haven's Paramount Theatre. A short film called *Alibi Racket* (1935), from an MGM series called *Crime Does Not Pay* was screened, after which students led discussions about the story, the casting, the acting, photography, lighting, and other categories; the students also restaged several of the scenes themselves; then the film was screened again, to show the audience what they may have missed the first time. That audience included local Rotary clubs, Kiwanis and Lions, the PTA, and also church groups. The featured speaker was Hal Hode, an assistant to the vice-president of Columbia Pictures, who spoke on the "Producer's View of the Movies." The location of the symposium and the featured speaker show the linkages between the classroom project and the film industry, with both school and industry combining in a brand of evangelical outreach to significant groups of local citizens, to convince them of the value of film education and the possibility of improving film consumption.

Indeed, the apparent improvement in consumption practices provides another measure of the success of the movement, and the test case in New Haven was the signifier par excellence of film quality, the Shakespeare film: MGM's 1936 version of *Romeo and Juliet*. In New Haven, "all performances were practically sold out, and nearly ninety per cent of all tickets were sold through the schools."[21] Just about everywhere else, the film failed at the box office. Evi-

The balcony scene from *Romeo and Juliet* (1936), one of the model motion pictures of film education in the late 1930s.

dently in New Haven, the film education movement fostered an interest in a Shakespeare film, and also created a relationship between schools and theaters to the extent that the former apparently acted as a kind of box office for the latter. In addition, according to sociologists at the time who were studying the film education movement, exhibitors in New Haven actively sought to book films that met with the approval of the student motion picture councils and that lent themselves to classroom study, so that a number of theaters booked *Romeo and Juliet*. Thus the film education program had worked, at least if we accept *Romeo and Juliet* as a film of undeniable high quality. The study of films led to a demand for better films, and the theater managers responded by booking those films and then working with schools to make sure that people attended.

The New Haven experiment was part of a loosely affiliated national program. As noted above, the ideological sweep of the movement was broad, mirroring the socialist to centrist scope of the progressive education movement, with teachers committed to cinema also linked by such mundane concerns as maintaining the interest of innumerable bored students. The various schools and educators practicing film pedagogy were also connected by such periodicals as *Educational Screen* and *The Motion Picture and the Family*, as well as Edgar Dale's textbook, *How to Appreciate Motion Pictures*. These film studies textbooks all served to give coherence to programs in different states, as did traveling exhibitions designed as film studies units, such as the Museum of Modern Art's 1934 program, "The Cinema as Art."[22]

Most aspects of the movement also stressed the organization of film clubs in schools, and especially the high school, and we can get a sense of the functioning of these clubs from the film education literature of the period.[23] In fact, one of the interesting aspects of the film education program is the way in which its supporters engaged in a kind of anthropological study of the students involved, trying to understand the culture of adolescent film fans and the social organization of their groups. As a result we know, from efforts to chart the groups, that the average film club met once a week, and that it had anywhere from twenty-five to fifty members. Membership dues usually ran about a dollar a year, although efforts to raise money were constant, through "film showings at school, benefit performances at neighborhood theaters, and the usual food sale or party."[24] Virtually every member of a club was also a member of a club committee—the better, according to researchers, to keep out members who just wanted to talk about movies. There might be as many as twenty different committees at a club: the technical committee, with members who could operate projectors, the scrapbook committee, which collected articles and star photos, the movie review committee, which gathered up reviews, and so forth.

A club meeting might concentrate on a single issue. Much early film education centered on an auteurist discourse of directorial quality, and at one of the meetings recorded by a 1939 national survey of club activity, the members discussed "The Work of the Director." The meeting ran by first identifying prominent directors and their films, and then discussing "such directorial touches as the fade-out." Afterward, the club members took part in "impromptu pantomimes, following the instructions of a student director."[25] But the interests of clubs weren't always on such purely aesthetic matters. A number of the clubs being surveyed ran meetings on "The Motion Picture as a Crime and War Preventative," on "Methods of Film Advertising," and also on "Block-booking." Thus political and industrial issues stood out as central to film education in the 1930s, with block-booking holding an important place as a practice that removed the consumer, and even the theater, from any apparent choice in the films being programmed.

Theater managers were themselves often engaged with the clubs, giving tours of their theaters and booking films that the clubs wanted to see. But when they came to speak to the clubs, it was often about block-booking. And here we can imagine a sort of bonding between managers and students, the businessmen and the consumers, against the film corporations that demanded the booking of their products. Throughout the period, the two evils for the film education movement were block-booking, first and foremost, and the double bill, which was often seen as a means of mismatching films in order to attract the widest possible audience, thereby pairing children's or family films with movies best suited for adults. In producing better consumers, the film education movement sought to foster an activist consumer position; viewers not only recognized the best films, they also learned that pressure must be applied on the industry to alter its business relationships with theaters.

There were some notable failures in the clubs, failures that did not seem apparent in New Haven. While the clubs appeared to spread an awareness among students of the best films, "parent education through club members was reported as futile" by one club.[26] Thus we see one of the interesting paradoxes of the film education movement. Here in opposition to the tenets of progressive education, the movement was in part marked by an assertion that children were, in a sense, miniature adults, capable of adult decisions and choices, about movies and other things, if only given the proper instructions.

But actual adults were themselves typically ineducable, damaged by previous systems that made them forever incapable of mature choices.

There were more mundane disappointments. The 1939 survey reported that "one ambitious club made miniature sets and figures representing the outstanding films of the year," apparently 1937. "But only Claudette Colbert's Puritan costume," from *Maid of Salem* (1937), "came anywhere near expectations." Generally in this exercise, "boys balked on making the sets and the girls lacked the skill."[27] Indeed, the notion of the gendered movie fan produced other difficulties. Many clubs failed, according to the survey, because of the difficulty of finding "common ground for movie-magazine-minded girls and trick-photography boys."[28] In other words, the usefulness of the film clubs could be measured by how well they elevated the discussion of film away from gossip and technology for its own sake, and also, of course, by their success in turning the discourse of quality into the practice of demanding and attending quality films. As one teacher lamented about the film education movement and the success of the various clubs and classes, "Our pupils . . . talk about the excellence of *Quality Street* [1937] and *Berkeley Square* [1933]," the first based on a play by J. M. Barrie, the second a historical fantasy starring Leslie Howard. Then the teacher added, but they "go to see Mae West."[29]

At least implicitly, then, teaching high school students to demand the best films might be addressing the issue too late. As early as 1934, the State of California Education Department acknowledged this problem and produced an extraordinary document called *Motion Picture Appreciation in the Elementary School*. It is difficult to determine the relationship between this pedagogical statement and the larger film education movement, but there are certainly significant linkages. Philosophically, the document echoes the movement: "The motion picture in its present stage is recognized as one of the most powerful influences now known in molding public opinion and thought," and so it must be determined exactly "what part . . . the public school [is] to play in directing the influence of this powerful factor in our national and international life."[30] Leisure needed to become part of a pedagogical project, and participation in that leisure needed to be directed, at least in part, by educators. After this assertion of an activist pedagogy engaged with the recreation of students, the education department exalted the possibilities of film: "What a power for education of young and old alike is present in the film industry!"[31]

In the exercise of this power, a useful, enlightened cinema became, really, a useful and enlightened cinema culture, the incorporation of the artifacts of

Students might have expert classroom discussions about *Quality Street* (1937), with Katharine Hepburn and Franchot Tone, but to the dismay of their teachers they far preferred seeing movies with Mae West.

the film industry, in addition to the films themselves, into the daily activity of the elementary school student at school. All of this was with an eye toward getting students to go to and demand the best films: *The Emperor Jones* (1933) and *Little Women* (1933) rather than Mae West. And the pedagogical practice would be to alter the school day, not by showing films, but by creating educational projects around them. Teachers might bring an 8mm camera to school, for instance, to acquaint students with the work of the cameraman and to teach students, in the words of the document, that the cinematographer "must never make the audience conscious of the camera's presence," but that also, in special films like *Alice in Wonderland* (1933), there might be a place for photographic tricks.[32] Students also needed to learn the history of the film industry in the United States, so they would understand the "development of photography in motion pictures from the time of Edison's kinescope to the present time."[33] In this history, the two great heroes were D. W. Griffith and Adolph

Zukor, apparently because they were the founding fathers of film style and of the studio system. The modern inheritor of their tradition was Walt Disney.

By studying Disney and his animated films, students could be taught the labor of film production—the thousands of drawings that needed to be made, the multitude of people who work on a seven minute cartoon. Indeed, in almost all educational venues, from elementary school to high school, this broad movement in film education always emphasized issues of labor and industry; from block-booking to the process of making a cartoon, an emphasis that probably is lacking in much film education today.

Even these elementary school students might, themselves, become laborers in a sense. The document proposed that a class could write a screenplay, with planning done from the point of view of the producer, director, scenario writer, and the audience. Students might also produce the sets that they see in films, and the kind of authenticity recommended by the document would be at home in an Erich von Stroheim film; one sixth grade class, after watching some films about the Middle Ages, reconstructed the castles they had seen and carefully cataloged the typical castle feast, from the work of musicians and servants to the shape and design of the table.

Much more so than in New Haven, or in the high school movie clubs generally, the California program also sought to incorporate play into the classroom in relation to movies, or what the document called the development of "free dramatic expression."[34] Here, Disney provided a model for childhood education. A fourth grade class in San Jose, apparently in 1933, was studying music in film and designed a skit around the theme song of *The Three Little Pigs*, the 1933 Disney cartoon that had a success that is difficult to imagine today for a short film. The students learned the song "Who's Afraid of the Big Bad Wolf," they had tryouts to cast the parts of the pigs and the wolf, and the children who were chosen for those parts danced a skipping routine while the rest of the class sang the song. They performed this on stage, and designed pig houses and pig and wolf masks, and, in fact, they pantomimed the entire cartoon while the class sang. They even created special effects to make the straw and twig pig houses fall down when the wolf huffed and puffed.

The details of the production show the place of film culture in the classroom of the 1930s, where a movie came to be transformed into a series of lessons, about music, about performance, about working with other students, and about graphic design, while the film itself was not part of the classroom at all. In this example from San Jose, a Disney film that has come down to us as significant because of its status as a parable of optimism during the Depression developed an entirely different use value and significance in the California classroom.

The discipline of film studies is perhaps the least historicized of all the humanities and social science fields. There are scholars doing important work on this history now, but many people in the discipline have little idea of the various manifestations of film studies, particularly in the United States and especially before 1960. We also tend not to think of film studies and film education beyond the university. But there were vibrant film education programs in a variety of places even in addition to the elementary, junior high, and high school cases examined here. During the 1930s and in these different places, educators developed a pedagogy of play and leisure, something that connects to other more or less progressive projects, for instance the national playground movement in the United States that began in the early twentieth century and was marked by the belief that valuable lessons could be learned from organized activity in the playground. With cinema, we see the possibility of turning leisure into education in order to create more enlightened students and also better consumers.

We also see the active participation of the film industry in this project, and the ways in which the industry and the schools used films to produce a broad film culture in the educational setting. The study of these educational practices during the 1930s changes at least somewhat the accepted historiography of the period. As it is studied, the history of relations between the film industry and the public in the 1930s is dominated by conflict, and particularly by the discussion of censorship, with the public demanding cleaner films from a reluctant industry. But the movement in film education encompasses a major pedagogical project on the part of the public school that endorsed the cinema generally, and aimed at improving aesthetic understanding, political awareness, and consumption practices of children and adolescents. The movement formed part of a significant public relations program on the part of the film industry that was only tangentially connected to issues of censorship. The work of the industry in education during the 1930s was part of a program designed to demonstrate the usefulness of movies and emphasize their benefits, benefits endorsed by sections of the public that believed strongly in the power of cinema to enlighten and educate.

1 "Department Stores Show Film," *Educational Screen*, September 1934, 185. The subject of the movie was Dr. M. W. Locke, who had pioneered in the practice of "manipulative surgery," which is designed to provide increased movement for joints, particularly when that movement has been impaired by adhesions.

2 Frutchey and Dale, "Testing Some Objectives of Motion-Picture Appreciation"; Stadtlander, "Relative Importance of Placement of Motion Pictures in Class-Room Instruction"; Frutchey, "Can Youth's Appreciation of Motion Pictures Be Improved"; and M. May, "Educational Possibilities of Motion Pictures."

3 "New York University Plans Film Course," *Educational Screen*, February 1934, 54.

4 Greene, Editorial, 64.

5 Emirbayer, "Beyond Structuralism and Voluntarism," 639.

6 Wilson, "A Short History of a Border War." The citation, from page 715, comes from Cremin, *The Transformation of the School*.

7 For a discussion of the period's anti-homework movement, see Gill and Schlossman, "'A Sin Against Childhood.'"

8 Addams, *The Spirit of Youth and the City Streets*. For a discussion of Hall, see Gill and Schlossman, "'A Sin Against Childhood,'" 34. Among the Payne Fund Studies, see in particular Dysinger and Ruckmick, *The Emotional Responses of Children to the Motion Picture Situation*.

9 See the Payne Fund Study conducted and written by Peterson and Thurstone, *Motion Pictures and the Social Attitudes of Children*, chapter 2, "The Effect of Single Pictures," 5–38.

10 Dale, *How to Appreciate Motion Pictures*. Mullen, *How to Judge Motion Pictures*. For studies of the place of film studies in elite institutions, see Wasson, *Museum Movies*; and Polan, *Scenes of Instruction*.

11 Dale, "A Comprehensive Program for the Teaching of Motion Picture Appreciation." Dale's assertion about "a new kind of world" can be found on 127.

12 Ibid., 125.

13 Greene, Editorial, 145.

14 This anti-censorship impulse, and this desire to produce more informed consumers, aligned many of these educators with the apparent "enemy," the film industry. It was the industry-sponsored National Board of Review that sponsored so many film clubs for young people during the period, as well as radio shows about film content, all of which were designed to create an idea of children and adolescents as potentially very intelligent consumers who could indeed demand that the film studios produce better films. See Smoodin, *Regarding Frank Capra*, 104–11. For a wider discussion of the National Board of Review see Jowett, *Film*, especially 126–35.

15 Eldridge, "Motion-Picture Appreciation in the New Haven Schools." Eldridge writes of New Haven becoming "movie conscious" on 175. All the information on New Haven in this section comes from Eldridge: the formation of councils and the ten-lesson plan on 175–76; the auditorium and electricity on 178; connections to other

groups and radio shows on 179–80; the symposium on 180–82; and *Romeo and Juliet* on 179.

16   Ibid., 175.

17   Ibid., 176.

18   Ibid.

19   Ibid., 178.

20   Ibid., 179–80.

21   Ibid., 179.

22   *Bulletin of the Art Institute of Chicago*, 35, no. 4 (April–May 1941), 59–60, noted the arrival of the Museum of Modern Art program, with such films as Erich von Stroheim's *Greed* (1924), René Clair's *The Italian Straw Hat* (1928), and Walt Disney's *Plane Crazy* (1928).

23   For information about the clubs, see McCullough, "A Preview of an Investigation of Motion-Picture Class and Club Activities," part 1. All the information cited in this section about the clubs comes from McCullough: the formation of the clubs on 122–23; the work of the director and block-booking on 123; failures of education of adults and the problems of *Maid of Salem* on 124–25; and Mae West on 128.

24   Ibid., 121.

25   McCullough, "A Preview of an Investigation of Motion-Picture Class and Club Activities," 123.

26   Ibid., 124.

27   Ibid., 125.

28   Ibid.

29   Ibid., 128.

30   *State of California Education Bulletin, Number 9: Motion Picture Appreciation in the Elementary School*, Sacramento, May 1, 1934, 1–2.

31   Ibid., 2.

32   Ibid., 13.

33   Ibid.

34   Ibid., 32.

"WE CAN SEE OURSELVES AS OTHERS SEE US"

WOMEN WORKERS AND WESTERN UNION'S TRAINING
FILMS IN THE 1920S

Stephen Groening

The 1927 film *Accuracy First* introduces viewers to Sally
Lee, an avid reader, dancer, and singer. She works in a
high-pressure job, spending hours a day in front of a keyboard, desperately trying to keep up with the tasks arriv-
ing at her desk. Distracted by a conversation with a friend,
Sally makes a critical error at work. Her high-powered male
clients subsequently lose thousands of dollars in a botched
stock trade. There is plenty of blame to go around, and the
film ends before we learn of Sally's fate. This training film,
produced by Western Union, mixes conventions of narrative fiction films with the direct address and visual demonstration techniques of instructional films. Western Union
made other training films in the next three years, including *Keyboard Errors* (1929), *Speed Killers* (1930), *Gumming*
(1930), *X Messages* (1927), and *Mechanical Call Distribution
System for Receiving Telegrams by Telephone from Patrons of
the Western Union* (1930).[1] Characterized by a static camera, medium shots (often just the torso), and substandard
lighting setups, these training films were by no means stylistically sophisticated, instead relying on the conventions

and techniques of both the popular and the educational films that preceded them. These films contained footage of Western Union offices and reenactments of procedures in the operation of telegraph apparatus. In what follows, I will outline how gender politics and labor relations affected Western Union's institution of film as part of its training regimen, the specific spectatorial and identificatory demands that these training films placed on viewers, and the ideological content of the films themselves.

In the early 1920s, the Taylor Society (initially the Society for the Promotion of Scientific Management) argued that "non-financial incentives" such as cultural and aesthetic activities would assist in regulating worker behavior.[2] These non-financial incentives often took the form of moralizing lessons communicated through films. In line with contemporary views regarding film's efficacy as an educational tool, companies took advantage of the presumed communicative transparency of film to increase training efficiency and overcome language barriers. The easy-to-comprehend films became a proxy manager—replacing the hands-on training of the apprentice system. Training films were an attempt to teach corporate values, moral character, and the ethics of capitalism to a population of workers not yet assimilated to the industrial organization of work.[3]

Several early film production companies sought to promote film as an efficient teaching tool—more efficient and effective than human teachers—and the use of film as a training or instructional aid was not uncommon in the 1920s. During the 1920s, many large industrial firms produced training films for their employees, including the Willys-Overland Motor Company and the Ford Motor Company.[4] Beginning in 1920, the Visual Education Institute began publishing *Visual Education*, a journal promoting the use of film, slides, and other visual aids in education at all levels. *Educational Screen*, the most enduring and influential journal in this field, also commenced publication in 1920. Calling itself "a source freely accessible to all interested in the progress of the new, nation-wide movement which seeks to broaden and deepen, by the use of visual aids, our national education in school, church, club, and community center," *Educational Screen* merged with *Visual Education* in 1923. Filled with advice columns, reviews of educational films, and advertisements for various distributors who specialized in non-fiction, educational, instructional, and industrial films, these journals claimed that film was a valuable educational and instructional tool due to the medium's interpretive transparency, the efficient manner in which film transmitted information, and the ability of the film apparatus to substitute for teachers and experts (thus automating education). These efforts to promote the use of film to educate, instruct, and train led to the production of thousands of educational films in the late 1910s and throughout the 1920s.

Because training films were site-specific—produced for a select audience bound by company operations—they serve as an example of the reach of film exhibition into spaces previously reserved for other sorts of activities. The growing prevalence of film exhibition in workplace settings dating from this period demonstrates that film was not just actively pursued by audiences, but that audiences were actively pursued by films. The notion that filmmakers chose the audience, rather than the audience choosing the films, runs counter to dominant ideas of spectatorship in this era of film history. Numerous studies of spectatorship and movie-going habits in the United States prior to World War II place film in a range of amusements and leisure activities actively sought out and chosen by viewers. While certain non-fiction educational films and industrial films were able to draw audiences into movie theaters during this period, the genre of educational films generally sought out an audience that had little control over programming. The largest contingent of this captive audience was schoolchildren, as demonstrated by guides aimed at integrating films into the classroom and public school curriculum, like Frederick Dean McClusky's *Visual Instruction: Its Value and Its Needs* of 1932. Not all film audiences were as captive as student audiences. For instance, the fiction and non-fictional films shown to workers during this period utilizing the YMCA film bureau program were voluntarily attended.[5] Training films, however, were a growing part of work life, particularly in industries like telegraphy that were undergoing rapid technological innovation in which continued employment and promotion were contingent on acquiring new skills.

The ability of film to reach these captive audiences depended in part on the introduction of 16mm film in 1923. This stock, cheaper and lighter than 35mm, was crucial to the growth of the educational film. The cheaper and more portable projection equipment that accompanied the standardization of this gauge allowed for the installation of film equipment in schools, churches, corporate offices, and homes during the 1920s and 1930s.[6] The transformation of spaces within these extant institutions into quasi movie theaters enabled the creation of captive audiences. The 16mm distribution networks, film exchanges, and rental agencies were dependent on widespread installation of 16mm exhibition technology for their financial success.[7] Thus Western Union's training films came at a confluence of several factors: the discursive positioning of film as a viable and valuable educational tool, the introduction of new film technology, and changes in the labor market.

The possibility of unionization of Western Union's telegraphers caused the company to react in a fashion that eventually led to the use of film as an instructional technology. First, Western Union attempted to dilute the organizational efforts of workers by hiring what was viewed as a separate category of worker: women. Second, Western Union took advantage of technological innovations in automated telegraphy to meet the ever-growing demand for telegraphed messages while simultaneously shedding skilled telegraph operators (usually men and often with years of experience). Third, Western Union established schools, recruiting students from within the ranks of its employees — often unskilled entry-level employees — to train on the automated equipment.[8] These efforts, which overlapped to various degrees for nearly thirty years, led Western Union to another form of automated communication technology — film — in its bid to efficiently train larger numbers of women workers in the protocols of telegraphy and Western Union corporate culture.

LABOR ORGANIZATION AND THE TRAINING FILM

The Western Union films were made during a period of labor transition. As Diane Waldman puts it, "The early part of the 20th Century was a period of intense industrial strife" marked by violent clashes between workers, management, and the agents of management.[9] During the period between 1915 and 1930, Western Union employed a variety of strategies to prevent unionization within its workforce.[10] Chief among them was the promotion of the idea that the interests of management and labor were the same, or at least coincided. Western Union's internal bulletin, the *Western Union News*, "edited by employes for employes [*sic*]" began publication in 1914 and its chief mission was to inculcate a work ethic in employees. The opening column of Western Union's president, Newcomb Carlton, stated, "In your charge is one of the important vehicles of commercial and social life. In your charge is its efficiency and success."[11] From the start, the newsletter concerned itself with cooperation between labor and management. Keeping relations peaceful was linked to the success of the company (which in turn was linked to the success of the employees) and to greater efficiency and productivity. A column in 1915 stated that the cooperative spirit between labor and management would lead to "an improved speed of service, a consequent reduction of expenses—in short, an increased efficiency."[12] The June 15, 1918 issue of the *Western Union News* was a special issue on unionization in all but name. It denied any conflict between the company and its employees. Furthermore, the issue blamed the attempt at unionization on foreigners, claiming most of the union members and organizers were Canadians.[13] Finally, it announced the formation of an employee association and sanctioned an employee association newsletter called *The Telegraph World*.

Besides giving workers "a chance to express themselves"[14] via the employee newsletter, Western Union's anti-union strategies included hiring a large contingent of women workers. The company justified the strategy of hiring women workers with a belief that women were more congenial, malleable, and tractable than men.[15] In addition, employers (and many male employees) expected women to leave their jobs upon marriage. High turnover in the workforce inhibits worker cohesion, collectivity, and solidarity, and so it is a crucial part of management's anti-union efforts.[16] These strategies were not without their perils for Western Union. *The Telegraph World* provided a forum for mild agitation (even if it was safely contained in the newsletter and counterbalanced by management views) and the expanding introduction of women workers was the subject of controversy and consternation. Additionally, while women may have been viewed as amenable to supervision, their ability to embody the work ethic crucial to the functioning of industry in the United States was an open question.[17] Due to the problem of training a large number of new workers—that is, new to the company and new to the workforce—Western Union turned to film.

SPECTATORSHIP AND SUPERVISION

According to the U.S. film industry's own research, women and children dominated the movie-going audience in the 1920s. Richard Koszarski has warned against putting too much stock in these statistics: "There are few reliable statistics on the proportion of women in silent-film audiences, but the Evansville survey suggests that males gradually lost interest during their teens. In 1920 W. Stephen Bush reported in the *New York Times* that 60 percent of film audiences were women, but in 1927 the *Moving Picture World* set the figure as high as 83 percent."[18] The importance of these numbers lay not in their relative accuracy, but in that they provided an argument for Hollywood to produce and market particular types of films (urban melodramas, for instance).

In other words, Hollywood acted upon these numbers *as if* they were true. Other trade magazines noted the importance of the lunchtime office crowd to the success of movie theaters during this period. Richard Abel draws our attention to "the special February 1912 issue of *Billboard*, [in which] Jos. F. Hennegan noted that, in downtown districts, 'clerks, stenographers, etc., employ their noon hour in seeing moving pictures' almost daily."[19] Examining the complex relationship between women and the film industry during the 1910s, Shelley Stamp claims that "there has been no other time in the history of American cinema when women's movie-going habits, tastes, and desires were talked about, catered to, and debated so thoroughly. A closer look at this period shows us that the cultivation of a female audience for the movies, as well as textual viewing positions open to women, were not incidental to the development of classical cinema in the teens but instrumental to it."[20]

In the ten to fifteen years leading up to Western Union's production of training films, the culturally dominant idea was that women were more likely than men to be interested in film, to be entranced by film, and to be susceptible to any given film's messages (not to mention that women were thought to be integral to the continued financial success of the film industry). Thus, in a time when the U.S. movie-going audience was perceived to be dominated by women and women's tastes, the training wing of Western Union deliberately chose to use the medium assumed to hold special appeal for women and to be an efficient and effective teaching technology.

Western Union reproduced this idea about women moviegoers in the employee association newsletter, a sign of the notion's pervasiveness. A passage in a "Woman's Affairs" column of *Telegraph World* in 1921 cautions women to take film seriously while briefly outlining some central tenets of the contemporary call for using film as a moral teacher: "The moving picture shows are doing a lot of good. For one thing, they teach us to study ourselves. We can see ourselves as others see us. They are educational too. Many people who will not take time to read let the 'Movies' give them the best stories ever written, as nearly all the big stories have been 'movieized.' To get the best out of the 'movies' do not take in the plot only, but the lessons, the acting, the life that is taught. And don't be a 'movie fiend'—be a 'movie fan.'"[21]

Urging a self-reflexive viewing mode, this advice illustrates why Western Union might have thought films to be particularly effective as a training technology for women workers. Film was seen as a powerful and effective didactic medium to the point that fiction films—adaptations of literature particularly—were presumed to bring moral uplift if viewed properly. The distinction between a movie fiend, who is an uncritical enthusiast, and a movie fan, who adheres to the protocols of film appreciation, has a logic applicable to the Western Union workplace, in which adherence to the protocols laid out by management was key to success as an employee. This comparison relies on a logic of exteriorization, in which the reader is advised to think of how others would see her. The spaces of amusement and work mirror each other because in this example both are spaces in which the woman is being watched. As Stamp and others have shown, women's behavior (and presence) in movie theaters was the subject of debate and their visibility at these venues was the primary impetus for these controversies. Likewise, in the workplace, the supervisory protocols of management took place in the visual register.

One of the stereotypes of the "movie-fiend," the "movie-struck girl," or the woman afflicted with "film-itis" was that she was unable to distinguish between the fantasy and romance of the movies and her own real life. Stamp points out that exhibitors took advantage of this; for instance, by installing picture booths in their lobbies, promoting them as an opportunity for women to take photographs of themselves as if they were in films. The discipline of film studies has resisted these portrayals of film audiences as enthralled, hypnotized, and easily influenced. And yet training films *depend* on their audiences imitating the characters, actions, and habits portrayed in film. In a few Western Union training films, including *Gumming, Keyboard Errors, X Messages*, and *Speed Killers*, workers were called upon to recreate the portrayals in the film. In other words, the form of identification *suggested* by fictional film is *required* by the training film.

For the training film to function properly, the viewer must project herself into the images on the screen. The viewer is called upon to exteriorize herself into the portrayals within the film at the same time that she is internalizing the lessons of the film. The column in *Telegraph World* takes this one step further, asking the female Western Union employee to, in essence, step outside of herself to see herself. The film screen is therefore supposed to act as a mirror for the viewer. The viewer is assumed to be the subject of the film as well as its object.

None of Western Union's films possess the shot/reverse shot sequence so familiar to scholars and viewers of classical Hollywood film (or contemporary film and television for that matter). The presumed fashion in which viewers are sewn into the film, by adopting the optical standpoint of the protagonist, is entirely absent from the training film.[22] The only shots that could be construed as point-of-view shots in the classical sense are close-ups of the various

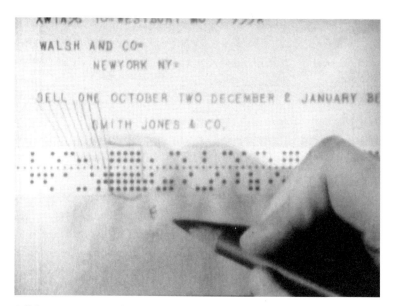

Still from *Accuracy First*: the hand of the supervisor correcting a telegram. Western Union Telegraph Company Records, Archives Center, National Museum of American History, Smithsonian Institution.

telegrams. But the illusion of point-of-view is shattered when, in each film, a hand appears with a pencil circling incorrect times, miscoded messages, spelling errors, and so on. This hand is not supposed to belong to the worker; it is the hand of the instructor or of the supervisor.

In essence, the trainees are called upon to position themselves as supervisors. Western Union's management valued self-regulation because it increased worker efficiency and productivity while easing the burden of supervisors and management. Making workers responsible for their own management thus saved money for the company by condensing two layers of office protocol to one set of workers.[23] Since the films portray worker activity from the point of view of supervisors it implicitly encourages sympathy with management and may have turned worker frustration against other workers for their failure to perform up to the demands of management. In addition, depicting employee errors as the product of misbehavior may have played to protocols and habits of maternal supervision of children, the conventions of which many women workers were no doubt familiar (regardless of their status as mothers). The portrayal of these actions from the perspective of management therefore is not a failure of imagination, but coincided with Western

Union's aspiration to create a docile, well-trained, and self-regulated work force.

In this way, these films called upon spectators to adopt the viewpoint of the bourgeois individual, not the collective worker. Western Union benefited from worker disregard for the collective nature of work and the collective viewing of these training films. Western Union pitted individual workers against one another in a competition, through the system of merits and demerits that penalized workers for errors and inaccuracy, and rewarded workers for speed and punctuality.[24] This system was effective only if each worker saw herself as having little commonality with other workers. This process required first that the viewer of the training film see herself in the film, through a process of exteriorization, and second that the trainee internalize the lessons of the film itself. In this way, the trainee isolates herself from other trainees and workers while connecting to the images on the screen. The process of isolation, in this case, results in a temporary form of class mobility, as the laborer is called upon to adopt the attitudes (and in some cases, the responsibilities) of management.

As Miriam Hansen shows in *Babel and Babylon*, early film audiences were engaged in social interactions within the theater. During the 1910s and 1920s, a new mode of spectatorship became dominant. Stamp and Hansen describe the process of disciplining women moviegoers through advertisements, placards, signs, and comics into a particular form of spectatorship. This new form involved silence, lack of interaction with other audience members, and concentration on the screen in front of the audience. The same form of attention—silent, absorbed, and concentrated—was advocated for all Western Union employees as part of a model work ethic. The new mode of film spectatorship matched the behavior specified by Western Union management, both within the training films and in various admonishments within the pages of *Telegraph World* and its successor newsletter, *Dots and Dashes*. The association of work with film is not an association of labor with fun; it is an alliance of two activities emphasizing focus, single-mindedness, and careful observation. These were the dispositions encouraged in the film appreciation movement, referenced earlier by the "Woman's Affairs" column, and the dispositions Western Union wanted to instill in its workers.

Despite its near monopoly of U.S. telegraphy at the time, Western Union's continued financial success depended on operators' ability to transfer messages accurately and quickly. Western Union offered ubiquity of service, but its service included the very qualities that it feared new women workers did not possess—concentration, precision, and assiduity. To ensure successful and accurate transmission, operating telegraphic technology required absorption similar to that required by classical film narrative. Thus the importance of film as a training technology lay in how the form itself was perceived as disciplining its audience, not just in its ability to transfer information efficiently, the viewpoint promoted by journals such as *Educational Screen*.

"THE WOMAN QUESTION IS NO LONGER A 'PROBLEM'"

The special position of women in the economy made the question of women workers' consciousness particularly fraught. The unremunerated domestic labor still typical for many women is a form of labor marked by its insularity from other workers performing the same tasks. In *The German Ideology* Karl Marx emphasizes the importance of space and place in creating worker consciousness. In this postulation (and many others that followed it), the factory floor provided the necessary space for worker interaction. Bonds of commonality could be formed in these spaces, where workers could see each other laboring and discuss workplace issues. Since social structures limited women to forms of domestic labor, they had fewer such opportunities for solidarity. As Sarah Eisenstein puts it, women "are not, through their roles in the family, involved in interactions with other women which would tend to encourage recognition of a common position as women in social terms. Rather, those roles structure a situation which is privatized and personal, and which tends to generate a conception of the category 'woman' in moral, biological or 'natural,' rather than social terms."[25] The entrance of women into the workplace, including the offices of Western Union, marks a radical change in this spatial relationship and thus the role of women in society.

As films of the Western Union telegraph offices show, women worked alongside men and other women, performing the same tasks at the same time, in full view of one another. Although, as we shall see, talking (or "chatting") was discouraged, the spatial arrangement of the telegraph office provides an environment better suited toward collective identification. Similarly, the strict protocols of the telegraph office, which owed much of their organization to the principles of scientific management and Taylorism, established a highly rationalized, regimented, and routinized workplace environment that clearly delineated boundaries between workers, managers, and customers.[26] Thus, even though the introduction of women workers would have a disruptive effect, the common experience of a highly controlled workplace would offer women workers the opportunity to recognize themselves and each other as workers.[27] One of Western Union's strategies — seen in various policies treating men and women differently, particularly in regard to pay — was to assure that women saw themselves and were seen by others as a separate category of worker and thus achieve internal conflict within the labor force.[28]

If Western Union's training films themselves do not address the tensions produced by a changing workforce directly, the newsletter of the Western Union Employee's Association, *Telegraph World*, took on the issue squarely. By 1919, a new feature had appeared that was directed especially to the women workers. At first the section was called "The Nameless Women's Page?" while the newsletter held a naming contest for a more permanent and suitable title. In April 1920, the new title, "Woman's Affairs," appeared with the following caveat: "This is the first name suggested and it will stand until some one thinks of a better one. If you don't like it say so and make a better suggestion." It was not until August 1922 that the name was switched to "Of Interest to Women." The double entendre of "Woman's Affairs" typified the newsletter's ambivalent treatment of women as suspicious and potentially untrustworthy. Indeed, when the section was first announced in the December 1919 issue, the editors wrote the following: "It would be interesting, first of all, to have an appropriate name for the department. Suggestions are now in order: Shall it be a dignified name — suggestive or trite. For instance: 'w o m a n'; 'Of Interest to Women'; 'We Girls' (Which might merge into the 'Wiggles Department'); 'Peach Pie Department.'"[29]

Based on the fashion in which *Telegraph World* incorporated the new section into the employee newsletter, it would be reasonable to assume that the incorporation of new women workers into the workplace met with similar equivocation. This ambivalence resulted in a delicate balancing act within the column. An early attempt to maintain and expand traditional notions of women's place in society was followed by notes on the latest fashion in footwear and hats, and a recipe for peanut salad. This sort of vacillation continued throughout the column's history. The first page often consisted of progressive declarations as to the status of women, working women, and labor. The image of the female office worker was associated with modernity and progress. Advice on beauty, fashion, manners, housekeeping, and cooking appeared after these assertions of women's rights. While women's accomplishments and abilities were acknowledged, winks and nods to so-called feminine foibles continued to be a regular topic.

Untitled comic, *Telegraph World*, March 1921. Western Union Telegraph Company Records, Archives Center, National Museum of American History, Smithsonian Institution.

"Why Most Girls Are Late," *Telegraph World*, June 1921. Western Union Telegraph Company Records, Archives Center, National Museum of American History, Smithsonian Institution.

For example, several satirical comic strips appeared in *The Telegraph World* portraying women as unsuitable for the type of work required by Western Union. These comics portray women as distracted and inattentive.[30] Work is a secondary concern to their personal lives. By proposing that women were perpetually prone to gossip the comics aimed to demonstrate that women were constitutionally unsuited for the particular service offered by Western Union. Western Union needed to portray its employees as trustworthy, in addition to being efficient, accurate, and fast. The image of women who either had little conception of time passing or willfully ignorant of the clock holds particular significance in a company that emphasized timeliness, punctuality, and the accurate recording of time throughout the process of telegraphic communication. Within the company, however, these portrayals of women workers as overly concerned about fashion and their appearance expressed, in no uncertain terms, male resentment toward this new type of worker. While these are enduring images of women, their presence at this particular time in *The Telegraph World* indicates a growing anxiety regarding the place of women in Western Union.[31]

Male worker resentment may have been rooted in the fear that women were taking men's jobs and driving down wages (two things management wanted). In particular, married women were objects of controversy. Since jobs became scarce in the 1920s, the idea of a married woman working, especially if her husband also worked, while men went unemployed troubled many employees. Western Union employees raised this issue in several employee association meetings during the 1920s.[32] In this way, the presence of women workers achieved much of Western Union's anti-union efforts by creating schisms and tensions within Western Union's workforce.

Alongside the question of whether women could perform the same work as men was the question of the moral status of women who chose to work side by side with men outside their family. Telegraph operators worked at the interface between private and public. In the 1920s the Western Union messengers who delivered paper messages from telegraph offices to residences and businesses were mostly boys; the operators who took messages either in person or over the phone, encoded and decoded those messages, and were responsible for the on-time and discreet transfer of those messages were women. In other words, the fact that women, whose position had been confined to the private domestic space except when escorted, had the opportunity (even obligation) to interact with strangers without a male family member present was the subject of anxiety. The introduction of large numbers of women to the workplace was met precisely with concerns about women workers' moral status.[33]

The affiliation of women with the home was in turn leveraged by feminists as a way of asserting women's abilities and skills in the workplace. In certain strands of early feminist rhetoric, the workplace and the public sphere were to be subsumed by the domestic sphere. Women were called upon to extend the virtuous order and cleanliness women exerted on their homes to other areas of life. For instance, the "Woman's Page?" column of February 1920 made the following assertions:

Suggestions that have come in from the women in the field indicate a desire for discussion of woman and her place in the sun. The woman question is no longer a "problem." Woman has made such progress in the past few years that the problem is solved. She has taken her place, tho [*sic*] there are some, both male and female, of our population, who do not realize it. To the minds of many of us it is astonishing that there ever was a thought that Woman's sphere is the home, meaning the care of the home exclusively. Woman's sphere is the home, but the home in our country touches every circumstance of life — schools especially, politics, government, religion and education.[34]

Simultaneously denying and acknowledging the home as the woman's place, the editors attempt to expand the reach of the home outside of what had been previously construed as a limited domestic sphere. The conclusion extends the formerly private and closed boundaries of the home into the realm of politics, government, religion, and education. Indeed, the point made in this column is that the private realm interacts with public institutions at all levels and that these relationships should not be denied. This set of ideas, which continue to position women as natural homemakers, may very well have been inspired by Jane Addams's "Civic Housekeeping" column in *Ladies' Home Journal* in 1910 in which she claims that civic and political activity is an extension of domestic labor. As Stamp has shown, the rhetorical strategy of linking women's "domestic virtue" and natural role as housekeeper to citizenship and the public sphere was a common strategy for the suffragist movement in the 1910s.[35] In other words, the woman worker was, from the outset, bridging the private and the public, the household and the workplace. As a result, the insistence on extending the domestic sphere to include the workplace divided women between private and public obligations rather than uniting these obligations because the institutions themselves had not changed, only women's role within them.

Some of Western Union's training films built upon the attempts by suffragists, feminists, and newly employed women to link the home to work. *Gumming* opens with a delivery of badly packaged groceries on a housewife's doorstep. When she attempts to lift the badly wrapped and poorly sealed packages and bags, the groceries spill all over her stoop, leaving her with damaged goods. The film compares the badly prepared grocery delivery with a sloppy and damaged telegram. By appealing to a domestic situation, the film positions the female viewer (presumed to be familiar with the irritations of grocery delivery) as sympathetic to clients of Western Union who receive telegrams that are improperly gummed. The rest of the film demonstrates the various techniques of gumming telegrams, from the proper amount of water to use on the adhesive, to the correct margins and spacing, to the importance of holding the tape straight and taut. The level of precision necessary "to uphold the standard of appearance and safety" is both mechanical and objective and an appeal to women's position as homemaker and presumed concern with cleanliness and neatness.

The message of *Accuracy First*, in contrast, relies on a clear distinction between domestic and workplace behavior. Sally, the telegraph operator in the training film, is able to sing and dance with a man at home. An opening title card states that she "loves to dance and have a good time — even as you and I," encouraging a form of identification between viewer/trainee and the character of Sally. At work, Sally interrupts the gumming of an X message (a telegram regarding a stock transaction) to socialize with her friend, the woman who played piano in the opening dancing scene. This interruption is blamed for the errors costing male stockbrokers at the receiving end of the message thousands of dollars. In other words, the behaviors that make Sally a modern woman at home do not make her a model worker at Western Union. Sally's flaw, according to this logic, is a failure to distinguish between work and home. The behaviors sanctioned for a young, educated middle-class woman in the private domestic sphere are opposed in the workplace. Certainly the film plays to stereotypes of women as chatty and gossipy, yet the film never *directly* addresses those characterizations of women. Instead, the film criticizes the telegraph operators for failing to pay close attention to the details of their work, for being distracted, and for not properly consulting with their supervisors. The film, therefore, was not meant to instruct workers in the operation of the telegraph, but to instruct workers in the proper habits and protocols of the workplace. *Accuracy First* took this form precisely because it was addressed to a new category of worker, one who was perceived as ignorant of the work ethic common to industrial America.

Thus *Accuracy First* grows out of a concern that even as working women transcended the private space of the domestic sphere, the behaviors associated with women in the home sphere would also be carried into the workplace. The film attempts to align the priorities of women workers with the priorities of masculinized high finance. In the communication circuit portrayed by *Accuracy First*, the sender and receiver are both men. The messengers (or transmitters) are women. Western Union feared that, in this situation, the priorities associated with men (profit, efficiency) would be superseded by the priorities associated with women (social relationships, talk). The unresolved tension of the film lies in the fact that the supposed priority women place on communication is the reason for their success *and* their failure as telegraph operators. The central concern is that women would be unable to subordinate the oral communication common to the domestic sphere to the written word crucial to business and commerce.

CLOCKWORK IN FILM AND TELEGRAPHY

By asking telegraph operators to identify with the characters portrayed in training films, Western Union encouraged its employees to imitate the very technologies under their supervision. In *Keyboard Errors*, for instance, women workers were admonished for what the film calls a "heavy thumb," which would produce too many spaces, and advised to use a "firm, flexed finger" to ensure that each keystroke would be recognized by the machine. *Keyboard Errors* also showed the dangers of long fingernails, which would accidentally key the wrong character. The film concluded by encouraging workers to keep an even, steady rhythm in their work to prevent the tickertape from looping or breaking. Western Union therefore attempted to instill in its workers machine-like characteristics. Chief among the qualities valued by Western Union were accuracy, efficiency, and productivity, which often manifested as rhetoric against wasting time.

The concern with wasted time extended down to some of the smallest units of time. The further breakdown of work time from days to hours, then to minutes, and finally to seconds is the result of increased complexity in the synchronization of tasks within Western Union offices and between Western Union and its clients. As E. P. Thompson shows, synchronicity of tasks between workers indicates an emergent emphasis on time-attentiveness and industrial labor's intimate relation with the clock.[36] The reliance on clocks to determine the proper execution of tasks externalizes control over labor. The operator is not in the position to determine how much time should be spent on a message: such a calculation is made by management and enforced by clocks and supervisors. The complexity of the tasks necessary for the functioning of Western Union offices and the need to coordinate and synchronize these tasks accentuated the need for precise time-keeping and time-telling technologies at Western Union. In turn, workers were alerted to the importance of these technologies and the significance of adhering to the dictates of the clock.

The "Of Interest to Women" column of August 1922 stated, "Time gets us everything we desire. How? By being used. Nothing can be accomplished without time. To waste one minute is a loss . . . Don't waste time. Get everlastingly busy. You will be filled with joy and happiness."[37] The continuing emphasis on "time-thrift," a movement that Thompson dates back to the 1750s, indicates Western Union's concern that its new employees had not fully internalized the ethos of ordered work temporality. "Fighting the Clock," an article in *Telegraph World* from April 1920, states, "To successfully FIGHT the clock, we must WATCH the clock and get to the job on time. Stragglers, three and four minutes late, disrupt organization to a greater extent than they probably realize."[38] The merit and demerit system at Western Union in 1920 penalized employees for being more than five minutes late. Getting workers to not take advantage of the three to four minute leeway was the job of "non-financial incentives." During this interwar period, the measurement of wasted time was further subdivided into smaller units, so that Western Union kept track of employee minutes and, as shown below, seconds.[39]

The concern with speed is also convergent with emerging trends in high finance and commerce. *Dots and Dashes*, the successor to *Telegraph World*, started regularly running stories highlighting the importance of speed. The telegraph was positioned as central to the increased speed of business, which in turn increased productivity, efficiency, prosperity, and profit. The very nature of telegraphy as a communications system keyed such changes: "In using a letter as a means of communication the transaction to which it relates is dying while the letter is in transit; the same transaction dies again when the answer is traveling back by mail. These two dead periods might be avoided by using the telegraph."[40] While associating death with idle periods in business, the article offers the telegraph as the solution to these deaths—faster communication reanimates your business. This portrayal of the telegram as a life-saver is followed by a series of anecdotes regarding business successes due to telegraph use or business failures due to the lack of telegraph use.

The training films also attempted to instill a practice of clock watching and precise timing in Western Union employees.[41] In *Speed Killers*, a telegraph operator is chastised for gumming an X message and then calling a supervisor over. In this sequence, the operator gums the message, looks around for a supervisor, raises her hand, waves her hand about, and then eventually the supervisor appears. In film time, forty-five seconds transpired between the operator first signaling for a supervisor and the supervisor's arrival. The operator is then chastised for allowing valuable time to be wasted (a title card reads, "all of this is time wasted"). In the second sequence, demonstrating the proper protocol, the operator signals for a supervisor immediately after hearing the bells signaling the arrival of an X message. The supervisor arrives in ten seconds in elapsed film time after this signal. In the film, the operator is admonished for her failure to signal for the supervisor at precisely the right moment, glossing over the sudden change in the supervisor's responsiveness. In *X Messages* the supervisor also instantaneously responds to the operator who signals an X message *prior* to gumming it, as if the supervisor somehow knows if an X message has been gummed before seeing it.

The time-stamping procedure portrayed in *Speed Killers* has similar internal contradictions. Delays are always the fault of operators, not supervisors or equipment. Clocks are never wrong but workers can misread them. The clock portrayed in *Speed Killers* has a minute sweep hand (one that is constantly in motion, rather than advancing from one minute to the next in a step fashion). When the X message is received to then be transmitted to another telegraph office, the clock is shown in the film with the minute hand halfway between 11:21 and 11:22. The title card then states that the time is closer to 11:22 than 11:21 (I was unable to discern this in repeated viewings). The operator records the time as 11:21, making it appear as if it took longer to process the message than normal; as a title card states, "there is no delay, but a discrepancy of one minute to start." Because of this "discrepancy," the message appears to have been received by the other telegraph operator two minutes later than it was sent. As the next title card states, this delay "obviously must be investigated by the receiving office." While the training film ostensibly wants to train employees to read properly a clock with a sweep minute hand, to round off seconds properly, and to make sure that no undue delays occur, this particular vignette in the film emphasizes the importance of record keeping. There is nothing, apparently, stopping operators from post-dating or pre-dating the X messages. Following the logic of the film, the sending operator could have recorded the send time as 11:22, and the receiving operator could have recorded the receive time as 11:23 by rounding off seconds. Because the film is careful to state that "actually no undue delay occurred," it encourages modifying the records in order to give the appearance of smooth, quick, and accurate transmission of the message.

The introduction and widespread use of mechanical technology, particularly in industrial contexts, has led many historians and social critics to lament the machine age as one in which humans have become objectified, quantified, and drained of any characteristics that distinguish them from the machines they operate. Western Union's training films exhorted workers to work with the same mechanical precision, steady rhythm, and attention to detail possessed by the telegraph apparatus and the film projection apparatus. These films demonstrate that it is the drive for profit—through increased emphasis on productivity, efficiency, accuracy, and speed—that causes employers to attempt a mechanization of their employees' labor.[42] The advantage of machines in production lies in their lack of idiosyncrasies, in their constancy, steadiness, and relentless obedience. The gumming machine was never bored or distracted, never late, never tired, and never hungry. In this context, efforts to make telegraph operators more like telegraph machinery appear logical and necessary. It is *not* the interaction with technology that made workers more machine-like. Rather, it is that the workers labored under the same conditions of industrial capitalism that necessitated (and relied on) machine technology. The machines and workers exhibit similar characteristics because they are called upon to perform similar tasks.

CONCLUSION: SOLVING LABOR PROBLEMS WITH FILM

The anonymous contributor to *Telegraph World*, from whom I take the title of this chapter, reminded women moviegoers to "not take in the plot only, but the lessons, the acting, the life that is taught." These are standard tenets applicable to appreciation of literature or the theater as well as film. The columnist's allegation that film reflects social reality—that it reproduces traces of actuality to which viewers can relate—is a directive to viewers to identify with actors and/or situations in film. Here, a pre-existing conception of what constituted proper viewing habits helps to produce identification. And yet, the identificatory process for Western Union's training films is reinforced by the nature of their exhibition. These training films were shown to a captive (but willing) audience of trainees. Thus, the exhibition context of these films structures their response (and I would argue this is true of all cinematic experiences). The trainees knew, before the projector was even turned on, how to view the films and the consequences of not paying attention.

Western Union's effective use of film as a training medium, therefore, relied on discourses of theatrical moviegoing and the structures of the classroom. The company specifically tried to refashion film-viewing spaces by combining the practices of disparate institutions. The content of the films likewise relied on eliding traditionally separated spaces—the home and the workplace—in an attempt to appeal particularly to women. Western Union employed film specifically to help assimilate a new category of worker, a category the company first introduced as part of a campaign against worker organization. The declaration that in films "we can see ourselves as others see us" offers a good explanation of how identification works in these training films to create a self-regulated and self-reflective audience. It asks moviegoers to watch films while keeping in mind that they themselves are also watched. By adopting the position of the watcher and the watched, the female Western Union employee was asked to put herself in the position of management and labor. By asking trainees to identify with the supervisor, the training films were part of a campaign to condense layers of office work, decrease management responsibilities, and therefore experience management and labor as having congruent interests.

The content and form of these films suggest that Western Union was concerned about the ability of women workers to conform to telegraphic technology and the work ethic desired by the company. It was, in part, due to the problem of training a large number of new workers that the company turned to film. Film was perceived as an efficient educational tool, able to present information quickly to large groups in a highly engaging way. This was particularly attractive in an industry invested in relatively rapid worker turnover and technological innovation. Alongside this discourse of film as the newest and most progressive educational tool was an image of women as avid moviegoers. Western Union's attempt to solve one labor problem created another; and the company found the answer to the second problem in film.

NOTES

I have enormous gratitude for valuable insights and commentary on earlier drafts of this article offered by Charles Acland, Keya Ganguly, Ronald W. Greene, John Mowitt, Haidee Wasson, and the anonymous readers at Duke University Press. The research for this chapter was conducted with the financial assistance of the University of Minnesota's Harold Leonard Memorial Film Fellowship and Grant, which allowed me to perform archival research at the National Museum of American History Archives Center and the Library of Congress. Thanks are due to the staff at the Archives Center who assisted me: Wendy Shay, Reuben M. Jackson, Kay Peterson, and Susan B. Strange.

1 These are the only films surviving from the period in the National Museum of American History Archives Center. I found no documents detailing their production, or if

any other films were produced. Nor did I find any documents detailing their exhibition. Most likely these films were shown in Western Union Telegraph Schools.

2   Jacoby, *Employing Bureaucracy*, 99–132.

3   See R. Greene, "Y Movies"; and Waldman, "'Toward a Harmony of Interests.'"

4   These films were mostly intended for sales personnel, rather than to instruct mechanics or other skilled laborers. The bias here seems to be that films were best suited to training employees whose main duties included communication. The Willys-Overland films included *Work Your Work Sheet* (1927), *Bring Them to the Salesroom* (1927), *Standard Presentation* (1927), *Intelligent Bullying Is as Important as Intelligent Selling* (1928), *Making Your Demonstrations as Impressive as Your Products* (1929), and *After Vacation There Is a Job to Be Done* (1930). The Ford films include the series *Communication Systems* (1920, 1921) and *Sales and Service Improvement Material* (1924–35). Leo Beebe notes, "The first training films of any consequence were produced for the U.S. Armed Forces in World War I. The Army used sixty-two films on such subjects as *The School of the Soldier* and *Elements of the Automobile*" and mentions that International Harvester, U.S. Steel, and Caterpillar Tractor were also making industrial films during this period. Beebe, "Industry," 88. By the 1930s training films had abandoned the hybrid approach mixing fictional narrative with direct instruction. In 1936 Audiovision produced *Selling to Women* for Plymouth Motor Company and *Service That Sells* for Delaware Lackawanna and Western Coal. These films, whose scripts can be found in the Library of Congress Copyright Collection, abandoned dramatic narrative in favor of a series of illustrative vignettes to demonstrate the effectiveness of certain sales techniques.

5   See R. Greene, "Y Movies"; and Waldman, "'Toward a Harmony of Interests.'"

6   See Beebe, "Industry."

7   For examinations of 16mm in a variety of settings, see Wasson, *Museum Movies* and "Electric Homes! Automatic Movies! Efficient Entertainment!"; Zimmermann, *Reel Families*; and Ruoff, *Virtual Voyages*, 217–37.

8   See *Industrial Relations: Final Report and Testimony Submitted to Congress by the Commission on Industrial Relations*.

9   Waldman, "Toward a Harmony of Interests," 42.

10 See Ulrikkson, *The Telegraphers, Their Craft and Their Unions*.

11 Carlton, "Introducing the News," 1.

12 Burts, "Operating Supervision," 4.

13 The reference to Canadians seems to stem from general anxiety about Canadians moving into industrialized urban areas in the northern United States and working in telegraph companies. In addition, Canadian Pacific Railway was the only company in North America prior to 1915 to have a contract with a telegrapher's union. See "Commercial Telegraph Companies" in *Industrial Relations*, 9291–541; see in particular the testimony of Newcomb Carlton regarding Canadian Pacific Railway on page 9295 and the testimony of T. W. Carroll, the division traffic superintendent of Western Union, regarding Canadian employees on page 9415.

14 I am of course referring to Walter Benjamin's remarks on Fascism in the epilogue to his famed 1935 essay "The Work of Art in the Age of Mechanical Reproduction." In

this way, the employee newsletter serves as a concession to workers that would miti-gate worker agitation.

15 Eisenstein, *Give Us Bread but Give Us Roses*, 26–27.

16 In 1915 Western Union was under investigation for employing "special agents" used to infiltrate the Commercial Telegrapher's Union, a practice that apparently began in 1911 (see *Industrial Relations*). Newcomb Carlton also testified, regarding prospec-tive employees, that "they all know that we do not favor their membership in the Commercial Telegrapher's Union" (*Industrial Relations*, 9308).

17 Newcomb Carlton testified to the U.S. Congress, in April 1915, "I am a tremendous believer in certain forms of woman labor. Some of the most efficient, up to a certain point, of our labor, is by women; but women have not the telegraphic capacity of men—that is, very few have—the average woman is considerably below man in her capacity for telegraphic work, and to that extent we have reduced her hours of labor" (*Industrial Relations*, 9307).

18 Koszarski, *An Evening's Entertainment*, 30.

19 Abel, *Americanizing the Movies and "Movie-Mad" Audiences, 1910–1914*, 90.

20 Stamp, *Movie-Struck Girls*, 199.

21 Scott, "Woman's Affairs," 199.

22 I am referring here to the system of the suture as put forward variously by Daniel Dayan, Jean-Pierre Oudart, and Kaja Silverman.

23 This point is made explicit in Elbert Hubbard's column "The Law of Wages," in which he states that "the less you require looking after, the more able you are to stand alone and complete your tasks, the greater your reward . . . do your work so well that it will require no supervision, and by doing your own thinking you will save the expense of hiring some one to think for you." *Western Union News* 1, no. 4 (October 1914), 6.

24 "Report on Merit and Demerit System," *Telegraph World* 2, no. 10 (1920), 365–67.

25 Eisenstein, *Give Us Bread but Give Us Roses*, 39.

26 For a history of the rationalization of office space and its relation to scientific man-agement, labor relations, and the military, see R. Martin, *The Organizational Com-plex*.

27 The role of spatial relations in worker consciousness and equal pay was remarked on during Newcomb Carlton's testimony to the Commission on Industrial Relations:

> Commissioner O'Connell: Are there any arrangements being made whereby the males and females are being separated in the office, or are they associated right together as I have seen them, sitting next to each other?
> Mr. Carlton: There is no segregation of the females from the males.
> Commissioner O'Connell: The females sit next to the males doing the same work, and yet there is a difference of $6 a week in their wages? (*Industrial Relations*, 9307).

28 See *Industrial Relations*, 9291–541.

29 "Announcement: Our Women Folk," *Telegraph World* 1, no. 12 (1919), 360.

30 Untitled comic, *Telegraph World* 3, no. 3 (March 1921), 167; and "Why Most Girls Are Late," *Telegraph World* 3, no. 6 (June 1921), 272.

31 No comics like these appeared in Western Union publications during the 1910s,

1930s, or 1940s. Within the employee newsletters, magazines, and company para-phernalia, graphic depictions of the crisis of women in the workplace was limited to the 1920s.

32 See, in particular, "Resolution Objecting to Married Women Working While Men with Families and Having Less Seniority Are Dropped from the Service," *Telegraph World* 3, no. 10 (October 1921), 508.

33 It should be noted that this concern also extended to messenger boys. See the tes-timony to the Commission on Industrial Relations regarding messenger boys and "houses of ill repute" (*Industrial Relations*, 9291–541).

34 "Woman's Page?" *Telegraph World* 2, no. 2 (1920), 46.

35 Stamp, *Movie-Struck Girls*, 179–80.

36 Thompson, "Time, Work-Discipline, and Industrial Capitalism."

37 "Of Interest to Women," *Telegraph World* 4, no. 8 (August 1922), 8.

38 "Fighting the Clock," *Telegraph World* 2, no. 4 (April 1920), 126.

39 "Report on Merit and Demerit System," *Telegraph World* 2, no. 10 (1920), 365–67.

40 "Speed Up Business by Telegraph," *Dots and Dashes* 1, no. 1 (April 1925), 1.

41 Western Union began measuring worker productivity in seconds starting in the mid-to late 1920s. The corporate literature during this period emphasized the importance of "split-second" timing and speed. "Cable Service Is Life-blood of 'Split-second' Banking," after a lesson in the complexity of the financial arbitrage, notes "the speed of these processes is indicated by the fact that the automatic timing machine which stamps time of service, registers the hour, minute, and second of all operations, and while the ordinary time for sending a message to London [from New York] and get-ting a reply has been given as less than three minutes, there are numerous instances of this complete service being performed in 90 seconds" (*Dots and Dashes* 3, no. 3 [March 1927], 1). Other cover stories during the 1930s included "High Speed Ticker Feels the Pulse of Business" (*Dots and Dashes* 9, no. 12 [December 1933], 1); a series of stories proclaiming that the installation of Western Union clocks with the second sweep hand have inspired athletes to new heights in athletic competitions ("Giant Clocks Used at Football Games and Rodeos Are Popular," *Dots and Dashes* 9, no. 12 [December 1933], 2); and "A Visit behind the Scenes Where Speed Is King," which includes a profile of women who skate around the Western Union office to increase the speed of message transmission (*Dots and Dashes* 7, no. 10 [October 1931], 1).

42 There is a relationship between automation, speed, and increased hiring of women workers by Western Union. The more automated telegraphy equipment required less skill on the part of its operators. Under the Morse system, an operator would have to distinguish and decode several thousand sounds per hour. The automated system provided typewritten transcriptions of the telegram. This enabled Western Union to shed some of its skilled highly paid male employees in favor of less skilled female employees, many of whom were trained in Western Union's schools. It is un-clear that these helped defray costs for Western Union, but it did allow the company to lessen the ranks of a particular category of employee. Sylvester Konenkamp, the president of the Commercial Telegraphers' Union of America, told Congress in 1915, "The telegraph business has been changing from the Morse system to what is known

as the automatic, where less-skilled labor is employed, and these employees are even making a greater record on the automatic than in the Morse. We have records taken from the Western Union News showing that women have maintained an average speed of a message every 21 seconds for 8 hours and 15 minutes in a day. In other words, 1,220 messages in 8 hours, or a maximum of 167 messages handled in one hour . . . In recent years the company has been trying its best, apparently, to eliminate the Morse operator and to use in its stead the automatic machine. Three to four girls and boys are usually required to do the work that one operator formerly did, thus eliminating the skilled worker." (*Industrial Relations,* 9312–13). Regarding the Western Union schools in the 1910s, T. W. Carroll told the commission, "We graduate a few female employees. We teach them telegraphy, and if they desire to continue on the Morse side of it, that is their privilege: but as a rule, we graduate them into the automatic service" (*Industrial Relations,* 9415).

HOLLYWOOD'S EDUCATORS

MARK MAY AND TEACHING FILM CUSTODIANS

Charles R. Acland

The scholarly and historical status of the Payne Fund Studies on children and the movies of the 1930s has always been uncertain. The existing literature is even inconsistent about how many there actually were, because of a difference between the number of studies and the number of volumes. Let's call it twelve studies, which includes Edgar Dale's film appreciation text and Frederick Thrasher's and Paul Cressey's unpublished work, but excludes W. W. Charters's and Henry Forman's summaries. Reading them, they are simultaneously impressive and bewildering. Some were ahead of their time methodologically and some were well behind. Despite a clear line to research developments in the sociology of the Chicago school, the studies were too quantitative and normatively driven to find a sure place in what would become the humanities-based field of film studies. And they are without directly continuous institutional influence, unlike the work of Paul Lazarsfeld and his cohort, to be considered anything but a curious anomalous effort for the field of mass communication.[1] In terms of reception, the project was momentarily popularly energizing but so deathly dull as to virtually guarantee few would read the complete works. It appears that the Payne Fund Studies are interesting more for the fact that they took place than for actual research findings and impact.

And the findings, tentative and contradictory as they are, are themselves part of the reason for this ambiguous status. The historical record has concentrated upon Henry Forman's commissioned summary volume of 1933, *Our Movie Made Children*, and his three *McCall's* articles in 1932 as the definitive public face of the studies.[2] But Forman notoriously twisted the detail of the research into an inaccurately coherent version of the negative influence of motion pictures on children. The summary volume did not reflect the actual studies, and some Payne Fund authors criticized its anti-movie sermonizing tone, saying so in print.[3] This has been well documented in the best work on the Payne Fund Studies, *Children and the Movies: Media Influence and the Payne Fund Controversy* by Garth Jowett, Ian Jarvie, and Kathryn Fuller.[4] But even in the 1930s, commentators noted the discrepancy between the presumed impact of the studies and what they actually documented. The immediate critical appraisals of the Payne Fund, scholarly reviews, Mortimer Adler's *Art and Prudence* (1937), and Raymond Morley's *Are We Movie Made?* (1938) made it clear that a debate was in process. Far from being uniformly influential or accepted, the Payne Fund Studies were described in 1940 by John Marshall, the eminence of the Rockefeller Foundation Humanities Division, as essentially discredited.[5]

Jowett, Jarvie, and Fuller put the studies and their reception in context, highlighting the dissension among the ranks of scholars involved, the variety of methods, and neglected efforts. They also pick up on an underdeveloped theory of society as the source of the studies' failings, rather than the sermonizing of the Forman volume. They confirm that the Payne Fund Studies' legacy is not easy to assess, noting that major reforms like the work of the Legion of Decency and the enforcement of the Production Code were already in the works before the appearance of the volumes. Still, some current research continues to see the studies and their reception as unified and singularly momentous. For instance, Nicholas Sammond, in his generally terrific book *Babes in Tomorrowland*, claims, "More than any other preceding discursive formation, discussions of the Payne Fund Studies would cement the notion of a generic child engaged in a uniform practice of viewing and deriving effects from that practice applicable to any other child, regardless of race, class, or gender."[6] In fact, their most basic finding was that there was no generic child, but instead that results depended on a range of factors including sex, education, familiarity with movies, family composition, neighborhood, and economic situation, to name just a few. Sammond claims that Samuel Renshaw, and his infamous studies with beds wired to measure sleep disturbances and tachistoscopic tests of the effect of flicker on young eyes, drew overly broad conclusions despite inconclusive data.[7] Actually, Renshaw complained to Forman about this misrepresentation, and here is what he and his authors summarize: "We can conclude . . . that seeing *some* films does induce a disturbance of relaxed, recuperative sleep in children. . . . On the other hand certain films may have an instructive or cathartic and sedative effect that is good. We do not believe that any sweeping generalization can be made about the 'type' of film, or 'type' of child most likely to be influenced."[8]

One issue at root here is the way that "behaviorist" psychological and social scientistic methods from earlier eras have become easy targets for humanities-informed contemporary scholars. I am especially concerned that the rush toward conclusions of ideological coherence can distort the historical record and result in an undervaluation of the significance of social science and psychology in the history of the study of film, if not "film studies" exactly. It remains essential to see what sets of knowledge, expertise, and understandings about media power were put into action in any given historical moment, even if such thinking does not match the epistemological frameworks favored by scholars of today. Doing so, as I discuss in this chapter, we can see how engaged scholars, reformers, progressives, and liberals willingly courted positions of co-opted managerial influence.

I am not proposing to re-evaluate, let alone rescue, the Payne Fund Studies, but to suggest that they are but one slice of a powerful shift in attention to educational reform, and that to understand them one needs to cut a wider swath to include other activities in media education. Doing this tells us something about the flow of debate and expertise between the academy, philanthropic foundations, industry, and schools on the subject of motion pictures. Through the 1930s, 1940s, and 1950s, the sheer volume of initiatives to deploy film to expand sites of learning, to establish new voluntary educational societies, to advocate new teaching methods and technologies, to test and assess these new directions, and to launch a fully functioning instructional film production and distribution industry remains remarkable, from the prewar American Council on Education (ACE) studies to the postwar film council movement. These reformers advocated a modified Deweyian model of progressive education through technological means, emphasizing experiential learning, group-led discussion, and structured debate. Broadly speaking, these efforts were part of an enactment of a modern mass-mediated public, as well as the production of related hierarchies of cultural authority.

As a way to indicate the limited influence of the Payne Fund, Jowett, Jarvie, and Fuller observe that few of the researchers had further interest in motion pictures once their contributions were complete. But among those few were some impressive long-term efforts, especially by Mark May, Edgar Dale, and Samuel Renshaw—all three innovators in the deployment and assessment of media in changing educational contexts. What follows concentrates upon Mark May's contributions to the institutionalization of the properly instructional deployment of motion pictures and of the role Hollywood was to play in this new technological pedagogical formation.

May trained in psychology at Columbia University, with much of his research concentrating on character—its formation, expression, and measurement. With Hugh Hartshorne and Julius B. Maller, he spent five years studying character, which was part of the Character Education Inquiry, Teachers College, Columbia University, in cooperation with the Institute of Social and Religious Research, under the supervision and with the participation of Dr. E. L. Thorndike. Published as *Studies in the Nature of Character* in 1928 and 1929, the first volume was *Studies in Deceit* and the second *Studies in Service and Self-Control*. The work tried to measure a wide range of social activity, including cooperation, charitable behavior, service, school morale, and the role of out-of-school experience. They measured self-control by observing persistence and inhibition, using party games and assessing contributing factors. In what was an expansive project, May and his colleagues studied more than a thousand children of various ages and various types of schools to do this work.

Though not the focus of this study, they did ask questions about and charted moviegoing among the children they observed. In one of their general conclusions on the relationship between frequency of moviegoing and participation in civic service activities, they found, "It is apparent that other factors than mere attendance at movies need to be taken into consideration, but even after we have noted such concomitants as have been recorded we still find larger differences in service tendencies between the regular and occasional moving picture attendants—between the addicts and the casuals—than it is easy to understand."[9] And on the relationship between moviegoing and self-control, they wrote, "Those who attend motion pictures less frequently than their schoolmates do are inclined to exert greater effort and greater self-restraint. It is a question whether this results as a direct effect of the pictures themselves

Teaching Film Custodians, Inc., logo.

or from characteristic ways in which habits of attendance on motion pictures develop among different sections of the population of a given community."[10]

These observations, showing some differences without conclusive claims of causality, echo in May's later Payne Fund study. Co-authored with his Yale colleague Frank Shuttleworth, May contributed *The Social Conduct and Attitudes of Movie Fans* (1933), gathering material from three hundred frequent movie-going kids (three films per week) and three hundred infrequent moviegoers (less than once per month). They used the same Character Education Inquiry developed in the earlier study. Among the general findings were that teachers look less favorably upon the movie fans, but that peers rank them higher as popular people and as "best friends." On attitudes about crime, prohibition, sex, parents, authority, and the like, they found essentially no difference between the groups, concluding that the community is a greater influence than motion pictures.[11]

At the time, May wrote studies of theology in practice and of driving safety. His most prominent work was at Yale University's Institute of Human Relations, an appointment he held from 1927 through to 1960, and of which he was director from 1935. At this Rockefeller-funded research center, May oversaw some celebrated research projects, including John Dollard's *Caste and Class in a Southern Town* (1937). The goals of this institute were broad, and it was an effort to take the epistemological stakes of psychology from the closed lab context out into messier social environments. The researchers saw categories like perception and personality as involving social structures. To examine this, the institute constructed what at the time was a fairly novel interdisciplinary context, in which anthropology, medical research, economics, history, primatology, statistics, and psychology would be in conversation with each other. As *Time* magazine put it, under May's direction, the institute studied an odd array of topics, including prejudice, satire, detective stories, war, crime, speech defects, frustration, and reactions to parking tickets.[12] The intellectual influences of the day were many, but Dollard gave special mention to Edward Sapir and Sigmund Freud.[13]

So, with this sense of new directions in research, contemporary social phenomena, and "real world" application, as well as his own academic prominence, May began to work in an advisory capacity with the Motion Picture Producers and Distributors Association of America (MPPDA). May's work on character education and ideas for a human relations series interested the MPPDA because of its potential appeal to a general audience of teachers and students.[14] Just as important, here was an accomplished academic, at a prestigious university, who was truly committed to the exploitation of the educational potential of film. Knowledge of how films might be used, what kinds of films benefit teachers, and what pedagogical advantage instructional use held was still scant at this time. In essence, there was a premium placed on those who could construct and interpret information about film in non-entertainment settings. Mark Lynn Anderson has examined the Payne Fund Studies in exactly this way, demonstrating their impact on the formation of a cohort of professional media experts whose primary goal was the exercise of social control.[15] In his efforts to work between academia and Hollywood, May was similarly fashioning himself an exemplar of the kind of influence these new media experts might exert.

In the 1930s, popular reports emphasized the MPPDA's longstanding interest in education, in particular repeating the fact that soon after the group's formation, William Hays, its head, expressed his interest in industry reform for the benefit of education to a meeting of the National Education Association (NEA) in Boston in 1922. Between 1930 and early 1936, the MPPDA collected a thousand school curricula, press clippings, and various published statements by educators in an effort to ascertain the possible educational value of non-current theatrical shorts.[16] This activity notwithstanding, education was hardly the core concern of the organization, to say the least, though it was a powerful public relations tool. Whatever advancement in education the MPPDA may have eventually subsidized, its primary focus never wavered from the well-being of its member Hollywood studios.

May's first contact with the industry lobby appears to have been attendance at the MPPDA conference of educators and civic leaders on film as a teaching tool in 1929. At this event, the MPPDA established the Committee on Social Values in Motion Pictures, with Howard LeSourd (the dean of Boston University Graduate School) as chair, and on which May served. This committee developed the experimental use of shortened features, which began in earnest in 1933, and became the "Secrets of Success" series.[17] The series consisted of eight prints of twenty one-reel works taken from "quality" films and made available to schools, running from 1934 to 1936. The films demonstrated excerpts of "social value" for use in character education, which was understood as a secular version of religious education.[18] School interest in the "Secrets of Success" series was substantial, but it was not easy to regularize usage as, with prints available in 35mm only, it required schools to negotiate cooperation with local theaters to open their doors to classes. The MPPDA estimated that over six hundred thousand students saw these films over two years, a sizable audience given that this program was essentially exploratory by design. Still, general distribution would require the ability to handle much larger numbers.[19] Too expensive to maintain, too complicated to organize, and too fraught with uncertainty about economic impact on theater owners, the program was unsustainable. Moreover, the MPPDA did not wish to continue supporting the "Secrets of Success" series in part due to concerns about releasing member films for distribution by non-member organizations.[20]

And yet, as a testing ground, the MPPDA appeared to convince many that ignoring the teaching role of film was not an option. In 1936, May and LeSourd designed a plan to build on the findings, and shift the goals, of the Committee on Social Values in Motion Pictures and of the Payne Fund Studies.[21] Their proposed program would offer illustrative films, depictions of human relations, coverage of world news, and methods of critical discussion of what students would be seeing, the latter described as "a psychologically sound method of censorship."[22] The first year of the plan would involve arranging for the films used by the Committee on Social Values, that is, the "Secrets of Success" films, and preparing some new ones, then testing them experimentally in about thirty schools. During the next year a wider selection of films would be offered. The members of the committee were to be retained in an advisory capacity. Distribution of the films was to return to the industry after that two-year period.[23]

One iteration of this proposal was the Commission on Human Relations film project of the Progressive Education Association, under the direction of Alice Keliher, but with significantly more ambitious plans.[24] The MPPDA agreed to Keliher's experimental use, provided films were in 16mm format only and were exclusively exhibited in school, which responded to some of the exhibitor and studio concerns about the "Secrets of Success" program. Keliher's more expansive project undertook the editing of other feature films, with special emphasis on questions of social life. Even though in May 1936 Keliher was not optimistic that she would receive support for this,[25] the Rockefeller Foundation, through the General Education Board, did back the effort. The project ran for two years, 1936–38, and then received a final year's grant for 1938–39. Topics selected were to "cultivate social democracy, promote a feeling of responsibility for war, and break down racial prejudice . . . [and show] parent-child relationships, effects of divorce on children, family adjustments, the obligations of friendship, the functioning of law in the community."[26] The Human Relations project treated the "Secrets of Success" films as an initial offering, soon adding newsreels, travelogues, and other subjects.[27] In other words, the character education programs were a starting point for a wider application of film in education, rather than the main focus. Using seventy-five truncated films to chart and study pedagogical uses, Keliher's program recorded the discussions following such films as *Black Legion* (1937), *Fury* (1936), and *Alice Adams* (1935). All these excerpted films were for the program's exclusive use, and did not go into general distribution.[28] Keliher made explicit the fact that her commission, and not the industry lobby, would have control over usage of the films, by which she meant critical analysis and discussion of the films in question. She was, reasonably, concerned about undue interference from the mainstream industry in her experiment. This request had the apparent blessing of May and Hays.[29]

Before the Human Relations series had been planned and launched, May visited Hollywood with Hays and other board members in July 1935 to discuss a possible appointment to an MPPDA educational film committee. May reported to Marshall at the Rockefeller Foundation that he had decided not to accept the position as a salaried member, preferring to act as an independent advisor.[30] The need for even more formalized study led to the invitation of Mark May to prepare a report through the summer of 1936 to recommend further action on the part of the MPPDA. His main point, one that was formally launched in September 1936, was the establishment of an Advisory Committee on the Use of Motion Pictures in Education, made up of leading educators and with May appointed its head.[31] Effectively, this was a transformation of the

MPPDA's Committee on Social Values into a non-salaried Advisory Committee so that the expertise and familiarity with the earlier program was not lost.[32]

Several factors encouraged the MPPDA and participating members of the need for such an Advisory Committee. These included praise for their work from educators at home and abroad, and the growing number of grants for other experimental instructional projects by the American Council on Education and the University of Minnesota. Other sparks of activity in the area of educational film included the aforementioned Human Relations project, and the formation of the American Film Center and the Association of School Film Libraries in 1938.[33] A perennial problem to the development of motion pictures in education was that schools were not investing substantially in projectors because of the lack of films, and few films were being released for instructional usage by the Hollywood majors due to the absence of projectors. With its special relation to the mainstream entertainment industry, the Advisory Committee was in a good position to lobby for the release of films "to break the deadlock in the educational film movement," which it did.[34] The members of the MPPDA still worried what effect such distribution would have upon their theatrical releases, so the focus rested upon films that had completed their theatrical run. But, beyond the public relations advantage of Hollywood supporting education, these experiments in educational film were also a way to test the waters for what secondary markets might exist for these old products. What new value might the studio libraries hold for educational markets? The Advisory Committee acknowledged that classroom use was still relatively uncharted territory for film, so it recommended intensified support for research on film and education. And, always mindful of the public perception of Hollywood involvement, all study was to be undertaken by a third party, rather than the industry or the Advisory Committee itself, even if one or the other would direct and make requests for certain kinds of research. This note of impartiality turned the research dimension back to educators, scholars, and philanthropies.[35]

Meeting for the first time on February 9, 1937, and then five more times in 1937, the Advisory Committee operated with the unshakable belief that cooperation between the film industry and educators was entirely possible. The members were well aware of the delicate nature of such an idea, and vowed to assure that schools would not sense an encroachment of advertising and that exhibitors would not feel they were losing revenue or facing a new competitor.[36] Even so, once operations were up and running, one of Hollywood's

THE SELECTED PHOTOPLAY

Selecting... THE USEFUL FOOTAGE

Preparing...THE ROUGH CUT

Checking... THE WORK PRINT FOR

Final Acceptance

TFC preview committee work process, from *The* TFC *Story*, 9.

requirements for releasing films for classroom use, and written into licensing contracts with schools, was that the logo of the originating studio would be clearly visible and presented with each screening. A first step was to take stock of existing films and to coordinate existing information on film use. The Advisory Committee spent quite a bit of time at these early meetings watching non-current shorts and discussing how they might be treated and assessed.[37] The idea to begin with a comprehensive survey of existing films and their classroom potential appears to have come from Hays himself.[38]

For this survey, analyzing films was on the basis of four criteria: content, presentation, and probable effects and function in relation to existing materials.[39] Accordingly, members of the committee assessed each film to fit one of several proposed film series, including citizenship, parenting, occupation, consumers, leisure, health and safety, and "personality adjustment," which were to fall in line with the Human Relations films.[40] Surveying trade journals, they constructed a list of about three thousand shorts, divided into travelogues, scenics, historicals, sports, animated cartoons, musicals, popular science, nature studies, melodrama, comedy, and vaudeville. Setting melodrama, comedy, and vaudeville aside, panels of educators reviewed corresponding films.[41] Reviewers recorded a synopsis, assessed possible subjects and grade levels, and proposed teaching uses. They also were to take note of limitations.[42]

This inventory was taken in the summer of 1937, with viewing panels for art, biological science, elementary education, music, physical education, physical science, and social studies. Participants previewed a total of 1,595 films, of which 903 were theatrical shorts and 692 were instructional films from Eastman, ERPI, and Bray, all of which were affiliated with the MPPDA. The panels' concluding assessments found 849 films acceptable as they were and 234 acceptable with minor modifications.[43] Panelists also screened some films of non-member companies on a limited basis, including those of Instructional Films, Inc., Gutlohn, Gaumont-British, and the YMCA.[44] A final 364 passed all stages and were made available for school use.[45] Recommendations to the MPPDA from the Advisory Committee were for funds to produce a catalogue of these select films, for immediate arrangements to make the films available to schools, for continued support for a film preview program, and for a grant to study in detail the data compiled during the previews in the summer of 1937.[46]

The previewing work of this committee through that summer received considerable public attention. *Film Daily* erroneously described it as a survey of fifteen thousand shorts.[47] The *New York Times* covered the NEA meeting in Detroit and the presentation of the Advisory Committee's work as a watershed moment for mechanized instruction. Under the banner "Machine Age Sets Education Trend," the article described experimental methods to teach safe driving to groups using simulated automobile controls, lantern slides, and point-of-view films shot through windscreens. Mark May, promoting the work of the preview panels, commented that the growing interest in "life studies" as a respected area of education would be greatly advanced by the use of film to depict realistic situations.[48]

With a catalogue in process, the details of how best to circulate recommended films, in a way agreeable to the Hollywood majors, still needed to be resolved. The Advisory Committee was not equipped to be a distribution outfit. So the committee was incorporated as a non-profit company, in the state of New York, and renamed Teaching Film Custodians (TFC) on December 8, 1938. The "custodians" part of the name was to make unambiguous the fact that they were but caretakers of the films and that ownership of the films remained with the original studios.[49] The Advisory Committee became its first board, with May as the head, a position he went on to hold for forty years until 1968. The committee continued to operate, serving the dual function of an MPPDA advisory organ and a separate incorporated entity, with the most obvious advantage of cosmetic appearance of arm's-length operation from Hollywood.[50]

The catalogue itemized the screened, evaluated, and recommended Hollywood shorts and was available in 1939.[51] The first year of TFC's film distribution—the 1939–40 school year—did not include advertising for specific programs for film, as the TFC was hoping instead to gauge market interest from school demand alone.[52] Films, including MGM's "Crime Doesn't Pay" series, *City of Wax* (1934), *Marine Circus* (1939), and *Pagodas of Peiping* (1933), cost a rental rate of $15 per year or $30 for three years.[53] Users of the TFC—which included schools, school boards, state departments of education, and university systems—entered into licensing agreements for either one-year terms or three-year terms.[54] The 1939 catalogue included about 450 films, though some were not yet actually available due to technical problems. In particular, the Technicolor films could not be supplied as a result of the challenge and expense of reducing them to 16mm.[55] Hays did promotional work for the TFC, appearing at an NEA conference and introducing the TFC as an industry response to the growing interest in classroom films. Reportedly, demand was highest for historical works and travelogues that focused on social and economic life.[56] Updating its offerings, the TFC completed a new catalogue, *Films for Classroom Use*, in 1941, adding 141 new films and dropping about 100 due to low demand or unavailability.[57] To assist in the deployment of films in specific classroom contexts, the TFC produced study guides to accompany film rental, doing so with assistance from the National University Extension Association.[58] In what was a notable source of bewilderment for the TFC's directors, demand for films in high school social studies classrooms remained low. As a consequence, they agreed to support a preliminary study on this need, conducted by Howard Wilson of Harvard University.

Initially, the TFC drew up contracts for the films it handled with each individual studio, emphasizing that only non-current films that had completed their theatrical run were of interest, with Paramount the last holdout until 1941.[59] The agreements allowed for the use of short subjects for exclusive, non-profit use in schools in the continental United States, though this eventually expanded to Canada and beyond. The TFC renewed the three-year contracts for the use of these films for another three years in 1942.[60] The goals of the TFC, as explained to member-company ERPI, only began with the laudatory expansion of educational service. Another goal was the stimulation of a market for projectors, and hence an eventually profitable educational film production and distribution industry. The TFC was "positive that this added encouragement has in many instances proved the determining factor in enabling school systems to equip their school buildings for the projection of classroom films."[61] A further objective saw the public relations benefits of putting an educational gloss on Hollywood enterprise. This "goodwill for the motion picture industry" among teachers and administrators would assist in "the softening of the charge of monopoly against the industry in educational circles," which arose when they found that desired films were unavailable for educational uses.[62] And all indications were that interest in the films the TFC offered was growing. By the end of 1945, more than 10,300 TFC 16mm reels were circulating at 423 film libraries.[63]

But these reels were all still short subjects. Other scholarly work has suggested that the TFC circulated excerpted features in the 1930s, which it did not.[64] Such truncated films were available in a limited and experimental basis first through the "Secrets of Success" program and then through Keliher's Commission on Human Relations, but they were not in general distribution in the 1930s. The release of features, however excerpted, remained a significant stumbling block. The market impact was uncertain, and it was not completely clear how permanent the turn to film education would be. Alice Keliher had plans to begin renting the Human Relations films openly. John Marshall commented on the unlikelihood of the Rockefeller Foundation supporting such a turn, as Keliher moved the commission away from its experimental and research stage.[65] Marshall addressed Carl Milliken, the MPPDA's executive secretary, on this subject, and Milliken reiterated the fact that the films remain the property of the original Hollywood producers. With the TFC gaining steam, Milliken, as one of its trustees, recommended that that organization might be in a position to divert some of its rental revenue to Keliher's commission.[66] Keliher became vice-president of the American Film Center (AFC) in 1939 and announced that distribution of the Human Relations films was then available from the AFC, though officially the Human Relations project had been completed and there were no contracts for such distribution.[67] She handed these films over to the TFC by April 6, 1943,[68] though the TFC did not yet have the green light for their distribution either.

To negotiate excerpted feature distribution, to work on an ongoing basis with the TFC, and to get the studios on its side, the MPPDA formed another committee in 1943 composed not of educators but of industry representatives: N. Peter Rathvon, president of RKO; J. Robert Rubin, vice-president of Loew's Inc.; and Joseph Haze, vice-president of Warner Bros.[69] The luminaries lent support and credibility in the eyes of the studios to the release of excerpted feature films. As a result, the next round of TFC contracts with the studios, in 1945, included both features and shorts. Unlike the previous two, this contract extended for an unlimited time period.[70] The revised contracts of 1946 allowed for excerpting of features, distribution to any educational organization, and opened up the possibility for selective international distribution. Shortly thereafter, *The Oxbow Incident* (1943) became *Due Process of the Law Denied* and parts of *Song of Love* (1950) became *The Schumann Story*. Later in the 1950s, the TFC offered a reel on racial prejudice clipped from *Something of Value* (1957), and a reel titled *The Executive Interview* cut from *The High Cost of Loving* (1958).[71] Selected and reconstructed films were only leased, shown without an admission fee, and required no royalty payment. And, important to the members of the newly renamed MPPDA—now Motion Picture Association of America (MPAA)—prints, as always, identified the originating studio.[72]

The postwar activities of the TFC were more aggressive and confident. In many respects, the prewar and war periods were times of information gathering, stock taking, and exploratory market testing; coordination and consolidation characterized Hollywood's relation to educational film during the postwar years. It was taken for granted that film did not simply inject ideas into the brains of audiences, but that the film viewing and film discussion situation was an indispensable vehicle for the promotion and maintenance of democratic life. With this view, the postwar MPAA made educational activities an even more solid aspect of its activities. In 1945, when Eric Johnston took the helm of the MPAA—incidentally only after Edmund E. Day, the president of Cornell University and a longstanding TFC board member, turned down the position—he continued strong support of the TFC and expanded its activities. The TFC, for instance, helped the development of specific audiovisual education programs, such as one elaborate distance education experiment run by the State of Nebraska. Johnston also established the Division of Educational Services at the MPAA in September 1946, with the TFC board member Roger Albright in charge. To keep things cozy, Albright took up the position of director of Educational Services of the TFC.[73] One primary activity of this division was to coordinate the increasingly varied efforts of the MPAA in educational matters. The TFC subsumed this division of the MPAA in 1958.

The MPAA set up the Commission on Motion Pictures under the American Council on Education with a grant of $25,000 a year for five years, beginning in 1944.[74] Betraying cross-membership of three individuals on the commission and on the board of the TFC, being housed at Yale, and Mark May again in the position of chairman, this body was supposed to operate independently to identify the classroom film needs and develop film series for "training for democratic citizenship." With this project, May addressed producers directly, itemizing the kinds of films needed, including those that motivate, inform, demonstrate, and build art appreciation and values.[75] This is extensively itemized in the final report of the Commission on Motion Pictures, appearing in 1949.[76] The commission's objectives were to help film producers meet the perceived educational needs of postwar America and, reflecting the period's interest in consensus building, "to organize film content along a middle course between the extreme educational philosophies."[77] The report identified five target topics and audiences: global geography for junior high schools, issues of democracy for senior high schools, math for secondary schools, and art and music appreciation for multiple levels. The commission prepared 141 film treatments, sending 117 directly to producers, hoping to directly influence the cooperation between the users and makers of educational films.[78] The recommendations were then to be acted upon by educational film producers, with the first a series of geography films produced by Louis de Rochemont for United World Films.

Another initiative, the Motion Picture Research Project, used controlled experimental situations to determine the best types of teaching films. Alternate versions of films would be tested with school children. Funds for this came from both the MPAA and the TFC, and the Institute of Human Relations ran these studies with May as one of the researchers. The results were published as *Learning from Films* in 1958.[79] Yet another effort was to produce experimental educational films whose construction and topics would be approved by the commission, would be tested by the Motion Picture Research Project, and whose final project would be distributed by the TFC.[80] Through Rathvon's committee, the MPAA put forward $100,000 for seven educational films, which Eric Johnston said would "serve as a standard for producers of classroom films." Arthur Mayer, the secretary of war's consultant on film matters, oversaw production with approval from a scrutinizing body of educators, and with the TFC distributing the films nationwide upon completion.[81]

In the expansiveness of this postwar activity, the efforts to coordinate all aspects of the educational field are apparent. Interrelated programs included a pilot film production wing, a film testing wing (Motion Picture Research Project), a market research wing (Commission of Motion Pictures for the ACE), and a distribution wing (TFC). The key terms used during this period were coordination and integration, and here a miniature version of a vertically integrated industry was being developed. The involvement of central figures in multiple initiatives, notably May himself, points to this integration. Impor-

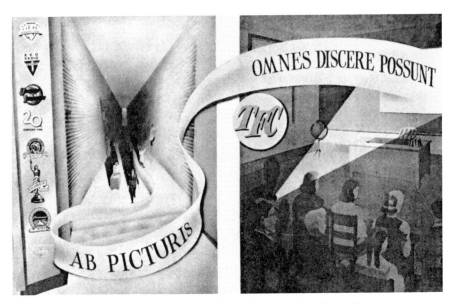

TFC, moving films from the Hollywood studios to classrooms, from *The TFC Story*, 4.

tantly, whatever educational or scholarly merits there were, the actions taken were monitored unambiguously and closely through the connections of the sponsoring industry, benefiting their own understanding of this rising market of 16mm instructional film. Where the Payne Fund Studies wondered about the nature of influence of moviegoing upon children, the Payne Fund author Mark May, and the TFC, developed instructional programs as the proper and "useful" function of film, never leaving industrial interests outside their activities. For its part, Hollywood, noted for its self-congratulatory nature, touted the public relations, legacy, and nascent market value of these projects. For instance, a dinner celebrating the industry's contributions to education took place at the Beverly Hills Hotel on the occasion of the TFC's fifteenth anniversary,[82] which included the release of a promotional film *The TFC Story*. At a parallel event on the East Coast, they patted themselves on the back at the Biltmore Hotel in New York City, where Mark May bestowed honorary scrolls to Eric Johnston and the eight MPAA studio heads for their commitment to education.[83]

Activity continued for several decades more, with increased attention to audiovisual technologies and television. From 1950 to 1954, the TFC ran several workshops and conferences, and supported the Lake Okoboji Leadership Conferences on audiovisual education of the NEA's Department of Audio-

Visual Instruction (DAVI).[84] The TFC provided financial support for DAVI's Field Service, which helped schools and universities get audiovisual programs off the ground.[85] The TFC acquired the rights to distribute "Cavalcade of America" television programs in the early 1950s, and developed films for language acquisition with the Modern Language Association, beginning in 1959.[86] All of the TFC's materials were handed over to Indiana University in 1973 as it ceased operations.

The TFC was just one organization advancing the place of film in educational institutions during this period. Comparable records of activity could chronicle the contributions of other initiatives. Mediating the interests of the mainstream commercial film industry, however, the TFC was in a uniquely influential position that kept Hollywood majors involved in this growing market and that assisted in promoting the very notion of screen education, further integrating moving images with other aspects of contemporary life. Let me reiterate that the activity documented here involved more than simply licensing films. It involved assessing film usage, compiling catalogues, writing study guides, testing usage and effectiveness in closed settings, monitoring discussions in classrooms, surveying teachers, proposing films, and editing features. In other words, this was a massive effort to study and advance particular kinds of film usage. This enterprise fell immediately on the heels of the Payne Fund Studies. That famous project offered a varied assessment of the effects of motion pictures upon children and helped galvanize a sense of concern about film entertainment. But to fully appreciate the period, we must also recognize the lasting contribution of the film educationalists to the development of ideas about how films are made to be "useful" and to the expansion of an institutional structure to serve those notions.

On the place of character education in this history, Eric Smoodin precisely describes it as a shift in American education to erase boundaries between classroom subjects and social life.[87] Most surely, the commitment to the idea of character education was a reason why the character education expert Mark May was swept into work with the MPPDA and the Payne Fund to begin with. And yet, reviewing the activity, it is important to understand that character education goals connected with other pedagogical, industrial, and organizational goals. The language of making education keep step with a changing world—modernizing the classroom and making it relevant—was evident in many initiatives, not all of which reflect the specific approach of character education as a subject. Character education was a way to generalize interests and values, and an ideologically riddled enterprise, to be certain. As a first step, to test and break the perceived logjam to the development of modern technologized education, and with it launch a new industry, character education was a way to produce material with the widest possible appeal to schools, without stepping on the toes of state and school board curricula. It was the first wave, to be followed by programs that responded to specific topics and subject needs, tied ever more closely to classroom lessons. The common element, as the subjects changed, was the situation, namely the promotion of screen-mediated teaching: the film occasion, with civil discourse, guided by a leader, prompted by some form of screen engagement.

This illuminates some of the work May published as an educational polemicist. In 1941 his tract titled *Education in a World of Fear* began by proclaiming, "The dominating emotion of the world today is fear. Never in history has the behavior of as great a proportion of the inhabitants of this earth been so extremely motivated by a common anxiety."[88] His concern was that the fear of totalitarianism would lead people to apathy and to reject the prospects of liberal democracy. Modern education figured as the best defense. He recommended an active management of fear: "In critical times we must steer a middle course between the alarmists whose anxieties are unduly high, on the one hand, and those who would lull us to sleep in a sense of false security, on the other. The task of education is to teach people how to manage their anxieties and hold them proportional to the realities of the danger."[89] The voice of a future "cold warrior" is already making itself heard. Postwar, he devoted more effort directly to the advancement of psychological warfare; while continuing as the director of the TFC, he also acted as the chairman of the U.S. Advisory Commission on Information, from 1953 to 1960, where he centralized all propaganda and psychological warfare operations, and drew stronger ties between government operations in this area and academics.[90] This was a liberal humanism that could sidle up nicely next to a cold war policy of information management.

In closing, what we confront in the figure of Mark May is one career-long illustration of the lasting impact of psychology and social science upon the emergence of a coordinated field of educationally useful film and of the involvement of major media corporations in the supply of educational materials to U.S. teachers and community leaders. Accordingly, this did not produce a generic national spectator or unified ideological formation at the level of subject matter. In fact, if anything, we see the methodological implements and categorizing schemas, from the surveys, evaluations, interviews, group discussion, and empirical experiments, putting forward ways to organize and segment a public as a fledgling educational market. This often addressed grade-level in addition to age, in so doing fortifying an idea about development and maturation. This is not the first moment of an interest in educational media, but it did represent the consolidation of ideas that put technology in the classroom, redefined the space of where learning takes place, made media appear to be indispensable to modern education and skill acquisition, offered evidence of the perceived advantages in quantifiable results, and saw a new balancing act between industry, government, and the engaged, albeit technocratic, scholar. In short, May and the organizations he led helped establish the procedures for participation in screen-mediated publics. This was a hegemonic moment in which industry and education contributed equally to postwar ideals of liberal citizenship while solidifying a stratum of media experts who spoke on behalf of that screen public and a business sector, eventually converting what began as good public relations into the lucrative world of educational technology.

NOTES

1   The lasting institutional influence of the Payne Fund Studies can be found in education, especially in what will come to be called "media literacy," but even here this influence has been only occasionally acknowledged.

2   Forman, *Our Movie Made Children*, "To the Movies — But Not to Sleep!," "Movie Madness," and "Molded by Movies."

3   See for instance Mark A. May, op-ed, *Christian Science Monitor*, January 3, 1933, 18.

4   Jowett, Jarvie, and Fuller, *Children and the Movies*, 101–3.

5   John Marshall Diaries, interview with Leo Rosten, September 17, 1940, Rockefeller Foundation, Rockefeller Archive Center (hereafter RAC).

6   Sammond, *Babes in Tomorrowland*, 62.

7   Ibid., 66.

8   Renshaw, Miller, and Marquis, *Children's Sleep*, 155.

9   Hartshorne, May, and Maller, *Studies in the Nature of Character, II: Studies in Service and Self-Control*, 232.

10 Ibid., 427.

11 Shuttleworth and May, *The Social Conduct and Attitudes of Movie Fans*.

12 "For Freud, for Society, for Yale," *Time*, March 6, 1946, 41–42.

13 Dollard, *Caste and Class in a Southern Town*, vii–ix.

14 John Marshall Diaries, interview with Mark May, August 2, 1935, RAC, 2.

15 Anderson, "Taking Liberties."

16 "Revue," January 28, 1939, Teaching Film Custodians file, Margaret Herrick Library, Academy of Motion Picture Arts and Sciences (hereafter AMPAS), 3.

17 Teaching Film Custodians, "The TFC Story," 28. Concerning his involvement on the

Committee on Social Values in Motion Pictures, some went further to give Mark May credit for the cooperation received from Hays for the "Secrets of Success" test program. John Marshall Diaries, interview with Mark May, August 2, 1935, RAC, 2.

18 "*Secrets of Success* Manual for Discussion Leaders," General Education Board, Rockefeller Archive Center (hereafter GEB), 1.1 series 632.7 box 284 folder 2966; "The Development of a New Technique for Teaching Character Education by the Discussion Method with the Use of Excerpts from Photoplays," January 1939, AMPAS, 1; and M. May, "What Is Character Education?," 21, 58, 60. This series has been discussed by Morey, *Hollywood Outsiders*; and Jacobs, "Reformers and Spectators."

19 "The Development of a New Technique for Teaching Character Education," 1.

20 David Stevens Interviews, with Alice Keliher, May 5, 1936, GEB, 1.2 series 632.7 box 283 folder 2960.

21 David Stevens Interviews, with Mark May and Howard LeSourd, March 24, 1936, GEB, 1.2 series 632.7 box 283 folder 2960.

22 Letter from Progressive Education Association (hereafter PEA) to GEB, stamped received June 19, 1936, GEB 1.2 series 632.7 box 283 folder 2960, 4–6. It is interesting that the development of critical and discerning spectators, ones that "would not so readily be carried away by inferior products," went by the name of censorship ("Request to Board of Directors for action on extension of Commission on Human Relations budget," stamped received May 7, 1936, GEB 1.2 series 632.7 box 283 folder 2960, 8).

23 Letter from PEA to GEB, stamped received June 19, 1936, GEB 1.2 series 632.7 box 283 folder 2960, 6–8.

24 David Stevens Interviews, with Alice Keliher, May 5, 1936, GEB 1.2 series 632.7 box 283 folder 2960; Joseph Losey was one of the key production personnel involved with this; for more detail on this important project see Kridel, "Educational Film Projects of the 1930s."

25 David Stevens Interviews, with Alice Keliher, May 5, 1936.

26 "Request to Board of Directors," 1.

27 Ibid.

28 Teaching Film Custodians, "The TFC Story," 28–29.

29 "Request to Board of Directors," 6.

30 John Marshall Diaries, interview with Mark May, August 2, 1935, RAC, 2.

31 "Revue," 3; and Teaching Film Custodians, "The TFC Story," 29.

32 "Request to Board of Directors," 3.

33 "Report of Advisory Committee on the Use of Motion Pictures in Education," ca. December 1937, AMPAS.

34 Witt, "How Hollywood Serves Education through TFC," 645.

35 "Report of the Advisory Committee on Motion Pictures in Education," October 1, 1937, AMPAS, 7.

36 Ibid., 1.

37 "Revue," 4.

38 John Marshall Diaries, interview with Mark May, August 2, 1935, RAC, 1.

39 "Report of the Advisory Committee on Motion Pictures in Education," 2.

40 Ibid., 3–4.

41 Ibid., 5.

42 Ibid., 6.

43 Ibid., 8.

44 Ibid., 8–9.

45 Witt, "How Hollywood Serves Education through TFC," 645. Five subcommittees reviewed the films: art education, chaired by Dr. Royal B. Farnum, vice-president of the Rhode Island School of Design; elementary education, chaired by Mrs. Bess B. Lane of the New York Ethical Culture School; science and nature study, chaired by Dr. Paul Mann of the New York City Public Schools; physical education, chaired by Dr. Jay B. Nash, an education professor at New York University; and social studies, chaired by Professor Karl W. Bigelow of Teachers College, Columbia University ("Old Films Studied for Use in Schools," *New York Times*, July 15, 1937, 14).

46 "Report of the Advisory Committee on Motion Pictures in Education," 14.

47 "Educational Group Eyes 15,000 Short Subjects," *Film Daily*, July 2, 1937, 1–2.

48 Eunice Barnard, "Machine Age Sets Education Trend," *New York Times*, July 4, 1937, 53.

49 Teaching Film Custodians, "The TFC Story," 29.

50 The first board of directors consisted of Dr. Frederick H. Bair, the superintendent of schools in Bronxville, N.Y.; Dr. Isaiah Bowman, the president of Johns Hopkins University; Dr. Karl T. Compton, the president of MIT; Dr. Edmund E. Day, the president of Cornell University; Dr. E. Givens, the secretary of the National Education Association; Dr. Royal B. Farnum, the vice-president of the Rhode Island School of Design; Dr. Mark A. May, the director of the Institute of Human Relations at Yale University; and Dr. Jay B. Nash, an education professor at NYU. In 1940 Dr. James R. Angell, the president of Yale University, and Dr. Francis Spaulding, the dean of Harvard University's Graduate School of Education, joined the board (Teaching Film Custodians, "The TFC Story," 29–30). The three trustees were Milliken, Angell, and Givens ("Revue," 6). Carl Milliken, a former Republican governor of Maine, served twenty years as the executive secretary of the MPPDA, resigning in 1947, but staying on as a managing trustee of TFC, a post he had held since 1939 ("Ex-Gov. Milliken of Maine was 83," *New York Times*, May 2, 1961, 37).

51 Teaching Film Custodians, "The TFC Story," 30.

52 "Report of the Work of Teaching Film Custodians, Inc.," May 24, 1940, AMPAS, 1.

53 Thomas M. Pryor, "Fulfilling a Promise: Film Producers Open Their Vaults to Promote Education by Pictures," *New York Times*, July 9, 1943, 113.

54 "Report of the Work of Teaching Film Custodians, Inc.," 1.

55 Ibid., 2.

56 Ibid., 3.

57 "Teaching Film Custodians, Inc.: Report of the President for the Year 1941," June 26, 1942, AMPAS, 1.

58 Ibid., 2.

59 Ibid., 1.

60 Teaching Film Custodians, "The TFC Story," 30.

61 Letter, Secretary, TFC, to T. K. Stevenson, ERPI, April 15, 1940, AMPAS, 3.

62 Ibid., 1.

63 Teaching Film Custodians, "The TFC Story," 30.

64 Jacobs, "Reformers and Spectators," makes this mistake, which many who refer to her ground-breaking article then repeat.

65 John Marshall Diaries, talk with Alice Keliher, March 13, 1939, RAC.

66 John Marshall Diaries, interview with Carl Milliken, May 17, 1939, RAC.

67 The address for the Human Relations film distribution is the same as that of the AFC, 45 Rockefeller Plaza, in October 1939 (Association of School Film Libraries, *Newsletter*, October 1939, 4, 5, 8, GEB series 1.2, box 225, folder 2158, RAC). Keliher resigned from the associate director position to return to her teaching post in education at NYU in the spring of 1940 (John Marshall Diaries, interview with Donald Slesinger, March 13, 1940, RAC, 2).

68 John Marshall Diaries, Conference on Motion Pictures, April 6, 1943, RAC, 1.

69 Teaching Film Custodians, "The TFC Story," 30.

70 Ibid.

71 "An Anniversary for TFC," *Educational Screen and AV Guide*, December 1958, 622.

72 Teaching Film Custodians, "The TFC Story," 17.

73 Ibid., 30.

74 Ibid.

75 M. May, "Films and Teaching Functions," 339, 340, 345.

76 M. May, *Planning Films for Schools*.

77 Ress, "The Literature in Audio-Visual Instruction," 358.

78 Ibid., 358–59.

79 May and Lumsdaine, *Learning from Films*.

80 M. May, "Educational Projects," 200–201, 232.

81 "Fund Set to Test Classroom Films," *New York Times*, April 2, 1946, 22.

82 Thomas M. Pryor, "Granger Refuses Role in U.-I. Film," *New York Times*, November 6, 1952, 37.

83 "Of Local Origin," *New York Times*, April 19, 1952, 18.

84 Witt, "How Hollywood Serves Education through TFC," 646.

85 Ibid., 647.

86 Ibid., 645.

87 Smoodin, *Regarding Frank Capra*, 78.

88 M. May, *Education in a World of Fear*, 1.

89 Ibid., 74.

90 M. May, "What Should the New Administration Do about Psychological Warfare?," 4, 6, and "Psychological Warfare," 191.

UNESCO, FILM, AND EDUCATION
MEDIATING POSTWAR PARADIGMS OF COMMUNICATION

Zoë Druick

> How much of the world's fear and hate stem from illiteracy and igno-
> rance it is impossible to say. But there can be no doubt that a great
> deal of its misery and suffering do, and [UNESCO] is therefore attacking
> these major ills at their roots to develop improved methods of education
> and instruction in visual training projects on all the continents.
> —ROSS MCLEAN, "UNESCO and Film" (1954), UNESCO Archives

Can visual education be a panacea for misery and suffering? Although this link may seem naïve and hope-
lessly dated, it is not so far removed from the idea of social
improvement through the enlightened application of technology that continues to characterize our own day. In the
years immediately following World War II, the mass media
took on a new significance and the study of communication
emerged to analyze the effects of these social technologies
and to direct their implementation, legacies of which are
with us still. The wartime experience of propaganda as well
as the polarization of the globe into the uneasy entente of
the cold war—a war of ideologies—gave ample reason for
attending to the importance of the mass dissemination of
ideas. The United Nations Educational, Scientific and Cultural Organization (UNESCO) was intimately involved with
the new landscape of mediated international communication. Although the interest in mass media took many forms
in this period, no activities in the field took place with as
much moral authority as those endorsed by an organization
with the mandate of global peace. Designed to foster peace

over the long run rather than solve immediate conflicts, in the years follow-ing its foundation in November 1945, UNESCO dedicated itself to a number of interrelated projects of education and the media. The organization's long-term objectives were to eliminate illiteracy and provide the basic lessons of modernization, thereby leveling the global playing field. The organization was the institutional machinery designed to put into place the ideals at the heart of the UN's declaration of the 1950s concerning the free flow of information.

Practically speaking, many of UNESCO's projects to teach the masses relied on some sort of media and, at least initially, this often meant an emphasis on cinematic technologies. In the years before the widespread introduction of television broadcasting, film was an educator's most important visual aid. In many of the so-called new nations of the rapidly decolonizing world, film was the first visual medium of mass communication with which rural people had contact. In addition, it provided the hope for indigenous forms of cultural ex-pression, a source of education and entertainment, and possibly the basis of a national cultural industry as well. Although certainly not the only organiza-tion devoted to media and development, UNESCO crystallized a number of the modernizing tendencies of the postwar period.

Working closely with American development experts in the long shadows of European colonialism, the postwar United Nations was often characterized by critics as a handmaiden to American foreign policy, insinuating Western technology and capital into oil rich buffer zones around the Soviet Union's sphere of influence.[1] Although the Soviet Union was an inaugural member of the UN Security Council (along with the other victorious nations of World War II, China, France, the United States, and the United Kingdom), the Soviet republics did not join the United Nations until 1954, leaving UNESCO's mass communication and film departments to work closely with Western powers for close to a decade.[2] Indeed, the Soviet and Chinese presence in the United Nations was a site of constant friction, with the Soviet representative vetoing the inclusion of de facto Western colonial states to the United Nations (such as India and the Philippines) and the West insisting on the exclusion of Soviet states. Finally, the issue of the elevation of the Republic of China (based in Taipei), which supported the United States, at the expense of the commu-nist People's Republic of China, which did not, brought the controversy over political leverage to a head and the Soviet Union boycotted its seat for most of 1950 (during which period the Korean war was declared).[3]

The constant maneuvering for dominance on the Security Council was reflected in the work of the first years of UNESCO's existence, which relied on funding, experts, and modes of center-periphery relations that promised to bring modernization and capitalist development to the third world and other strategic, nonaligned nations. I have argued elsewhere that UNESCO continued the work of the League of Nations Intellectual Cooperation Committee, and this included its Eurocentric emphasis.[4] Its officers argued for the need to use cinema for "fundamental education," a mix of literacy and agricultural training directed at adults. Yet these otherwise unobjectionable projects were often executed in conjunction with former colonial administrators, missionaries, and experts from the Ford Foundation and the U.S. State Department, and their efforts could be perceived as mere window dressing for more instrumental cold war geopolitical strategies.

But even granted UNESCO's Western bias, there were different paradigms at work. The connection of UNESCO's work during this period to American development communication is undeniable. However, through its links to the British educational and documentary film tradition UNESCO was also committed to providing an alternative to Hollywood theatrical film. In the realm of communications in general and film in particular, UNESCO marshaled a number of often conflicting interests. For example, UNESCO pursued quite different policies in developed and underdeveloped worlds and therefore its influence on the local use of film was different in industrial and non-industrial contexts. In underdeveloped regions, this work included establishing screening and distribution infrastructure, often through mobile cinemas driven into communities and screenings made part of formal schooling for children and adults. In the developed world, UNESCO's policies about educational and redemptive uses of cinema provided a complementary, rather than competitive, model with Hollywood. This is hardly surprising as UNESCO's mass communication division was closely connected, through personnel and orientation, with the Colonial Film office in Britain, which had pioneered large-scale nontheatrical cinema in order to forge a distinctive cinema culture.[5] In its emphasis on non-theatrical and educational cinema, UNESCO's film program thus distinguished itself from the more spectacular success of Hollywood's cultural exports.

By the end of the 1960s, things had changed dramatically. The United Nations Educational, Scientific and Cultural Organization had become a mouthpiece for opposition to American hegemony, representing and endorsing a politicized response by the economic south to Western capitalism and commercial culture. In the 1970s and 1980s, as the field of development communication came under fire, and revolutionary media such as Third Cinema heated up, UNESCO changed its policies and began to endorse indigenous media. By the early 1980s, just before the American and British withdrawal from the organization (in 1984 and 1985 respectively), UNESCO stood on the side of multi-vocal discourse, endorsing its *New World Information and Communication Order*. Today, UNESCO reiterates the importance of diversity and cultural difference.[6]

Rather than use this about face in UNESCO policy to discredit the organization, or to suggest that its policies have been overly faddish, in this chapter I posit that UNESCO's involvement with film and its study in the decades following World War II should be examined in all its complexity and contradiction. The organization incorporated—and arguably continues to incorporate—a complex of forces and perspectives from progressive to reactionary, democratic to authoritarian, making it a compelling case of the application of theories of the institutionalization, technologization, and instrumentalization of culture, as well as the shifting of common sense around notions of film and society.

In what follows, I explore some of the themes of UNESCO's publications and policies on film and education in the 1940s and 1950s and discuss the development of their particular cold war social-scientific positions on communication in relation to American and British interests and film traditions. Utilizing material from the UNESCO Archives (Paris), I consider Ross McLean, the head of the film education section from 1950 to 1957, as a compelling example of the balance achieved by UNESCO between various political forces, spanning old and new worlds, and divergent models of national media. The organization's discourses of media, democracy, and education have shifted over the years, but so too have political contexts and academic and industry trends. My goal is not to single out UNESCO among postwar forces, but rather to see it as a useful heuristic for examining the social role of film in the postwar period more generally.

The nation-based notion of culture was dominant in postwar social science, and was often linked to concepts of national character and aptitude. Through its association with the United Nations, UNESCO contributed to the vision of each country, eventually producing characteristic national cinemas.[7] This approach reified culture as a form of national difference while simultaneously naturalizing the nation as a source of the traits of individuals. By altering the way a nation communicated with itself and with other nations, one could conceivably engineer behaviors at the national level. This approach also tacitly endorsed the nation as the natural form of human organization, against the Soviet Union's "unnatural" transnationalism. Where an emphasis on nationalism must certainly be seen as ideological, it also potentially led to spaces in global media culture for cultural products — even nationalistic ones — from many lands. The number of international film festivals, for instance, grew quickly in this period. With their focus on the celluloid representations of national culture and stories, they were the perfect forums for both the expression of national culture and its interrogation. In international film culture of the 1950s, for example, many celebrated artists explored the questions and contradictions of national history and modernity itself, as can be seen in any survey of world cinema. That the nation remains an important category in film studies and cultural policy alike is indicative of the tenacity of this logic.

The support for national cultures is mirrored in one of UNESCO's first major projects, the study of national media. This was the first undertaking of its kind and although its rationale was linked to wartime reconstruction, it seems clear that the revelation of facts about national patterns of media consumption could serve a range of functions, from identifying nations in dire need of targeted aid to those that were the site of pitched ideological battles. The undertaking began modestly in 1947 with a survey of the media in ten countries whose infrastructure had been affected by the war, mostly in Western and Central Europe, but also including Pakistan and Haiti. In 1948 the survey grew to include seventeen other countries, mostly in the developing world. These two studies provided detailed primary research on each nation's communication infrastructure with special attention to the source of media content. In 1950 the study was expanded and repackaged — arguably obscuring its cold war roots — as the first empirical communication studies textbook, *World Communications: Press, Radio, Film*, published by the Division of the Free Flow of Information of UNESCO's Department of Mass Communication.[8] The information on each country in this edition is more concise than in the earlier reports, but a significant addition is in the presentation of data visually in a series of colorful charts. Tables chart the population, the size of each territory, the rate of illiteracy, the diffusion of news agencies, presses, radio receivers, transmitters, and so on, as well as the existence of radio program exchanges and school broadcasting. In the film section, tables chart the number of cinemas, make note of whether ownership is private or public, the seating capacity, the number and type of films screened (feature, newsreel, educational), as well as the provenance of their production and distribution.

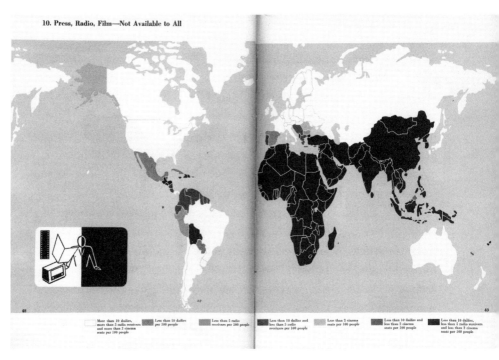

A color-coded map from the 1956 edition of *World Communications*.

This comprehensive data definitively situated India and Japan as important global film producers alongside the United States, thereby providing empirical evidence for a view of international fair competition with Hollywood.

Television was added to the title and subject matter of the 1951 edition, but film retained an important place in the book's conception. Documentary and educational films are identified in the 1956 edition as an important part of the school curriculum in many parts of the world. "Allied to television, [film] is bound to play an increasingly important role as a medium of education and information among the world's peoples."[9] The textbook continued to expand over the years until, by the final edition of 1975, it covered two hundred countries.

This survey not only helped to highlight the national formation of mass media, it was also foundational to a certain type of communication studies. As Christopher Simpson has compellingly shown in his essential study of cold war communication studies, *Science of Coercion*, much of the research done through American social science research institutes with any relationship to psychological warfare in the 1950s was covertly or semi-covertly underwritten by American defense funds. The fact that the survey began with the middle ground countries of Europe and the third world, which provided the most hotly contested battlegrounds of the cold war, certainly supports this view.[10] What appeared to be an innocuous inventory would most certainly have produced results of strategic importance to the United States and Western Europe. Cold war politics are evident in other ways as well. The UNESCO surveys are at pains to indicate which countries have access only to Soviet newsreels and other media and, under the guise of free flow of information, the survey is clearly an attempt to argue for the need for openness of all countries' markets to Western media.

Wilbur Schramm, whom Simpson characterizes as "the single most important definer of U.S. mass communication studies of his day,"[11] was involved in the international survey from 1949 on, providing the information on the United States and its "dependent territories," as well as helping gather information about Canada. According to the historian Timothy Glander, at about this time Schramm recommended to the U.S. State Department that intelligence reports be gathered on "communication and opinion-forming patterns of particular countries" of Western Europe, the "Arab region," and South Asia. Studies of media diffusion were the perfect front for such enquiries into national opinion.[12] As Glander puts it, "Masking espionage and intelligence gathering as scholarship and legitimate inquiry was a useful way in which the influences of the United States on the internal affairs of other nations could remain opaque and not easily detected."[13] Schramm worked with UNESCO for decades, publishing a number of key studies, including *Mass Media and National Development* in 1964.[14] A famous study of 1956, *Four Theories of the Press*, which Schramm co-authored, presents a one-sided American perspective that situates American liberalism as the progressive antithesis of Soviet totalitarianism, even in the midst of America's communist "witch hunts."[15] The kind of work undertaken by Schramm and others was crucial to the establishment of communication studies as a cold war discipline, where free flows of information and free markets of media products served the American agenda of capitalist expansion and where obstructions to the transmission of messages — technological and political alike — represented "noise" in the communications circuit.[16]

The issue of the free flow of information was intimately connected to that of literacy. Where people could not read, the existence of a local press was irrelevant. To create literacy would, by this logic, establish one of the basic conditions for democracy. The advocacy of literacy neatly avoided the discussion

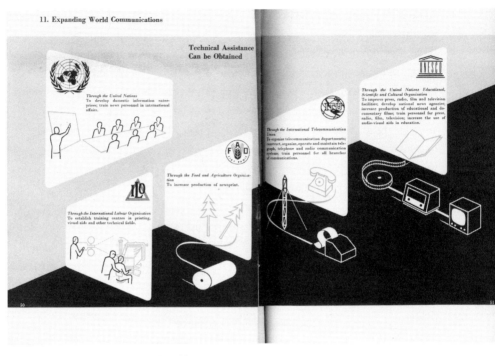

A page from the 1956 edition of *World Communications*.

of content by turning reading into a neutral technique, not unlike the valorization of a free marketplace of ideas. Like freedom of expression, literacy worked as a seemingly non-ideological ideal of Western states exerting influence on the developing world. Often working closely with representatives of the American military-industrial complex, much of UNESCO's work fit within the American communication studies model of the transfer of messages, what Simpson has identified as the hegemonic cold war "domination" model of communication.[17] The anthropologist Mark Peterson has described this tradition as follows: "Early work in development communication sought to yoke mass communications with linear, evolutionary models of social changes to create a powerful tool for pursuing goals of economic modernization."[18] A somewhat contradictory state of affairs emerged. Literacy became a synecdoche for progress, modernization, and democracy, as though reading automatically produced a particular political point of view. In practice, communication policy makers posited the availability of the mass media as a magic bullet for both literacy and democracy. In this way educational media often took the place of reading, while purporting to fulfill the same function. But visual media, with its ability to transport viewers technologically, promised to do even more.

In his study of the Middle East, *The Passing of Traditional Society*, the famous cold war media theorist Daniel Lerner makes clear the connection between media and modernity, and casts it in terms of psychological evolution, the capacity for empathy:

> The media teach people participation of this sort by depicting for them new and strange situations and by familiarizing them with a range of opinions among which they can choose. Some people learn better than others, the variation reflecting their differential skill in empathy. For empathy . . . is the basic communication skill required of modern men. Empathy endows a person with the capacity to imagine himself as a proprietor of a bigger grocery store in a city, to wear nice clothes and live in a nice house, to be interested in "what is going on in the world" and to "get out of his hole." With the spread of curiosity and imagination among a previously quietistic population come the human skills needed for social growth and economic development.[19]

Not only does Lerner connect media exposure with the development of psychological maturity, he also posits curiosity and empathy as stepping stones to capitalist visions of entrepreneurial success and material luxury. In this tendentious equation, we see some of the short cuts taken in the communication and development discourse exposed.

Supported by funds from the U.S. State Department, Lerner's study was extremely influential in development communication circles. The media experts at UNESCO, too, pushed for the deployment of visual media, which could be "read" by the illiterate. In particular, film, and to a lesser degree filmstrips and posters, could be a source of the introduction of modern technology and of the role of the modern educator into developing countries. Media provision might, in this way, take the place of literacy.

This conclusion about the usefulness of visual education for the illiterate is apparent as early as 1948 when the Film Sub-Commission of the Technical Needs Study noted,

> While the achievements in most of the countries under review are modest, there is a very active interest in the development of the production, distribution and use of educational films. This is particularly true in those countries of Asia and Latin America which have large problems arising from

the illiteracy of a high proportion of their populations. Educational films have an enormous contribution to make in conquering illiteracy and disseminating information in those countries. . . . There is a high proportion of illiteracy in all the countries reviewed in Latin America. Educational films not only provide a means for communicating important ideas to illiterate people but they also provide an excellent method for eliminating illiteracy itself. It is important, therefore, that the work of the experts in fundamental education should be closely co-ordinated with the work of experts in mass communication, so that the quickest possible results might be achieved.[20]

Clearly, UNESCO rested its hopes for the achievement of peace on mass education, which relied, in turn, on the efficiencies of the mass media. Just as the endorsement of literacy was unobjectionable, so by extension was the promotion of educational visual media.

Yet literacy and its corollary "media literacy" both presume "illiteracy" and bear complex legacies of colonialism and neo-colonialism.[21] Western notions of literacy have often served to deny and even eradicate indigenous forms of knowledge. As Roy Armes puts it in *Third World Filmmaking and the West*, "Literacy itself is not an unqualified boon, if it serves merely as a channel for foreign influences and loosens the links that bind the colonized to their own society and their own history."[22] Currently, literacy is much more likely to be regarded as a situated practice rather than a neutral thing in itself.[23] The emphasis on modern media by UNESCO was tied to an unquestioned belief in the necessity of rapid modernization all across a networked globe that tended to ignore indigenous forms of knowledge.[24]

Media literacy borrows the metaphor and value from reading and makes the comprehension of and reliance on visual media itself a barometer of modernization. To this day, the visual literacy field resorts to a discussion of cultural competencies, in effect delineating "literate" from "illiterate."[25] The historian J. M. Burns calls the stories about media illiterate Africans—a feature of the visual literacy literature—"colonial folklore" that established differences between colonizers and colonized and was used to justify colonialism.[26] For example, Burns reveals that the famous story about the inability of African film viewers to see anything on screen during a film, except a hapless chicken wandering into the scene, had to do with the content of the films they were shown, which were exceptionally static. British colonial film operatives developed the theory that African film audiences were incapable of handling the sophisticated film language of edits and the elision of time. As a result they

An instructional program is recorded in the Ivory Coast.

Workers watch the program during a French literacy class at an industrial firm.

made single shot films with no camera movements. To an audience faced with such films, a chicken running spontaneously across the screen could understandably bring a moment of excitement.[27]

Another story of media illiteracy is equally fallacious, according to Burns. In one particularly humorless educational film about how mosquitoes transmit malaria, a close-up of a mosquito brought the comment from an audience member, "We're lucky that our mosquitoes aren't so big as that one!" The British audience monitors interpreted this comment to mean that the African viewers did not understand the concept of the close-up. But African audience members were injecting a moment of irony and levity into an otherwise patronizing exercise.[28]

Despite these more recent reassessments of the politics of media literacy discourse, in the 1950s development communication was a dominant force. The *World Communications* publication contributed to the setting up of normative terms about national media and modernization. Yet the infrastructure study would prove to have other important results as well. The commission recommended the implementation of a free flow of educational films among UNESCO's member countries. The resulting convention ratified by member nations in 1952 provided a template for the exchange of independently produced educational and non-theatrical films. And UNESCO would continue to attempt to push the free flow doctrine into the exchange of educational television in the 1960s. Thus although free flow has been shown by commentators as diverse as Wilbur Schramm and Herbert Schiller to have disproportionately favored the nations with the most developed media industries, when applied to non-theatrical audiovisual goods aspects of the free flow policies also potentially opened up new channels for international distribution and new forms of oppositional modernity. The same set of potentials and ambivalences applies equally to both literacy and media literacy.[29]

Aside from the massive survey of world media infrastructure, in the 1950s UNESCO released a series of publications on mass communication. Immediately following the war, UNESCO underwrote an extensive series of media studies under the rubric of *Press, Film and Radio in the World Today*, which began appearing in 1949. Demonstrating their profound belief in film as a tool of modern education, the studies include *Use of Mobile Cinema and Radio Vans in Fundamental Education* (1949), *The Entertainment Film for Juvenile Audiences* (1950), *The Film Industry in Six European Countries* (1950), and *Professional Training of Film Technicians* (1951). The studies highlight the use of film to modernize national cultures by either former colonial powers or national government representatives. Throughout the 1950s, UNESCO published a series entitled *Reports and Papers on Mass Communication,* many of which concerned film as an educational tool. The organization also sponsored the publication of film catalogues, such as the occasional publication *Films on Art* (1949 and after).[30]

Throughout the 1950s UNESCO also organized a number of conferences and workshops. Starting in 1951, UNESCO coordinated the international annual meeting for the study of ethnographic films, which brought together experts to discuss subjects such as the place of the filmic reconstruction and the role of entertainment in ethnography.[31] A seminar of film experts was convened in Paris in 1951 and charged to report on how film could help further the purposes of UNESCO. Subcommittees reported on newsreels, documentary film, educational films, and children's media. The organizers of international film festivals were called upon to eliminate confusion and to become more coordinated.[32] The visual aids and language-teaching workshops of 1952 and the seminar "Fundamental Education and Visual Aids" (Messina, Sicily) in 1953 were the basis for a number of the papers published in the UNESCO *Mass Communication* series and showed the network of international communication, education, and development experts who were in contact around these issues. Many colonial filmmakers and administrators, such as William Sellers and Norman Spurr, as well as André Renaud of the Canadian Indian Welfare Division of the Canadian Citizenship Branch, were enthusiastic participants in the fundamental education workshop of 1953, which lasted four weeks. A follow-up meeting considered the question embedded in its title — an "Experiment on the Use of Films with Audiences Other Than Those for Which They Have Been Made" — and invited prestigious participants from the colonialist film world.[33]

Conferences on media-related topics were abundant in the mid-1950s. A meeting in 1955 considered the possibility of an international center for entertainment films for children and adolescents, prefiguring a center dedicated to that end in Brussels.[34] The United Nations Educational, Scientific and Cultural Organization also encouraged cooperation between "films and television at the international level" at a conference held in Tangiers. A meeting in 1956 discussed the need to study the influence of mass media on children. Another meeting in the same year explored the possibility of establishing an international center of educational, scientific, and cultural films for television. In creating forums such as publications and conferences, as well as endorsing educational and film exchanges and film festivals, UNESCO continued the work associated with the British documentary film movement of accommodating Hollywood by creating a non-commercial, non-theatrical, and educational alternative.

As these conferences and publications show, educational cinema theories that predated the cold war were also called upon in force by UNESCO. For example, the preeminent world model of educational film was gleaned from the documentary makers in the Grierson circle and owed a good deal to the British colonial vision of filmmaking. John Grierson himself was the first director of the mass communication division at UNESCO between February 4, 1947 and April 30, 1948, in which capacity he presided over the Commission of Technical Needs in Press, Radio and Film discussed above.[35] In January 1948, Grierson presented at a conference called "The Film in Colonial Development," which was held in London by the British Film Institute and the British Colonial Office.[36] In his wake, the filmmakers Arthur Elton, Paul Rotha, and Basil Wright were involved in an ongoing basis with UNESCO until the late 1960s. Rotha and Wright sat on a number of committees and made conference presentations on UNESCO's film work at the Edinburgh Film Festival, among other places.[37] As late as 1967, Wright penned a UNESCO mission report on the development of a Ugandan film unit. Wright and Rotha also spent many months in 1952 making *World without End* (1953), a fifty-three-minute film about UNESCO's development and educational programs in Asia and Latin America. The film was shown widely at film festivals and was broadcast in the United Kingdom on the BBC and in the United States on ABC's national network.[38]

The famed Scottish-Canadian animator Norman McLaren, of the National Film Board of Canada (NFB), took a number of postings with UNESCO in the 1940s and 1950s, including to China and India where he taught non-camera animation techniques for films and filmstrips.[39] He also advised on the applicability of these experiments with Aboriginal people in Canada. William Sellers and Norman Spurr, longtime colonial administrators and filmmakers, lent their expertise to UNESCO's fundamental education campaigns.[40] Not part of the main documentary tradition, to be sure, Sellers and Spurr were nonetheless contributors to the imperial uses of educational and documentary film by the British government.

Perhaps the most important link to Grierson's legacy, however, was the work done for eight years in the 1950s by a little-known Canadian public servant, Ross McLean. McLean played a key role in the institutionalization of documentary film in Canada. He was Vincent Massey's secretary when

Massey was Canadian high commissioner in London before the war and introduced Massey to John Grierson. In 1938, he wrote a historic report suggesting that Grierson be encouraged to come to Canada. Later he worked as Grierson's deputy during the war and then valiantly attempted to keep the imploding Film Board together after his charismatic predecessor's departure under a cold war cloud in 1945.[41] McLean's contract as film commissioner was not renewed in February 1950, but by then he had already been offered and accepted a post at UNESCO as head of its film division, where he stayed throughout the 1950s.[42] Indeed, as early as 1948, McLean chaired the Film Sub-Commission of the Technical Needs Commission.[43]

A true inheritor of the British documentary film tradition's administrative aspect, McLean was at the center of UNESCO's film work during this crucial decade.[44] He organized the fundamental education conferences, liaised with film organizations around the world, oversaw publications by experts, and produced the occasional film. He also liaised with American philanthropic organizations. On one trip in the winter of 1951 he visited Canada "to consult with the National Film Board of Canada and with other officers of the Canadian Government regarding the contribution which might be made by the NFB to the development of UNESCO's audiovisual program, particularly in the Fundamental Education and Technical Assistance fields."[45] On the same trip he met with UN Film Board officials in New York to discuss the *Films on Art* catalogues as well as cooperation between UNESCO, the World Bank, the Food and Agriculture Organization, and the World Health Organization. He traveled to Washington to discuss the U.S. State Department catalogue *Motion Pictures Available and Suitable for Use Abroad*, which had been sent to all UN member states.

A second trip, in 1954, shows the degree to which McLean pursued different goals in industrial and non-industrial contexts. He discussed fundamental education initiatives with officials in Puerto Rico and Mexico and then traveled to Hollywood, where he had extensive weeklong meetings with educators and film industry representatives about how Hollywood could contribute to the goals of UNESCO. No doubt he was buoyed by his extensive contact with David Selznick who, since 1950 had been offering an award, the Golden Laurel (as well the Silver Laurel and the Lifetime Achievement Laurel), to European films deemed by an American jury to have best demonstrated the humanitarian values of the United Nations. These awards were given out at European festivals — Venice, Berlin, and Edinburgh — with the endorsement of UNESCO. Among others, Alexander Korda and Vittorio de Sica were recipients.[46] Integrating and rewarding positive messages in Hollywood films was suited to the American film industry, while outside the United States, educational films took on a different cast.

In 1956, McLean traveled to south Asia and the Middle East to assess the work film could do there. He wrote lengthy reports on the educational film facilities of India and Pakistan. His reports would provide a template for what became known as mission reports in the 1960s, where Western media experts would visit developing countries and make recommendations about their film and television production. It also harkens back to the same process of the 1930s and 1940s when British experts would travel to dominions such as Canada and Australia to make similar recommendations.[47] In fact, the Canadian National Film Board, a prime example of a dominion film scheme, was often invoked in these reports. At about the time of Lerner's research on media and modernity, McLean was in Lebanon meeting with officers of the Ford Foundation to discuss the question of a regional audiovisual center in the Middle East. Based on his meeting McLean concluded: "The Foundation is ready to help in the development of a realistically conceived project, and would also, I am sure, be ready to channel that help through UNESCO."[48] In the example of Ross McLean, we see a complex of activities undertaken by UNESCO in the realm of film in the 1950s. Whether it was engaging in technology transfer and fundamental education through film, trying to influence national media policies, or rewarding mainstream commercial cinema for its humanitarian themes, UNESCO insinuated itself into prevailing debates, many of them heavily influenced by cold war social science, about visual communication, nation building, and the networks through which information would be exchanged and controlled.

The fifteen years following the conclusion of World War II saw an unprecedented utilization of film for political ends, intensive and extensive, covert and explicit, educational and entertaining. I have argued that UNESCO's film activities played a role in this deployment. The 1960s saw the beginnings of another kind of useful film: Third Cinema. Led by revolutionary Cubans, filmmakers from across Latin American and Africa strove to make films that would resist imperialism in both form and content. Third Cinema manifestos (by the Brazilian Glauber Rocha, the Argentineans Fernando Solanas and Octavio Getino, and the Cuban Julio Garcia Espinosa, among others[49]) made quite clear the desired distance from politically complacent formulae of Hollywood, and reignited the connection between culture and politics. This widespread post-colonial opposition to cultural imperialism affected the disciplines of communication and film studies, which immediately began to disavow the close connections that had previously held between U.S. foreign policy, development, and media, and in which UNESCO had played an important role.

In the process, cinema studies lost track of an important historical link between culture and politics, one that had utilized film explicitly—if problematically—as a motor of progress and modernization. The film and mass media departments of UNESCO can certainly be seen to have acted as handmaidens to colonial and neo-colonial powers. However, it is just possible that they also offered the documentary tradition as an alternative model of imperialism to Hollywood. In their emphasis on national filmmaking and distributing capacities and in their attempts to smooth the way for non-theatrical distribution, they may have helped to produce a model of low-budget, non-theatrical cinema that was later seized upon and used against the imperial centers. As Paul Willemen notes in a discussion of Third Cinema, "both neo-realism and the British documentary were examples of an artisanal, relatively low-cost cinema working with a mixture of public and private funds, enabling directors to work in a different way and on a different economic scale from that required by Hollywood and its various national-industrial rivals."[50] Given the British documentary tradition's direct influence on UNESCO's film policies, it is possible that Willemen's comments signal the success of these interventions. At any rate, neglecting the connection has tended to obscure the ways cinema operated outside the theatrical circuit in much of the world.

In the early 1960s UNESCO's work shifted to match the new political realities. In 1961 leaders of twenty-five newly independent nations in Africa, Asia, and Latin America forged the Non-Aligned Movement, but not before the UN General Conference adopted a resolution on decolonization on December 12, 1960.[51] The United Nations Educational, Scientific and Cultural Organization endorsed the work of the pan-African film organization, Commission Permanente Interafricaine du cinéma, involving Ousmane Sembene and a group of other French African directors. It sponsored meetings on the use of broadcasting for education in Asia (1960, 1962, and 1966) and Africa (1964), conferences that featured a preponderance of African and Asian representatives, rather than Europeans, for the first time.[52] Although the push for national broadcasting replayed the problems of free flow seen in press and film, often serving as Trojan horses in the third world, ensuring reliance on expensive technologies and providing only limited use, a shift was underway nonethe-

Children watching educational television as part of their lessons in Niger.

less.[53] By the late 1960s, it seemed as though much of the development communication model of film and media had, after twenty years of entrenchment, largely given way.

In this essay I have given a broad overview of the involvement of UNESCO with film in order to explore the ways that UNESCO's activities in the postwar media landscape demonstrate the complex of forces it coordinated on the topic of film and how they could be most usefully applied. While on the one hand UNESCO contributed to the transfer of technologies of modernization with problematic results, on the other hand it possibly helped to create spaces for the cultural expression of post-colonial filmmakers. In the developed world, UNESCO strongly supported the production and circulation of non-theatrical cinema, both nationally and internationally, through film festivals and educational television alike. An examination of the activity of UNESCO in the realm of film shows the degree to which its work at the margins of global media production and distribution, but most importantly in applied theories of communication, consolidated a number of key ideas — and different paradigms — concerning film and education.

NOTES

This research was made possible by a grant from the Social Sciences and Humanities Research Council of Canada. I gratefully acknowledge the assistance of Mahmoud Ghander and Jens Boel of the UNESCO Archives, Paris. My thanks also go to Cassandra Savage and Laurynas Navidauskas for research assistance.

1 Samarajiwa, "The Murky Beginnings of the Communication and Development Field."

2 Of the twenty founding nations of UNESCO, the United States and the United Kingdom were by far the most powerful. The other members were Australia, Brazil, Canada, China, Czechoslovakia, Denmark, the Dominican Republic, Egypt, France, Greece, India, Lebanon, Mexico, New Zealand, Norway, Saudi Arabia, South Africa, and Turkey. See "The Organization's History" on UNESCO's Web site, http://portal.unesco .org/en/ev.php-URL_ID=6207&URL_DO=DO_TOPIC&URL_SECTION=201 .html (accessed May 21, 2008).

3 For more on this complex history see Frederking, *The United States and the Security Council.*

4 Druick, "'Reaching the Multimillions,'" 79–81. The directors general of UNESCO for the first thirty years were Julian Huxley (United Kingdom), Jaime Torres Bodet (Mexico), John W. Taylor (United States), Luther Evans (United States), Vittorino Veronese (Italy), and René Maheu (France). "Director Generals List," UNESCO Web site: http://portal.unesco.org/en/ev.php-URL_ID=3657&URL_DO=DO_ TOPIC&URL_SECTION=201.html (accessed May 22, 2008).

5 See Dickinson and Street, *Cinema and State.*

6 UNESCO, *A New World Information and Communication Order,* and *Universal Declaration on Cultural Diversity.* See also MacBride and Roach, "The New International Information Order."

7 Peterson, *Anthropology and Mass Communication,* 47. See also Mead and Métraux, *The Study of Culture at a Distance.*

8   Wilbur Schramm's anthology *Mass Communications* (1949), published a year earlier, takes a decidedly more humanities-inspired approach.

9   UNESCO, *World Communications*, 23.

10 Samarajiwa, "The Murky Beginnings of the Communication and Development Field," 5.

11 Simpson, *Science of Coercion*, 54.

12 Glander, *Origins of Mass Communications Research during the American Cold War*, 160. Glander reports on a mysterious trip taken overseas by Schramm in the summer of 1950 to work on a "survey of international communication" (159). It seems likely that this trip was related to Schramm's UNESCO-sponsored research for the *World Communications* textbook.

13 Glander, *Origins of Mass Communications Research during the American Cold War*, 162.

14 Schramm, *Mass Media and National Development*; and Schramm, Coombs, Kahnert, and Lyle, *The New Media*.

15 Siebert, Peterson, and Schramm, *Four Theories of the Press*.

16 See Jarvie, "Free Trade as Cultural Threat."

17 Simpson, *Science of Coercion*, 9.

18 Peterson, *Anthropology and Mass Communication*, 42.

19 D. Lerner, *The Passing of Traditional Society*, 412.

20 "Conclusions and Recommendations of the Film Sub-Commission" to the Technical Needs Commission, Second Session (August 25, 1948), 2, 5, UNESCO Archives.

21 Although the term "media literacy" did not come into widespread use until the 1980s and 1990s, the idea of being able to "read" the screen is at least a century old. Stories about the astonished spectator of silent films have been publicized widely since the 1890s. Despite the probable origin of the stories in publicity campaigns, they bolstered a sense that only "modern" spectators could watch films with the requisite detachment. See Gunning, "An Aesthetic of Astonishment"; and Bottomore, "The Panicking Audience?"

22 Armes, *Third World Filmmaking and the West*, 11.

23 Peterson, *Anthropology and Mass Communication*, 233.

24 See for example Schramm, *Mass Media and National Development*.

25 See Messaris, *Visual Literacy*. See also Gunning, "An Aesthetic of Astonishment," and Bottomore, "The Panicking Audience?" for discussion surrounding the "reading" competencies required of silent film audiences.

26 Burns, *Flickering Shadows*, 46.

27 See Notcutt and Latham, *The African and the Cinema*. For a further discussion of British colonial mobile cinema see Druick, "Mobile Cinema in Canada in Relation to British Mobile Film Practices."

28 Burns, *Flickering Shadows*, 40–41.

29 Schramm, *Mass Media and National Development*, 61; and Schiller, "Genesis of the Free Flow of Information Principles." See also Preston, Herman, and Schiller, *Hope and Folly*.

30 Loukopoulou, "'Films Bring Art to the People,'" 416.

31   *UNESCO Chronicle* 3, no. 12 (1957), 333.

32   "Report on the Committee of Film Experts Convened in Paris on April 2–7, 1951," UNESCO/MC/13 (Paris, June 27, 1951), 14.

33   "Experiment on the Possibility of the Use of Films with Audiences Other Than Those for Which They Have Been Made," UNESCO Archives file 307 778.5 A 859/67.

34   "Report on the Meeting to Study the Creation of an International Centre for Entertainment Films for Children and Adolescents," Edinburgh, September 6–10, 1955, UNESCO/MC/27 (Paris, May 3, 1956); "Final Report on the Meeting of Experts to Promote International Co-operation Between Film and Television," Tangier, September 19–30, 1955, UNESCO/MC/26 (Paris, April 4, 1956); "Meeting of Experts for the Establishment of an International Centre of Educational, Scientific and Cultural Films for Television," UNESCO House, Paris, June 13–20, 1956, UNESCO/MC/30 (Paris, July 11, 1956); and "Expert Meeting on the Creation of an International Body to Study the Influence of Mass Media on Children," Final Report, UNESCO/MC/31 (Paris, November 29, 1956).

35   According to Grierson's personnel file at UNESCO, Grierson's entire tenure was marred by a disagreement about salary and Grierson notified his wish to terminate his contract on January 30, 1948.

36   Grierson, "The Film and Primitive Peoples."

37   "New Directions in Documentary," Edinburgh Film Festival International Conference (1951). Wright participated on the panel "New Horizons," discussing UNESCO's work on using film to raise standards of living and education in underdeveloped countries. Wright and Rotha both participated on the panel "The Sponsor and the Creative Artist."

38   See Druick, *"World without End."*

39   The material published in his *Cameraless Animation*, a classic NFB pamphlet, was originally published in UNESCO's *Fundamental Education: A Quarterly Bulletin* 1, no. 4 (1949).

40   Sellers, "Making Films in and for the Colonies." See also, Smyth, "The Development of British Colonial Film Policy, 1927–1939," and "Movies and Mandarins."

41   See Ellis, *John Grierson*, 122; and Evans, *In the National Interest*, 6–12.

42   According to documents in McLean's UNESCO personnel file, discussions about the appointment were already underway in December 1949. The official offer of appointment, dated March 2, 1950, was signed by McLean on March 10, 1950, but his curriculum vitae on file indicates that he resigned from the NFB film commissioner's post in January 1950. Cf. Evans, *In the National Interest*, 12. McLean was replaced as the NFB commissioner by Arthur Irwin, who promptly dispatched the staff members seen to be security risks whom McLean had been protecting. See Druick, *Projecting Canada*, 91.

43   UNESCO, *Report of the Commission on Technical Needs*, 19.

44   Archival material found in UNESCO Archives files 307 778.5 A 57(7) "McLean Film Missions to Central and North America"; 307 778.5 A 859/67 "Experiment on the Possibility of the Use of Films with Audiences Other Than Those for Which They

Have Been Made"; 307 778.5 A 871 "Golden Laurel Awards (Selznick)," Parts 1 and 2; and 375 A 302/074 (45) "53" 173 "Seminar on Visual Aids in Fundamental Education, Sicily 1953."

45 Ross McLean, "Report on Mission to Canada February 23, 24, 25, 1951," 1 UNESCO Archives 307 778.506.6.

46 "Golden Laurel Awards" files, UNESCO Archives 307 778.5 A 871.

47 Dennis, *The Tin Shed*; Dawson, "The Grierson Tradition," 139–41; and Ellis, *John Grierson*, 124.

48 Memorandum from Ross McLean to UNESCO Director-General, "Regional Audio-Visual Centre for the Middle East" (April 4, 1956), 1, UNESCO Archives, 307 778 506.6.

49 See Pines and Willemen, *Questions of Third Cinema*; and Downing, *Film and Politics in the Third World*.

50 Willemen, "The Third Cinema Question," 5.

51 Preston, Herman, and Schiller, *Hope and Folly*, 295; and UNESCO, *A Chronology of UNESCO, 1945–1987*, 23.

52 "Meeting on the Introduction and Development of Television in Africa," Lagos, Nigeria, September 21–29, 1964, UNESCO/MC/51 (Paris, November 3, 1964); and "Meeting on Broadcasting in the Service of Education and Development in Asia," Bangkok, May 16–23, 1966, UNESCO/MC/53 (Paris, August 5, 1966).

53 Katz and Wedell, *Broadcasting in the Third World*.

HEALTH FILMS, COLD WAR, AND THE PRODUCTION
OF PATRIOTIC AUDIENCES
THE BODY FIGHTS BACTERIA (1948)

Kirsten Ostherr

In the postwar frenzy of audiovisual education, physicians, nurses, insurance agencies, hospitals, pharmaceutical companies, civic groups, schoolteachers, and others became involved in the production of health films that were clearly designed to instruct their viewers while also persuading them of the sponsor's cause or point of view.[1] In this era, organizations in all sectors of society got into the business of filmmaking, retooling the techniques of propaganda for the ostensibly benevolent purposes of education and enlightenment. Insurance companies made short films on seatbelts and safety; dentists offered movies about the social value of a nice smile; the U.S. government produced films about how to survive a nuclear attack and avoid venereal diseases (though not at the same time). All of these films espoused civic virtues while simultaneously pursuing their own self-interest in the name of community service.

As the other essays in this volume demonstrate, educational films had once been screened alongside Hollywood films in motion picture theaters, but by the postwar era, these films occupied distinctly different exhibition contexts. While Hollywood films were still mostly shown in the fixed location of a motion picture theater, instructional films were shown in a wide variety of settings, including churches, civic clubs, YMCAs, classrooms, and other locations whose primary purpose was not film exhibition.[2] Theatrical exhibition of Hollywood films took place at consistently scheduled intervals, for a fixed price, while non-theatrical exhibition of instructional films took place at irregular intervals, with free admission. Feature films usually lasted approximately ninety minutes and were accompanied by newsreels and other short subjects; educational films were themselves short subjects, and were often shown alongside other shorts addressing a diverse array of topics, or to illustrate a lecture on the same subject matter.

The differences between Hollywood and educational exhibition settings reflect the different production and distribution contexts of these films as well, and collectively these varied facets of the postwar educational film movement shaped a mass audience trained in the virtues of patriotic film spectatorship. Moreover, this film-going public cultivated a sufficiently diverse range of interests to sustain a regular viewership for the thousands of instructional films that were produced in the postwar period. It is my contention that the creation of this audience was a direct result of the shared experience of mass exposure to World War II propaganda films, both in the United States and abroad. This essay will present a case study of a particular kind of educational film, examining its production contexts and one of its products (a health film of 1948). By focusing the analysis on a specific historical period (the post–World War II era), and paying close attention to distribution, exhibition, and the rhetoric that shaped postwar film practice, this essay will chart the shifting function of educational film from its service to government in wartime to its employment in the cold war pursuit of industrial health and citizenship. Thus, this chapter will also serve as a case study of the ways that the tropes of state and wartime propaganda profoundly shaped what was widely thought of as "educational" after the war. The specific context that will frame our analysis of postwar educational film is the American College of Surgeons (ACS), whose extensive medical motion picture program set the standard for health film production, distribution, and exhibition in this period.

Founded in 1913, the American College of Surgeons is the primary professional association for surgeons in the United States. The college provides board certification for surgeons, as well as ongoing education through annual meetings and other activities dedicated to improving patient care and surgical training.[3] The Motion Picture program of the ACS was established in 1926 by recommendation of the Committee on Approval and Development of Motion Picture Films. In this year, a committee of ACS fellows met with George Eastman, the head of the Eastman Kodak Company, and Will Hays, the president of the Motion Picture Producers and Distributors Association of America (MPPDA), to assess the viability of pursuing a medical motion picture production program.[4] The proposal was greeted with enthusiasm and offers of assistance from all quarters, and production promptly began.[5] The ACS produced its own films, selecting topics based on the committee's recommendations for important subjects of general interest to surgeons, and starting in the early 1930s any producer of medical or health films, whether aimed at a specialist or general audience, could also send a copy of his or her film to the ACS for review.[6] Films were reviewed by "a committee consisting of recognized authorities on the subject matter portrayed," and were evaluated primarily on the basis of their "teaching value," but "professional technique" and "photographic quality" were also taken into account. If the film met "basic standards" in these areas, it would be approved by the college, and the producer would then be permitted to insert a title card at the beginning of the film, which read: "Passed by the Committee on Medical Motion Pictures of the American College of Surgeons."[7] As indicated by the seal preceding the opening credits, our case study title, *The Body Fights Bacteria*, was reviewed and approved by the American College of Surgeons.

In ACS documents, the pre–World War II period is largely described as a period of research rather than full-scale film production. A widely publicized resolution adopted by the Board of Regents of the ACS after the meetings with Eastman and Hays in 1926 declared that "the year's work has demonstrated that much fundamental and experimental work must be done in what is practically a new field," and "we approve of the principle that this fundamental and experimental work should be done before proceeding to volume production of pictures that would be inadequate and not present the high ideal that we believe to be possible."[8] Numerous films were nonetheless made in the years before the war, but the scope of the endeavor was relatively limited in com-

AMERICAN COLLEGE OF SURGEONS

Guiding Principles in Evaluating Medical Motion Picture Films

The principles which guide the American College of Surgeons in evaluating medical motion picture films are as follows:

PROFESSIONAL STANDPOINT:

1. Subject matter.
2. Method of presentation.
3. Selection of case for the procedure indicated.
4. Relevancy of subject matter to material presented.
5. Technique.
6. Teaching value.
7. Sacrifice of efficient service to the patient to photographic quality.
8. Originality of presentation.
9. Possible better portrayal of subject by other existing films.
10. Elements introduced.
11. Ethics.
12. Distribution:
    a. Profession in general.
    b. Specialists only.
    c. Medical students.
    d. Hospitals.
    e. Lay public.
13. Suggestions for improving the film.

MECHANICAL STANDPOINT:

1. Method of presentation.
2. Logical sequence.
3. Photographic quality.
4. Clearness of operating field.
5. Illumination.
6. Terminology.
7. Legends.
8. Possibility of better portrayal of subject matter through:
    a. Animation.
    b. Diagrams.
    c. Drawings.
    d. X-rays.
9. Quality of:
    a. Animation.
    b. Diagrams.
    c. Drawings.
    d. X-rays.
10. Unnecessary duplication.
11. Condition of the film.
12. Date of production.
13. Suggestions for improving the film.

"Guiding Principles in Evaluating Medical Motion Picture Films."

parison with the unbridled enthusiasm apparent in postwar publications and film catalogues. The shift to large-scale educational filmmaking may have been shaped in part by the college's decision to switch from 35mm to 16mm film gauge for its postwar productions. In 1927, the ACS and Eastman Teaching Films, Inc. submitted a proposal to the ACS board that clearly identified 35mm as the preferred filmmaking gauge, and the first ACS films were produced and distributed on 35mm film.[9] However, the ACS lost Eastman funding in 1931 as a consequence of the stock market crash and subsequent economic depression, and sometime between this date and 1940 the decisive shift to 16mm film was made.[10]

The ACS Committee on Medical Motion Pictures systematically gathered information in an attempt to identify and standardize a set of best practices for medical filmmaking, and a pamphlet obtained by the committee provides a particularly valuable perspective on the postwar educational film scene. The pamphlet, called "Let's Make a Movie," was published by the Visual Information Section of the Soil Conservation Service, U.S. Department of Agriculture (USDA) in 1948, and it states, "Non-theatrical motion pictures were being used by industrial concerns, government departments and other organizations before the start of World War I. World War II demonstrated *to the general public* the ability of the motion picture to sell, train, inspire, teach and convince in the most effective manner. Eleven-odd million veterans, now returned to peacetime pursuits have great respect for the motion picture. They want to see more films used in business and they expect their children to have the advantage of educational films in school."[11] *The Body Fights Bacteria* was one of the films that satisfied this postwar expectation that audiovisual aids be incorporated into state-of-the-art pedagogical techniques. As the USDA pamphlet suggests, both veterans and the general public saw the motion picture as a technology of national betterment that enabled victory in World War II and would continue to improve the lives of Americans and their allies in the postwar period.

Following this logic, the ACS publication "Medical Motion Picture Films" of 1949 describes its outreach and educational activities in the United States and abroad, and the text explicitly links its "Foreign Distribution of Approved Medical Motion Picture Films" to wartime activities and maintenance of American postwar scientific and cultural dominance abroad. Here, then, is an added incentive for increased efforts to produce and distribute health films after the war. Just as commercial entities in the United States used educational films as advertisements in disguise to cash in on the postwar economic boom, so the ACS used instructional films to advertise the surgical innovations that were an important part of American medical prestige in the World War II and postwar periods.[12] The ACS pamphlet describes the organization's cooperation with the Department of State and the Office of Inter-American Affairs in two programs that loan "approved medical motion picture films" to Latin American countries. Between 1940 and 1949, the ACS distributed 121 different films to "recognized medical groups in the countries of Latin America which . . . requested this service."[13]

The pamphlet identifies the Latin American audiences of the ACS films as comprising several different publics: the primary audience was an elite group consisting of government officials, military and police groups, industrial executives, and medical professionals; secondary viewers were adults and children in the population at large. The ACS materials claim that, with the assistance of more than 100 "mobile film units in sound film trucks owned by commercial firms," over 2,800 screenings of health and medical films took place between 1948 and 1949, reaching over 1 million viewers. Indeed, "The health films for the public [were] reported to be so popular that in many instances local theaters provide[d] their facilities for morning showings to as many as 3,000 children at a time."[14] While it is hard to imagine many movie theaters that could accommodate 3,000 children at once (even without their chaperones), the statistics nonetheless indicate some measure of success for the program. The list of "Films for the Laity" that were shown to general audiences of adults and children in Latin America included the following titles, which were simultaneously circulating in the United States and other parts of the world at this time:

> *With These Weapons: The Story of Syphilis* (American Social Hygiene
>   Association, 1939);
> *Choose to Live* (One woman's encounter with cancer) (U.S. Public Health
>   Service and American Society for the Control of Cancer, 1940);
> *Body Defenses against Disease* (ERPI Classroom Films, 1937);
> *Heart and Circulation* (ERPI Classroom Films, 1937);
> *Defense against Invasion* (Vaccination) (Walt Disney, 1943);
> *Eyes for Tomorrow* (Prevention of blindness from disease and industrial
>   hazards) (Coordinator of Inter-American Affairs, 1943);
> *Nursing the Americas* (The nursing profession) (Coordinator of
>   Inter-American Affairs, 1943);
> *The Winged Scourge* (Malaria) (Walt Disney, 1943);

Water — Friend or Enemy (Walt Disney, 1943);

Help Wanted (Basic principles of first aid and general procedures in caring
    for victims before the doctor arrives) (Johnson and Johnson, 1940);

Another to Conquer (Native Americans and tuberculosis)
    (National Tuberculosis Association, 1941);

Cloud in the Sky (Tuberculosis in Hispanic population)
    (National Tuberculosis Association, 1940);

Fight Syphilis (U.S. Public Health Service, 1943);

Know for Sure (Syphilis) (U.S. Public Health Service, ca. 1941).[15]

As their titles suggest, many of these films employed military combat imagery
and rhetoric to make their case; terms such as "weapons," "defenses," "invasion," "conquer," and "fight" all encourage viewers to imagine battling the
enemy disease and preserving their personal health as matters of patriotism
and national security.

In addition to the films for the general public, many of the more technical
ACS films were distributed exclusively to specialized medical audiences in the
Americas. These films had been approved by the ACS Medical Motion Picture
Committee, usually in advance of their premiere at an annual ACS Clinical
Congress, and were then exhibited, upon request, at medical schools in the
United States and abroad. A brief sampling of these titles includes *Hernio-
plasty for Direct Inguinal Hernia* (Lawrence S. Fallis, M.D., 1941); *Transfusion of
Unmodified Blood (Demonstrating Transfusion Needles and Continuous Flow In-
strument)* (Michael E. DeBakey, M.D., 1938); *The Mechanism of the Heart Beat
and Electrocardiography* (Lewis M. Hurxthal, M.D., 1932); *Reconstruction of
Cleft Lips* (James Barrett Brown, M.D., 1940); *Aseptic Resection of Stomach for
Carcinoma and Ulcer* (Emile Homan, M.D., 1940); and *Diagnostic Procedures
in Tuberculosis* (National Tuberculosis Association, 1938).[16]

The ACS partner in this program, the Office of Inter-American Affairs
(OIAA), "was directed to formulate and execute programs in the commercial and economic fields and the fields of the arts and sciences, education
and travel, the radio, the press, and the cinema that would further national
defense and strengthen the bonds between the nations of the Western Hemi-
sphere."[17] To conduct this work, the OIAA collaborated closely with the Department of State. As Seth Fein, Lisa Cartwright, Brian Goldfarb, and others
have explained, during and after World War II the OIAA was directly engaged
in struggles with Axis powers over ownership and control of mass communications media in much of Latin America, and cinema was at the forefront of

this battle.[18] Indeed, much of the cold war was fought on the cultural front, thus extending the relevance of the military metaphor for educational film activities well beyond the immediate postwar era.

The ACS pamphlet of 1949 goes on to describe film distribution activities in China and many other countries, concluding with a critical and telling understatement of the condition that enabled these programs to exist: World War II had interrupted medical education in all the countries that were occupied or saw military action. For this reason, the U.S. Office of War Information asked the ACS to step in and fill the void with its instructional program of medical motion pictures. As a result the pamphlet claims, "The American College of Surgeons has been a great factor in extending medical education throughout the world."[19] The rationale for the active pursuit of foreign markets by an ostensibly non-commercial entity is explained here in terms that clearly acknowledge that the American medical community was exploiting the same overseas opportunities that Hollywood exploited after the war.[20] As the ACS *Bulletin* summed up the situation, "The development and availability of films of the highest type is especially important at this time in view of the disruption of medical education and medical practice throughout the world. . . . American medicine is destined to leave its imprint throughout the world into the indefinite future."[21] Here, medical motion pictures are depicted explicitly as vehicles for benevolent international medical education, and implicitly as commodities that facilitate global market dominance by the U.S. health-care industry.

The example of the American College of Surgeons demonstrates how films that were conceived as technical vehicles of pure education nonetheless also functioned as vehicles for the management of populations of specialists and the general public, at home and abroad.[22] In this light, the filmed "operations" that these surgeons performed take on a metaphorical power; not only is the human body a placeholder for the national body, but the power to "play god" on one anatomical specimen is extended through these films to a geopolitical scale of omnipotence. Despite the fact that most ACS films were created by and for medical specialists, the organization's motion picture program was part of a larger transformation of the public sphere as electronic media and screens became increasingly ubiquitous around the world in the second half of the twentieth century, providing a key stage for a new kind of global biopolitics. From this perspective, we can see that the ACS film program defined the context and functions of "education" in terms that were fundamentally shaped by the rhetoric of wartime propaganda.

During World War II, educational films had been used to train combat troops, to persuade the general public of the merits of U.S. engagement, and to frame the privations of war as patriotic duty. Many of the wartime films were health films aimed at producing and maintaining the vigorous population of recruits and home front laborers needed for mass military mobilization.[23] These films, with titles such as *Fight Syphilis* (1941), *Enemy X* (1942), and *Health Is a Victory* (1942), framed health in terms of battle, and after 1945 they continued to utilize military metaphors to explain their rationale and methods of instruction, as well as the pathophysiology of disease itself.[24] The seemingly powerful impact of propaganda films during World War II was directly cited as the incentive for non-military organizations to attempt using film for their own persuasive purposes after the war. Our primary example will be a fourteen-minute-long film from 1948, *The Body Fights Bacteria*, produced by Audio Productions, Inc. in association with McGraw-Hill Text-Films. The film was part of a series of seven "text-films on health education" produced for use with the *Textbook of Healthful Living* by Harold S. Diehl, a college-level text that was first published in 1935, with several subsequent editions each decade up to the late 1960s.[25] The other films in the series were *Emotional Health*; *The Nose, Throat, and Ears*; *Body Care and Grooming*; *Human Reproduction*; *Hormones and the Endocrine Glands*; and *Diseases of the Heart and Circulatory System*. While this catalog of titles may evoke images of scientific neutrality more than propagandistic sensationalism, the title of our film, *The Body Fights Bacteria*, is clearly suggestive of the combat mentality that characterized many wartime propaganda films.

To underscore the film's approach, the chapter of the *Textbook of Healthful Living* correlated with the film, called "Major Health Problems," opens by laying out its own pedagogical combat strategy: "In planning a campaign, the military strategist surveys the entire field of action, appraises its strong points and its weaknesses, and then concentrates his efforts where the dangers seem greatest and the possibilities of success brightest." The chapter then displays a series of tables providing "a composite view of our major health problems." Following the stated campaign strategy, the text continues, "Let us examine these [tables] and then direct our attention to those conditions which offer the greatest possibilities of improvement."[26] The chapter systematically proceeds to implement this tactical model in explaining health problems and their potential solutions. Notably, the post–World War II editions of the textbook include new sections that explicitly frame health issues in relation to the war; the reader thus learns, for example, that "the total number of . . . casualties during the first 10 days of the Normandy invasion was less than the number of casualties from automobile accidents for an average 10-day period in 1946."[27]

Corresponding to the textual metaphor, the opening sequence of *The Body Fights Bacteria* underscores the military mentality that the film seeks to elicit in its viewers. The film opens with documentary footage of a fighter plane in flight followed by the explosion of an atomic bomb, while the voiceover announces, "We respect the atom bomb. We respect it because we have seen, at one breathless glimpse, the awful destructiveness of its power. But how many of us respect this"—here the image cuts to a close-up of a petri dish—"a glass dish containing colonies of organisms." At this point a hand reaches into the frame and removes the glass cover of the dish, allowing the camera to cut in to an extreme close-up of its contents. "And yet, this dish full of disease-producing organisms, if allowed to grow unchecked, may be capable of more widespread loss of life than a dozen atom bombs." To underscore this dramatic point, the film cuts back to another shot of a nuclear bomb exploding.

Continuing the theme, the image of a mushroom cloud dissolves to an aerial shot of Hiroshima, Japan, followed by a montage of street-level scenes of destruction in the city. In a menacing tone, the voiceover remarks, "One atom bomb, dropped on a city of 300,000 population, created tremendous local destruction." To ensure that the analogy is not lost on any viewers, the image dissolves to an animated close-up of a petri dish, then zooms out, leaving the dish in the upper left side of the frame, while the remaining screen space fades in on a world map, with continents slowly becoming shaded as the narrator describes the world history of pandemics. "But a colony of virulent disease-producing germs on a single petri or culture dish might initiate an epidemic of such proportions as to engulf the entire earth, and run up a death toll in millions, as bubonic plague did in the thirteenth century, and smallpox in the sixteenth century, and influenza in the twentieth century. What are these organisms, whose destructiveness is literally beyond the scope of calculation? We know them as bacteria, but how do they attack us? And what defenses do we—you and I—have against them?" Shifting back to live action, a new scene opens with a medium close-up of a young man at a microscope, placing a slide underneath the scope and leaning in to examine it. Here we cut to an extreme close-up, point-of-view shot of cinemicroscopic images of bacteria. As the film launches into its more overtly instructional phase, the voiceover begins a technical description of the different types of bacteria. But even in the more

"The awful destructiveness" of the atomic bomb in *The Body Fights Bacteria*.

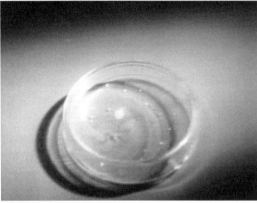

"A glass dish containing colonies of organisms" from *The Body Fights Bacteria*.

scientific sequences of the film the hyperbolic rhetoric of military engagement remains: "Bacilli, Cocci, Spirochetes — big names for little fellows. But they're armed with more potential destructiveness than a fleet of bombers."

The film's use of military language and imagery in the opening sequence is none too subtle, and the voiceover continues to use martial metaphors to refer to bacteria and viruses throughout the film, asking, "With bacteria and viruses so plentiful and dangerous, why haven't they already won their endless war against mankind?" and noting, "The first line of the body's natural defenses against bacteria is the skin. Skin is like armor covering the body's surface." Later in the film, bacteria are described as "invaders," and white blood cells are "special defense cells," whose job it is to "corner the enemy." The film even returns to the imagery of the opening sequence by reminding us that "in spite of these many body defenses, we have diseases. Diseases which, if they become epidemic, can strike us with greater impact than an atomic bomb."

This leads into a discussion of antibodies and vaccines, described as "a strong defense," generated from "an actual attack of the disease itself." The film ends with the exhortation, "Only with your help can disease be conquered. The battle is yours. Fight bacteria."

Not only does the voiceover in this film repeatedly emphasize the war-like intentions of bacteria, it also repeatedly utilizes direct address to declare that viewers may become the target of these attacks. By employing inclusive pronouns throughout *The Body Fights Bacteria*, the narrator encourages the audience to share his perspective, though this egalitarian gesture is temporary; the film's final statement clearly transfers responsibility for winning the battle against bacteria from "us" to "you." The narrator's apparent willingness to identify with the film's viewers is further undermined by the comparison of bacteria with atomic bombs; this scare tactic reinstates the narrator's superiority by placing viewers in the subordinate position of needing his expert advice to avoid the fate of Hiroshima's citizens. The use of war imagery as an analogy for the body's interaction with bacteria frames the exercise of viewing and implementing the film's instructions as a citizen's patriotic duty. In the college classroom setting, the persuasiveness of these techniques may have been enhanced by the added incentive of earning a good grade in the class. Moreover, 49 percent of American college admissions in 1947 were World War II soldiers receiving their education through the G.I. bill; thus, almost half of the students enrolled in 1948 were veterans.[28] Having already trained this portion of the audience with instructional films during the war, the filmmakers continued to utilize the familiar military combat metaphors as they shifted their focus from the management of wartime populations to the regulation of health in postwar civilians and veterans.

The Body Fights Bacteria was not alone in its thematic linkage of health education with military propaganda; numerous other films from the postwar period utilize this technique.[29] Many scholars have noted the prevalence of military metaphors of disease, using this observation to think about conceptions of the body, health, and illness historically and up to the present day.[30] But I want to suggest further that the military analogy also played an active role in shaping the postwar boom in non-theatrical film exhibition. More significant than any technological development in the rise and fall of educational film were the social conditions that created a mass, civic-minded audience willing to view regularly the thousands of instructional films that were produced in the postwar period, and I would argue that the creation of this audience was fundamentally linked to the shared wartime experience of propaganda film viewing, both in the United States and abroad. Richard Dyer MacCann and others have documented the extensive use of 16mm film exhibition to train (and entertain) American civilians and military troops, both before mobilization and once they were overseas.[31] As a consequence of this continuous use, 16mm film came to be seen as a medium at the vanguard of the postwar pedagogical revolution, even though the film gauge had been available since the early 1920s.[32] Thus, it was not a technological shift but rather a discursive shift that legitimated the expansion of non-theatrical exhibition after the war. While film propaganda acquired negative connotations through its use in Nazi Germany, it simultaneously achieved a newfound respectability as a medium that facilitated the victory of the Allies, both as a training tool for soldiers and as a vehicle for news gathering and morale boosting on the home front.[33]

This is not to suggest that a robust network of non-theatrical film distribution only came into existence after World War II. On the contrary, as Ronald Greene and Gregory Waller have shown, the preconditions for the postwar explosion of 16mm film production already existed before World War II.[34] However, it is my argument that the mass-mediated social experience of the war enabled those existing networks to serve as vehicles for the rapid expansion of audiovisual education after the war with a larger scale of production and a more varied viewership. Moreover, the mode of address employed in wartime propaganda films provided a familiar framework for engaging viewers in the postwar era; both civilians and veterans were accustomed to the rhetoric of patriotic sacrifice and toil through newsreels and educational shorts, and nongovernmental production companies did not hesitate to borrow this rhetoric for their own films after the war.

CONCLUSION: HEALTH EDUCATION MEDIA FROM 16MM FILM TO DIGITAL SIMULATION

The continued linkage of educational film with military endeavors in the postwar era underscores the importance of examining the strategic functions of mass media initiatives conducted in the name of public interest. *The Body Fights Bacteria* is one example among many of a post–World War II instructional film that links bodily processes to military metaphors while simultaneously securing exhibition outlets through state-sponsored activities that were directly linked to global military expansion. As Martin Quigley observed in 1937, "The dictum, 'trade follows the flag,' has been revised to read 'trade follows the film.'"[35] In this case, however, viewers were encouraged to believe that "health follows the film." *The Body Fights Bacteria* was designed to enhance audiovisually college students' understanding of their text-based curriculum on human health. Many of these same students would view more sophisticated ACS-approved films as part of their future medical training, learning not only advanced surgical techniques but also the professional codes of conduct for possessors of specialized forms of knowledge about the human body. For such viewers, health films may have served the instrumental purpose of career advancement, in addition to the more basic function they were meant to fulfill for their audiences: helping them to avoid illness and attain better health.

In the ACS production context, the success of a training film might be evaluated on the basis of surgical outcomes for the viewers' patients. While it would be difficult to isolate the effectiveness of the teaching film from all the other factors that could contribute to patient morbidity and mortality, the introduction of new techniques into a medical practice after surgeons' exposure to motion pictures explaining those techniques would qualify nonetheless as a strategic function of filmmaking. Another evaluation of the effectiveness of health film production and distribution might focus on the extent to which innovative techniques were disseminated across a large geographical expanse, thus measuring the influence of a specific surgical team beyond their local sphere of contact, much as one might measure the impact of a propaganda campaign.

Alternatively, these films might also be assessed in terms of the viewers' professional conduct. To what extent does the privilege of viewing these films, with all the socially and medically intimate information they convey, make their viewers "feel" like surgeons, with the elite cultural connotations that such an identity implies? Since the mid-twentieth century, so much medical training has taken place through virtual experience that the process of becoming a doctor and then a specialist has become a process of viewing, internalizing, then replicating the onscreen performance of doctoring. In this sense, at least one clear objective of these motion pictures is the propagation of physicians who share a particular way of seeing the body that in turn shapes the transformation of that body through medical intervention. As we can see from the strategic global outreach of the ACS film program in the cold war era, these films produced medical authority in their viewers even as they fostered relations of dependence between foreign medical schools in need of postwar reconstruction and the U.S.-based surgeons, whose expertise and wealth of resources helped to define American superpower status in this era.

By cultivating these geopolitical alliances through the benevolent donation of medical knowledge, the ACS assisted in the expansion of American spheres of influence, using education instead of military force, and thus extending ways of seeing the body into ways of seeing the nation.

Mass-mediated medical ways of seeing the body have continued to change over time. Just as 16mm films such as *The Body Fights Bacteria* were part of a postwar educational movement toward increased use of films in classroom settings and elsewhere, so experiments with educational television, videotape, and computer software have marked subsequent trends in media-based learning.[36] One of the key factors that led to the eventual demise of 16mm film production was the widespread availability of videotape, and many scholars have emphasized the impact of television news switching from 16mm film production to electronic production in the early 1980s.[37] More research needs to be done in the area of non-theatrical exhibition, but I would suggest that social factors, in addition to technology, played an important role in the rise and fall of 16mm educational film. The propaganda function of 16mm film during World War II not only created a market for the medium, but also created a mass audience motivated by patriotic duty to attend non-theatrical film screenings. The proliferation of production and distribution companies, treatises on audiovisual education, and 16mm films themselves throughout the 1950s and 1960s suggests that the wartime enthusiasm endured for some time after 1945. But these same sources had dwindled by the 1980s, as the social cohesion needed for a robust non-theatrical exhibition circuit staffed by unpaid, civic-minded Americans declined in the wake of a less popular war, protest movements, and the Watergate scandal.[38] And yet, the space vacated by 16mm non-theatrical exhibition did not remain empty; non-theatrical video exhibition played a critical role in the very political movements that rejected the top-down model of 16mm educational film.[39] Low-budget, often amateur, do-it-yourself activist videotapes such as those promoting erotic safer sex practices during the early years of the AIDS pandemic in the late 1980s most likely circulated among different viewers than those who dutifully attended screenings on tuberculosis and the polio vaccine in the 1950s, but both crowds were engaged at least in part by the pursuit of social betterment and improved personal health.[40]

Today, digital video continues to fulfill the educational function for medical training once served by 16mm film; the ACS Committee on Medical Motion Pictures was initially replaced by the Committees on Video-Based Education and Informatics, and now the ACS Division of Education provides the

E-Learning Resource Center, including educational DVD listings, Web casts, and an online "Medical Modeling and Simulation Database."[41] Meanwhile, health films for the general public have been replaced by medical reporting on television newsmagazines and direct-to-consumer pharmaceutical advertisements. As a survey by the Centers for Disease Control and Prevention reported in 2001, more Americans get their health information from television than from any other source, though recent reports identify a growing trend toward online health education.[42] Moreover, while the United States may continue to be a global leader in medical innovation, the accessibility of American health care has fallen far behind international standards, a point of ongoing debate in the context of health-care reform.

Just as the current health education landscape is characterized by the ubiquity of media messages in an ever widening array of electronic formats, the postwar context featured such prolific educational film production that viewers may have learned more about the educational imperatives of a society transitioning from wartime propaganda to superpower propaganda than they did about the specific content of any given film. This may be the single most important point for scholarship on instructional films: despite the pointed self-interest of the firms that sponsored these productions, non-theatrical educational films were often treated by exhibitors as somewhat interchangeable, especially within a given subgenre, such as health films. Some were certainly better than others when evaluated according to the criteria of the American College of Surgeons, but the very ubiquity of the films during their golden era, coupled with their lack of distinctive stars and their frequent distribution and exhibition en masse, suggests that the significance of these films may only be adequately understood in aggregate. Representative films such as *The Body Fights Bacteria* provide clues to the distinctive modes of address that characterized postwar instructional films and shaped audiences' responses to them. But the most powerful effects of these films emerged from the postwar social setting in which masses of Americans, through curiosity or compulsion, viewed educational films as part of daily life.

NOTES

1   For a description of sponsored film as it encompasses educational and instructional films, see Prelinger, *The Field Guide to Sponsored Films*, vi.
2   On non-theatrical exhibition sites, see Prelinger, *The Field Guide to Sponsored Films*, vii–ix. While Hollywood films were later shown in a wide range of settings, including

airplanes, drive-in theaters, and television, their exhibition in the immediate postwar era was primarily confined to traditional theaters. For a complete history of Hollywood's exhibition settings, see Gomery, *Shared Pleasures.*

3   "What Is the American College of Surgeons?" American College of Surgeons Web site, http://www.facs.org/about/corppro.html (accessed June 26, 2007).

4   Stephenson, "Visual Education in Surgery," 9.

5   The success of this collaboration is interesting in light of the MPPDA's inclusion of "surgical operations" in its list of "Don'ts" and "Be Carefuls" one year after this meeting, suggesting that the alliance with the ACS may have been partly a strategic decision to identify clearly the appropriate domain for such excessively realistic documentary images, leaving Hollywood films free to imagine a more idealized version of the medical encounter.

6   Stephenson, "Visual Education in Surgery," 11.

7   "Medical Motion Picture Films," *Bulletin of the American College of Surgeons* 34, no. 4 (1949), 381.

8   "Development of Medical Films Praised," *The Motion Picture,* December 1, 1928, 5. American College of Surgeons Archives, Committee on Medical Motion Pictures, Correspondence and Data on Films, 1926–97 RG5/SG2/S2 Box 1, Folder "Med. Motion Picts — Articles in Trade Journals 1926–1929."

9   American College of Surgeons, "Medical Motion Picture Films," September 1927, 2. American College of Surgeons Archives, Committee on Medical Motion Pictures, Correspondence and Data on Films, 1926–97 RG5/SG2/S2 Box 1, Folder "Medical Motion Picture Library Lists." See also Stephenson, "Visual Education in Surgery," 10.

10 "Inter-American Distribution of Approved Medical Motion Picture Films," Reprint from *Bulletin of the American College of Surgeons,* September 1943, 1. Committee on Medical Motion Pictures, Correspondence and Data on Films, 1926–97, RG5/SG2/S2 Box 6, Folder "U.S. Information Agency, 1943–1975." For valuable historical context on the fates of other educational film projects in this period, see R. Greene, "Selling Reputation."

11 Emphasis in original. American College of Surgeons, Committee on Medical Motion Pictures, Correspondence and Data on Films, 1926–97, RG5/SG2/S2 Box 1, Folder "Medical Motion Pictures Committee — Production 1942–1977."

12 See Prelinger, *The Field Guide to Sponsored Films* for over four hundred examples of films that aim to persuade their audiences of the sponsor's perspective, which often emphasized the desirability of purchasing the sponsor's product. *The Field Guide* can be downloaded from the Web site of the National Film Preservation Foundation at http://www.filmpreservation.org/index.html.

13 "Medical Motion Picture Films," 382.

14 "Inter-American Distribution of Approved Medical Motion Picture Films," reprint from *Bulletin of the American College of Surgeons,* September 1943, 2. Committee on Medical Motion Pictures, Correspondence and Data on Films, 1926–97, RG5/SG2/S2 Box 6, Folder "U.S. Information Agency, 1943–1975."

15 "Inter-American Distribution of Approved Medical Motion Picture Films," 6–7. *Heart and Circulation* and *Know for Sure* are available for viewing on the Internet at http://www.archive.org/ (accessed June 13, 2008). *The Winged Scourge* is available on a DVD collection of Walt Disney's World War II cartoons, called *Walt Disney Treasures—On the Front Lines* (Disney, 2004).

16 "Inter-American Distribution of Approved Medical Motion Picture Films," 3–6.

17 National Archives, Records of the Office of Inter-American Affairs (RG 229) http://www.archives.gov/research/holocaust/finding-aid/civilian/rg-229.html.

18 Fein, "From Collaboration to Containment"; and Cartwright and Goldfarb, "Cultural Contagion."

19 "Medical Motion Picture Films," 382.

20 See Jarvie, *Hollywood's Overseas Campaign*; Miller, Govil, McMurria, Maxwell, and Wang, *Global Hollywood 2*; Stokes and Maltby, *Hollywood Abroad*; and Trumpbour, *Selling Hollywood to the World*.

21 "Medical Motion Picture Films," 382.

22 For a more extensive discussion of this issue, see Ostherr, *Medical Visions*.

23 See Parascandola, "Syphilis at the Cinema" and other essays in Reagan, Tomes, and Treichler, *Medicine's Moving Pictures*. For a discussion of women and postwar health films, see Cartwright, *Screening the Body*, especially chapter 6, "Women and the Public Culture of Radiography."

24 Examples of wartime health films include *Enemy X* (Prod. U.S. Public Health Service/American Society for Control of Cancer/CBS, 1942); *Fight Syphilis* (Dir. Owen Murray, Prod. U.S. Public Health Service, 1941); *Health Is a Victory* (Prod. American Social Hygiene Association, 1942); *In Defense of the Nation* (Prod. Jam Handy/U.S. Public Health Service, 1941); *Keep 'em Out* (Prod. Stark-Films/U.S. Public Health Service, 1942); *Local Health Problems in War Industry Areas* (Prod. Division of Public Education, New York State Department of Health, 1942); *Magic Bullets* (Prod. U.S. Public Health Service/Warner Brothers, 1940); *Middletown Goes to War* (Prod. National Tuberculosis Association, 1942); *Military Sanitation: Disposal of Human Waste* (Prod. War Department/U.S. Army Signal Corps, 1943); *The Mosquito* (Combat Film Report, No. 157) (Prod. Army Air Forces, 1945); *On the Firing Line: A Travel-Tour to Scenes of the Fight against Tuberculosis* (Prod. National Tuberculosis Association/Courier, 1939); *Reward Unlimited* (Prod. U.S. Public Health Service/Office of War Information/War Activities Committee, 1944); *Save a Day!* (Prod. Federal Security Agency/U.S. Public Health Service, 1941); *They Do Come Back* (Dir. Edward G. Ulmer, Prod. National Tuberculosis Association, 1940); *To the People of the United States* (Dir. Arthur Lubin, Prod. Walter Wanger/U.S. Public Health Service, 1944); *Tsutsugamushi: Prevention* (Prod. U.S. Navy/Audio Productions, 1945); and *Your Health Department* (Prod. National Motion Pictures Co., 1941). For a discussion of these films, see Ostherr, *Cinematic Prophylaxis*.

25 Additional editions were published in 1939, 1945, 1950, 1955, 1960, 1964, and 1968.

26 Diehl, *Textbook of Healthful Living*, 26.

27 Diehl, *Healthful Living*, 29–30.

28 See Mettler, *Soldiers to Citizens*; and the U.S. Department of Veterans Affairs statistics at http://www.gibill.va.gov/GI_Bill_Info/history.htm.

29 Examples include *Prevention of the Introduction of Diseases from Abroad* (Prod. U.S. Public Health Service/Bray Studios, 1946); *The Eternal Fight* (Prod. United Nations Film Board/Madeline Carroll Films, 1948); *The Fight against the Communicable Diseases* (Prod. U.S. Public Health Service, 1950); *For the Nation's Health* (Prod. Communicable Disease Center, 1952); *The Silent Invader* (Prod. Westinghouse Broadcasting/U.S. Public Health Service, 1957); and others listed in the text of this essay. See Ostherr, *Cinematic Prophylaxis*, for a discussion of these films.

30 See Sontag, *Illness as Metaphor*; W. May, *The Physician's Covenant*; Rothman, "Ethics and Human Experimentation"; E. Martin, *Flexible Bodies*; Annas, "Reframing the Debate on Health Care Reform by Replacing Our Metaphors"; and Mongoven, "The War on Disease and the War on Terror."

31 MacCann, *The People's Films*, 118–72; Winston, *Technologies of Seeing*, 75; Zimmermann, *Reel Families*, 90–111.

32 Rossi-Snook, "Persistence of Vision," 3.

33 The medium also served as repurposed propaganda when captured Axis footage was integrated into the American propaganda series called *Why We Fight*. See Thomas Doherty, *Projections of War*, especially chapter 2, "Leni Riefenstahl's Contribution to the American War Effort," 16–35. See also Zimmermann, *Reel Families*, 90–91.

34 See Ronald Walter Greene, "Pastoral Exhibition: The YMCA Motion Picture Bureau and the Transition to 16mm, 1928–1939," in this volume; and R. Greene, "Y Movies". See also Waller, "Distributing 16mm."

35 Quigley, "Public Opinion and the Motion Picture," 131. Quigley was a prolific film critic, Hollywood insider, and co-author of the text of the Production Code.

36 See Goldfarb, *Visual Pedagogy*.

37 Slide, *Before Video*, 134–35; Winston, *Technologies of Seeing*, 86.

38 For an overview of these social changes, see Patterson, *Grand Expectations*, and *Restless Giant*.

39 Despite the decline in non-theatrical exhibition of 16mm educational films, non-commercial screenings continued on videotape, especially as the medium became widely available and affordable in the 1980s. See Juhasz, *AIDS TV*; and Eberwein, *Sex Ed*.

40 A crucial difference lies in the AIDS videos' explicit critiques of the federal government's failure to respond promptly or adequately to the pandemic, in contrast to the wholehearted patriotism of most postwar health films. For an excellent discussion of AIDS activism in relation to government funding of scientific research, see S. Epstein, *Impure Science*.

41 ACS — *Davis and Geck Surgical Film-Video Library Complete Catalog*, rev. April 1988. American College of Surgeons, Committee on Medical Motion Pictures, Correspondence and Data on Films, 1926–97 RG5/SG2/S2 Box 3, Folder "Davis and Geck Published Articles 1950–1977." See also http://www.facs.org/education/index.html. For a history of ACS involvement with motion pictures, see Stephenson, *American*

College of Surgeons at 75, 7, 68, 74–93. For an excellent discussion of the significance of digital technologies for medical practice, see Curtis, "Still/Moving."

42 See the CDC Healthstyles surveys of 1999–2005 at http://www.cdc.gov/Health Marketing/entertainment_education/healthstyles_survey.htm (accessed June 13, 2008). See also Fox and Jones, *The Social Life of Health Information.*

2 CIVIC CIRCUITS

Gregory A. Waller

The 16mm gauge—as film stock, camera type, and projection format—was first made available to the general public in 1923. By the late 1920s, as Haidee Wasson demonstrates in her essay on commercial film libraries and "the domestication of cinema," 16mm was regularly marketed as a technology especially well suited for the showing of motion pictures in the home and for the production of amateur cinema.[1] When did it come to dominate the broader field of non-theatrical cinema beyond the home? In July 1931, the *Motion Picture Herald*, a trade magazine geared particularly toward theatrical exhibitors, predicted—somewhat prematurely, it turned out—that the "educational field" for 16mm offered vast, imminent promise as a "potentially great division of the motion pictures industry."[2] Other declarations waxed even more optimistic about 16mm's progress in the American motion-picture marketplace. The executive secretary of the newly formed 16mm Motion Picture Board of Trade claimed in September 1931 that three hundred thousand 16mm projectors had already been sold in the United States alone.[3] The Victor Animatograph Company, a major supplier of cameras and projectors, pointed that same year to "the almost universal adoption of 16mm film and motion picture projectors for practically all non-theatrical uses."[4]

But the shift in the early sound period from 35mm to 16mm for the non-theatrical market was not this clear-cut and categorical. Victor's claim hardly jibes with, for instance, a survey concerning visual education programs in Indiana conducted during the 1930–31 school year, which noted that while 35 percent of the state's public schools owned 35mm projectors, only 8 percent were equipped to screen 16mm film.[5] Three years later, the numbers seemed more promising. Based on a survey of 116 cities in 1934, a writer in *Educational Screen* speculated that American schools might be "half-way through a general change" from 35mm to 16mm.[6] This ongoing shift also registered well beyond the classroom: for instance, the Civilian Conservation Corps (ccc) — established by President Franklin Roosevelt immediately after he took office in March 1933 — made extensive use of 16mm in its camps, and during the run of Chicago's highly publicized Century of Progress International Exposition in 1934 a majority of the many sponsored exhibits using motion pictures relied on 16mm, often screened in loops by automated sound projectors.[7]

It was, however, the period between 1935 and 1945 that saw 16mm — by then readily available as a moderately priced, sound-on-film technology for recording and displaying motion pictures — rise to prominence as the chosen apparatus for what appeared to be an ever expanding non-theatrical terrain that stretched beyond the classroom, home, and church. Here was a realm rich in utopian promise and entrepreneurial opportunity — or so the discourse often averred. Did the portability and cost of 16mm mark it as the small-gauge and, thus, inevitably less prestigious and less valuable ancillary to commercial cinema's 35mm gold standard? Was 16mm merely a delivery system or was it somehow the fulfillment of the motion picture's long claimed promise as a universally accessible, powerfully effective, eminently useful medium of communication?

This essay examines 16mm's flourishing in the United States from the mid-1930s through World War II, not so much in terms of the mode and output of production, the marketing of affordable cameras, or the specificities of exhibition, but in terms of the distribution — or, better put, the discursive circulation of 16mm projectors and motion pictures. Relying primarily on the trade press and advertising material produced by major equipment manufacturers like DeVry, Bell and Howell, rca, Ampro, and Victor, I will examine in roughly chronological order how the circulation of 16mm was imagined, promoted, and practiced. I am interested in what marked 16mm as novel, handy, convenient, and practical—and more: what made 16mm appear to be truly important as a multi-purposable, broadly applicable, readily deployable motion picture technology capable of serving, constructing, and linking a host of audiences, and in so doing transforming everyday life in the classroom, the nation, and around the globe. In other words, how did 16mm figure as a blend of the mundane and the modern, of practical appliance and world-altering technology? How did the selling of projectors—and hence the selling of the promise of 16mm—change in the years before and during World War II as the usefulness of 16mm became a matter of special urgency, nationally and globally?

THE POWER OF PORTABILITY

The 16mm gauge, of course, was neither the first nor the only motion picture format sold as a cheaper and safer alternative to 35mm.[8] There were also, for instance, Pathé's non-flammable 28mm and 9.5mm formats and, most notably, 8mm, which Kodak put on the market in 1932.[9] For the purposes of this study, the prime context for 16mm was not other small-gauge formats but rather 35mm. To foreground the relation between 16mm and 35mm is inevitably to raise or beg the question: where to draw the (imaginary but meaningful) line between theatrical and non-theatrical practices, between the movies and useful cinema? Film stock of the 16mm type, for example, might be understood as a vehicle for delivering—by downsizing—content originally shot on 35mm. And while 16mm projectors, which were almost always characterized as being compact, moveable, and transportable, looked to be absolutely distinct from the anchored-down behemoths casting images from safely sealed booths in movie theaters, it is worth recalling that 35mm projectors, too, could be portable and commercially viable, as various companies had demonstrated from at least the early 1920s. For example, the Zenith Portable Motion Picture Projector (billed as "safe-simple-sound-sure") and the American Projectoscope (compact enough to "take it any place—any time") were among the various portable 35mm projectors advertised in *Visual Education*, a "magazine devoted to the business of American education" that was published from 1920 to 1924 before being absorbed by what would become the premiere journal in the field, *Educational Screen*.[10]

DeVry's advertising campaign for its portable 35mm projector in *Educational Screen* in 1924 articulates themes that would later echo through promo-

DeVry Portable Projector in Operation

DeVry portable 35mm projector, *Educational Screen* (1924).

tional material for 16mm equipment. DeVry offered a user-friendly motion picture apparatus built with industrial sites, churches, and schools in mind.[11] A decade later, after 16mm equipment had become the preferred option for forward-thinking visual education programs, Simplex—a well-established manufacturer of 35mm equipment—continued to underscore the suitability of its "portable" 35mm projector for all manner of non-theatrical venues, from steamships to colleges.[12] Unlike the Simplex machine, DeVry's product, however, was literally a projector-in-a-suitcase, dependable and ready to take "abuse," as transportable as a salesman's sample case. With an adequate power supply (including, if necessary, an automobile battery), there was no limit to where this 35mm projector could venture, no "adverse" circumstance that could not be turned into a successful screening occasion. Operation was presumed to be so easy, in fact, that a standard feature of DeVry's *Educational Screen* ads in 1924 was a photo of the portable 35mm machine "in operation," closed up suitcase-style, plugged into a wall socket, and casting a beam of light—all with no operator in sight.[13] Such ads underscore that "portability" was more than a matter of size, weight, and wiring. As a marketing claim and discursively constructed goal, "portability" signified the open-ended promise—at once ideological, social, and pedagogical—of motion pictures once this potentially multi-purposable medium was set free from the constrained conditions of commercial cinema.

The first wave of ads for 16mm portable sound projectors in 1931 reiterate many of DeVry's claims that its suitcase 35mm was unparalleled in "simplicity, efficiency and ease of operation." Thus RCA billed its $1,075 "Theatre in a Suitcase," which consisted of projector, amplifier, and loudspeaker, as the "smallest, lightest and simplest operated portable sound reproducing equipment," while Western Electric assured customers that its new sound-on-disc portable 16mm projector (weighing more than 125 pounds) "has been simplified in every respect so that anyone can operate it in a few minutes' time."[14] "Anyone" meant any teacher, specifically, the female teacher-as-projectionist, a figure often represented in advertising for 16mm classroom films and projectors during the 1930s, rivaled only by the young male student-as-projectionist.[15] Such ads underscore the user-friendliness and what we might call the gender-friendliness as well as the dependability, no-risk promise of the 16mm projector as a highly functional modern appliance. The portable projector might be the "Aladdin's Lamp of the Classroom" (to cite a Victor ad of 1931), but it required no secret incantation or technical savvy to enable its wizardry. In fact, Universal claimed that its sound projector "operates almost as simply as your radio," though unlike a home radio, this projector can play "for audiences 50 to 2000."[16] From this perspective, 16mm projection offered a professional product without the need for—and the expense of—a professional, unionized, adult male operator. Alleged to be powerful in its pedagogic effects and always open to greater improvement in design and further economy in cost, 16mm projection, the product of the modern media corporation's investment in research and development, was ready to begin service as an invaluable (and necessary) tool with everyday utility in and out of the classroom.

As both the price and weight of portable 16mm projectors dropped during the 1930s, manufacturers insisted even more emphatically that ease of operation and overall simplification in design in no way meant diminished cinematic quality, as measured by 35mm "professional," that is, theatrical, standards.[17] Here was one more acknowledgement that the non-theatrical—implicitly, at least—could not help but define itself in relation to the theatrical, though the reverse was rarely the case. Victor promised "theater-quality performance" for its Animatograph, while RCA's sound-on-film 16mm projector was guaranteed to deliver "theatrical brilliance and clarity of picture and sound."[18] Bell and Howell went even further, attesting by the end of the decade that its projectors were designed "by the same engineers who create the preferred studio equipment of Hollywood. The standards of Hollywood cinemachinery are the standards of Bell and Howell school projectors."[19]

RCA "theatre in a suitcase," *Educational Screen* (1931).

A similar point about the relation between the classroom and the movie theater was made graphically in 1935 in a comic-style ad for Bell and Howell that pitched Filmo projectors as "more than mere machines." In the first panel, a young boy and girl—appreciative and experienced viewers—are watching a film featuring a large elephant with tusks raised; the boy exclaims with delight, "Our [classroom] movies are just as bright as the ones we see in the theater." The two female teachers in the second panel, meanwhile, are "amazed" at the "rock steady" image projected (which therefore poses no danger to students' eyesight) and by the fact that the Filmo allows them to "keep the room light enough to maintain discipline."[20] In this 16mm configuration of the exhibition space, no secure booth necessarily separates the operator/provider from the audience, which can readily be observed in the semi-darkness. Here, Bell and Howell implies, is a viewing experience perfectly suited and perfectly safe for the progressive classroom of the 1930s—fully up to the audiovisual standards of theatrical exhibition while still allowing for necessary monitoring of youthful spectatorship, long a dream of movie-wary reformers.

At the same time, portability mattered. Projectors for 16mm film could be whisked from classroom to classroom, carried from classroom to auditorium,

. . . that's because of Filmo's powerful direct-lighting system and the scientific air-cooling which permits use of high-wattage lamps—up to 1000 watts! Lenses are critically sharp and highly precise in correction.

. . . that's because of Filmo's exclusive, scientifically correct 9-to-1 film movement mechanism and perfect film registration. Brilliant illumination eliminates need for extreme darkening of the room.

THERE'S A SCIENTIFIC REASON
BEHIND FILMO PROJECTOR QUALITY

Filmo School Projectors and Filmosound Sound Movie Reproducers are more than mere machines. They combine the science of optics with those of physics to produce moving screen images whose superlative brilliance, clarity, and steadiness bespeak the careful design and painstaking manufacture of the projector itself. The fact that the Filmo Projector is preferred in the leading schools of America, whose tests are of the severest kind, points again to the underlying value of the machine, its scientific design and careful craftsmanship.

1000-Watt Filmo Projector

Adequate illumination for the largest auditorium. 1600-foot film capacity (one-hour showing); F 1.65 lens; variable lamp resistance; voltmeter; variable speed governor (16 to 24); separate motor for take-up and fast power rewinding; pilot light; interlocking controls; two-way tilt; film conditioner; low center of gravity; adequate cooling for the 1000-watt lamp.

750-Watt Filmo Projector

Similar in appearance to the Model 130, but for smaller audiences. 1600-foot film capacity (one-hour showing); power rewind; two-way tilt; pilot light; reverse; still projection. The 750-watt lamp may be replaced with a lower powered lamp when less illumination is needed and greater economy is desired. Variable resistance and voltmeter are optional.

500-Watt Filmo Projector

A low cost projector, but with the same basic operating mechanism as Filmo 129. Has 2 inch F 2.1 lens; two-way tilt; power rewind; lamp switch; reverse; still projection; 400-foot film capacity. 500-watt and 750-watt models.

Filmosound Sound Movie Reproducers

Sound movies—real, professional-quality sound movies on 16 mm. safety film—are now available for every school. The Bell & Howell Filmosound is the machine for the purpose. 1000-watt and 750-watt models. Highly perfected, simple to operate, and giving theater-quality results, the Filmosound may be had from a nearby dealer on a low-cost rental plan. The Filmosound Library provides the latest and finest sound films for education and entertainment. See your dealer today for full particulars.

BELL & HOWELL
FILMO

16 mm. Movie Cameras and Projectors
1817 Larchmont Ave., Chicago; New York, Hollywood, London (B & H Co., Ltd.) Established 1907

Bell and Howell classroom screening, *Educational Screen* (1935).

even transported from school to school in the same district or beyond. An Ampro ad of 1935 featured a testimonial from the William H. Dudley Visual Education Service, which was using sixty-five portable Ampro projectors to handle a circuit of over six hundred schools.[21] But the potential mobility of 16mm projectors extended much further, giving them a boundless capacity to reach, in Wasson's words, "a range of audiences in limitless locations."[22] The sound-equipped "theatre in a suitcase," introduced by RCA in 1931, may have weighed more than two hundred pounds, but it was still guaranteed to be "easily transportable in [a] small automobile."[23] DeVry's first 16mm sound version of its suitcase projector actually required two suitcases, each weighing forty-four pounds, a hefty load that nonetheless posed no problem for the smiling white-collar worker toting this unit in an ad in 1931.[24]

Complementing the classroom projectionist (usually pictured as a female teacher or male student), the suitcase-projector-bearing man on the move became another signifier of the capabilities of 16mm. He appeared, for example, in an Ampro ad of 1936 that promised "professional performance, easier portability, greater economy."[25] Predictably, this figure, who had occasionally figured in ads for portable 35mm projectors, also surfaced in *Business Screen*, a trade magazine first published in 1938 and dedicated to the use of motion pictures in business and industry. Victor's ad in the September 1938 issue of *Business Screen* features a dapper man carrying and operating a suitcase projector, to which a microphone and a turntable can be easily attached, making it "the greatest of all modern sales tools."[26] (This notion of the 16mm projector as part of an expandable audiovisual system encompassing radio, public address capability, and recorded sound would also be a key aspect of Victor's 1939 advertising campaign in *Educational Screen*.[27]) Clearly, adult men as well as women and adolescents could handle this convenient apparatus without relinquishing anything in the way of stable gendered identity. The many ads representing these various users and transporters suggested that 16mm was an audiovisual delivery system that was as easily deployable as it was widely applicable.

THE SITES OF 16MM

Capturing clients and training sales staff with unparalleled efficiency, bringing history, biology, and geography lessons "to life" with theater-level quality—these were central to the promise of 16mm by the late 1930s, signified most often by the portable, affordable, dependable, easy-to-use projector being carried by a salesman or casting compelling images onto a classroom screen. Of course, there were churches, department stores, and other actual or potential screening sites regularly mentioned in periodical sources like *Educational Screen* and *Business Screen*. Distributor catalogues, too, often enumerated the venues for 16mm beyond homes, churches, and schools. Such lists emphasize the broad coverage and saturation of 16mm across a range of non-theatrical sites, some socially and ideologically apart from the audiovisually equipped public school classroom (such as prisons, convents, and asylums) and others more likely assumed to be relatively contiguous with the school (such as hospitals, factories, and YMCAS).

A two-page spread in the *Ampro 1940 Precision 16mm Cine Equipment* catalogue offers perhaps the most striking representation of 16mm's extended purview, far beyond any single company's circuit of schools or any itinerant exhibitor's rural route. Supporting the claim that "Ampro Is Used Everywhere," this illustration arranges fifteen sites into a symmetrical grid that includes, to borrow Ampro taxonomy, churches, hotels, gymnasiums, schools, industry, and govt. depts., as well as institutions, parks, dance halls, colleges, and CCC camps. All are locations for exhibiting and viewing films, sites for generating what is implicitly understood to be a nation of audiences, though, in fact, there are no projectors, projected films, or spectators pictured in this illustration. Each zone of Ampro's "everywhere" is rendered as an equally important and equally abstract visually complementary icon, one component in a film-ready, orderly, modern

Model 33 assembles into one small compact unit. Removable top of case houses reel arms, reel and attachment cord. Speaker in baffle case is easily detached.

Victor, salesman with projector, *Business Screen* (1938).

AMPRO IS USED EVERYWHERE

CHURCHES   HOTELS   GYMNASIUMS   HOMES   SCHOOLS

AUDITORIUMS   INDUSTRY   GOVT. DEPTS.   STADIUMS   CONVENTIONS

INSTITUTIONS   CCC CAMPS   COLLEGES   PARKS   DANCE HALLS

Ampro catalogue, the 16mm grid (1940).

America that 16mm has somehow made possible by linking home and school, leisure and work, the state and the private sector. As totalitarian as this 16mm grid might seem in its visual design and its claims for uniformity, order, and comprehensiveness, Ampro's vision features no privileged center or choreographed, mesmerized masses à la *Triumph of the Will*. This illustration offers no information about where the films might come from, how they might be seen in these various places, or how Ampro's precision projecting machines might actually be used. It provides no clue as to whether the presence of 16mm technology across the public sites of a mediated and networked nation might constitute the conditions for utopian democratic promise — or the reverse.

Ampro's grid, as we will see, offers a telling comparison to the discourse celebrating 16mm that circulated during World War II, but even before the mobilization of the motion picture industry in the wake of Pearl Harbor, projector manufacturers circulated quite different visions of the brave new world of 16mm. In an ad in 1936, for example, DeVry posed its Challenger model sound projector with film threaded, ready to cast its illuminating beam through the threshold of a misty, ivy-covered cathedral of learning.[28] That same year Victor emphasized less the formidable power of 16mm entering (or invading) a familiar bastion of culture than its successful targeting of North America, pictured as an aerial map dotted with sites served by Animatophone projectors, including schools, universities, industry, CCC camps, and churches, as well as ships and trains. In the same ad, Victor announced that "even in far-flung South Africa Animatophone predominates in Schools and among all other non-theatrical users," and it boasted of serving markets "North, East, South and West—At Home and Abroad."[29]

Victor's expansive claim concerning the worldwide reach of American motion picture technology from CCC camps to South Africa exemplifies what we might call the rhetoric of global 16mm. The later 1930s saw a marked increase in the United States of "foreign" and "foreign-language" films on 16mm, along with all manner of non-fiction motion pictures across different genres that took up peoples, places, and events beyond U.S. borders. Projectors were thus marketed as a means of "bringing the world" to the local classroom, lodge, or church. "Ampro Circles the World," an ad from December 1937, takes a different tact. While Hollywood filled the firmament with stars, Ampro envisioned a sky full of mobile 16mm projectors: seen from a point far in space, an unbroken ring of identical Ampro machines circumnavigates the Earth, ready to unreel their usefulness, primed for whatever celluloid has to offer. Again, as in Ampro's vision of the 16mm grid, operators, films, and audiences are absent in "Ampro Circles the World."[30] Perhaps these satellite projectors constitute a powerfully useful, global (and globalizing) technology precisely because they can be operated by anyone, can show any 16mm film, can reach any audience. In contrast to this transcendent or at least supra-national position, during World War II, the American-ness of projector, operator, film, and audience was endlessly underscored by Ampro and its competitors.

MOBILIZED 16MM

As has often been noted, motion pictures were intimately linked with America's national project during World War II.[31] The wartime careers of industry celebrities like Clark Gable and Frank Capra and, especially, the wave of Hollywood-produced patriotic shorts, combat films, and war-related serials, cartoons, and newsreels have understandably come to define, in retrospect, this period. Yet as Richard Dyer MacCann claims in his study of U.S. government motion picture activity, World War II also had a significant effect on the increased use of and—we can add—attendant public discourse concerning 16mm in the United States.[32] That gauge of film was, for instance, the

Ampro, global 16mm,
Educational Screen (1937).

preferred format for training films, in and out of the military, and newsreel footage in "digest" form marketed by Castle Films and other distributors became quickly and readily available for purchase or rental on 16mm (as well as 8mm). Most importantly, non-theatrical exhibition in the service of the war effort at home and abroad attested to and signified 16mm's ubiquity and increasing prominence as a media delivery system extremely well-suited for present exigencies and future opportunities.

Especially prominent in this regard was what *Billboard* called the "overseas movie program," which involved the wide distribution of 16mm prints of new Hollywood product for viewing by GIs.[33] This service began in February 1942, and according to *Educational Screen*, within two years more than 8,500 prints of 300 different films had been exhibited, while the number of 16mm projectors in military use throughout North America and overseas from Iceland and Algiers to Fiji and India had grown from 370 to 2,500.[34] The historian Thomas Schatz claims that these 16mm screenings became "part of everyday military routine," and the program soon constituted "the largest distribution and exhibition circuit in the world — and one that eventually encompassed the entire globe."[35] As would be expected, the non-theatrical trade press made much of this program, recounting impressive statistics to prove that 16mm was already realizing its enormous potential. In February 1945, the Army Overseas Motion Picture Service reported to the War Activities Committee that it had utilized over 25,000 16mm prints of feature films and 27,000 prints of shorts for screening to 1 million servicemen daily.[36] Near the end of the war, the Army's distribution center was requesting 117 copies of each new feature film to meet the daily entertainment needs of a military audience that topped 1,450,000.[37] By the time this program wound up on October 31, 1945, the military had received from Hollywood studios 43,000 16mm "gift prints" of feature films and a like number of shorts.[38]

On the home front, 16mm projectors also had important roles to play. "Your Projector Has a War Job This Summer," announced the June 1943 newsletter published by the Audio-Visual Center at Indiana University, which here took its cue from the Bureau of Motion Pictures of the Office of War Information. Owners of projectors were strongly encouraged to loan their machines to churches and clubs, take them into war plants, collaborate with civil defense organizations, and "arrange showings of films at public meetings — band concerts in public parks, war rallies in courthouse squares."[39] This call to engage in civic/cinematic activism became most strident when it came to the Treasury Department's fifth, sixth, seventh, and eighth war loan drives in 1944–45. Before the final loan drive in the fall of 1945, the Treasury Department announced that 33,402,950 people had seen 16mm films at 141,615 free showings during the seventh war loan drive (up almost 15 percent from the sixth drive).[40] These screenings at a broad array of sites had been arranged for and promoted by autonomous state organizations, loosely under the bureaucratic auspices of the Nontheatrical Division of the Bureau of Motion Pictures (within the Office of War Information).[41]

Predictably, the loan drives made headlines in *Film World*, a new trade magazine first published in February 1945 that was "devoted exclusively to non-theatrical 16mm . . . that branch of motion pictures which has overnight become internationally important in entertainment and education."[42] *Film World* dedicated the cover and a special section in its May 1945 issue to the seventh war loan drive, praising the work of state organizations, outlining strategies for the widest possible exhibition, and calling for full mobilization of all 16mm projectors in the land, including those owned by individuals and businesses. *Educational Screen* similarly insisted that "every [16mm] projector, every operator, every hall, every volunteer worker" should be prepared to play its part for the eighth and final loan drive, set for the fall of 1945.[43]

Even as more people were viewing 16mm prints and additional spaces were pressed into service as non-theatrical exhibition sites, the supply of new 16mm equipment available for purchase by amateurs, traveling exhibitors, and institutions dropped during the war, since motion picture equipment manufacturers either retooled for war-related production or filled government contracts, a situation that lasted until the end of 1945.[44] Thus at first glance it seems counterintuitive that the major manufacturers of 16mm projectors ran so many full-page advertisements during 1943–45 in *Educational Screen* and *Film World*, and even in *Home Movies*, a large-format monthly geared toward amateur filmmakers (and published by Van Halen Publications, the same firm responsible for *Film World*). Since few, if any, projectors were for sale to consumers, these ads seem designed to promote corporate brand identity, to encourage future sales in what promised to be a competitive postwar market, and, most interesting for my purposes, to sell 16mm as an essential wartime technology that should prove to be no less essential in postwar America.

The relatively small number of ads for 16mm projectors in *Home Movies* during 1940–41 focused on home screenings: "Have you *really* seen your summer movies?" asked Bell and Howell, while Ampro encouraged the family to "Make your Living room a Theatre."[45] But by late 1943, these same companies, along with Victor (and, to a lesser extent, DeVry), were highlighting a more serious, urgent, and demanding mission for the transportable, hardy 16mm projector than providing a better-than-8mm experience in middle-class living rooms. And while there were ads in 1944 touting Victor's record of "Progress in Education" and in modernizing the "Little Red Schoolhouse,"[46] the focus shifted almost completely away from the classroom per se to other sites of audiovisual instruction across the United States. "In schoolhouses and other social centers throughout the land," announced a Bell and Howell ad in the 1943 edition of *Visual Review*, "projectors are running films that help us to win the war and prepare us for the peace to come. Films that train civilian and soldier alike, and soldier-to-be also, how to work and to fight; films that keep high our resolve that the free way of life shall prevail."[47] Thanks to Bell and Howell's Filmosound projector, miners could watch a screening underground, while five factory workers in a Victor ad gave full attention as another worker ran an Animatophone—a sight that was supposed to demonstrate "the vital dynamic way to victory training for government, for industry, for all education."[48] Each of these groups constituted one of what were suggested to be innumerable micro-audiences served by 16mm.

Magazines like *Educational Screen* and *Film World* pointed to the role of

Ampro, Victory Loan,
Home Movies (1945).

training films and the successful victory loan campaigns in 1944–45 as undeniable proof that 16mm was providing an invaluable contribution to the national war effort, largely by reaching so many citizen-spectators. The schematic grid that Ampro had used in 1940 to suggest the pervasiveness and powerful capacity of 16mm took on a different configuration in an ad in December 1945 that celebrated the utilization of 16mm on the home front. By attracting "millions" of viewers, the victory loan drives, Ampro claimed, had forged a quite tangible link between retail stores, churches, schools, and industry (all exhibition sites), and 16mm had proved to be an ideal means of reaching diverse audiences: women's clubs, farm and labor groups, and citizens gathered for "public forums."[49] In this ad, Amprosound projectors become a sort of public utility, demonstrably useful in their capacity to mobilize citizens across different sites and groupings to achieve a state-dictated goal.

Such civic mobilization depended in part on the mobility of 16mm projectors, which were thereby able, according to manufacturers' ads, to contribute mightily as well to the American military effort. Loaded as "vital cargo" into

Victor, Death pauses for Mickey Mouse, *Home Movies* (1944).

trains and transport planes and carried by hand onto combat-zone beaches, these durable and workmanlike projectors made it possible, Ampro contended, for "American Fighters" to see sound movies "projected brilliantly clear right in the middle of the steaming, malaria ridden, insect infested jungles of the Solomons."[50] "Death pauses for Mickey Mouse," announced an ad that Victor ran in *Home Movies* and *Educational Screen* in March 1944: it shows smiling GIs being revitalized by a night at the movies.[51] Notably, in these ads (and in the entire coverage of the military's extensive overseas exhibition system), 16mm becomes not so much a competitor with Hollywood (and with 35mm) as an indispensable means of keeping the entertainment pipeline — and cultural lifeline — open. Bringing Mickey Mouse to the troops expands the reach of the movies, one of the surest signifiers of America.

The exhibition of Hollywood product on 16mm "from the Aleutians to the Solomons, from the Caribbean to Iceland," as an Ampro ad in *Home Movies* in 1943 phrased it,[52] was surely a testament to the movies as a necessity of life for Americans. But it was also evidence of the global reach of 16mm, literally

Victor, beach landing,
Home Movies (1945).

in the tracks and on the backs of the advancing U.S. military during the war years. Victor favored the image of its boxed-up but still portable projector being carried ashore on the shoulder of a GI. This image of transportability complements the drawing in another Victor ad of a projector superimposed on a map that charts its route "through Algeria, Syria, Egypt and Italy."[53] In two other ads, both featuring globes, Victor promised and claimed access to the world at large: first, its sound motion picture projectors could "unfold new worlds" through 16mm "films of every description in an unprecedented array"; and, second, its "world wide service" reached to the "far off corners of the world."[54]

The broader implications of Victor's vision were made explicit in 1944, when the company celebrated what it called the 16mm industry's "Coming of Age" on the twenty-first anniversary of Alexander F. Victor's introduction of his Cine-Camera and Cine-Projector. With its wartime responsibilities, 16mm was now fully "grown to manhood," the company announced, and "in the peaceful world of tomorrow, its horizons and possibilities are limitless."[55]

Victor, 16mm Comes of Age,
Educational Screen (1944).

A related Victor ad offered a more apocalyptic prospect: against an ominous red and black sky, a single projector casts its illuminating beam almost as if it were channeling or lighting the way for the "world-changing new day [that] is dawning"—a day defined by "the new ways and impact of sound motion picture training, teaching and selling."[56] In a widely circulated pamphlet that echoes countless other claims for other communication media—motion pictures, radio, television, the Internet—before and after 16mm, a Victor executive declared, "16mm is available in a desert village or a remote mountain settlement as it is in the largest city." Further, it "is a language the whole world can understand. It is a language that can show to all a better way of life, better methods, the wonders of modern science and the worth of modern products."[57]

In contrast to Victor's 16mm projector now screening Disney cartoons in a combat zone and soon to be delivering modernity's blessings and capitalism's bounty to all corners of the earth, Bell and Howell's ads in *Home Movies* insisted more bluntly and simply that every projector, like every camera, is a

Ampro, wartime Amprosound,
Educational Screen (1944).

"WEAPON" with a "fighting job" to do.[58] The 16mm projector as a weapon, however, found its fullest articulation in Ampro's 1944 advertising campaign, which featured Sanford Rubin's meticulously wrought, black-and-white rendering of the Amprosound projector in images that look like intricate photo-realist engravings.[59] This 16mm machine is no mere appliance or tabletop tool; it is an impressive piece of cutting-edge technology, indeed. Seen from various angles in different ads but always dominating the design and pushing beyond the boundaries of the page as if in constant motion through the world, Ampro's aestheticized vision of sophisticated engineering and mechanized power has little in common with the familiar suitcase projector or Victor's boxed-in Animatophone. Described as having been perfected "in a world-wide laboratory" and subjected to the "grueling tests of war," the monumental Amprosound sometimes resembles a massive tank or battleship, except that all its gears and controls are visible. Or it appears like a flying fortress, casting a powerful beam of light as it patrols the night sky, even more imposing because it is operator-less and far distant from any audience that might be watching. Would the 16mm projector ever look this powerful again? Given the date of this ad campaign, Rubin's Amprosound resonates not only as a symbol of non-theatrical 16mm motion pictures as a force to be reckoned with, but also of unmatched American military and industrial prowess and of unchallengeable American might that became only stronger through the crucible of a worldwide war.

And yet, the written text on these ads sometimes offers a surprisingly mundane and reassuring promise to potential Ampro customers: the imposing Amprosound is, in fact, described as being "compact" and "portable," perfectly designed to "enrich your home life" for it can deliver much in the way of sweetness and light (that is, "the world's finest dramas and operas, important world events, travelogues, cartoons, educational subjects . . . in your own living room").[60] "Tomorrow's Goal" for 16mm, another ad in this campaign affirms, is not American global dominance but "sound motion pictures in all schools."[61] Perhaps the pitch here is that the imposing machine and the tabletop appliance are one and the same, meaning that the benefits of war-honed motion picture equipment will register in the home and the school as well as, somehow, in the vast foreign territory patrolled by American technology. The 16mm projector is both means and end, not only a signifier of how we fight, but also why we fight—to win a technologically equipped, film-enhanced future. Or that the technologized home front, saturated with 16mm projectors, is why we fight, that is, the civilized outcome of war, the fruits of suffering.

The "tomorrow" promised by projector ads couldn't arrive fast enough for the 16mm film industry. By December 1945, instead of showing its machine illuminating the future or traveling from Algiers to Italy, a Victor ad showed a row of projectors moving down a stylized assembly line "on their way to you!"[62] Within months, each issue of *Film World* would be almost bursting at the seams with press releases and news reports about the expanding, entrepreneurial postwar non-theatrical market. Victor's ads in early 1946 no longer heralded utopian possibility but testified to the Animatophone's "unsurpassed sound fidelity, easy threading, brighter images and greater safety"—a claim no different than what Bell and Howell would make for its projector or Ampro for its no longer larger-than-life Amprosound.[63]

Advertising for 16mm projectors captures well the shifting and hardly uniform sense of 16mm's possibility and promise in the years leading up to and including World War II. A fuller history of 16mm during this formative decade would need to look beyond projector manufacturers and take other practices, participants, and discursive strands into account, most notably the roles of commercial distributors, Hollywood studios, government agencies, non-profit film libraries, and foundations as well as the multi-sited debate about the relations between entertainment, sponsored film, and educational cinema. But the historically grounded claims about audiovisual technology, globalization, mobility, expertise, access, and audiences that I have been examining—claims that were stridently marshaled or merely implied in advertising for Ampro, Bell and Howell, Victor, and their competitors—these, I would argue, are crucial to understanding 16mm as "new" media, mundane appliance, civic tool, and deliverer of useful cinema.

NOTES

1   Wasson, "The Reel of the Month Club." It is unusual to find evidence of 16mm sponsored films before 1927; one notable exception was General Electric, which advertised that its "educational films" were "available in both Standard 35mm and 16mm sizes" (*1000 and One*, 55).

2   "Educational Field Opening Way to Huge Non-theatrical Growth: Big Division of Industry to Use 16mm Film," *Motion Picture Herald* 102 (July 11, 1931), 9, 24.

3   "National 16mm Exchanges Planned," *Educational Screen* 10 (1931), 234.

4   "Victor Builds Special Projector with Powerful 250 Watt–20 Volt Lamp (16mm)," *Educational Screen* 10, no. 2 (1931), 64.

5   McIntire, "Visual Instruction in Indiana," 139.

6   Andrews, "The Visual Program: Its Equipment and Cost."

7   See "Film and Slide Showings at CCC Camps," *Educational Screen* 13, no. 5 (1934), 132; and Farr, "The CCC," 236. On the exposition of 1934, see "Motion Pictures in 1934 at Century of Progress," *Educational Screen* 13, no. 7 (1934), 183, 185.

8   Kattelle surveys earlier small-gauge formats in *Home Movies*, 52–92.

9   See Mebold and Tepperman, "Resurrecting the Lost History of 28mm Film in North America."

10 Zenith ad, *Visual Education* 2, no. 1 (1921), 63; American Projectoscope ad, *Visual Education* 2, no. 2 (1921), 64. See the chapter on projectors in McKay, *Motion Picture Photography for the Amateur*, 207–19; and the discussion of self-contained, portable 35mm "suitcase" projectors in Ellis and Thornborough, *Motion Pictures in Education*, 227–29. The frontispiece for this book is a photograph of a portable suitcase projector set up in a classroom, with the caption: "The correct way to teach with motion pictures."

11 DeVry ad, *Educational Screen* 3, no. 3 (1924), 104–5. The same year, *Educational Screen* also ran ads for Power's Projectors, which offered "non-theatrical institutions" the same stationary 35mm projectors "used in thousands of theatres" and for the Movie Supply Co., based in Chicago, which advertised "slightly used portable projec-

tors," including machines from DeVry as well as from Acme, Cosmograph, National American, and Graphoscope (*Educational Screen* 3, no. 9 [1924], 336, 361).

12 Simplex ad, *Educational Screen* 12, no. 10 (1933), 264.

13 DeVry ad, *Educational Screen* 3, no. 3 (1924), 104–5.

14 RCA ad, *Educational Screen* 10, no. 8 (1931), 221; "Electrical Research Products Announces New 16mm Talking Equipment," *Educational Screen* 10, no. 7 (1931), 216.

15 The female teacher as projectionist had long figured in accounts of the progressive classroom equipped for "visual instruction." "Anyone who is capable of operating an automobile can learn to operate any type of motion-picture projector. Women teachers and women principals often operate the professional standard machines as successfully as the average man," concluded Anna Verona Dorris, in her *Visual Instruction in the Public Schools*, 207. The accompanying photo of a classroom in this book is captioned "A classroom teacher can easily operate a portable motion-picture projector."

16 Universal ad, *Educational Screen* 15, no. 9 (1936), 287. In 1921 the American Projecting Company had pitched its portable 35mm as being "as easy to operate as a phonograph . . . a schoolboy can do it"; *Visual Education* 2, no. 2 (1921), 64.

17 The Bass Camera Company, a major mail order retailer based in Chicago, offered the following prices for portable 16mm projectors in October 1940: Sound 16mm Bell and Howell Filmosound $276–410; Sound 16mm Ampro: $320–345; Sound 16mm Victor Animatophone: $275–320. One 1940 dollar equaled approximately fifteen dollars in 2007, putting the cost of these 16mm portable sound projectors, in 2007 dollars, in the $4,000 to $6,000 price range.

18 Victor ad, *Educational Screen* 10, no. 10 (1931), 230; and RCA ad, *Educational Screen* 14, no. 3 (1935), 79.

19 Bell and Howell ad, *Educational Screen* 18, no. 3 (1939), 109. See Zimmermann, *Reel Families*, 56–89, for a detailed account of the implications of "professionalizing amateur-film equipment" in this period.

20 Bell and Howell ad, *Educational Screen* 14, no. 10 (1935), 276.

21 Ampro ad, *Educational Screen* 14, no. 3 (1935), 62.

22 Wasson, *Museum Movies*, 46.

23 RCA ad, *Educational Screen* 10, no. 8 (1931), 221; "RCA Photophone Portable Sound Equipment," *Educational Screen* 10, no. 8 (1931), 249.

24 DeVry ad, *Educational Screen* 10, no. 8 (1931), 223.

25 Ampro ad, *Educational Screen* 15, no. 5 (1936), 134. Six years later, the figure again appeared in an Ampro ad, this time in *Home Movies* 9, no. 4 (1942), 139. For an example involving a 35mm portable projector, see the American Projecting Company ad, *Visual Education* 2, no. 5 (1921), 55. See also Gray, "Can Educators Profit from Industry's Experience with the Motion Picture?"

26 Victor ad, *Business Screen* 1, no. 3 (1938), 4.

27 Victor ad, *Educational Screen* 18, no. 7 (1939), 257.

28 DeVry ad, *Educational Screen* 15, no. 9 (1936), 267.

29 Victor ad, *Educational Screen* 15, no. 9 (1936), 285.

30 Ampro ad, *Educational Screen* 16, no. 10 (1937), 335.

31 See, for example, Doherty, *Projections of War*, 60–84; and Koppes and Black, *Hollywood Goes to War*.

32 MacCann, *The People's Films*, 118–72. See also, for example, Slide, *Before Video*, 101–2.

33 "Overseas Movie Program Expanding; Wins GI Okay," *Billboard* 56 (September 16, 1944), 44.

34 "Overseas Film Showings to Troops," *Educational Screen* 23, no. 1 (1944), 40.

35 Schatz, *Boom and Bust*, 144–45; see also Doherty, *Projections of War*, 75–78.

36 "Over Million Servicemen See Motion Pictures Daily," *Film World* 1, no. 2 (1945), 45.

37 "Army Boosts Demand," *Film World* 1, no. 6 (1945), 198.

38 "Praises Value of Films Shown to Armed Services," *Film World* 1, no. 11 (1945), 405, 439.

39 *A-V News* [Indiana University] 3, no. 9 (1943), 1.

40 *How, When, Where to Show 16mm Victory Loan Film* (Washington: Treasury Department, 1945). This information circulated, for example, in "16mm Industry Again Active in Eighth Victory Loan, Oct. 29–Dec. 7," *Educational Screen* 24, no. 7 (1945), 300.

41 MacCann, *The People's Films*, 135–37.

42 *Film World* 1, no. 1 (1945), 3.

43 "The Final Battles," *Educational Screen* 24, no. 2 (1945), 55.

44 For example, Revere, which specialized in 8mm equipment, announced in an ad in *Home Movies* 9, no. 12 (1942), 453 that it was "now fully converted to the production of precision-built aircraft instruments and war supplies."

45 Bell and Howell ad, *Home Movies* 8, no. 10 (1941), 502; and Ampro ad, *Home Movies* 8, no. 4 (1941), 185.

46 Victor's "Pioneer in Education" ad ran in *Home Movies* 11, no. 11 (1944), 450, and *Educational Screen* 23, no. 9 (1944), 372. Versions of the Little Red Schoolhouse appear in Bell and Howell ad, *Educational Screen* 23, no. 4 (1944), 179, and Victor ad, *Home Movies* 11, no. 8 (1944), 308.

47 Bell and Howell ad, *Visual Review* (1943), 3.

48 Bell and Howell ad, *Film World* 1, no. 6 (1945), 190; Victor ad, *Home Movies* 12, no. 3 (1945), 86; *Film World* 1, no. 2 (1945), inside front cover; and Victor ad, *Visual Review* (1943), 89.

49 Ampro ad, *Home Movies* 12, no. 12 (1945), 515.

50 Ampro ad, *Home Movies* 10, no. 5 (1943), 135.

51 Victor ad, *Home Movies* 11, no. 3 (1944), 86; Victor ad, *Educational Screen* 23, no. 3 (1944), 96.

52 Ampro ad, *Home Movies* 10, no. 1 (1943), 83.

53 Victor ad, *Home Movies* 12, no. 7 (1944), 266.

54 Victor's "Unfolding New Worlds" ad appeared in *Home Movies* 10, no. 11 (1943), 342; Victor's "A World Wide Service" ad appeared in *Home Movies* 11, no. 12 (1944), 494; *Educational Screen* 23, no. 10 (1944), 412; and *Film World* 1, no. 1 (1945), 2.

55 Victor ad, *Home Movies* 11, no. 9 (1944), 370–71; and *Educational Screen* 23, no. 7 (1944), 274–75.

56 Victor ad, *Home Movies* 11, no. 6 (1944), 218.

57 *The 16mm Industry Comes of Age* (Victor, 1944), n.p.

58 Bell and Howell ad, *Home Movies* 10, no. 12 (1943), 428; and Bell and Howell ad, *Home Movies* 10, no. 2 (1943), 64.

59 See the following Ampro ads that utilize some version of this image: *Educational Screen* 23, no. 1 (1944), 6; *Home Movies* 11, no. 2 (1944), 55; *Educational Screen* 23, no. 3 (1944), 101; *Home Movies* 11, no. 4 (1944), 139; *Educational Screen* 23, no. 4 (1944), 150; *Educational Screen* 23, no. 7 (1944), 272; *Educational Screen* 23, no. 8 (1944), 336; and *Educational Screen* 23, no. 9 (1944), 379. All the images of the Amprosound in these ads are signed by Sanford Rubin. This advertising campaign continued after Ampro was purchased by General Precision Equipment Corporation, which included among its other subsidiaries a producer of 35mm motion picture equipment for theaters (*Educational Screen* 23, no. 7 [1944], 326).

60 Ampro ad, *Home Movies* 11, no. 4 (1944), 139.

61 *Educational Screen* 23, no. 3 (1944), 101.

62 Victor ad, *Home Movies* 12, no. 12 (1945), 506.

63 Victor ad, *Film World* 2, no. 5 (1946), 184; Bell and Howell ad, *Film World* 2, no. 5 (1946), 187; and Ampro ad, *Film World* 2, no. 6 (1946), 247.

A HISTORY LONG OVERDUE

THE PUBLIC LIBRARY AND MOTION PICTURES

Jennifer Horne

I n 1871 *Appleton's Journal of Literature, Science and Art* published a profile of the Boston Public Library, the first municipally funded library system in the United States. The author celebrated the institution for the remarkable way that it served its diverse public: "At all hours of the day groups of people throng it and quietly pursue their objects. . . . The assembled crowd is often motley. But, the more motley, the more various and dissimilar its ingredients, the better the proof of the wide-spread influence of the library. Rich and poor assemble together and alike in this narrow dispensary, and a great many of them too."[1] This picture of harmonious social mixing at the library contrasts with our contemporary experience of central and branch libraries as spaces of racial and economic stratification. The lack of concern of the *Appleton's* author over intermingling might also be strikingly unfamiliar to readers of film history, who are used to accounts of Progressive Era reformers speaking out against the dangers awaiting children and the unchaperoned in dark and crowded recreational spaces of all kinds, accounts that have often been summoned in order to describe the middle classes' attempt to control the new spaces of commercialized leisure available to the working classes. To the observer of the Boston Library's patrons, the public library's civic body was just a crowd. Largely unconcerned with books and reading, or the private and contemplative reader, the report's recommendations hinged on the social production and efficiencies of space. Championing the library's capacity for creating a heterogeneous public, the *Appleton's* writer set the disorder of that utterly modern mass against the ordered shelves of new and old knowledge.

The dominant view of the library as a utopian social space finds its stark opposition in cultural institutions where activities of reading, viewing, or learning (in all their guises) are restricted to a private clientele. The open doors of the library building capture the imagination of commentators who seek to locate the public library as a pillar of civic education and a symbol of the benefits of individual pursuits of reading to the general public good and to the promotion of full citizenship. In 1883 the critic Matthew Arnold had been charmed by a shoeless boy in a Boston Public Library. "What a tribute to democratic institutions it is to say that, instead of sending that boy out to wander along in the streets," Arnold marveled, "they permit him to come in here and excite his youthful imagination by reading such a book as *The Life of Washington!*"[2] Not many years later, Hugo Münsterberg, a professor of psychology at Harvard University (and later, of course, the author of one of the first psychological studies of film), turned a social-scientific eye to this cultural apparatus in his book *The Americans* (1904), where he celebrated the American public library as a "general meeting-place and substitute for the saloon and the club."[3] In addition to seeing exemplary instrumentalism in its structure, he was most impressed by what was precisely public about it. By Münsterberg's assessment, the library had superseded the church as a monument to self-discipline and correction; as he observed, "the American taxpayer supports [public libraries] more gladly than any other burden, knowing that the public library is the best weapon against alcoholism and crime, against corruption and discontent, and that the democratic country can flourish only when the instinct of self-perfection as it exists in every American is thoroughly satisfied."[4] Seeing the library as instrumental to "social reconstruction," Münsterberg fashioned his view of the library according to the guiding tenets of Progressive Era reformers whose embrace of educational and recreational sites was prefaced upon the American post-industrial demand to bring the divergent goals of self-improvement and social control closer together. The public library would fit neatly, but never without controversy, into narratives of bootstrap individualism and Yankee self-determination. It is true that, whether established by a charitable donation, philanthropic gift, or legislative act, the public library is founded on the belief that a democratic state should provide its citizens free access to tools of education, expression, and self-improvement. That a community might be perceived, even today, as incomplete, remote, or cut off from streams of knowledge or other cultural goods without a public library suggests the force of this notion.

To think of the public library only as a utilitarian site would be to overlook its many social functions in a changing cultural landscape. As Thomas Augst has persuasively recounted in his treatment of public library architecture, the public library gained cultural legitimacy by presenting itself as the space of a new secular faith, aspiring to become a place of worship and a temple of learning. Augst keenly observes how the rituals of reading life that public libraries promoted followed older models of traditional religious education. Making reading, or, to be more precise, scripturalism, one of the central "pieties of secular modernity," public libraries, Augst argues, "helped to institutionalize leisure as moral education" and "became a temple to a civil religion, a site not only to borrow books but also to practice devotions of self-realization that embody freedom in liberal democracies."[5] Civic institutions might evoke "religious" feeling through a masterful organization of the past, through the recording of information, or through the protection of sacred documents of public importance.

For many scholars of non-print media cultures, the didactic social function and non-commercial, bureaucratic status of the public library has inhibited analysis of it as a vital network of knowledge and information circulation. In fact, the public library has been all but overlooked by scholars of literature and film alike, treated as merely a repository of popular publications, a bastion of censorious forces, or the domains of the large-type casual reader and other marginal audiences. But patterns of readership and moving image spectatorship have long existed in a complicated latticework of entertainment, education, and social control; in other words, precisely those realms the public library was designed to circumscribe. The quaint metonymy between the public library and the book has also obscured how integral multimedia collections had become to libraries as early as the beginning of the twentieth century, and how public libraries have helped to keep outmoded recording technologies from immediately passing into obsolescence.

As public libraries shed their 16mm film and VHS collections and library administrators struggle over decisions about new media acquisitions and access, past debates over the public value of moving images become all the more relevant, precisely because they return us to the origins of the library's self-conception as a public utility. The seeming uselessness of media formats that have been removed from use often makes it difficult to recall the "usefulness" that encouraged their incorporation into library collections in the first place. In what follows, I offer an overview of the introduction of motion picture use into library services in order to illustrate how cinema pressured libraries to decide how they could be useful to their patrons or to the civic sphere more generally.

As one might expect, debates over cinema's respectability and its purported potential to degrade or elevate its spectators deeply influenced librarians' attitudes to film. The beginning of library-film services coincided with the controversies over the public exhibition of entertainment film and the period of the film industry's self-regulation, a particularly active period for organizations such as the National Board of Censorship (1909–22), the National Board of Review (NBR), and the Motion Picture Producers and Distributors Association of America (MPPDA), begun in 1922, and its Studio Relations Committee. The actions of state and municipal censor boards and studio public relations offices, as well as the legal decisions that, as Lee Grieveson puts it, guaranteed the "social functioning of the cinema," determined in large measure how the library would utilize particular types of motion pictures.[6] Under the Studio Relations Committee's "Open Door" policy, a policy that Richard Maltby describes as "a containment exercise" in the larger project of fending off the reform lobby and cementing the cultural legitimacy of the motion picture industry, representatives from the American Library Association were invited to participate in preview events and to offer criticism of new releases.[7] The end of the period I am concerned with here overlaps with Martin Quigley's crafting of the code of ethics in 1929 and the adoption of the code in 1930. Grieveson's approach to the cultural context of the cinema, especially his emphasis on the productive aspects of regulation, is particularly germane to my interpretation of library concerns over and interests in motion pictures, moviegoing, and film culture. What I attempt to illuminate in what follows are librarians' attitudes toward motion pictures. Given public libraries' deep investment in cultural respectability, these attitudes are more varied than one might expect and the desire to treat the cinema's inherent publicness itself as a social good equally surprising.

During the years in which the public library became an auxiliary site for motion picture spectatorship, several phenomena critical to our understanding of the cinema intersected: competing ideological agendas, motion picture regulation and legislation, exhibition practices, economic interests, and technological innovations. The function of the public library as a juncture or source of these contending and intersecting film-cultural phenomena was part of the library's institutional self-understanding. The physical site of the library helped cultivate habits of moviegoing that were often regionally inflected and community-based, and the policies and profession of the librarian established lasting taxonomies of motion picture subjects. By looking more closely at the intersection of the two sites — the public library and the movie theater — and their respective publics we can ask a number of questions about their reciprocal impact: Where did the library's public and the cinema's public overlap? Where did they diverge? To what extent were these otherwise discrete social formations mutually affected by emerging habits of spectatorship, modernizing conceptions of information and knowledge, and the respective publicness or privacy of both media sites? And what accounts for the persistent characterization of these two spaces as separate and dichotomous: contemplation versus distraction, education versus entertainment? The public library was not alone in shaping or being shaped by moving image culture. But without an account of the vital role municipal and state libraries have played in motion picture study and appreciation, distribution, and exhibition, we are left with an account of cinema history skewed toward entertainment.

Of course, the library is an older institution than the cinema.[8] The first American public library dates back at least to 1835, when the state of New York passed legislation allowing its school districts to operate libraries, open them to the public, and finance them by collecting taxes.[9] These early educational libraries loaned books to alumni only, but eventually did replace all the so-called social libraries of the mid-eighteenth century that had been based on a much more exclusive subscription system. According to George Bobinski's critical history of the Carnegie libraries, it was these school-based collections that helped to establish the doctrine by which a free library system would be expected to operate in the service of the public. Bobinski identified a tripartite structure for integrating the library into the government and revenue structures of the state ("taxation for free library service, state aid to libraries, and recognition of the library as an educational agency"). Successful inauguration of this financing system, however, depended upon the agreement of shared public values: the belief in doctrines of self-improvement, the commitment to the idea of an informed citizenry, and the conviction that knowledge and learning is a common right.[10] Cultural factors, such as the rise of popular forms of literature, expansions in publishing, and increasing literacy rates, helped to separate the public library from its association with schools and cleave it to the idea of community welfare as a whole.[11]

It is significant that these two institutions, the cinema and the public library, both claiming a unique capacity to inform and address a mass public, simultaneously underwent critical and rapid expansion under the banners of modernization and what we might call the literary imperative of progressivism. The public library had been struggling against its nineteenth-century reputation as an elite cultural institution and, guided by new social-scientific ideas of civic engagement, adjusted its library services to respond to the needs of new immigrant groups and the changing workforce. By some measures, the library underwent a more rapid expansion than the cinema. Theatrical motion picture exhibition had scarcely been around for two decades, while many public library systems in the United States and Canada were marking a half-century of service. For instance, in 1896, when Edison's Vitascope was given a public demonstration at Koster and Bial's Music Hall in New York, there were already close to one thousand libraries across the United States with print collections of one thousand volumes or more. When the number of movie theaters in Canton, Ohio had grown to twelve in 1926, the number of non-Carnegie-funded public libraries alone in that state had more than doubled.[12] But if new library construction was outpacing theater construction at this time, administrators of public libraries also expressed a need to compete with the spread of "movie madness." To better appreciate the contours of this anxious response, consider the variety of screen fare audiences encountered in a single visit to a theater: in addition to serials and feature-length films, programs included "screen magazines," nature films, travelogues, sponsored and factual films, and newsreel. The Pathescope Company of America even likened itself to a public library in its advertisements, targeting the educational circuit with its 28mm film rentals.[13]

To be sure, all public institutions, from museums and parks to schools and libraries, were under pressure to justify their existence and stay relevant to modern civic life. In her article chronicling the expansion and retraction of public libraries' smaller gauge film holdings, Elena Rossi-Snook recounts the variety of service upgrades spawned by the library reform movement: "Determined to become an institution to actively develop society rather than merely reinforce public school education, public libraries multiplied services, which included free access to shelves, children's rooms, interlibrary loans, longer hours of operation, user-friendly catalogues and lists, lending books for home use, opening neighborhood library branches, and incorporating lectures and exhibits to reinforce and promote the reading of topically related books."[14] In 1908, the president of the American Library Association (ALA), Arthur E. Bostwick, began in earnest what Rossi-Snook refers to as an "ideological renovation," a services-based set of improvements that abided by the previous moral code of intellectual and social uplift while drastically transforming the librarian's task. Accessibility became the public library's guiding principle, and under this principle the librarian's function was also modified: now it would include the active matching of book to reader.[15] The types of circulation and access enhancements pioneered under Bostwick were used to sell this modern notion of the library as a meaningful destination and a communal location, even if uplift and betterment remained the unstated goal of its varied services.[16]

The restructuring of the public library included the redesign of its buildings in ways that were meant to bring the institution in line with progressive educational theories of the day.[17] The brightly lit, open-access stacks and self-service reference areas that are today quite common were once revolutionary new library ideas. As a result of these initiatives, patrons who entered these less intimidating spaces were supposed to experience a newfound permission to browse. These new public libraries were designed to seem less austere and restrictive. This change was particularly important to smaller and more remote branch and county libraries. The size of the buildings changed too. Smaller buildings in the arts and crafts style, like those designed by Cass Gilbert in St. Louis and Detroit, were replacing the grand style of Beaux-Arts architecture used to build central libraries and state archives. Some branch libraries were located in storefront spaces. Indeed, under the new philosophy of access these locations promoted book circulation, a new statistical measurement of a library's health. The library building was accessible to even those who could not travel to it. "Sunshine libraries" mailed books to shut-ins, and bookmobiles and traveling libraries of various sorts toured rural areas. Particularly in smaller cities without museums or similar educational venues, architects designed multipurpose buildings with meeting halls and lectures, display foyers, exhibition halls, and theatrical spaces.

Ideological though it may have been, the shift from the austere private library to a vernacular public library seemed rather more urgent in the face of a burgeoning leisure industry. Library reform, linked in some areas to free

speech activism, was taking place at the same time that the nickelodeon, famous for accessibility of a different sort, was booming. These proliferating
sites for lively and small film exhibition existed somewhat apart from the sanctioned and sanitized zones of commercial life. Robert Sklar has described
these novel spaces as "free of middle-class observation," implying that such
sites had a momentarily counter-public status in the years before their un-
savory reputation raised the interest of reformers and lawmakers. Sklar offers
as an example the anecdote told in 1909 by the social critic Simon N. Patten,
who describes walking down a "provincial Eastern city" street divided into
passivity and activity, one side dark and the other light. Patten sees on one
side of the street, the dark side, "'the very Institutions of Civilization itself,' the
library, the high school and the church, all locked, closed for the evening or the
season. Across the street were the people, noise, enthusiasm, life—clustered
around soda fountains, fruit stands, popcorn wagons, penny shows and the
nickel theater."[18] As unchaperoned as these operations were, the amusements
were still strongly tied to middle-class tastes and ideas. In 1905–7, what was
shown on screens at storefront nickelodeons "was much closer to the average
novel or legitimate stage play than middle-class opponents of the movies ever
admitted."[19] To these demographics and exhibition venue descriptions we
can also add the more complicated aspirational address to the viewer by the
cinema, such as the one Miriam Hansen has outlined, which in its imaginative
structure lurched from "distraction and absorption, between specific memories and shared ambitions, between intersubjective experience and alienated,
universalized forms of subjectivity, between a cinema relying on the social
space of the theater as a public sphere and a cinema that initiates its viewers
into a larger consumer culture."[20] Never so cleanly opposed in practice as the
library and the cinema were in the rhetoric of reform, each became an agent
of the other; the public libraries and the cinema proffered new modes of address and, albeit in different ways, expanded patrons' horizons in tandem.

Most of the historical accounts of North American public libraries date the
introduction of educational film services to around 1930, and usually in relation to two types of audiences: adult learners and children.[21] Annual reports
and bulletin announcements, the sources for many of the aforementioned histories, refer to motion picture programs aimed at younger readers, recommending the use of films based on plays, children's literature, and poetry for
afternoon and weekend educational programs. In many cases, the use of other

types of performance—puppet shows were common—was noted as an encouraging new effort to entice younger patrons into the public library. Fred Lerner cites an earlier origin of these services, writing that "after World War I, public library service to children became widespread, and was extended even to those who were too young to read. To encourage preschool children to find enjoyment in books, libraries offered picture book collections and story hours. Films, puppet programs, and other activities enticed children and their parents into the library."[22] In fact, direct cooperation between librarians and motion picture distributors and exhibitors actually began in a diffuse and gradual way at least seven years before the conclusion of the war.

At the Madison Free Library in Wisconsin, children's librarians began to include motion pictures in story hour programs in late 1910. Spotting the trend, the "Madison News and Notes" section of the *Wisconsin State Journal* announced in its issue of December 5, 1910 that "the use of moving pictures is coming into vogue at the free library, adding to the instruction and entertainment of the story hour for children. Great success attended the first of such entertainments Saturday afternoon in the auditorium of the library."[23] The main library was housed in a new Carnegie-built, Elizabethan Gothic-style structure that had opened in 1906. The large auditorium, located in the basement, seated 350 people.[24] The motion picture operator and supplier of the films was J. E. Sherwood, who was identified with an outfit called Fair Play.[25]

The library profession took notice. Contemporaneous accounts of the Madison library program were published in the American Library Association's professional publication, *The Library Journal*, in the *Wisconsin Library Bulletin*, and in *Public Libraries*.[26] The items are so similar in their details that they are likely the work of one publicity office. Each referred to the story hour presentations as "experimental" and emphasized the broader value of motion pictures as instruments of education. *The Library Journal* dryly noted "the purpose of the experiment is to prove the value of moving pictures as an aide to the educational efficiency of the library."[27] Taken together, the descriptions suggest that the audience was composed of seventh and eighth graders who had received tickets for the event from their teachers. The students were presented a mixed program of live storytelling, illustrated lecture, and story films. The two librarians, Marion Weil and Harriet Imhoff, recited the stories of Sir Lancelot and Elaine and *Oliver Twist* before the films were shown. (There were at least four filmed versions of *Oliver Twist* available in 1910; none of the descriptions indicate whether the librarians screened Vitagraph's *A Modern*

Oliver Twist, or the Life of a Pickpocket [1906], or J. Stuart Blackton's version for Vitagraph made four years later, simply titled *Oliver Twist*, or one of the two French adaptations released in the United States in 1910, by Pathé and by Film D'Art.) The unsigned item published in the journal *Public Libraries* described the display of films with a degree of attention to program order that the other journal accounts lacked, observing the interplay between the lesson and the picture, emphasizing its anti-spectacular pedagogical purpose. Reflecting the service to school systems that so many regional and municipal librarians provided, *Public Libraries* generally took more of an interest in the role of the librarian as educator than other journals for the library profession. Without any sustained discussion of the film or the story it tells, *the library idea* appears to be supported by the moving picture apparatus, and not the other way around:

> Miss Wilde [*sic*], the children's librarian, on a recent date told in a simple manner the story of Launcelot and Elaine, explaining that this story, which was to be illustrated by the pictures and other stories of a similar nature, would be found at the loan desk of the institution.
>
> The moving picture then portrayed the leading scenes of the story, the scenery and costuming of the characters being in perfect accord with the spirit of the time. Miss Imhoff then outlined the story of Oliver Twist, giving a little account of Charles Dickens and his other interesting books, and then for about 20 minutes the story of Oliver Twist was retold by a moving picture apparatus.
>
> The stories were told simply, without any effort at dramatic art, with the single thought of interesting the children in the literature and the characters of the story chosen.[28]

An editorial in *Wisconsin Library Bulletin* by the secretary of the state's library commission, Matthew S. Dudgeon, emphasized the instrumental use of such programming to stimulate book circulation and cultivate readership, but qualified the experiment in visual entertainment as what would later be referred to as "book bait": using films for the singular purpose of increasing interest in other books.[29] Two years later, a local exhibitor in Madison would cooperate with the library by showing adaptations of Thackeray's *Vanity Fair*, a book that was likely on many "bad book" lists.[30] In defense of this first public library screening, Dudgeon advocated the "wonderful efficiency" of images. He parsed the difference between film and the cinema:

From this use of moving pictures it should not be assumed that library authorities give moving picture shows their indiscriminate endorsement. In fact, indiscriminate endorsement of the moving picture show as an institution is the thing that should be avoided. It is to be noted that the moving picture is made use of only under the most favorable circumstances. In the case spoken of, the pictures were shown in the library building, in the day time in a room not entirely darkened. The machine an excellent one, producing almost no flutter. The films were fire proof. The pictures were not only harmless, but they were literary and educational in their nature.[31]

Through the most conventional lenses of film history, this statement sounds like a condemnation of the dangers of cinema, echoing outsized public fears about film-going: film and unsafe theaters pose optical, physical, psychological, and sociological threats to viewers, especially children. But within the broader progressive discourse of library reform, the author's refusal to endorse motion pictures "as an institution" is a reaffirmation of the trust between the library and its public: it alone can authorize proper cultural selection. In other words, cinema served a homeopathic function for the public library, which was at this time seeking to shore itself up on the notion of legitimate spaces for media reception. In general, the *Wisconsin Library Bulletin* was among the more liberal publications, supporting the professional autonomy of librarians and reflecting anti-censorship views about popular culture.[32] Public funding often required doublespeak; to reject an "indiscriminate endorsement" of cinema was still an endorsement of motion pictures.

In Ohio, the Cleveland Public Library was also beginning to experiment with film programming. The St. Clair Avenue branch library, a small Carnegie library serving a community of 35,000 predominantly German, Polish, Slovakian, Slovenian, and Irish immigrants on the near-east side of Cleveland, hosted a motion picture event in the library's large second-floor auditorium June 29, 1911.[33] The poster, which issued the invitation to "be our guest at a free moving picture show," promised a "pleasant evening" free of charge. Sponsored by the Cleveland Independence Day Association, the show promoted public safety and national pride. The evening program featured the patriotic-themed short subjects *Stars and Stripes, Washington at Valley Forge*, and *1911 Cleveland Sane Fourth Pictures*.[34] A note on the poster in a scrapbook refers to an "illustrated talk" at which a "large audience was present." A handwritten note in a librarian's daybook reads, "a moving picture show was given in the auditorium Thursday night to illustrate the wisdom of the sane fourth."[35] The

Children at the South Brooklyn Branch, Cleveland Public Library, 1939. Courtesy of the Cleveland Public Library Archives.

MADISON NEWS NOTES

Blake Reappointed—Judge A. L. Sanborn of the federal court has re-appointed Chauncey E. Blake United States commissioner. He is a member of the law firm of Sanborn & Blake, his associate being John B. Sanborn.

Moving Pictures at Library—The use of moving pictures is coming into vogue at the free library, adding to the instruction and entertainment of the story hour for children. Great success attended the first of such entertainments Saturday afternoon in the auditorium of the library.

A Xmas Present Free With Each Purchase.—Mothers will do well to purchase their boy's winter outfit at the Crescent Clothing Co., as with

Item in "Madison News and Notes" column, *Wisconsin State Journal*, December 5, 1910.

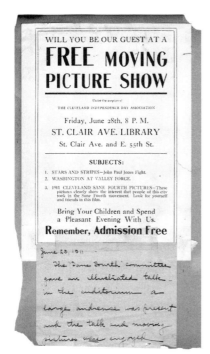

Poster from the St. Clair Branch, Cleveland Public Library, 1911. Courtesy of the Cleveland Public Library Archives.

inclusion of a local film ("Look for yourself and friends in this film") in a program celebrating American revolutionary figures was a visible assertion of the connection between spectatorship and citizenship and a direct encounter between an example of useful cinema and the "useable past" of a type of heritage film.[36]

While the Madison Free Library story hour may have been the earliest American library film screening, the Cleveland Public Library event stands out for several reasons: it was *not* an instance of book baiting or children's programming (though parents were encouraged to bring children); it was a library screening in a city already fairly flush with theaters and vaudeville houses;[37] in theme, content, and location the program directly addressed its local audience; the screening evidently escaped notice in the professional journals and local papers. Together, these features imply a challenge to our practice of film historiography. How exactly might we factor an off-the-grid, yet fundamentally public screening such as this into our developing understanding of film exhibition and spectatorship in this period, given that this understanding is commonly based upon evidence taken from trade press publications, theater listings in newspapers, and city zoning maps — in short, the usual evidence of a *theatrical* film history?[38] The Madison and St. Clair branch screenings appear marginal only with respect to the industrial-commercial history of cinema.

Many more libraries across the United States began to integrate motion picture use into their services between 1911 and 1918, demonstrating the compatibility of moving image culture to the library idea. Public libraries in Edgewater, New Jersey, Gary, Indiana, Milwaukee, and Seattle had added projection equipment to auditoriums and lecture halls and offered weekly film screenings by 1916. In the years immediately following, municipal and state libraries used motion pictures in library promotion and added theater cross-promotion to weekly activities. At the same time, the American Library Association (ALA) began information-sharing partnerships with both the National Board of Review (NBR) and the MPPDA.

On the pages of the ALA publications, brief boastful accounts of film programs for children rarely offered anything as elaborate as a theory of spectatorship. Audiences are described in terms that could only be taken as indicating favorable responses to the librarians' work, quantifiable in the post-screening increase in book circulation. The Reddick Library in Ottawa, Illinois, began its in-house story hour programs in 1913 in an effort to appear to be a "modern, democratic, and progressive" public institution.[39] Modeling the use of motion pictures in a letter to *Library Journal*, the Reddick librarian Vera Snook simply stated that their screenings were successful: "practically all the children who are old enough take books and the little tots are anxious to begin."[40] As a part of these events, children were also instructed on how to behave at the movies. Crowd control was maintained at the forty-five minute screenings by a local Ottawa Boy Scout troop, used as ushers and ticket-takers to "march" the groups of 150 in and out of the auditorium. Snook offers two rules of exhibition drawn from her observation of her audiences' passion for perceiving: that the recorded musical accompaniment be instrumental only ("as a rule vocal pieces are not very effective") and that the program must be balanced ("it is wise to balance strictly educational pictures with a comedy, otherwise the children think they have been treated a little unjustly").[41] The Gary Public Library began a popular series of Saturday matinees at a local theater in 1917, the five-cent admission still able to turn a small profit to the house.[42] This particular partnering moved the library assistants into the role of theater usher. A librarian reported that the library retained control over the matinee audience: librarians were placed in the theater to monitor the children who attended these screenings.

Librarians complained about the difficulty they experienced trying to find age appropriate films for young spectators. In 1917 George Kleine advertised a series of films directly to librarians in the hopes that the Edison name, a revered brand name for the educational and scientific communities, would imply high-minded entertainment.[43] The *Library Journal* promoted the Edison studios' Conquest Pictures series, which included adaptations of literary classics and American short stories, to those "who have motion picture machines in their libraries or who co-operate with the proprietors of commercial moving picture theaters."[44] While lists of distributors of educational, scientific, and "wholesome" films were available, in this new venture, as with books, librarians turned to outside networks of expertise to locate films that would not stir controversy.[45] In the parlance of librarians, all films were "passed on" before being screened with public library approval. Methods for recommending "good" films and "better" films, a kind of lay expertise in film criticism, were shared among librarians. Motion picture equipment, while harder still to operate and maintain, was but a small part of the apparatus of a modern library. As might be expected, the traffic in film spectatorship, whether inside library auditoriums or organized with a local theater, was also shaped by a paternalism intended to uphold middle-class mores and aesthetic values. Broader literacy networks involved in the socialization of reading (such as school curricula and magazine markets) as well as regional tastes, too, guided library decisions about screen content.

Children's matinees at public libraries represented a convergence of interests and movements fueled by concerns over child welfare and child labor. Apprehensiveness about primary identification with the apparatus was often fused with fears of the theater space as alien and offensive to a child's mental outlook. In 1914 Ida May Ferguson of the Minneapolis Public Library wrote, "anyone who is with little children very much must realize that motion pictures play a tremendous part in the life of a child, but the conditions under which they see the pictures are far from ideal. The theaters they frequent are usually cheap and ill-ventilated, and the pictures are poor. The chief objection to the photo-play for children is that it is sophisticated, grown-up, and out of their experience. It is on a par with the story in the fifteen-cent magazine, which no one would think of offering to a little child as a steady mental diet."[46] Libraries offering weekend and afternoon matinees were counter-programming against an entertainment sector that promised wholesome amusements and trustworthy chaperones, even if the films they booked were the same ones that were shown on neighborhood screens.[47] The theatrical matinee movement was organized by industry and industry-friendly groups defending against popular rhetoric that claimed that so-called harmful pictures were deteriorating both the family and the experience of childhood. Since matinees cordoned off a child audience but cultivated habits of spectatorship, "children's matinees," Richard deCordova points out, "were thus among the least radical solutions to solve the problem of children and movies. Matinees involved no state censorship, no laws restricting children's access to films, and no change in the basic structure of production and exhibition. They were preferred most by those who believed that the power of movies could be harnessed for the good of children. They were also favored by those most closely aligned with the industry, and, at least by 1925, by the industry itself."[48] While the distinct function of the theatrical matinee was to produce a new audience demographic and elevate the place of the cinema in general, the same could not be said for library matinees. Motion pictures shown in libraries, sponsored by libraries, or organized by librarians, for audiences of children or young adults, were subject to library decisions about appropriate content, cultural value, and the public good.

Just what kind of good is an interesting question. Unlike the history of entertainment films shown in theaters, which can be gleaned from a wide variety of sources, many of them highly critical of the commercial enterprises of cinema, the history of film in libraries must be gathered almost entirely from the professional organs of the libraries. The evidence of the good that children's matinees did or intended to do, in other words, exists precisely because these services were a point of pride for libraries and a way for them to claim cultural relevance. We know about children's matinees—a prominent example of library-film industry cooperation—because children were a population of high priority to libraries in this period, and because many library systems were housed within state education systems.

We also know that other new groups of interest to libraries—recent immigrants, for instance—were the beneficiaries of new media services at libraries. Cinema served as the model for this service. For if the movies competed for the leisure time of library patrons, the cinema—or to be more precise, public spectatorship in theaters—was just as often held up as a path to social literacy and civic participation. For this reason, John Cotton Dana, the director of the Free Public Library of Newark, New Jersey, editorialized on the cinema's potential in 1913, noting daily theatrical attendance in Newark of twenty-six thousand. "The latest rival of the public library and of the reading of books is the moving picture." However, film, he wrote, must be reckoned with, and on the whole greatly approved. It promises to become one of the most important educational factors that man has added to his equipment since the invention of printing. It is quite possible that it will inform the world, interest the world and broaden the world even more rapidly than the printing press ever has. It will doubtless lead to changes in mental habits, just as printing has checked, for example, the growth of memorizing; but in the field of instruction it may prove to be the greatest instrument ever devised.[49]

Advocates for film within the library system at this time were often also advocates for newspaper reading rooms, photography collections, and community activities. Surveying the professional publications in this period—a period especially significant because it precedes any of the social-scientific surveys of audience and reception—it becomes clear that motion pictures were only one of the many new media forms being incorporated into library practice. Furthermore, it was the *theaters*, not the films, that stirred the library professionals' unease.

In April 1914 the *Library Journal* published an article written by Everett Perry, a librarian with the Los Angeles Public Library, listing the commercial recreations competing for the attention of library patrons. "Public opinion actively supports the moving picture; the picture theater," Perry wrote, "is the greatest competitor of the public library, and the very people whom the library serves the least are the mass of men and women who patronize these theaters."[50] To produce high circulation figures, he argued, libraries needed better publicity and modernized marketing practices. He detailed opportunities such as designing store window displays, orchestrating mass mailings, handing out free bookmarkers, publishing book lists in newspapers, delivering multigraph circulars directly to homes, placing posters in public spaces, and circulating postcards. A key component of this strategy was official collaboration with film exhibitors. The most important of these publicity methods, according to Perry, was exploiting the public's widespread enchantment with the movies. Perry advocated partnering with those sophisticated local film exhibitors who recognized the educational value of their structures and would already be "well disposed toward the public library." These exhibitors would then show slides between films stating that "this theater gladly aids library extension."[51] Perry speculated that this would help the library as well as the exhibitor. Such statements aimed to integrate the cinema with the library's operations, connecting it publicly to the spirit of goodwill and interest in personal enlightenment. The practice was likely fairly widespread. In 1915, for instance, in Binghamton, New York, an exhibitor inserted handwritten slides written by librarians between short film programs addressing the spectator's aspirations of upward mobility and financial freedom: "'How to get a better job,' 'Trade opportunities,' 'Learn how to cook and make a home happy,' 'Best tips in salesmanship and advertising,' 'After school what?' 'What shall I do for a living?' 'Cut out the cost of high living,' and 'Dressmaking at home,' are some of the slogans that are flashed on the screen between acts."[52] Showmanship and librarianship, unlikely bedfellows, came together in surprising ways, as when librarians offered fifteen-minute illustrated lectures during vaudeville programs. Such tactics were then taken into the theaters as spectacular enticement to local libraries' growing collections of professional training materials.

The best and best-known example of library–film industry cooperation occurred at the Cleveland Public Library. Celebrated by Margaret Farrand Thorp in her book, *America at the Movies* (1939), Cleveland had become a national leader in film-library cooperation. "One cites Cleveland," writes Thorp, "only because the librarians there have been pioneers in taking the movie into partnership and because they are zealous and interested in compiling figures."[53] Not only did the library construct elaborate lobby displays of photoplay adaptations to provoke readers' curiosity about literary classics, but it documented their exhibits in photographs as well. In 1923 the Cleveland Public Library began to insert into every book that passed over the circulation desk to patrons a bookmark that had printed on it the title of a film showing in a theater locally. Each one listed titles of local films, with narrow reminders with suggestions of books to read prior to seeing the film and books to read afterward to continue the subject.

Book baiting and promotion of the "book film," the short-lived term for a film adaptation, were activities easily incorporated into the library services of even the smallest branches; but in some areas, full-scale film projection and film production also took place. Milwaukee's South Side Library installed a Simplex projection system in a fireproofed projection booth in 1916 for use in its 550-seat auditorium during Saturday nights "and perhaps oftener."[54] The public library in Edgewater, New Jersey responded to irregular attendance at its free lecture series by showing films instead. Without so much as a note of compromise, a librarian wrote that "To this end we are now planning to give a series of weekly entertainments, running through the late fall and winter months, these entertainments to be entirely free to the public."[55] The Seattle Public Library held and filmed "an aeroplane contest" for children in 1914

Movie tie-in display at the Cleveland Public Library's History Reading Room, 1926.
Courtesy of the Cleveland Public Library Archives.

and the camera operator also photographed the opening of the Yesler library branch. The resulting film was shown at local theaters and then purchased by the public library, which hoped to use the film for publicity.[56]

The California State Library planned to open a film exchange in 1915, primarily for the distribution of educational and industrial films, and soon found itself involved in the production of an industrial library film.[57] That same year, *American Library Annual* announced that the "work done by libraries in California was graphically shown [as part of a library exhibit] at the Panama-Pacific Exposition in a moving-picture film." A state librarian oversaw much of the production of this film, which was certainly one of the earliest to showcase library activity. The hour-long film connected reading life and rural life in a panoramic tour of sites of book circulation and collection. The film is not known to be extant; describing the life of the film after its screening at the Panama-Pacific Exposition, *American Library Annual* offers a possible explanation: "Since the exposition closed the film has been cut up and made into twenty-minute reels. One of these is shown in Los Angeles, one is at the California State Library, one went to China for use with the American Library Association material there, and one is in the possession of the Cali-

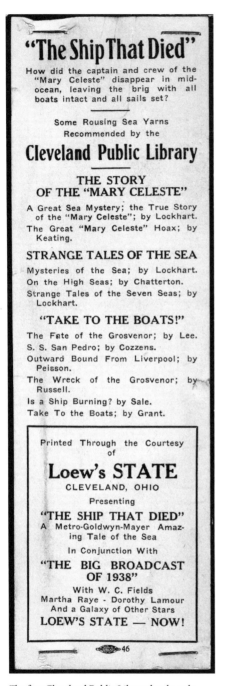

"The Ship That Died"

How did the captain and crew of the "Mary Celeste" disappear in mid-ocean, leaving the brig with all boats intact and all sails set?

Some Rousing Sea Yarns
Recommended by the

Cleveland Public Library

THE STORY
OF THE "MARY CELESTE"

A Great Sea Mystery; the True Story of the "Mary Celeste"; by Lockhart. The Great "Mary Celeste" Hoax; by Keating.

STRANGE TALES OF THE SEA

Mysteries of the Sea; by Lockhart. On the High Seas; by Chatterton. Strange Tales of the Seven Seas; by Lockhart.

"TAKE TO THE BOATS!"

The Fate of the Grosvenor; by Lee. S. S. San Pedro; by Cozzens. Outward Bound From Liverpool; by Peisson. The Wreck of the Grosvenor; by Russell. Is a Ship Burning? by Sale. Take To the Boats; by Grant.

Printed Through the Courtesy of

Loew's STATE
CLEVELAND, OHIO
Presenting

"THE SHIP THAT DIED"
A Metro-Goldwyn-Mayer Amazing Tale of the Sea

In Conjunction With

"THE BIG BROADCAST OF 1938"
With W. C. Fields Martha Raye - Dorothy Lamour And a Galaxy of Other Stars

LOEW'S STATE — NOW!

46

The first Cleveland Public Library bookmark to feature short subject films. Courtesy of the Cleveland Public Library Archives.

fornia Library Association. Less cumbersome than the whole hour run, these films are even more interesting to the ordinary observer."[58] This dispassionate view of print life reveals something of the utilitarian conception of the library film no less than of the library as a cinematic venue.

The force of this movement within the library systems for a direct engagement with all areas of cinema, from spectatorship to production, was undeniable. In the space of only four years, public library partnerships with local exhibitors were all but replaced by budget allocations for circulating film libraries and other film ventures. Key to decisions regarding library acquisition or rental of a particular film was the broadening of the institution's mission, an expansion of ideals intended to make it operate more like a public utility, to, as Elena Rossi-Snook puts it, allow it to "surpass a merely literary function" by serving the growing population of lifelong learners.[59] This democratizing doctrine pitted the attractions of *the good* against the requirement of *the good for you*, producing a lasting effect on the design of individual library collections.

The National Board of Review (NBR), an organization also funded by the film industry but not, in fact, an industry body, established a connection with the library community early on in its operation.[60] Principally an anticensorship front, the board had maintained its position by promoting the vague and often equivocating standard of "quality" motion pictures. It did so by means of a policy of inclusive pressure politics, aimed at a wide swath of special interest groups and civic organizations. In 1916 the board formed an umbrella group, the National Committee for Better Films, through which it orchestrated a national anti-censorship movement and campaigned vigorously through local women's clubs and national organizations.[61] As Richard deCordova has shown, the sprawling associated clubs and volunteer networks maintained a focus on the child audience and exhibition to that market. In this venture, given the record—tradition, even—of public libraries' use of motion-picture story-hour tie-ins, the overlapping terrain suggested logical alliances between librarians, better films advocates, and the matinee movement supported by the MPPDA.

The National Committee for Better Films issued lists of recommended films through its own bulletins, leaflets, newsletters, the *National Board of Review Magazine*, and, beginning in 1920, *Exceptional Photoplays*.[62] These recommendations were then reprinted with regularity in full-page spreads in the *Library Journal* under headings such as "Motion Pictures for Religious Book Week" and "Motion Pictures Based on Literature." Entire sections of the *Library Journal* were devoted to library motion pictures in February and March 1918. It is important to resist interpreting the public libraries as having been exploited to further the goals of either the MPPDA or the NBR. The libraries had interests of their own in these partnerships. These interests were reiterated by Orrin G. Cocks, the secretary and a strategist for the NBR. Cocks addressed regional and national library associations on several occasions, delivering messages of self-sufficiency in film selection and cooperation with local exhibitors.

On one such occasion in 1914, Cocks had antagonized librarians even while the board was courting the library system to join its anti-censorship activities. The National Board of Censorship, as it was then called, submitted announcements to the *Library Journal* identifying distributors with hefty catalogues of educational films and providing the names of film bureaus able to provide evangelical film material.[63] Cocks's article, "Librarians and Motion Pictures—An Ignored Educational Agency," stands as an important argument regarding film's place in the library.[64] Though his tone is at times inflammatory—libraries, Cocks insists, "must pay the price for their earlier indifference!"—his article also explains, in a generous tone, the rudimentary procedures of film handling, booking, and film programming to a presumed audience of neophytes, coolly assuring the librarianship that the only real dangers are permanent eye damage and sudden uncontrollable conflagration. Aware that the industry's competitive pricing structures prohibited the libraries from purchasing, lending, or exhibiting film prints, Cocks proposed negotiation and coalition building between the industry and nongovernmental organizations to establish accessible and useful public film libraries: "The only other solution which has occurred to thinkers on this subject is the purchase at a large initial cost of a supply of films for rental and exhibition by some philanthropists or philanthropic foundation."[65] This statement announced the board's interest in infusing existing systems of distribution with new sources of capital. More importantly, it demonstrated the board's intention to put some economic and intellectual muscle behind the categorization and taxonomy of screen fare, to assist in the separation of the excellent from the good, the good from the better, and the better from the worst, and, in the process to create a second-rung circuit of better films. The educational film, a staple in movie house fare, was, in the eyes of the board, adding to economic congestion in the traffic of pictures. The solution Cocks proposed to the problem of low circulation figures of informational programs was the feeding of the educational film into the library. This action he insisted, would also stimulate the secondary and tertiary markets for the manufacture and sales of small-gauge machines and gear. The underlying desire was for the creation of a stable, state-supported, public distribution system for that second-class category of film, films the National Board of Review would later refer to as "by-products of the entertainment film."[66] Film classification and film indexing is a significant, if rarely touched upon, aspect of the appeal of the library and the library profession to the film industry. Orrin Cocks's interest in the skill of the library cataloguer can also be traced back to 1914, when the National Board of Censorship had identified a need for a more systematic and recognizable method for erecting a classification system for film genres, particularly in the area of educational film. A standardized and authoritative practice of moving image description and discrimination was needed. For this, the National Board of Review sought to benefit from the cataloguing and classifying expertise of librarians. At a time when the film industry—especially the distribution exchanges—was not yet stabilized, the visible and growing library profession, the object of much public respect, appeared to control a vast network of information circulation, one that was supported by the state, county, and municipal libraries. One item in the National Committee for Better Films's *Bulletin* metaphorically suggested how the apparatus of film might fit into the information retrieval systems, practically drooling over the well-established and state-funded distribution and lending system: "The public library has become so widespread in its ministrations, and its directors have done so much to encourage the wide use of its resources in every possible direction, that it might very well phrase its invitation to the public in those words. . . . The motion picture machine, itself, has come into the library. . . . The narrow band of film may become a straight path leading from a lower to a higher cultural plane."[67] Such milquetoast advocacy frequently appeared in the committee's *Bulletin* and was ubiquitous in literature and other pamphlets circulated by the better films movement's various agents.

The issue of the day for librarians, however, remained the decline of reading. In an article titled "Motion Pictures and Reading Habits," published in the *Library Journal* issue of February 1918 that was devoted to motion pictures, Cocks tried a different approach to elitist concerns about misuse of leisure time. In it, he called for the use of a new library-film slogan of "Intelligent Cooperation." Reaching the "impressionable minds" of non-readers (in barely veiled references to the working class, the poor, and children) was the civic duty of the librarian: "show these beginners that there are still finer things and still larger vistas behind the doors of libraries."[68] If the discourse around motion pictures and libraries was previously oriented to an ideal of *communitas*, the ground had now shifted. With the war as backdrop, discussion was shaped by a more restrictive climate of *civitas*.

Perhaps as a result of the number of films addressing patriotic, pacifist, or Americanizing themes or what promoters of quality films would call "civic motion pictures," the notion of a free library of films available for screenings in community education programs received more attention in the better films circuits. As this message radiated outward, many, such as Ina Clement, who was a better films activist but also a reference librarian in New York, seized on the need for public film libraries:

> There is more need for a public library of films than there ever was for a public library of books, and for the following reason: the book is an individual property; it can be read in solitude; the individual can purchase it if he wants it. But the motion picture is essentially a collective commodity. The individual can have a desired motion picture only on condition that a large number of other people want the same picture at the same time. This fact makes it peculiarly out of question [*sic*] to leave motion pictures to the exploitation of unlimited commercialism. . . . The public film library, dealing with a sufficiently large number of schools, churches, and other

agencies, would be able to draw on the world's supply for whatever film it wanted, and to ransack the film output for the past ten years.[69]

The demand for a public film library, to be funded by philanthropic organizations or the state, should not be confused for a plea for film archiving. The concept of collection was remarkably detached from that of conservation: what Clement wanted was for films to be *used*, and she encouraged a public consumption of film prints. The public film library she envisioned would involve librarians as scavengers of footage who would "ransack the film output of the last ten years." About the archiving standards of film producers at the time she was optimistic and naïve: "Most of the negatives (the original copies) of good films, no matter when or where made, have been preserved, and fresh copies can always be prepared." However, her vision of the film library is significant for the expression of an early understanding of a material film history. The librarian would act as part programmer or curator, and part reference librarian, assisting with selection and suggesting a well-balanced film program, drawing material from a wellspring of masters, dupes, or compilations. A different call for a public library of film would be made, almost ten years later, by Charlotte Perkins Gilman, who imagined the building of publicly financed, free film libraries on the scale of a national public works project: "For every reason which justifies a public library of books we should also have public libraries of motion pictures. . . . Private benefactors like Mr. Carnegie, could help; there should be state aid, perhaps Federal aid; every village could offer a steady series of good pictures, free."[70]

It wasn't until 1923 that the ALA would formally acknowledge motion pictures as a significant cultural force and educational instrument. When it did, it would set up national committees and task forces within libraries as well as between the ALA and the motion picture industry.[71] Over the next few years, a number of duplicative and inconsistent recommendations, procedures, and policies for the collection, storage, and circulation of educational film issued forth from these committees. While trepidation over teaching technical expertise in the field of librarianship lingered, greater emphasis continued to be placed on the appropriateness and quality of the visual material for the public, and on the special expertise of librarians to evaluate film from a learned and trustworthy perspective. In 1924 Carl H. Milam, who headed the ALA's Committee on Relations Between Libraries and Moving Pictures, a committee formed mainly to interact with the MPPDA, expressed concern over the feasibility of libraries distributing films at all. But he nonetheless equated the cinema with an educational apparatus that was destined to be a part of a modernized library system and could not be ignored: "there has grown up a great institution—moving pictures—which is affecting the lives of millions of Americans in one way or another. It concerns education and recreation, the same field, in other words, as the libraries. No general effort has been made to define the relations between libraries and motion pictures."[72] Milam appealed to the profession for action in three areas: collections, distribution, and, notably, a direct and formal partnering with the MPPDA. From the perspective of the MPPDA, libraries held a unique and localizing potential, cutting across each of its distinct functions and departments: public relations, self-regulation, legal relations, and exhibitor relations. In a presentation at an ALA convention that year, Gladys Caldwell, a librarian with the Los Angeles Public Library, described with a glamorizing and star-struck tone research work that her art and music departments had provided to costume and set designers. The library had issued "corporate" library cards to motion picture studios to facilitate their long-term borrowing of reference books during productions. An even greater service to its public than showing films, she argued, and the best way to utilize the unique abilities of the reference librarian, was to help to ensure that motion pictures were accurate in their presentation of historical details.[73]

In 1925, the ALA Motion Picture Relations Committee made three recommendations on film use in public libraries: 1) that all public library information services should include film indexes and distribution catalogues; 2) that a number of regional public libraries begin the collection and distribution of films "for the use of schools, clubs and other organizations in their respective regional areas"; and 3) that a new position be created at the ALA or the MPPDA to oversee "the task of developing and sustaining a consecutive program of co-operation between the public libraries and the moving picture producers."[74] Book-film promotion, partnerships with local theaters, and matinee film screenings—the types of film use that were the innovations of regional librarians—were not mentioned. The conspicuous absence of such local initiatives from the committee's recommendations indicated that the years of experimentation and library-exhibitor partnerships had given way to a period characterized by excessive bureaucracy that would later be referred to as "apathy and confusion" about "the basic film question."[75]

Backed by a strong visual education movement, the introduction of 16mm and 28mm film in the 1920s in libraries would drastically alter the landscapes of educational film exhibition and spectatorship found there. But the importance of the earlier period of films in libraries, a period dominated by the 35mm gauge, is that it demonstrates that the spaces of mass instruction and amusement parallel to the cinema were also affected by it. Indeed, if the public library seemed at times to be the least favorable context for *film*, it was a most ideal environment for *cinema*, one best able to exploit the artistic, educational, and technological aspects of the medium. In these spaces, cinema—the "democratic art"—became emphatically local.

I have suggested that libraries, public libraries in particular, are important to our understanding of film history, and not only our understanding of nontheatrical film. The use of film by libraries can be understood as a measure of the cultural expansion and consolidation of mass media forms, necessarily balancing the traditional with the modern, the national with the local. Recovering this overlooked history, we can see how social and commercial forces within and without the library system produced a remediating exhibition circuit for film, one that addressed viewers as local citizens rather than American moviegoers. The public library, in other words, contended with the cinema by introducing a negotiated type of civic spectatorship, one that was, at least in the period I have covered here, peculiar to its patrons. The various microhistories of public library film use waiting to be written would only demonstrate the force of this contradictory ideal and its hold on a particular civic imaginary of cinema.

NOTES

1 Whitehill, *Boston Public Library*, 80–81. The article describing the Lower Hall delivery room was written by Albert G. Webster and published in *Appleton's Journal of Literature, Science and Art* 7 (1871), 629–31.

2 Quoted in Whitehill, *Boston Public Library*, 240–41.

3 Münsterberg, "Public Library in America," 84.

4 Ibid., 85.

5 Thomas Augst, "Faith in Reading," 153–54.

6 Grieveson, *Policing Cinema*, 4.

7 Maltby, "The Genesis of the Production Code," 11.

8 A fuller consideration, not possible here, would certainly include the pre-history of the cinema. Especially relevant would be magic lantern shows, lyceum slide lectures, and other more didactic and instructional uses of optical devices.

9 Bobinski, *Carnegie Libraries*, 4–5.

10 Ibid., 4.

11 Ibid.

12 Learned, *The American Public and the Diffusion of Knowledge*, 73.

13   Mebold, "'Just like a Public Library Maintained for Public Welfare,'" 269–70.

14   Rossi-Snook, "Persistence of Vision," 6.

15   Cramer, *Open Shelves and Open Minds*, 74.

16   Rossi-Snook, "Persistence of Vision," 6.

17   This is no less true in the Carnegie model, especially as discussed in Bobinski, *Carnegie Libraries*, and by Van Slyck, *Free to All*. See especially Van Slyck's discussion of the rise of professionalism and library design (chapter 2) and of gendered spaces in Carnegie-built libraries (chapter 4).

18   Sklar, *Movie-Made America*, 122.

19   Ibid., 30.

20   Hansen, *Babel and Babylon*, 59.

21   See Manlove, "The Educational Motion Picture Film in Public Library Service"; Waldron, *The Information Film*; Blair, "Films in Public Libraries"; and Dykyj, "Cinema Collections."

22   F. Lerner, *The Story of Libraries*, 156.

23   "Moving Pictures at Library," *Wisconsin State Journal*, December 5, 1910, 11.

24   Levitan, *Madison*, 150. The building was razed in 1965.

25   In some accounts the operator is identified as Sherwood and McWilliams, which may or may not have been Fair Play. "Library for Year," *Wisconsin State Journal*, August 15, 1911; and "Moving Pictures in Library Work," *Wisconsin Library Bulletin* 6, no. 6 (1910), 138–40.

26   "Madison (Wisc.) P.L.," *Library Journal* 36, no. 2 (1911), 89; "Moving Pictures in Library Work," *Wisconsin Library Bulletin*, 139; and "Moving Pictures in Library Work," *Public Libraries* 16, no. 1 (1911), 19.

27   "Madison (Wisc.) P.L.," 89.

28   "Moving Pictures in Library Work," *Public Libraries*, 19.

29   "Moving Pictures in Library Work," *Wisconsin Library Bulletin*, 139.

30   "Reading and Aids," *Library Journal* 37, no. 4 (1912), 224.

31   "Moving Pictures in Library Work," *Wisconsin Library Bulletin*, 139–40.

32   Geller, *Forbidden Books in American Public Libraries, 1876–1939*," 108. Geller includes John C. Dana and Marilla Freeman on a chart of liberal, anti-censorship voices in the library field. Both headed libraries — Newark and Cleveland respectively — that programmed with local motion picture exhibitors early on.

33   The library auditorium had a capacity of four hundred people. Designed to meet community needs, the floor plan included a space for women's club meetings and children's activity rooms.

34   Cleveland Public Library Archives, Box: Branches, St. Clair Branch: Scrapbook 1905–17, Folder 11 (St. Clair Branch 1911–14). The poster gives the date as "Friday, June 28th"; since June 28, 1911, was a Wednesday and two other sources say the event was on a Thursday, the most likely date is June 29.

35   Cleveland Public Library Archives, Box: Branches, St. Clair Branch: Daybook October 4, 1909–11.

36   See chapter 2, "The 'Useable Past' of Civil War Films," in Abel, *Americanizing the Movies and "Movie-Mad" Audiences, 1910–1914*.

37 Abel's meticulous survey of newspapers, trade press, city directories, and demographics in 1911 lead him to the conclusion that "Cleveland can be taken as a model of picture theater status, size, and geographic distribution for many large to medium-sized cities at the time" (*Americanizing the Movies and "Movie-Mad" Audiences, 1910–1914*, 49).

38 This question is answered, in part, by ongoing micro-historical research on the contexts of film circulation and reception, beginning with the debate between Robert C. Allen and Ben Singer published in *Cinema Journal*: Allen, "Manhattan Myopia"; and Singer, "New York, Just Like I Pictured It. . . ." More recently, Richard Abel's composite treatment of national distribution and local advertising in his "The 'Backbone' of the Business" seeks a more nuanced topography of spectatorship, as does Paul S. Moore's archeology of showmanship in his *Now Playing: Early Moviegoing and the Regulation of Fun*.

39 Snook, "Getting Pictures for Small Children," 157–58.

40 Ibid., 158.

41 Ibid.

42 "Moving Pictures," *American Library Annual*, 1917, 86.

43 "Moving Pictures," *Library Journal* 42, no. 7 (1917), 572.

44 "Library Work — Motion Pictures," *American Library Annual*, 1917–18, 61.

45 The extensive outside network of experts to which I am alluding deserves more space than I have here, but would include state censor boards and, after 1917, the Committee on Public Information.

46 "Library Work, 1915," *American Library Annual*, 1915–16, 77.

47 deCordova, "Ethnography and Exhibition," 235.

48 Ibid.

49 "The Library and 'the Movies,'" *Library Journal* 38, no. 3 (1913), 168; and Dana, "The Library in 1912."

50 Perry, "Aims and Methods of Library Publicity," 259.

51 Ibid., 264–65.

52 "Moving Picture Theaters," *American Library Annual*, 1916, 76.

53 Thorp, *America at the Movies*, 239.

54 "Moving Pictures," *American Library Annual*, 1916, 76.

55 Ibid., 77.

56 Ibid.

57 "Moving Pictures," *American Library Annual*, 1915–16, 77; and "Motion Pictures," *Library Journal*, January 1917, 72.

58 "Moving Pictures," *American Library Annual*, 1917, 86.

59 Rossi-Snook, "Persistence of Vision," 2.

60 Reliable, brief summaries of the formation of the National Board of Review are found in Inglis, *Freedom of the Movies*, 74–96; and deCordova, "Ethnography and Exhibition," 236–37.

61 Antonia Lant's excellent, scrupulously documented survey of the public participation of clubwomen in censorship debates and previewing activities between 1914 and 1930 — a context critical for understanding the library and film cooperation — is the

most comprehensive published account to date. See the introduction to "Cinema as Power," in Lant and Perez, *The Red Velvet Seat*, 249–79 and notes, 756–75.

62 Inglis, *Freedom of the Movies*, 76; Koszarski, *An Evening's Entertainment*, 209; Budd, "The National Board of Review and the Early Art Cinema in New York."

63 Slide, *Before Video*, 59.

64 Cocks, "Libraries and Motion Pictures: An Ignored Educational Agency," 666–68.

65 Ibid., 668.

66 Carl E. Milliken, "Increasing the General Usefulness of Films: Educational Pictures, Religious Pictures, Medical Pictures, and Films in Industry Are Given Encouragement," *The Motion Picture*, August 1928. Cited in Morey, *Hollywood Outsiders*, 148.

67 *Bulletin of the Committee for Better Films*, July 1917. National Board of Review of Motion Pictures Collection, New York Public Library, Box 96.

68 Cocks, "Motion Pictures and Reading Habits," 67.

69 "Need for a Film Library," *Bulletin of the Affiliated Committees for Better Films* 2 (September 1918), 2; and National Board of Review of Motion Pictures Collection, New York Public Library, Box 96.

70 "The Motion Picture in Its Economic and Social Aspects," *Annals of the American Academy of Political and Social Science* 128 (November 1926), 143–45.

71 Accounts of the ALA motion and formation of motion picture committees appear in Waldron, *The Information Film*; Slide, *Before Video*; Manlove, "The Educational Motion Picture Film in Public Library Service"; Dykyj, "Cinema Collections"; Adam, *Motion Pictures in Adult Education*; Blair, "Films in Public Libraries"; Galvin, *Films in Public Libraries*; Thorp, *America At the Movies*; and Rossi-Snook, "Persistence of Vision."

72 ALA *Bulletin* 22 (September 1928), 434, cited in Manlove, "The Educational Motion Picture Film in Public Library Service," 17–18.

73 Caldwell, *The Public Library and the Motion Picture Studio*.

74 Sherman, "Relations between Libraries and Moving Pictures," 210. See also "Libraries as Distributors of Educational Films," *Library Journal* 49, no. 1 (1924), 87–88.

75 Blair, "*The Information Film* by Gloria Waldron," 207.

BIG, FAST MUSEUMS / SMALL, SLOW MOVIES

FILM, SCALE, AND THE ART MUSEUM

Haidee Wasson

New York's Metropolitan Museum of Art (the Met) is the quintessential American example of the "universal survey museum," a museum that seeks to display and thus order everything within its walls.[1] Founded in 1870 by wealthy industrialists and urban reformers determined to establish New York as the capital of American civility, the building and the collections it housed self-consciously mimicked its European predecessors, from the princely gallery to the stately Louvre. Its architecture borrows freely from Romanesque and Greek styles, making present the ideal of an immaculate if mummified past. Long derided by its critics as a mausoleum — an elitist space where dead art died again and again — the wealthy trustees and patrons (Morgans, Rockefellers, Vanderbilts, alike), along with various museum presidents, have defiantly presided over a collection that includes two million objects, spanning five thousand years, dispersed across two million square feet of prime Manhattan real estate.[2]

Alongside its rhetorical efforts toward the timeless and universal, the Met has also long adopted so-called new

The Metropolitan Museum of Art, 5th Avenue Façade and Main Entrance, photographed 1939. Image copyright © The Metropolitan Museum of Art / Art Resource, New York.

technologies and display techniques in an effort to educate and engage its public. Augmenting lantern slides, electrically illuminated display cases and photographic and lithographic reproductions, films, film projectors, and reflective screens became fully integrated and permanent elements of museum architecture and programming during the 1920s. Among its art museum peers, the Met adopted film reasonably early, and by 1925 made and showed its own movies at the museum, as well as distributed and exhibited these (and titles made by other organizations) to interested institutions.[3] A year later, these films appeared twice weekly in the museum's Lecture Hall, gradually expanding to four regular showings, two during the week and two on weekends. The museum bulletin indicates that screenings were extremely popular, with audiences frequently exceeding the Lecture Hall's capacity.[4] In 1928, the museum began reducing its 35mm prints to non-flammable, 16mm gauge acetate, making its films compatible with the growing network of 16mm projectors, helping to further catalyze their exhibition.[5] The new self-operated portable projector allowed any would-be projectionist to comply with city fire codes and avoid the elaborate projection infrastructure required of 35mm exhibition apparatus; the new machine potentially turned any darkened space into a display venue for films. Subjects of the Met's movies reflected the museum's diverse constituencies and vast collections, and included Egyptian digs, home decor, and ancient weaponry. Some titles employed the conventions of nonfiction in their presentation of museum objects and activities; others borrowed freely from the language of fictional storytelling. A few of the films were stylistically hybrid, sharing qualities of non-fiction and fiction, didactic illustration and playful fantasy. Noteworthy among the films were numerous tours of particular collections or museum wings;[6] such films either augmented views of museum space for those already present in the museum or made this same space mobile, transporting galleries and collections to a dispersed public.[7] In other words, the museum itself figured prominently in the films it made.

During the 1920s many major urban museums either made or sponsored the production of films, and many more showed films as part of their public programming. This practice was most common at museums of science, industry, and natural history, but as previously mentioned it was in evidence at art museums as well. Previous work on museums and cinema has emphasized the ways in which museum educators used films to enliven and even sensationalize museum content, or to immerse museum-goers in a kind of wondrous technological sublime. Such goals, of course, were mediated by the museum's foundational status as a site of authoritative knowledge and respectable leisure. Alison Griffiths and more recently Theresa Scandiffio have shown definitively that film and its cognate media have long been an integral element of American museums' efforts to simultaneously differentiate themselves from entertainment and spectacle, and, yet to borrow from these same sites in order to engage and educate as wide a public as possible.[8] This has entailed using films to illustrate lectures, to animate museum objects (people, rocks, paintings), to spectacularize science, and to dramatize the extent of the museum's imperial reach by showing images captured from distant places and cultures. In concert with this scholarship, it must be said that some of the Met's individual films are helpfully understood by resorting to ideas about the exotic, the imperial, and to a lesser degree the sensational. Yet, what I want to argue here is somewhat different.

In the most general sense, the Met used cinema—films, projectors, and screens—in order to de-sensationalize and to simplify the experience of art and museum, often conceived as overwhelming in the context of its expansive collection and staggering spaces. The Met was, after all, the single largest museum on the continent. Thus, the attractions of cinema at the Met lay less in the capacity of projected celluloid to surprise or seduce or shock, and more in its capacity to diminish the size, direct the eye, order the clutter, and tame the experience of a vast museum and its art. In other words, at the Met there was an aesthetic, operational, and spatial specificity to the museum's experiments with the cinematic apparatus. The museum film's short length but long takes (that is, their slow pace) and the relatively small, standardized frame of the screen — spatially confined to an auditorium — connected intimately with the museum's effort to manage time and viewer attention. Film and its established conventions of spectatorship (seated and not moving; centralized rather than wandering focus) offered the capacity to condense, dynamically manipulate, reconfigure, and ultimately control viewing time in an automated fashion far more than previous museum display techniques, the diorama or the lantern slide for instance. Thus, during the period under examination, the Met's films should be understood as examples of a didactic and directive kind of cinema, one that articulates a specifically museological gaze that more efficiently directs the museum-goer's eye in how and for how long to look.

The Met's permanent film screen worked to naturalize this new museum view, augmenting the museum's cavernous architecture, gallery design, and glass display cases. The film screen provided a circumscribed site to experiment with new display techniques that included prescribed viewing angles, proximities, and duration. Shot length and editing worked together to provide an ostensibly ideal or at least museum-sanctioned viewing time. The screen also rearticulated museum space. In the most literal sense, the film screen became a part of the museum's built environment. Permanently situated in a purpose-built space for audiences and for multiple modes of projection, the film screen added to the numerous ways in which museum space and display techniques transformed old things into significant objects, and turned people into museum visitors — and audiences — in the first half of the twentieth century. Films of museum space shown in the museum and beyond extended this architectural function of the screen by re-presenting long hallways, multiple galleries, and steep vertical walls. Museum films and screens then provided a method by which sizable museum spaces and often cluttered display techniques appeared in repeatable and standardized language providing a particular viewing scale.

Anne Friedberg writes about the intimate relation between screen and window, suggesting that both transform the materialities of built space, creating

The Great Hall in the Metropolitan Museum of Art, photographed February 1926. Image copyright © The Metropolitan Museum of Art / Art Resource, New York.

a "delimited virtuality," an opening of space outward to a particular world be-yond.[9] At the Met, the film screen certainly served this function. Yet, in the context of an exhibition space that can only be understood as itself an expan-sive articulation of the virtual (making the past present through five thousand years of art displayed across two million square feet) the museum screen also served as a diminutive view inward, a miniaturized virtuality in concentrated form.[10] Individual films directed the view through this new looking glass, making the vast whole of the museum into smaller more manageable vectors of sight. Filling this screen with museum-designed content, the Met's films — shrunken, two-dimensional, glowing in the dark, ten, twenty, or thirty minutes long — offered *a particular viewing speed* as well as a unique scale by *which to see the museum and its objects differently*. Thus, through examining this particu-lar case study, this chapter shows that film was used by the museum to further its institutional goals, within and beyond its walls, by providing an unusual and specific manifestation of cinema that helped to refashion both museum and art in a more manageable scale. That is, film helped the museum to offer a smaller, simpler, slower version of itself in a standardized, reproducible form, enabling the timeless museum to operate in a more timely, spatially efficient, and optically tidy fashion; the cultural authority of the museum was fortified by a technological network and the comparative precision of moving images and screens. To borrow from Tony Bennett's work, film served as a method by which the museum could extend its "exhibitionary complex," using cinema to render its art more comprehensible and its publics more visible, not just as edified and well-behaved museum visitors but now also as an ever expanding assemblage of film audiences, gathered inside and outside of the museum.[11] Both art and the museum public were being extended and reframed, transformed by a collaboration between an authoritative institution and a very particular use of cinema.

MUSEUMS AND THE AMBIVALENCE OF MOTION

We have much to learn by examining the interface between these two prominent institutions of visuality, museum and cinema. This is particularly true given that the museum clearly served as a site for multiple articulations of cinema that were reasonably distinct from the well-established conventions of the American film industry at the time. As recent work in film studies has shown, by linking cinema to other forms of movement and other modes of temporality, we can observe the ways in which the moving image reflected and refracted a moving world.[12] But what specifically does the modern trope of movement mean for an ostensibly static space like the museum? By the 1920s, the motionless nature of museum space was increasingly seen by museum reformers as a problem. In other words, as the universal survey museum became a fixture in the American cultural scene, and the hierarchies of class and taste that it promulgated became solidified, the very *still* aspects of its art and architecture were seen as an impediment to engaging a larger public immersed in a world of moving pictures and things. In short, the museum's efforts to invoke a static timelessness were seen as a symptom of both its elitism and its aversion to public engagement.[13] As the historian Neil Harris has written, during the early part of the twentieth century, museums competed successfully with other urban attractions, world's fairs, and department stores as authoritative articulations of the newest and most appealing modes of visual display. By the 1920s, however, museums had become subjected to a deeper ambivalence because of their reluctance to further adapt to the mediated modes of display and dissemination transforming American culture. These critiques appeared in middlebrow literature and urban newspapers. While some commentators celebrated the museum's efforts to appeal to "the living," just as many decried the museum's utter failure to keep pace.[14] Radio, cinema, advertising, and department stores all seemed more vital and accessible modes.

The idea of a mobile museum became familiar during this period. Popular and specialist discourses invoked the image of a museum set in motion by technology. For instance, one journalist for the *New York Times* imagined that by using "special railway trains" museums would soon "ramble over whole states."[15] The train here became a museum technology, albeit an imagined one, making the physical site of the museum incidental to the way people would some day encounter museum objects and spaces. This idea of a dispersed museum set in motion was forwarded to different ends. On the one hand, left-leaning cultural reformers sought to demystify the museum, to dissemble its sacred shrine, and to spread its art everywhere in service of a democratic educational mission.[16] On the other hand, more conservative reformers sought to carefully navigate the new world of moving museums, anxious to ensure appropriate content, respectable form, and desired influence within the new motion-bound ideal.

As a sizable and formidable institution, the Met occupied a range of positions on this spectrum. The museum's Education Department housed moderate reformers, who then operated as subordinates to the prized departments, curators, and connoisseurs working elsewhere in the museum. Thus, as the ideal of the museum diversified, and criticism of its display techniques and elitism mounted, the Met began gradually and cautiously to adapt elements of its curatorial efforts and display techniques, particularly those generated by the Education Department. These efforts resulted in an augmentation of the museum's physical structures as educators accelerated efforts to circulate its art and its lessons. During the 1920s, the Met used not just photography, lithography, and lantern slides (long an element of museum programming) but also newspapers, magazines, radio, and film in order to spread the museum's images and words. The Education Department also worked in collaboration with local department stores, offering classes to clerks to improve their role as tastemakers; the museum also lent art and objects for retail displays.[17] The Met's status as one of the most prestigious American art museums was rewarded with sizable annual attendance that by the mid-1920s was well over a million visitors per year. In addition, the number of those exposed to its art and its discourses about art increased significantly when considering the growth of the museum's presence across and through these other largely ephemeral media forms.[18]

MUSEUM FATIGUE

At one level the museum was structurally more nimble, with its art appearing and then disappearing in disposable dailies and weaving across airwaves. Yet, there remained a broadly based and substantial discussion about how to make sense of motion *within* the museum. Artists of the period, particularly members of the avant-garde who critiqued *institutions of art* as much as they disrupted traditional ideas about form, began asserting new models for art exhibition. Such models also grew naturally from the need to display works generated from expanded art practices. Multimedia art entailed new ideas about exhibition; installation-based work and experiments with site-specificity became more common. Viewer engagement, for some, became a constitutive aspect of the art object. Experiments throughout the 1920s, 1930s, and 1940s by Frederick Kiesler, Moholy-Nagy, Herbert Bayer, El Lissitzky, and others refashioned exhibition design to incorporate the kinetic, the quick view, and chance into the experience of curated art, integrating elements of the urban spaces and media forms that undergirded so much avant-garde work during the period.

Mary Anne Staniszewski suggests that Frederick Kiesler's experiments inspired many of these exercises.[19] In 1924 he proposed to exhibit art on freestanding display units using vertical and horizontal beams that were adjustable. Such a system (known as the "L and T") broke up the space of the conventional four-walled, right-angled gallery, allowing art to be cantilevered and moved in relation to the plane of the wall and in relation to other art.[20] Many of these installation designs incorporated photography, film, and art reproductions, important because these forms allowed further fracture of singular perspective and also enjoined apposite and cognate plays with scale. Photographs were used to display objects enlarged from their normal state; or photographs themselves were blown up, dwarfing more conventionally sized art. Some hung from the ceiling to be seen from below or were placed on the floor to be seen from above, playing deliberately on expectations governing the proximity and angle of viewer to thing viewed.

Several years after his initial "L and T" provocations, Kiesler designed four galleries for Peggy Guggenheim in New York. One of these four galleries was

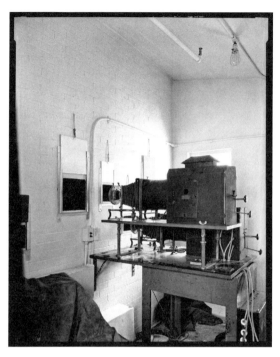

Moving Picture Projection Room in the Lecture Hall, Metropolitan Museum of Art, photographed September 1923. Image copyright © The Metropolitan Museum of Art / Art Resource, New York.

a library where visitors could consult books and examine reproductions. The other three overtly broke up gallery space by combining surrealist and dadaist practices creating dreamlike environments that employed automatic devices, intermittent lighting, and sound effects.[21] These galleries embodied the ideals of mobile and flexible art display, combining the movement of art and viewer with plays on scale in an overt and integrated fashion. Kiesler's "Abstract Gallery" featured art suspended by ribbons that could be moved, rotated, or otherwise manipulated by the viewer. The "Surrealist Gallery" featured movable furniture, curved walls, and spotlights that went on and off every several seconds. The sound of a train's engines added intermittent ambient noise. The "Kinetic Gallery," named and designed as the most literal incorporation of movement into installation design, included two particularly compelling provocations. First, a machine allowed for the automated display of seven small, reproduced works by Paul Klee using a conveyor belt. When broken, an invisible beam of light triggered the belt into motion; a push-button paused the device, allowing the visitor to view a selected piece for a longer period of time.[22] Second, a tiny peephole beckoned gallery-goers to look while turning a large oversized ship-like wheel. Through this peephole appeared fourteen reproductions from Marcel Duchamp's expansive *La Boîte-en-Valise*, itself a series of miniaturized museums, featuring shrunken reproductions of Duchamp's oeuvre, displayed in portable boxes with handles.[23]

In such installation experiments, art appeared throughout a now malleable gallery. Images unimpeded by frames moved at various locations throughout a room, appearing and reappearing in slightly different positions, sometimes altering the viewer's footpath or even body position, ostensibly setting in motion the associations available between and among artworks. Active chance and random connections across the many pieces perpetually rearticulated the spaces of art; the viewer's presence supplied a unique catalyst as each view, each path through the mobilized space ideally yielded a new, embodied, temporally bound encounter.[24] Meaning too was theoretically set in motion, unmoored from the singular and the still, and re-formed in a persistently moving constellation of brush strokes, forms, and frames (absent and not). The working idea was to break out of the static, two-dimensional wall of the museum and to energize the spaces of art by calling attention to the mobile and kinetic possibilities entailed by the encounter between viewer and art object, allowing for montage-like associations and an ever evasive instantaneity to constitute the meaning and experience of art. Plays of scale were crucial for these provocations. Larger geometrically straight gallery spaces broke into multiply sized and multiply angled planes that expanded and contracted in variable fashion using light, moveable art, sound, and mobile viewers. In some instances, the gallery shrunk to the size of a peephole. In others, such as many of the Bauhaus installations, viewers looked skyward to large photographs mounted on the ceiling, or downward from above at the floor, emulating the aerial view. Big art and small art vied for attention in gallery spaces that themselves gestured toward a sliding spatial and temporal scale. Dynamics of scale were a constitutive component of efforts to energize and activate the spectator in a paradigmatically new kind of art and exhibition space.[25]

If avant-gardist provocations against the museum resonate with some of cinema's own—offering technologically reproducible and seemingly infinite plays with stable framing and points of view—the American art museum adopted a more cautious and disciplined approach to film and the question of motion and meaning it inevitably imported. To be sure, efforts to understand and direct movement inside the museum became an enduring element of American museum reform. This controlled movement, however, had less to do with experiments in hanging its Rembrandts across clotheslines, or nurturing the distracted and wandering spectator, and much more to do with directing the movement of people and especially directing their eyes. In other words, select museums began focusing on how *people* moved through museum spaces, and thus examining how museum-goers looked at—or more precisely how long they looked at—displayed art. Thus, the provocations that mechanically reproduced images and sounds offered the avant-garde became part of a wholly different display strategy at the Met, and at the American art museum in general. Museum educators did not use moving images to reimagine and reinvigorate the whole of its spaces. Rather, films and screens were spatially confined to the auditorium—where they would stay for decades— such that cinema's stationary seating and singular immobile screen provided a controlled and safe opportunity to experiment with new display techniques. The museum's in-house concession to the moving image thus remained marginal, maintaining the sanctity of its grand halls and endless galleries.

This relegation of cinema to the museum's auditorium takes on fuller meaning in the context of other shifts in museum culture of the period. One contemporary element of museum reform was shaped by the social sciences, and experimental psychology in particular. Beginning in 1928, and with a slew of studies following in the 1930s, Edward S. Robinson, a professor of psychology at Yale, published a report entitled "The Behavior of the Museum Visitor."[26] Sponsored by the American Museum Association, and endowed with funds from the Carnegie Foundation, Robinson oversaw a study of museum visitors at four unnamed museums in the New York–Philadelphia corridor. Resonating strangely with researchers of time-motion studies who were seeking to make factory workers and housewives more efficient, Robinson and his researchers, armed with stopwatches and notebooks, observed museum visitors throughout their visits to the selected museums. They made their observations on days of free admission because, they reasoned, this facilitated discrete record taking of "casual visitors" rather than educated ones, sustaining the distinction between the museum's devoted and serious public and the general one.[27] Each researcher would choose an unaccompanied adult and follow him or her as he or she moved from room to room and painting to painting. As the visitor did so, the researcher discreetly measured and recorded how much time he or she spent looking at each piece of art. Much to the dismay of those who cherished the ideal museum-goer as a committed and contemplative type, results indicated that the average museum-goer looked at the average piece of art for about three seconds.[28]

Anxiety about attention, in this instance the attention of the museum visitor, is echoed throughout writing that wrestles with the question of how to

Lecture Hall, Screen View, Metropolitan Museum of Art, photographed 1919. Wing E, Room 100. Image copyright © The Metropolitan Museum of Art / Art Resource, New York.

Lecture Hall, Metropolitan Museum of Art, showing seating and apertures into projecting room, photographed 1923. Image copyright © The Metropolitan Museum of Art / Art Resource, New York.

make sense of modernity's flurry of sensory stimulation, as well as of the new forms of subjectivity, perception, and sometimes pathology these conditions enabled.[29] Museum officials too sought to categorize the unique modern experience of the magnitude and density of museum exhibitions. During the late 1910s and frequently during the 1920s, "museum fatigue" served as a catch-all phrase that indexed a kind of sensory overload or exhaustion, described variously as emotional, physical, and intellectual. Museums simply overwhelmed most people by offering too many objects in a vast disorienting environment. Put differently, the scale of the average viewer to things viewed was disproportionate, compromising the ideal museum experience.

Robinson's stopwatch study confirmed museum fatigue and the barriers it posed to the museum's mission. With his findings, he supported a common-sense assumption held by museum workers that there was a clear division between educated, purposeful, and attentive visitors and those disoriented, inattentive, and unknowledgeable wanderers.[30] Museums — especially science museums — responded to museum fatigue by devising ways to better orient and guide the visitor. This included experimenting with new and adjustable electric lighting mechanisms, new display cases, and "satisfying vistas and restful retreats," which were simply places where people could sit.[31] Some new museums countered museum fatigue by lowering ceilings to eliminate the "eye strain" of looking upward, softening lighting to eliminate glare, and replacing hardwood floors with rubber and linoleum to help the feet and legs.[32]

One of the other common responses to the condition of museum fatigue was to argue that the museum-goer could only alleviate her symptoms by better training her eye to see museum displays more efficiently and thus properly. For museum professionals committed to maintaining the museum's authority and effectiveness, museum fatigue was also caused by the undisciplined eye, the eye that was always darting about from object to object — this wandering irrational eye being in a sense the very eye embraced by the avant-garde.[33] One museum in Dayton, Ohio described its new modern theater with state-of-the-art projection facilities as key in its strategy to combat museum fatigue; it allowed museum-goers to relieve their tired feet and to watch less taxing visual forms on screen. In short, cinema (and other staged forms of presentation) provided a reprieve from the overwhelming demands — physical and perceptual — made by the museum and its contents.[34] Films ostensibly calmed the harried eye with a clear line of sight to a plainly displayed object, deciding for the viewer where to look (steady and straight ahead) and for how long. The wandering eye and wandering museum-goer, conceived as a problem, found their cure in this useful form of museum cinema.

While the idea that the museum overstimulated visitors applies to patrons of both art and science museums, the condition of museum fatigue did pose problems that were specific to the art museum. The Met, and other such institutions, had been slowly moving away from the salon-style of hanging paintings, a style in which paintings hung according to size, shape, and the whims of the connoisseur, often filling walls left to right, top to bottom. Paintings that spanned hundreds of years, styles, and subjects, might all share space on the same wall or in the same room. Increasingly throughout this period, more rational classification schemes became prominent, dictating that paintings should be hung by chronology or geography (and eventually by formal attributes, schools, or movements), in a manner that allowed logical connection to be observed from painting to painting. Nevertheless, responding to museum fatigue remained a certain kind of challenge to the Met. While newer museums worked to accommodate visitor comfort from the design stage forward, the Met remained one of the oldest and the largest museums in the country, burdened in this respect by its stubbornly large proportions. Furthermore, classifying art by new and more rational criteria and then adapting display techniques that reflected these classifications clashed with the fact that wealthy collectors who had donated many of the institution's objects often required that their objects stay together. At times, display logic remained beholden to a patron's individual taste or habits of acquisition. The more modern criteria for displaying art, which included single works mounted in clear isolation from others — a style of exhibition that would dominate at the Museum of Modern Art, New York (MOMA) during the 1930s — arrived much slower to the Met. Nonetheless, the trend in American art museums was toward eliminating what some critics called the problem of "art clutter."

FILM AT THE MET

As I have argued elsewhere, the film program at the Met can be understood as one response to a visual culture that was increasingly conceptualized as a threat to the museum's mission.[35] Using film in a very particular and controlled way, as a part of a new display strategy, was an explicit attempt to conscript cinema to the imperatives of the museum, to make cinema useful to the project of engaging museum-goers in the importance of the institution's art. Huger Elliot, the head of museum education during this period, explicitly attacked commercial films and movie theaters in his advocacy of this new form of museum programming.[36] As opposed to those crass Hollywood melodramas, these were movies that were good for museum-goers to watch, confirming the moral imperative of the museum to sanction some kinds of cultural activity over others.

The use of films and screens at the Met grew in the context of the dialogue about museum fatigue and changing modes of display. Films simplified and ordered museum art and exhibitions, providing relief to the exhausted museum visitor. While individual films achieved this in distinct ways, all the films in one way or another can be understood by resort to this claim. Take for example films that were explicitly designed to re-present museum collections *in situ*, that is, films that showed museum objects as displayed in the museum habitat. One such film, the Met's tour of its American Wing, highlighted housing design and interior decoration as arranged chronologically by curators in its exhibition halls. A prominent feature of the museum, the American Wing opened in 1924 to much national acclaim, particularly in popular media and women's magazines.[37] The forty-five-minute film surveyed the halls of the wing in chronological order, emphasizing pertinent furniture and tapestry details, using close-ups and long-takes to punctuate and dramatize them. Armoire and armchair participated in narratives of patriotic assent. The film is structured chronologically, moving steadily forward through different phases of American art and design. The presentation of each gallery begins with a slow pan that serves as an establishing shot; select objects then appear in isolation and close-up. Such inserts functionally enlarged and emphasized objects in order to provide opportunities for more studied perusal; some items were placed on a revolving stand in order to allow for examination from all angles. Rotating in their often magnified state, select items such as chocolate pots or tea kettles acquired a larger role in the exhibit's loose historical and nationalist narrative. Furniture appeared whole as well as in detailed close-ups; kitchen tools and flower vases were shown stretched to several times their original size. Put simply, even though the objects ranged in physical size from several inches to ten feet, their framing and thus appearance on screen had the effect of transforming differences in size into the standardized frame of screen size. All items were center framed and shown in proportion commensurate with the didactic function laid out by the intertitle, respecting the limits of the film frame and thus screen.

The slow movement of the camera offered a steady panoramic view of period rooms. A stationary camera recorded individual objects. Still or moving, these images provided a new kind of mechanical museum view: not too fast so as to irretrievably transform the objects or distress the spectator, but not too slow as to simply emulate the static museum space. The camera here replaced the movement of a head or the motion of a crowd, becoming curator and tour guide, providing a distinct kind of museological gaze and rendering quite differently the static objects that (at least) some could just as easily see with their own eyes, at their own pace, down the hall.[38] Shot length declared the significance of each mechanically divined *objet*, exercising a slow and steady curatorial hand, working to focus the eye and alleviate the anxiety of art overload.

The ability of film to play with the scale of found objects created another dynamic to museum display, speeding up, slowing down, setting in motion, enlarging, and shrinking an endless assortment of objects into the new display window. These qualities shaped a contemporaneous discussion about how to make films useful to museums. Commentators wondered about how to create adequate interest and sustain attention, never assuming that just because something appeared on a film screen that the job of education and appreciation was done. Museum staff deemed short narrative films efficient and appealing organizational tools to "sustain attention as the more or less technical facts are unfolded."[39] Some of the museum's films pushed the limits of the fledging visual experiment by introducing elements of narrative fantasy, which augmented the didactic use of scale to help museum spectators more fully understand the smaller bits in relation to the larger whole. In *A Visit to the Armor Galleries of the Metropolitan Museum of Art*, viewers engaged in slow tours of chain mail and gothic plate armor displayed on walls and in cases. Similar to *The American Wing*, this film provided a slow moving view to the galleries, with single objects isolated for more detailed exegesis. Yet, the straightforward didacticism of these segments was augmented by adding fantastical journeys. This visit to the armor gallery, for instance, included meeting an ambitious knight who "comes to life by the light of the moon." The intrepid knight wanders out of his display case, through the museum, and out into the world. While on his journey he encounters an enemy. A duel ensues with Central Park as the backdrop. The knight makes quick business of his challenger and then promptly returns to his case just in time to be used as an object lesson in the mechanics and design of his armored suit by a museum docent. A knight's suit is then broken apart by a series of close-ups on chain mail, leg and thigh armor, helmet, and bodice, with intertitles explaining the function or providing details about each. The intrepid knight is dissected for your viewing pleasure.

This recasting of the museum's exhibitionary drama reinforced a certain density to the museum's visual fabric. Films became a tactic in an ever expanding museum strategy: new technologies used to stabilize old viewing regimes. While asserting control over how at least some of its exhibitions would be seen (very few films featured paintings, for instance), the Met multiplied its film screens and also extended previous display techniques, providing a different kind of venue for the vast views that formed the basis of the museum's spatial majesty, offering short films that featured five-, ten-, and twenty-second fragments instead. And, to be sure, compared to the three-second rapid view of the museum-goer observed by Robinson, museum films functionally slowed the museum-goer down, weaving steady shots of single (but sometimes multiple) items, ranging from five to fifteen seconds on average, formed into a new whole through editing and made newly digestible by their standardized size, static frame, comparatively long takes, and short overall length. Such techniques of visual display served to effectively address not simply a more *attentive* museum-goer but a more *retentive* one, that is, a museum-goer who ostensibly learned more. Lastly, watching films got people off of their feet and into a seat, a physical comfort that was hoped would focus the mind.

Within this idea of the art museum's increasingly dense visual field was more than a multiplication of views to selected art objects it held and exhibited. Equally important is that these new museum display techniques also reproduced particular views of the museum itself, setting these views in motion, with particular spatial and temporal sequencing. Yet, each film did so in reasonably distinct ways. *The American Wing* was a highly didactic, chronologically arranged inventory of items in the exhibit hall, with brief intertitles announcing the period or pedigree of what was coming next. It presented in highly ordered, rational terms an exhibit that was itself highly ordered and rational. Indeed, it would be easy to mistake this for an inventory film, or a film that was more a utilitarian record than curatorial flourish. Yet, to be sure, these films implicate subtly the museum and its contents in a wide range of popular discourses forwarded contemporaneously by other media. In the case of *The American Wing*, there are clear links to women's magazines and home decor, and also to ideals of domesticity and patriotism. In the case of our brave knight, there is a self-conscious attempt to index a range of educational but also fantasy and adventure genres. Yet, the potential excesses of these genres are largely contained by the heavy-handed didacticism that frames each film.

Further, the interest in new incarnations of reasonably familiar technologies, films being familiar and museum movie theaters and cinematic museum views being reasonably new, is here made concrete by our fragmented knight's magical resurrection and by slow camera pans of old furniture, whose aesthetic appeal is difficult to recreate out of context. Yet, the act of the museum turning the camera's gaze upon itself, transforming the displayed objects and venerated halls into two-dimensional, black and white, silent, small and portable moving images proved sufficiently compelling to authorize a new genre of film: the museum film — as well as a new use for cinema — offering a museum in a can, a museum that alleviated museum fatigue by *instructing* the eye and also *relieving* the eye with a newly simplified screened environment.

Perhaps most interesting of all for the question of how the museum was making use of film and forging a new mode *for its own visibility* is a film entitled *Behind the Scenes at the Museum*. This film presents the inner workings of the institution with a kind of privileged front-stage/back-stage structure. Museum workers punch clocks, don aprons, and tend to the inner machinations of the museum's public displays. The museum becomes a place of rationalized and methodical work. In other words, this film spends less time on Persian pottery and Roman statuary and more time on the other sorts of operations the museum undertakes that have nothing to do with its art per se: the inventory and cataloguing department, the photography and film divisions, and the publicity division. Paramount within the rhetoric of the film is the need of the museum to configure itself as a bustling hive of activity, fully engaged with the latest technologies of dissemination and display — as a place where relevant, efficiently managed things are always happening. In this respect, the museum was making itself visible to its public by extending its mannered and authoritative exhibitionary impulses, linking the inner workings of the museum to the motion of the camera, the circulation of photographs, and the pulse of the press. This controlled and particular exhibitionary impulse includes the newness of the specific display techniques that brokered this view. That is to suggest that new and old display techniques worked together harmoniously here, furthering a particularly modern technological view to old art and ostensibly timeless spaces.

Specifically, each of these museum films entirely avoids the problem of art clutter, emphasizing instead ordered operations and controlled, slow views of still but ostensibly overwhelming art.[40] The films also avoid the problem of other museum patrons, who are almost entirely absent from these museum scenes. In sum, while museum administrators understood that the museum

must adapt to the moving pleasures of a moving world, they worked to develop a form of cinema—the short, slow film—that satisfied the needs of
the institution. The film screen, understood as irretrievably tethered to sym-
metrically arranged, forward-positioned, stationary seating in a theater-like
environment fortified the museum's long function as a site of congregation,
not only as a site of individualized wanderers. Cinema became a technology
for corralling museum visitors into an audience. The museum's use of moving image technology also further confirmed the impulse to make films *useful*
within the context of an institution whose modes of display were deemed
dated, static, and overwhelming but whose leadership was largely resistant to
radical revisioning of museum space; film was banished from the Met's galleries for decades.[41]

CONCLUSION: NEW INSTITUTIONS OF ART

The Met stopped making films in 1935, but continued to show those films, and
films made by others, in its auditorium and beyond. In general, films at art
museums became increasingly commonplace. By 1932 a survey conducted by
Marion Miller (incidentally an educator at the Met) for the Progressive Education Association indicated that roughly 25 percent of American museums
had active film programs.[42] A similar survey conducted several years later confirmed the growing presence not just of films but of projectors and dedicated
screens.[43] Some seventy-five years later, moving images are now integral to
museum operation, gallery spaces, and even the most basic idea of the museum.[44] Specialty television stations, DVD tours, and endless YouTube entries
ensure that the Met and other art museums continue to adapt and be adapted
by moving images large and small, professional and amateur, spatially specific
and decidedly wandering. Such screens ensure a kind of everyday quality to
museum movies, despite the enduring majesty of actual museum space. The
contemporary museum is a compelling site for studying the complicated relationship between representational and built space, each interdependent on
the other for its vitality, each multiply mediated and ever expansive.

   The history I have outlined here helps us to understand an earlier iteration
of the art museum and its relationship to moving images. The idea of the didactic, public display of art in a museum has long complicated the simple view
of the museum as a mausoleum. The Met's use of film is but one symptom of
this, indicating the museum's continuing struggles to respond to changing
visual technologies and also to evolving public expectations of engagement

that were being transformed by popular leisure and other modes of visual culture. Shown within the museum's walls, as well as beyond them, the Met's short films worked to refigure the space and time of the museum as well. These films, exhibited to a seated audience, promised to alleviate the demands on the museum-goer of the lengthy trek down palatial museum halls or the disordered wandering the elaborate architecture of the museum allowed. They helped to order the proliferating assemblage of things, directing the eye to one particular object, for a predetermined amount of time, in a mechanized viewing frame. They instructed the spectator to look at significant fragments of specific objects rather than be overwhelmed by the comparatively vast museum whole. At the Met in the 1920s and 1930s, film was a safe respite from and appealing alternative to what we might call the attractions of the museum.

So, what does this new mechanical gaze at the museum tell us specifically about useful cinema at the Met? From this case study, we can see that scale is a relational concept. There can be no idea of small without some comparable concept of what might constitute big; time cannot be understood as slow or brief without some contrasting idea about speed and duration. First and foremost, a close examination of a particular institutional context demonstrates the importance of understanding scale in cinema as a relative and therefore situational term, requiring consideration of the varied standards and measures attendant throughout film history as it is known, and as it is being discovered. Here I have suggested an expanded idea about what counts as film history, stretched to include other institutions that effected particular ideas about cinema's form and function. The category of the "short," "the small," and "the slow" takes on particular meaning in this context. The small screen, short length, and slowness of these films allowed cinema to become more useful to the spaces and temporalities of the museum. It allowed flexible programming, physical relief, and manageable modes or glimpses of art and objects that seemed otherwise unmanageable, particularly to cultural reformers eager to maximize the wider impact of museum exhibits. Thus, the very term "scale" invites us to think not just about the temporality of a film's whole and its parts, but also of its institutional frame. By this I mean to say that we might think of the film's scale (temporal and spatial) as not just a quality intrinsic to the image, or to institutions of cinema, but also as irretrievably tied to the other kinds of institutions and other scales of representation that inevitably interface with cinema and its component parts. That is, what informs our understanding of something as short or long, big or small, fast or slow is also tied to the structures and institutions that undergird the context of display and of watching, making cinema useful within integrated and complex networks of visuality.

The concept of the useful becomes more salient here when set in dialogue with the concept of scale. By scale I mean the sense of identifiable relations between like and unlike things. As Anna McCarthy has recently written, concepts of scale "enable conceptual movement between argument and evidence, generality and specificity, concreteness and abstraction."[45] In other words, by investigating a specific site and its changing representational practices, the concept of scale becomes a productive tool in seeking to understand the concrete specificity of the film screen, and its many contexts, as well as the abstract implications of its hybrid and ever evolving forms and functions (film at the museum and beyond). Scale also allows for considerations of size and speed (absolute or relative) across, within, and beyond the screened image. In other words, examining the question of scale allows us to explore the relationship between the sized screen and the aesthetic, ideological, social, material networks of which it is a part. The implications of this help to disarticulate the film screen from the film camera and in a sense the celluloid strip in order to think about screens as distinct elements in a range of visual apparatuses, and as a far more mobile and malleable element of "the cinema" than we usually tend to think of them. In the context of the Met, scale allows us to consider modes of visual presentation in specific and dialectical relation. Structurally we can see qualitatively different concerns being brought to bear both on the image and on the screened environment. In the end, these museum movies are but one chapter in the complicated history of moving images as screened cultural forms, inviting us to think about movies beyond the museum and everywhere else.

NOTES

1   Duncan and Wallach, "The Universal Survey Museum."
2   There are two standard histories of the Met. See Tompkins, *Merchants and Masterpieces*; and Howe, *A History of the Metropolitan Museum of Art, 1905–1941*.
3   The first screening of Met films appears to have been in October 1923 when the Department of Armor and the Department of Egyptian Art each respectively showed a film to the museum's trustees. These films were overseen and prepared under the direction of George Pratt, who was then the chairman of the recently established Committee on Cinema. The first film was about the museum's firearms, and the second an expedition film about the museum's excavation of Tutankhamen. In December 1925 screenings were opened to museum members; programs were arranged from at least

nine available titles. This same year, the Met began distributing and exhibiting films made by Yale University Press. The Chronicles of America Photoplays included fifteen films of a planned thirty-three. Each covered a topic in American history; titles included *Columbus* (1923), *The Pilgrims* (1924), *The Puritans* (1924), *Alexander Hamilton* (1924), and *The Frontier Woman* (1924), ("Cinema Films," *Bulletin of the Metropolitan Museum of Art* 20, no. 1 [1925], 2). Educational leaflets were also prepared and circulated with these films; all museums and museum members as well as schools were encouraged to rent them. See also "Historical Films Available," *Museum News* 20, no. 23 (1925), 3.

4   See "Showings of Motion Picture Films to Members," *Bulletin of the Metropolitan Museum of Art* 20, no. 12 (1925), 302.

5   Untitled, *Museum News* 23, no. 9 (1928), 222.

6   Such films included *A Visit to the Armor Galleries of the Metropolitan Museum of Art* (1922), *The American Wing* (1925), and *Behind the Scenes at the Museum* (1928); portions of other films featured images of museum workshops or galleries, including *Tapestries and How They Are Made* (1933), *The Hidden Talisman* (1928), *Firearms of Our Forefathers* (1923), and *The Gorgon's Head* (1925). These films ranged in length from fourteen to thirty minutes, with *The American Wing* the longest at forty-five minutes. The museum published a film catalogue in 1938 that lists the films it distributed as well as the conditions under which they were lent. See Metropolitan Museum of Art, *Cinema Films*.

7   These films were loaned without charge to public schools in New York City. For others, a fee of $5 for 35mm and $2.50 for 16mm per reel applied. Converted into 2008 dollars this equals approximately $82 and $41 respectively per reel. See Metropolitan Museum of Art, *Cinema Films*; some information about these films is also available in "The Chronicles of American Photoplays," *Bulletin of the Metropolitan Museum of Art* 20, no. 7 (1925), 186.

8   By the 1920s the use of film at museums was promising enough that the Akeley Camera company advertised in the professional literature for museum workers. The camera was sold as a way to enlist public interest and to illustrate lectures. The ad promoted it as something that "no museum can afford to further be without." See for instance "The Power of the Moving Picture" [advertisement] *Museum Work* 6, no. 6 (March–April 1924), 204. For more on the early use of film at American museums see Griffiths, *Wondrous Difference* and *Shivers Down Your Spine*. See also Scandiffio, "'Better'n Any Circus That Ever Come to Town'"; Staples, "Safari Adventure." For a contemporaneous case study in Canada see Jessup, "Moving Pictures and Costume Songs at the 1927 'Exhibition of Canadian West Coast Art, Native and Modern.'" For a study of museum practice that uses cinema as a cognate and contextual development, see Sandberg, *Living Pictures*.

9   For a fuller exploration of the idea of the film screen as window see Friedberg, *The Virtual Window*, especially chapters 3 and 4.

10   The outward gaze of the museum is made literal in its expedition films, which documented archeological digs and other such excavations. Such films by 1938 included *The Temples and Tombs of Egypt, The Daily Life of the Egyptian — Ancient and Modern,*

and *Digging into the Past*. Precise dates for these films are difficult but some of the footage used would date from as early as 1923. Also, films such as *The American Wing* largely focused on the furniture and domestic design objects displayed in galleries but also contained shots of domestic exteriors, something made difficult and often impossible by the physical impossibility of moving buildings or reconstructing multiple facades.

11 Bennett, "Useful Culture."

12 See, for instance, Doane, *The Emergence of Cinematic Time*; Gunning, "The Cinema of Attractions"; Rabinovitz, *For the Love of Pleasure*; and Charney and Schwartz, *Cinema and the Invention of Modern Life*.

13 The Met was inevitably named as a primary promulgator of the museum as a site of elite collection and overt display of wealth. The following is typical of left-leaning critics: "Instead of refracting the light of improved artistic standards into the practical affairs of their sprawling localities, they store the culture brought to them through leisure and wealth in the sterile salons of self-sufficient cliques." T. R. Adams (1939), quoted in Low, *The Museum as a Social Instrument*, 30.

14 Harris, "Museums, Merchandising and Popular Taste." Despite the importance of museums for establishing municipal status, even those at city hall espoused skepticism about museums and their elitism: see *Report on New York City Museums*, submitted to Mayor F. H. LaGuardia prepared by Robert Moses, March 1941 (New York Public Library).

15 Waldemar Kaempffert, "Vital Museums of the New Era," *New York Times*, March 20, 1932, SM12.

16 See, for instance, Dana, *The Gloom of the Museum*, 24–25; and Low, *The Museum as a Social Instrument*.

17 For more on the Met's relationship to consumer culture and media during this period, see Wasson, "Every Home an Art Museum." For a general discussion of the politics of these relations, see Duncan, "Museums and Department Stores."

18 Its educational "extensions programs" grew rapidly throughout the first quarter of the century and by 1925 there were as many as 3,427 loans made (more than 10 per business day), consisting of 115,954 individual items (*Annual Report to the Trustees*, the Metropolitan Museum of Art, 1925, 44). Ten years later these numbers had increased to 4,369 and 179,239—an average of 13 loans per day, representing an increase of almost 30 percent (*Annual Report to the Trustees*, the Metropolitan Museum of Art, 1935, 51). These reports are available in the Metropolitan Museum of Art's Library.

19 See Staniszewski, *The Power of Display*, chapter 1.

20 Kiesler is well-known in film studies for his design of a modernist movie theater for the International Film Arts Guild in New York in 1929, which featured an adjustable screen (which he called "screen-o-scope") and a total elimination of the ornamentation that characterized other theatres of the period. For more on this, see McGuire, "A Movie House in Space and Time."

21 When asked why his lighting design was so complicated, Kiesler replied, "because

it's dynamic, it pulsates like your blood. Ordinary museum lighting makes painting dead" (quoted in Goodman, "Frederick Kiesler," 93).

22 Ibid., 94.

23 Ibid., 94; see also Staniszewski, *The Power of Display*, 22. *La Boîte-en-valise* was a miniaturized collection of Duchamp's works mounted in suitcases — portable museums — begun in 1935, and serialized over the next three decades to eventually exceed three hundred editions. For a fascinating discussion of the *Boîtes* in relation to Duchamp's flight from Paris and the general state of exiled artists and intellectuals, see Demos, *The Exiles of Marcel Duchamp*. All the art objects displayed in the Art of This Century exhibition were owned by Peggy Guggenheim; many of them had survived the German occupation of France and been shipped to the United States despite occupation. A catalogue for the show was published as Guggenheim, *Art of This Century*.

24 Staniszewski, *The Power of Display*, 26.

25 Though all of these efforts resonate with the inspiration of cinema, not all of them integrated film. There were, however, some such examples. For instance, Moholy-Nagy built a room called "The Room of our Time" (1930, Germany), in the center of which was a machine (*Light Machine*) that projected patterns of abstract light when a button was pressed. In this same room a double-glass screen was mounted where two films were to be shown, one a documentary and the other an abstract experimental film. It may be relevant to note that the film and slide projection equipment did not work properly and the room opened without them functioning (Staniszewski, *The Power of Display*, 22).

26 Robinson, *The Behavior of the Museum Visitor*. Robinson was a respected psychologist who went on to become the editor of the *American Journal of Psychology*. Even though his methods may seem moderately disturbing, he was in many ways a progressive reformer, arguing that museums must change with the times by responding to their publics. Robinson's study was predicated on a simple and basic assertion that in order to answer public interest and need, you must by some method come to know your public. He rejected the proposition that you could know your audience by divination or simply devout prejudice. He argued such things until his untimely death in February 1937. See for instance "Museum Advised to Lead Education," *New York Times*, May 13, 1936, 14.

27 Robinson, *The Behavior of the Museum Visitor*, 17.

28 "Stop-Watches Held on Museum Visitors," *New York Times*, October 9, 1927, 13. The museum in question sought to adapt to the perceived change in people's attention spans, which this study showed diminished throughout the visit. And, as a result of this study, a new model for museum curation emerged. The Philadelphia Museum of Art, under development at this time, was to be organized around a style intended to resemble that of a "main street," mimicking the urban stroll, allowing visitors to move leisurely through paintings and sculptures arranged in chronological order, making it easier for museum patrons to make sense of paintings quicker, without causing undue stress and enforcing the pressure to see everything. This was a kind

of synoptic view, a "historical pageant" of art, ostensibly made familiar because it resembled the experience of walking down a nicely ordered city street. This conceptualization of the street as a safe, familiar, and manageable space, easier to make sense of than the museum, presents an idea of the city that is counter to many of the contemporaneous ones that fashion the city as an environment of overwhelming stimulus suitable only to rapid montage and quick viewing.

29 Schivelbusch, *The Railway Journey*; Simmel, "The Metropolis and Mental Life"; and Crary, *Techniques of the Observer* and *Suspensions of Perception*.

30 Robinson, *The Behavior of the Museum Visitor*, 31–42. This study recognizes the vague and unspecified manner in which the term "fatigue" is used. Yet, the vague complex of conditions it indexes is nevertheless presumed to be troubling and "one of the most prominent of problems facing museum men [sic]" (31). On a related note, this study also determined that the median number of paintings that could be viewed before the effects of fatigue (diminished attention) set in was thirty-five (55).

31 Benches were an innovation in several newly designed museums during this period. See, for instance, "Dayton's Museum," *New York Times*, May 9, 1930, 129. For a fascinating attempt to attract and maintain attention that worked by the logic of isolating objects from all other stimuli, and providing comfortable seating and educational pamphlets, see Whiting, "Isolation of Museum Objects for Emphasis." Similarly, a redesign of the Brooklyn Museum in 1937 was reported to have resulted in the "best equipped, best arranged and pleasantest of our modern American museums; one that can demonstrate the virtually entire disappearance of the albatross, 'museum fatigue.'" Among the features working against this fatigue were organ recitals, radio broadcasts, folk dancing, and educational movies (Edward Alden Jewell, "Brooklyn's 'New' Museum," *New York Times*, October 10, 1937, 182).

32 "Buffalo Museum Combats Fatigue," *New York Times*, April 6, 1930, 144. Several smaller art museums opened during this period, including the Frick Museum, in New York, in 1935. Articles about the museum cited the museum's small size, carpeted floors, and air conditioning as sure-fire improvements to help avoid the "museum fatigue" encountered in many other museums ("Frick Art Museum Opened to Public," *New York Times*, December 17, 1935, 20). When the Whitney Museum, founded by Gertrude Vanderbilt Whitney, opened in 1931, the *New York Times* singled out the museum's "immediately established atmosphere of intimacy and charm" as a way to successfully alleviate the "dire malady" of "museum fatigue" ("Hoover Lauds Aims of Whitney Museum," *New York Times*, November 18, 1931, 21). Period rooms also ascended during the 1920s and 1930s, at least partly because it was believed that seeing objects in their "natural grouping" rather than on a plain background helped to alleviate "the usual fatigue to eye and body" ("Frequenters of Museums," *New York Times*, November 27, 1929, 19).

33 See, for instance, "Museum Fatigue," *Museum Work* 7, no. 1 (1924), 21–22. "Museum fatigue" became a general call for more museum education in general. See, for example, *Bulletin of the Metropolitan Museum of Art* 23, no. 9 (1928), 218–20, and "Art Museum Names Winlock Director," *New York Times*, January 19, 1932, 23.

34 The question of fatigue and gender was also important to the way that museum fatigue was discussed. One museum in Columbus, Ohio reported attempting to increase male patronage and to create more appealing ways to engender art appreciation. "Art smokers" were initiated wherein once a month an evening was set aside in which men were invited to the museum. As this new male patron entered the gallery he was given a pipe filled with "well selected" tobacco: "As he stretched himself out in the easy chairs that had been provided he found himself as comfortable as in his own club. While thus at ease, officials of the gallery or others discussed in the most informal fashion the current exhibition or matters of general art interest. They stressed the relation of art to business and home; art was elevated to masculine standing and understanding" ("Art Smokers for Business Men," *Museum Work* 6, no. 5 [1924], n.p.).

35 Wasson, "Every Home an Art Museum."

36 Elliot, "The Museum's Cinema Films," 216.

37 For instance, the *Ladies Home Journal* declared the wing proof that "Americans are a home-loving race" (Seal, "The American Wing of the Metropolitan Museum," 20).

38 "A New Museum Film," in "Notes," *Bulletin of the Metropolitan Museum of Art* 30, no. 7 (1935), 150.

39 C. R. R., "Editorial: Interpretive Museum Films," *Museum Work* 7, no. 2 (1924), 52. This editorial singled out the Met's film *Vasantasena* as a promising example of film experimentation. This film was made in collaboration with members of the Pratt Institute and was described in museum literature as telling "a tenth-century East Indian story" ("Cinema Films," *Bulletin of the Metropolitan Museum of Art* 20, no. 1 [1925], 2).

40 Museum officials clearly felt some need to justify their use of film within museum programming. In order to do so, they predictably preached their distaste for spectacular, commercial cinema, while they also conceded the medium's importance and "its place among recreational plans" of the people (George C. Pratt, quoted in "Dove and Donkey," *Time Magazine*, January 28, 1924). Museum movies were offered expressly as a correction to the commercial movie house. Huger Elliot, the head of Museum Education, declared in 1926 that "thousands of people are looking for motion pictures which have artistic, instructive, and entertaining value, but the average motion picture producer does not show such films. He has overlooked his latent public and has sought to please only those who enjoy the type of pictures now generally shown, with their cheap love scenes and impossible plots." They equally if defensively asserted that the "quiet contemplation of a thing of beauty" remained the keynote of aesthetic enjoyment (Elliot, "The Museum's Cinema Films," 216).

41 Other ideas emerged but did not become realized. For instance, a learning laboratory and theater was planned, which would invite museum-goers to choose a film upon entering, and to project the film more than once if need be, "to fix it more firmly in memory." The short film here was part of a repertory theater, sufficiently efficient in form and function to facilitate better mental retention in an otherwise crowded museum mentality ("Accessions and Notes," *Bulletin of the Metropolitan Museum of Art* 23, no. 9 [1928], 222).

42   Marion E. Miller, *Summary of Types of Education Work in the Museums of the Country* (February 1932), General Education Board Series 1; Subseries 2 Box 317 Folder 3313, Rockefeller Archive Center.

43   For more, see Robert Tyler David, *Educational Activities of Art Museums: An Analysis of Questionnaires Answered by 41 Art Museums in the United States, 1938*, General Education Board Series 1; Subseries 2 Box 320 Folder 3333, Rockefeller Archive Center, p. 52. This study also indicated that one of the primary reasons that more museums did not have more motion picture and other educational technology was lack of resources.

44   A full catalogue of available films was published as Metropolitan Museum of Art, *Cinema Films*.

45   McCarthy, "Cultural Studies and the Politics of Scale," 25.

PASTORAL EXHIBITION
THE YMCA MOTION PICTURE BUREAU AND THE
TRANSITION TO 16MM, 1928–39

Ronald Walter Greene

For one Italian communist, the Young Men's Christian Association (YMCA) was synonymous with America(nism). Antonio Gramsci assessed the role of the YMCA analogically: "America has Rotary and YMCA; Europe has free masonry and Jesuits."[1] While the YMCA had many national manifestations, Gramsci experienced the YMCA as an American institution, perhaps due to the Italian contacts established by the International Committee of North American YMCAs during World War I.[2] Just as the Industrial Department of the International Committee of the YMCA contracted with Rockefeller in the United States, representatives of the YMCA would join with Giovanni Agnelli, the head of Fiat, to bring the YMCA's services to the Italian factory floor. Gramsci remarks on the lack of rhetorical success and on opposition from the Catholic Church, but encourages his comrades to avoid smirking condescension. For Gramsci, the representatives of the YMCA were "professional, political, and ideological intermediaries" involved in "the biggest collective effort to date to create, with unprecedented speed, with a consciousness of purpose unmatched in history, a new type of worker and of man [sic]."³ The name Gramsci gave to this collective effort was Fordism, and while the success rate was uneven, the YMCA's role in crafting this modern subject was extensive.

Film had a role to play in this Fordist revolution. Beginning in the second decade of the twentieth century, the International Committee of the YMCA invested in the power of film by establishing the YMCA Motion Picture Bureau and Exhibits (MPB) as a branch of the Industrial Department between 1911 and 1914.⁴ The MPB was initially designed to leverage the popularity of movies for the purpose of promoting the YMCA's industrial welfare programs. This industrial welfare work took place at the point of production and contributed to its urban outreach. By the 1920s, the YMCA "had built 158 buildings devoted to special industries such as railroads, textile mills, and mining [and] they had established industrial extension work in over 143 cities throughout the United States."⁵ Educational programs in automobile repair, bricklaying, mechanical dentistry (making crowns and bridges), traffic management, and public speaking brought men and women into the local Y building. Similarly, as the Motion Picture Bureau transitioned into being, movies were identified as useful for attracting young men to the local YMCA. For example, by 1912, *Association Men*, the corporate journal of the YMCA secretary, was running advertisements for movies and projectors with the advice: "If the moving picture shows in your locality are drawing young men away from you, meet this competition by offering them better moving pictures in your association rooms."⁶ The Motion Picture Bureau would attempt to fill the need of the Y secretary by distributing "better movies." Moreover, it would increasingly encourage the exhibition of those movies beyond the YMCA's buildings in city and country, linking the Y secretary and movies to such well-known crucibles of modern subjectivity as factories, mines, lumber yards, schools, and parks.⁷

Film historians often note the importance of the YMCA for distributing and exhibiting films outside the typical pathways of classical Hollywood cinema. For example, Diane Waldman notes the YMCA's exhibition of ideologically conservative Hollywood genres and narratives at Rockefeller's Colorado Fuel and Iron Company.⁸ Furthermore, Steven Ross leaves no doubt as to the economic motives lurking in many of the "better movies" promoted by the YMCA: "the companies most active in crushing unions . . . were also the most aggressive in producing nontheatricals . . . shown at local YMCAS."⁹ In a radical idiom, the YMCA promoted a "class collaborationist" ideology in its industrial work. Yet, such an ideological indictment of the movies shown at any particular YMCA building leaves unaccounted the Motion Picture Bureau's role in establishing the infrastructure for a non-theatrical film culture.

By the end of the 1930s, according to Anthony Slide, "the YMCA position as a non theatrical film distributor was formidable" as the organization had reached as many as 26 million people, exposing them to a host of genres, including scenics, government productions, sponsored films, and educational, religious, and entertainment features.[10] The YMCA Motion Picture Bureau lasted nearly forty years before it severed its ties with the International Committee of the YMCA and became Association Films, Inc. The Motion Picture Bureau's history deserves closer investigation to appreciate the technological, economic, cultural, and ideological dimensions of non-theatrical cinema. Not only was the YMCA Motion Picture Bureau a central actor in the establishment of a non-theatrical film culture, its role as a distributor set the stage for the adoption of 16mm film in the non-theatrical domain *before World War II*. As Brian Winston has observed, "the final diffusion of the [16mm] gauge" would occur "between the 50s and the 70s."[11] But, as I will argue in this chapter, while its adoption of 16mm was not without false starts, the YMCA Motion Picture Bureau had established a viable 16mm infrastructure by the end of the 1930s.

In my previous work, I argued that the YMCA's use of (silent) film modernized pastoral power by supplementing the voice of the YMCA secretary.[12] For Foucault, pastoral power describes a relationship of governance among humans illustrated by the care of a shepherd for his (or her) flock.[13] A chief characteristic of pastoral power is its claim to the salvation of its flock; in more worldly language, its claim to do good, to protect and improve the well-being of those under the shepherd's care. Moreover, the modernization of pastoral power merges two tendencies, a desire to care for the individual and the population simultaneously. As such, a key modern solution to this pastoral task was the deployment of popular forms of education. The initial history of the YMCA Motion Picture Bureau within the YMCA's broader social welfare work in its Industrial Department harnessed film to this pastoral relationship. The silent film projected to an audience was to be accompanied by a Y secretary ready to care for the needs of an individual soul. While the Y's early exhibition of 35mm was to be done in the presence of a Y secretary, the YMCA Motion Picture Bureau's transition to 16mm took place within a more expansive moral constellation of religious, educational, and civic organizations.

A few key points are noteworthy during this period of technological transition to 16mm. First, the pastoral educational relationships traversing non-theatrical film culture encouraged the use of silent movies. The reasons for the staying power of silent cinema in non-theatrical exhibition were multifaceted, but this chapter will argue that film's mediation of the pastoral arrangement between a cultural authority and his or her audience formed one such reason. Second, this chapter will claim that the modernization of pastoral power expressed by the YMCA's involvement with other moral authorities during the 1930s is an important social factor enabling and, at times, constraining the diffusion of 16mm. The YMCA Motion Picture Bureau did more than distribute films, it also nurtured a preferred mode of exhibition, which I call pastoral exhibition. The defining characteristic of pastoral exhibition is the role of the cultural authority as a moral mediator regulating the encounter between audiences and movies. The articulation of this pastoral mode of exhibition was partly accomplished by the technological and textual forms of film and, as such, pastoral exhibition appears as a crucial context disassembled and reassembled by the technological invention and diffusion of 16mm.

NON-THEATRICAL CINEMA AND THE CULTIVATION OF PASTORAL EXHIBITION

The emergence of "classical Hollywood cinema" describes a key feature of film culture from roughly 1917 until the 1960s. As a theoretical concept, classical Hollywood cinema explains a deep structure underwriting the making of feature film narratives, a technological apparatus, and the ability of Hollywood to create vertical monopolies controlling the production, distribution, and exhibition of films.[14] To explore film culture from this Hollywood-centered perspective can, unintentionally, limit our understanding of movies to the uses designed for theatrical exhibition. For example, James Hay notes how focusing on the school as an exhibition site calls for a different take on genre studies:

> By focusing primarily upon the narrative conventions and production codes of Hollywood filmmaking, and by generalizing the site of cinema (as movie theater), genre criticism not only has privileged a particular kind of film (the feature-length film) but also has been particularly ill-prepared to consider the significance of the classroom film both in its relation to schooling, as a deeply institutionalized knowledge integral to the shaping of citizens, and in its relation to other sites where cinema and youth intersected and where schooling became part of broad social arrangement.[15]

In the 1920s alternative spaces of exhibition like the school, the church, and the Y building provided non-theatrical cinema with its geographical difference from classical Hollywood's theatrical preference for turning sites of exhibition into movie palaces. The YMCA Motion Picture Bureau increasingly cultivated these non-theatrical sites of exhibition as they aligned with producers, technology companies, churches, and other exhibitors to constitute a moral, economic, and educational interest in non-theatricals. For example, in 1923, George Zehrung, who was the director of the YMCA Motion Picture Bureau between 1918 and 1944, nurtured and protected the market for non-theatrical cinema by joining forces with the likes of William R. Kelly, the vice-president of Pictorial Clubs, Inc.; Arthur James, the director of Christian Herald Non-theatrical Pictures; Edward P. Earl, the president of the Nicholas Power Company; and F. S. Wythe of Wythe Educational Pictures to write the constitution of the "Motion Picture Chamber of Commerce of America (for non-theatrical films)."[16] As the *New York Times* reported in the winter of 1923, at the founding of the Motion Picture Chamber of Commerce, "at least twenty-five church and other organizations were present," including the YMCA, the Masons, and the Knights of Columbus.[17] While the Motion Picture Chamber of Commerce of America "desired to work in harmony with the motion picture industry and theatres, and was devoid of the slightest desire to form a censorship of pictures or do anything that would seek reforms in motion picture production" it was also aware how Hollywood might impinge on its interests.[18] Thus, its charter declared its commitment to "further all legitimate non-theatrical motion picture interests" and defined its primary purpose as "legislation that would not restrict the use of the motion picture apparatus exclusively to the theatres."[19] Its concern was motivated by the effort of Hollywood to establish its vertical integration through techniques like block-booking and exclusive rights to the first run of movies. Unlike some of its allies, such as the independent Motion Picture Theatre Owners of America, the Motion Picture Chamber of Commerce attempted to steer clear of an outright fight with the Motion Picture Producers and Distributors Association of America and the likes of the Famous Players-Lasky Corporation. Yet, the emergence of a non-theatrical market allowed for a reconfiguration of corporate, political, moral, and educational interests alongside and, at times, in opposition to the vertical and horizontal consolidation of classical Hollywood.[20]

As Haidee Wasson argues, non-theatrical cinema is concerned with more than finding different places for watching movies. It is also about the ways in which audiences are cultivated to watch movies, and the different technologies that mediate the exhibition of film.[21] Regarding the cultivation of the audiences, the YMCA Motion Picture Bureau committed early to the use of movies for educational purposes. As early as the 1910s, representatives of the YMCA began to persuade each other that movies would be an effective mode of instruction. Writing in the *Association Seminar*, H. E. Dodge advocated the exhibition of movies at the Y building for religious education by claiming, "With the motion picture as an educator, instruction will be received not only thus through the ear gate but the eye gate as well, and thus be more effective and lasting in every way."[22] The YMCA's initial interest in religious education put the YMCA in conversations with those Protestants committed to what Terry Lindvall calls "sanctuary cinema": a concerted effort to use movies to promote the religious and social work of churches.[23] George J. Zehrung, before taking the reigns of the Motion Picture Bureau, was a teacher for thirteen years. Featured in the *National Board of Review Magazine* in 1931, Zehrung recalled how he came to the conviction that film offered educational value:

> Eighteen years ago I had my first experience with motion pictures as a visual aid. One of my boys had been given a projector head, which had been discarded by a nearby theater, and he had constructed his own carbon lamp house and magazines. We used this machine after school hours. Subjects concerning metals, wood, leather, paper, etc., were obtained through the aid of the motion picture operator of the theater. Our experiment was of short duration as the supply of films was soon exhausted, but it left no doubt in my mind concerning the value of motion pictures. The boys grasped and retained the information to a remarkable degree.[24]

Throughout the 1920s and 1930s the YMCA Motion Picture Bureau never ceased to preach the educational virtues of film.

In its faith in the educational power of film, the MPB was not unique. Faced with the popularity of film in the first decade of the twentieth century and the cultural anxieties generated by women, children, and immigrant men congregating at the nickelodeon, both film industry boosters and social reformers looked to the educational uses of film. As such, Lee Grieveson notes, "Rhetoric on the educational potential of cinema drew on period conceptions of the function of education in both molding a moral and responsible citizenry . . . and in the reproduction of class distinction."[25] By the end of the 1950s, the YMCA was less of an evangelical association and more of a "general leisure-time and character-development organization."[26] Yet, earlier in the twentieth century, the organization had linked its evangelical sentiments to a host of practical issues associated with the emergence of the assembly line and the rationalization of work. Beginning in the 1920s, the YMCA's evangelical sentiments found a new expression in the emerging philosophies of progressive education, especially the idea that learning was best accomplished through doing. Whether more closely in touch with the factory floor or the classroom, the YMCA often imagined educational work in pastoral terms, terms reminiscent of how Ian Hunter describes the two concerns animating the constitution of popular schooling: a "religio-philanthropic concern with the moral well being for individuals and the governmental concern with the moral and physical condition of the population."[27]

The blending of the religious and governmental concerns can be illustrated by noting the front cover of the promotional catalogue of 1928–29. Printed on green card stock, roughly at the center of the catalogue is the Y's signature inverted red triangle; the base is at the top with the tip of the triangle pointing down. In the base of the triangle, "spirit" is printed, at the left side of the triangle appears "mind," and on the right side appears "body." Behind the triangle, visually supporting the triangle, is the Christian X P (*Chi Rho*) with the P sticking above the base of the triangle. Inside the triangle is an open book with the word "John" across the top of the two pages and the numbers 17–21 centered below the word "John" straddling the left—J O—and right—H N—pages. The passage is a part of Jesus' prayer to God prior to his ascension. At John 17:21 Jesus says: "That they all may be one; as thou, Father, art in me, and I in thee, that they also may be one in us: that the world may believe that thou hast sent me."[28] While the evangelical dimensions of this passage are obvious, it is wise to place the evangelical sentiments within the pastoral as a technology of power, that is, a relationship of care that manages to merge a concern for individual welfare to a collective concern about the flock as a whole. The passage invites those affiliated with the YMCA Motion Picture Bureau to identify with this prayer of communion by embodying the spirit of sacrifice and service.

It is the power of film to assemble an audience that provided its use value for pastoral relationships. By the beginning of the 1920s the YMCA's Industrial Department had begun to harness group activities to modify the behavior of workers. Thomas Winter writes, "Equipped with a suitable set of cultural instruments . . . expertly guided group activities would help to transform disruptive and destructive emotions of adult working men into constructive social impulses by giving outlet to their productive energies. . . . The YMCA officials

believed that the interaction of the workers in group would lead to modifica-
tion of each individual[']s thought through emotional elevation."[29] If movies
could assemble a group then the YMCA secretary (or other cultural authority)
could guide the group to govern the individual.

From the standpoint of pastoral education it mattered how an audience
watched a movie, the type of stories it watched, and what life lessons were
learned. Thus, pastoral education transformed movie watching into a domain
and a technique of social management. Moreover, pastoral education provided a mechanism for cobbling together different elements of non-theatrical
cinema. Not unlike the role of Sunday school narrated by Ian Hunter, movie
watching from a pastoral direction allowed for "specifically religious norms
and practices related to the care of the individual soul" to be "linked to quite
different ones associated with new forms of social investigation and administration, whose object was the moral and psychic condition of the population."[30] For the YMCA, this entailed grouping a population with a Y secretary
so that individuals might learn proper deportment through imitation.[31] The
blending of the religious and the governmental merged the teacher and the
preacher into a virtuoso performer more important than the content of the
movie. Zehrung writes that "many successful experiments have convinced us
that it is not so much a matter of content, as it is appropriate application. The
teacher who has the patience and ingenuity to discover a cubic content problem in a trail of coal cars, or to find the practical application of a laboratory experiment in hydraulics in a coal mining film, will inject new interests in otherwise dull subjects. The clergymen [sic] who finds a parable in the film story of
an orange and convey[s] a practical application of Christ's precepts will give
his congregation new spiritual interpretation and information."[32] The lecturer
and the practice of lecturing as a persuasive means of film application deserve
comment.

First, as Charles Acland argues, the mere presence of a lecturer pushes a
moving watching context toward the norms of education and away from the
norms of entertainment.[33] Second, the emphasis on application expresses
how the lecture works as a technique of pastoral power. The teacher/preacher,
through the act of application, demonstrates and models the proper relationship the audience should have toward the film. What was needed for successful application was, according to Zehrung, a "deliberate goal, careful preparation, and wise selections."[34] Regardless of the content, what is communicated
in a pastoral relationship is a proper disposition, a way of interacting with
oneself, others, and, in this case, movies. The cultural authority alongside the

film embodies the deliberateness, preparation, and discernment that should underwrite the audience (or group) assembled to watch the movies.

The modernization of pastoral power is partly accomplished by the tendency of modernity, according to Charles Acland, to authorize the "technological expansion of the sites of, and language about, education."[35] Articulated to a pastoral commitment, film can become a "moral technology."[36] The pastoral interaction between film and education does not explain all educational relationships traversing the non-theatrical, nor does it imply that other governing relationships, ones extracted from economic, cultural, or political discourses, did not traverse non-theatrical cinema. A defining feature of pastoral interaction requires a close relationship between the cultural authority of an individual teacher, preacher, or reformer and the exhibition of the film to properly guide how an audience might watch a movie. This pastoral relationship between exhibitor, film, and audience was warranted by the assumption that any religious, educational, welfare, business, and industrial organization could promote its programs with motion pictures. The growth of the YMCA as a distributor of non-theatrical films put a premium on the cultivation of relationships between the Y secretary and the cultural authorities associated with civic organizations and educational institutions.

The YMCA Motion Picture Bureau grew increasingly committed to linking itself to a vast civic apparatus infused with the potential of pastoral relationships. The back page of the promotion catalogue for the 1928–29 season notes: "[The Motion Picture Bureau's] purpose is to provide suitable film material at the lowest possible cost, and to discover and promote the most effective methods of presentation and adaptation of motion pictures to the programs of churches, clubs, industries, grammar, high and technical schools, colleges, community and welfare organizations and similar institutions, in addition to YMCAs. Upon request gratis service is given in regard to projection equipment, and appropriate subjects for special programs."[37] Most of these organizations — churches, schools, colleges, and community and welfare organizations — were involved in pastoral relationships that merged a concern with an individual to the governmental needs of caring for a population.

In contrast to the catalogue for 1928–29, the catalogue for 1920 was primarily addressed to Y secretaries and was titled "Use of Industrial and Educational Motion Pictures in the YMCA Practical Program." The idea that an initial use of movies was to move folks toward the Y secretary and the Y secretary beyond the association building was expressed halfway down the front cover: "In and Out of the Association Building."[38] In other words, at the beginning of the 1920s it was expected that the YMCA secretary would accompany the films, but by the end of the decade the catalogue announced that "the films listed in this catalogue are available to any organization or institution in the United States."[39] While the Motion Picture Bureau was committed to moving films beyond the internal confines of the vast Y bureaucracy to insinuate itself into the new playing field of non-theatrical exhibition, it still hoped to link the local Y secretary to this expanded field of exhibition by asking that the exhibitors' applications be "countersigned by their local YMCA."[40] In its role as a distributor, the YMCA Motion Picture Bureau would use movies to introduce the local Y secretary to other civic organizations engaged in non-theatrical exhibition. While the requirement to countersign might be a minimal form of contact and would be lifted by the end of the 1930s, with or without the traveling Y secretary, the Motion Picture Bureau imagined itself in a potentially pastoral relationship with exhibitors, providing suitable material and needed advice with programming, equipment, and projection just as those organizations were often involved in pastoral relationships with their audiences, whether imagined as members of a congregation, students, and/or clients.

The Motion Picture Bureau's deployment of religious references and symbols only appeared once. Yet, the sentiment of John 17:21 symptomatically expresses the pastoral uses of film and the YMCA's role in the modernization of pastoral power by merging religious and governmental concerns. To do so, the YMCA Motion Picture Bureau pulled different economic, cultural, and moral concerns of non-theatrical cinema together into an alliance by promoting a particular interaction that encouraged non-theatrical exhibitors to use films in the company of a cultural authority to guide an audience's experience of watching a film. We might refer to this peculiar interaction as pastoral exhibition. A pastoral mode of exhibition describes the use of movies by cultural authorities to simultaneously care for an individual's well-being while harnessing the practice of movie watching to alleviate social, political, and moral problems of a population. The blending of the individual and the social is partly accomplished by a cultural authority that attaches movie exhibition to other communicative techniques and technologies to extract value from the movie that exceeds its semiotic and narrative content. To be clear, the pastoral mode of exhibition is not a general condition of all non-theatrical cinema, but it is one articulation, potentially available when film is used educationally to solve social problems. Moreover, pastoral exhibition can work with or against Hollywood's mode of theatrical production. My argument is that the YMCA and its Motion Picture Bureau cultivated the pastoral mode of exhibition in the 1910s and tended to it in the 1920s by expanding its economic, political, and moral alliances. As the MPB began to reach out beyond the Y building to other civic organizations and cultural authorities in the later 1920s, it prepared the ground for a new deployment of pastoral exhibition. It would be a new generation of moral reformers questioning the norms of classical Hollywood cinema that would provide the social necessity for the pastoral mode of exhibition to make its way to the 1930s.

In 1933, Henry James Forman's *Our Movie Made Children* was published. This popular version of the Payne Fund Studies, a set of studies about the consequences of mass communication on youth, partly conditioned a new round of reform targeting movies. Eric Smoodin notes that the Payne Studies constituted Hollywood as a threat by tending "toward a notion of childhood and adolescent spectatorial passivity, of a mass audience that because of its immaturity could generate little resistance to what they saw on the screen."[41] In response, a "film education movement," as Lea Jacobs names it, arose to intervene, once again, into the viewing habits of children.[42] From the history I have outlined so far, the film education movement was a new articulation of the pastoral mode of exhibition nurtured and refined by the YMCA. In effect, as an organization, the YMCA took the Payne Studies as a call to action.

Able Gregg introduced the Payne Studies and film appreciation to the YMCA in the early 1930s. Gregg was active in the Christian Citizenship Program of the YMCA affiliated with the Y's work with boys. After joining the national staff in 1919, he quickly began to use "natural social groups" among the boys as a way to promote more active learning strategies. The key innovation of this work over the pastoral group work of the Industrial Department previously discussed was on how the group dynamics were to be managed to create group leaders. The YMCA relied on these group leaders as a moral technology of supervision and imitation.[43]

In the Y publication *Christian Citizenship*, later renamed *Christian Citizenship for Group Leaders*, Gregg represented film education as a way to redeem movies from a purely economic motive: "To bring about the rescue of this modern medium of amusement and education from the hands of a group which seeks to use it for selfish economic ends may take some little time. But it will be done. The pathway to this rescue is *increased understanding of the motion picture as art and as education on the part of all who go to the movies*."[44] Drawing on a host of resources, especially Edgar Dale's *How to Appreciate Motion Pictures*, Gregg encouraged Y secretaries and other cultural authorities to use group dynamics to have youth discuss the films they watched. Group discussion techniques modeled on the instruments provided by the film appreciation movement joined the lecture as a communicative technique useful for transforming movie exhibition and reception into a pastoral relationship. Due to their attachment to the film appreciation movement one advantage of these group techniques was the ability to incorporate more theatrical releases into a pastoral mode of exhibition.

These more proximate communicative techniques (lecturing and group discussion) helped to format the reception practices of youth into a new pastoral mode of exhibition. Different efforts at film appreciation, therefore, also relied on a dispersed constellation of cultural authorities. But as the film appreciation movement required cultural authorities for their uptake, the literature associated with the movement did as much to influence the cultural authorities as it did the kids. As Wasson notes, "A good portion of the study guides and remaining literature published throughout the 1920s and 1930s was aimed at interpellating middle-class adults . . . in ways of thinking about film that would arm them in their own practices of professional and community intervention."[45] In other words, the moral alliance of cultural authorities assembled by organizations like the YMCA Motion Picture Bureau did not come ready-made with the proper disposition toward movies; that disposition needed to be produced and a certain competence in discussing films was required to secure one's moral authority in and through film exhibition.

PASTORAL EXHIBITION AND THE MAKING OF THE 16MM NETWORK

It is arguable that 35mm harmed the constitution of a pastoral mode of exhibition. As Brian Winston notes, 35mm projectors were not easily moved from place to place and the size and cost of 35mm projectors and cameras made it hard to establish an amateur cinema market.[46] These problems were only magnified with the coming of sound. Moreover, the use of nitrate in 35mm film stock made it highly flammable. As Winston remarks, "Thus virtually unnoticed behind the fantastic spread of cinema all over the world, 35mm nevertheless meant that non-theatrical exhibition was, however marginal, more limited than it might have been while an amateur market could not develop for cinematography at all easily."[47]

While Winston may be underestimating the amount of non-theatrical cinema by privileging film making over its exhibition, the invention of 16mm gauge in 1923 did provide a more affordable, safer, versatile, and portable film gauge. More than a technological innovation in film gauge, it was, as Haidee

Wasson notes, an "expansive network of ideas and practices, supported by an amalgam of cameras, projectors, and film stock."[48] Wasson names this constellation the "16mm network."[49] Through this network, the value of 16mm was constructed, negotiated, and harnessed to a host of moral, governmental, and economic programs. For some, as Wasson highlights, the 16mm network represented a utopian dimension, "a whole new way of thinking, seeing, and being in the world," while, for Hollywood, the emergence of the educational market in film rentals brought with it a desire to repurpose and rescale its 35mm films into 16mm educational films.[50] This section of the chapter will document how the YMCA distribution dynamics attempted to manage the mobility and flexibility of 16mm for pastoral exhibition.[51] In so doing, the point is to encounter the 16mm network in process, not so much a totality of all things done with and to 16mm but to explore the potential and actual uses embodied by the network. The Motion Picture Bureau's initial effort to distribute 16mm can be noted in the catalogues for 1929–30 and 1930–31. While the catalogue for 1928–29 makes no mention of 16mm and all the films seem to have characteristics of 35mm (theater standard width or flammable), the catalogue for 1929–1930 made the following pitch: "[The MPB] now offers 16mm on free and rental basis. Write for catalogue."[52] I have yet to locate a 16mm-only catalogue for this year, but the pitch indicates the capability to distribute. Moreover, in the rental section, three important references to 16mm require comment. First, a genre of film lessons produced by DeVry for elementary and junior high schools was available in both 16mm and 35mm. Second, renting 16mm "substandard" films was less expensive than renting 35mm "standard." Since the previous year's catalogue discusses films as possessing theater standard width, I take the reference to 16mm substandard to represent the YMCA's adoption of the professionalism discourses that divided 35mm from 16mm. Third, 16mm was rented from the YMCA's new film exchange in Chicago. Chicago, not Hollywood, was destined to be the capital of non-theatrical production and distribution. More rhetorically direct, the promotional catalogue addressed an educational audience:

> Leading educational authorities, collaborating with motion picture experts, have produced more than a hundred film lessons for schools. These film lessons are the most complete courses of teaching motion pictures yet available which cover the entire content of the average course of study. Each fifteen-minute film lesson has been prepared under the supervision of practical teachers, acquainted with the needs and problems of the class-

rooms; hence they fit into the class time period and the classroom recitation. Workable teaching plans and helpful suggestions for every lesson will be found in the teacher's manual supplied each user.[53]

The claim that new 16mm films might increase the efficiency and quality of education provides the continuity between the YMCA's goals and its promotion of the new film gauge. However, it is noteworthy that the promotion of the films is predicated on the claim of an educational expertise in the production of the films. As noted earlier, the alignment of pastoral care with more secular forms of expertise marks an important moment in the modernization of pastoral care. In other words, while one might expect the classroom to provide a pastoral situation, the MPB and its educational and corporate alliances were offering a pastoral relationship between themselves and their educational exhibitors by providing the educational applications that the exhibitors' teachers might emulate.

The catalogue for 1929–1930 mostly promotes 35mm, but it is signaling a change in direction through the invocation of new educational films and the economic incentives to rent 16mm. The next year, 1930–1931, the MPB distributed a 16mm-only catalogue, requesting that its potential exhibitors write for the 35mm catalogue. Thus the MPB made an early attempt to secure its role in the distribution of 16mm by speeding up its own transition to 16mm. Moreover, the catalogue for 1930–1931 is noteworthy for the explosion of advertisements for 16mm projectors, movie cameras, and film. Perhaps providing an alternative revenue stream, these advertisements included sound technologies, movie screens, and the film review magazines associated with the *National Board of Review* and *Moviemakers*.[54] The culture of 16mm was in full force.

Recognizing the need for technological adaptation beyond the gauge was the topic of an editorial by Will Whitmore entitled "What Are You Going to Do about Sound?" This editorial is a unique rhetorical touch, as no other promotional catalogue has such a direct appeal to adapt to the shifting technological environment. Since the appeal was to sound and not to 16mm, the Y may have assumed an easy turnover to 16mm. In very direct terms, Whitmore's editorial addresses non-theatrical exhibition in relation to Hollywood's technological and generic advantage. The editorial directly compares how the use of silent films with a "religious, historical, recreational, and informational" content will increasingly lose touch with its audience as the audience gets accustomed to entertainment genres that speak. Whitmore pleads, "Yes, what are you going to do about sound? This question must be answered soon. Soon you will be without silent commercial entertainment pictures to show. The theatrical field will soon be 100% sound. The silent picture is becoming obsolete as a commercial entertainment facet and audience tolerance, acceptance or preference will determine how much longer the non theatrical field may continue to use the silent film."[55] The question calls forth the reader's response: transition to sound as soon as possible in order to adapt to the tastes of the film-going public. The ability of non-theatrical cinema to attract audiences may no longer be possible with silent movies. Whitmore's appeal is primarily based on a claim about the changing expectations of potential audiences and what is likely to happen as they move from entertainment to educational encounters with film. On the one hand, he claims that while the "audience of non-entertainment or non-theatrical organization[s] will continue for years to accept the silent films in their instructive programs, it is also possible that the silent films may soon lose some of their effectiveness." On the other hand, he leaves unanswered what made them effective and how film was coded as educational.[56] In both cases, silent film's ability to be assigned an educational dimension was, in part, imagined to be due to its exhibition alongside a lecturer or some other cultural authority to mark the seriousness of the context.[57] Thus, it may be that the pastoral mode of exhibition was still transitioning to the coming of sound as it imagined what the role of the cultural authority was to be, if sound replaced the need to narrate or apply the lesson from the film.

One more advertisement deserves mention for its ability to register Hollywood's reaction to the non-theatrical field. An advertisement from Universal Pictures Corporation encouraged exhibitors to rent directly from its new "Non-theatrical Department."[58] Hollywood did not stand idly by as the non-theatrical market emerged. Universal, and later Columbia, would advertise in the MPB catalogues with newly cut, adapted, and repurposed films especially designed for the educational sites of non- theatrical film. The fact that the YMCA Motion Picture Bureau was willing to enter into an alliance with Hollywood suggests that it, and Hollywood, found a convergence around education as a general social force and as a potential market. While they were potential competitors for the educational market, Hollywood and the YMCA Motion Picture Bureau were willing to work together to incorporate repurposed entertainment genres into a pastoral exhibition.

In 1931 the promotional catalogue of the MPB records the different technological forms and economic interests trying to establish the pathways of the 16mm network. For example, the repurposing and "shrinking" of 35mm to 16mm, advertisements for 16mm movie projectors and movie screens, corporate promoters of sound installations, new 16mm production companies, and Hollywood are represented in the advertisements of this catalogue. As such, these advertisements express how old and new agents adapted to and contributed to the contours of the network. However, the Motion Picture Bureau's desire to make the quick transition to 16mm was thwarted. One reason may have been slower than expected adoption of 16mm equipment by key exhibitors, especially local Ys.[59] While the MPB's distribution of reels to organizations beyond the Y would reorient the Y's alliances, the need to promote 35mm films might be due to the capital investment in 35mm film projectors during the Y's building boom of the first quarter of the twentieth century. While I do not have sales figures, a review of *Association Men* during the years between 1912 and 1918 indicates a constant stream of advertisements for 35mm film projectors. Likewise, the MPB's desire to move movies from the Y building to the classroom may have run into pre-established 35mm installations. For example, E. I. Way reported in the fall of 1928 that "the city of Detroit is reported to have over 300 standard equipped motion picture projectors in use among the Detroit public schools."[60]

While the YMCA Motion Picture Bureau was capable of working with enough filmmakers (especially educational and industrial) to provide 16mm films, the exhibition context seemed to slow the uptake of 16mm. It is possible that these new 16mm educational and industrial films were not the preferred genres of more established 35mm non-theatrical exhibition contexts. Winston argues that the suppression of 16mm had to do with distinctions between professional and non-professional filmmaking and Hollywood barriers to adoption. Furthermore the lack of what he calls a "supervening necessity" retarded the diffusion of 16mm.[61] Arguably, the educational necessity and the pastoral form of exhibition may have been too wedded to 35mm for the Motion Picture Bureau's distributive power to provide the energy for 16mm to take off in exhibition sites nurtured by the Y. Although 16mm was more mobile, the social need for that mobility had not saturated the social justifications for adopting a 16mm infrastructure for those who had already invested in a 35mm infrastructure. Moreover, the chaotic technology context after the introduction to sound may have engendered caution.[62] The transition to 16mm was partly put on hold, and the YMCA's Motion Picture Bureau would spend the 1930s managing the mobility of 16mm.

The second step in the Y's effort to constitute a 16mm network is expressed in terms of its effort to displace 35mm by 16mm in its promotional catalogues.

The slow displacement of 35mm and the continued life of silent film can be charted by paying attention to what I am calling the hybrid catalogues distributing both 35mm and 16mm film. The hybrid catalogues lasted from the 1931–32 season through the 1937–38 season. The silver anniversary catalogue for 1938–39 completes the journey back to an all 16mm catalogue quickly followed by rhetorical preference for 16mm's sound over silent. I will discuss the significance of the re-emergence of the all 16mm catalogue below. Some particular dimensions of the distributor-exhibition relationship during this hybrid period deserve attention. To wit, the catalogues always signaled a preference for the transition to 16mm and the reach of the exhibitors tended to grow. Beginning with the catalogue for 1931–32, films were now coded: marked as available to exhibitors in 16mm, 35mm, or both. Economically, 16mm would remain cheaper to rent, insure, and ship. While 35mm would rhetorically have top billing on the front of the catalogue and in the table of contents until the 1935–36 season, the catalogues offered more 16mm films than 35mm films as early as 1933–34. The cultural market, however, was decidedly moving in the direction of 16mm; all the ads pitched 16mm with a growing emphasis on 16mm sound after the mid-1930s. While the Motion Picture Bureau's preference for 16mm was visible, the archive does not comment as to the preferred gauge requested by the three thousand organizations served by the Motion Picture Bureau.

The promotional catalogues in the hybrid period also offer an important glimpse into the emerging cultural and economic alliances that would be crucial to the YMCA's effort to assemble a pastoral mode of film exhibition. Beginning with the 1931–32 season, the MPB's promotional catalogue noted the existence of an advisory committee. This early advisory committee was heavily weighted toward the concerns of industrial uses of film. The ability of the YMCA to provide free films was due to contracts it signed with industrial interests that sponsored these films and asked the Y to distribute them. The first advisory committee represented the interests converging on the Y's distribution network: the economic interests of Charles Barrell of Western Electric, G. N. McMillan of Associated National Advertisers, and Clinton Ivins of Pathescope Company, with the economic/educational interests of H. A. DeVry and I. R. Rhem of Atlas Educational Film Company, and the cultural authority of Wilton Barrett of the National Board of Review.[63] It is worth noting that the industrial and educational interests making up the MPB's alliance had already committed to 16mm.

The catalogue for 1932–33 asked exhibitors to inform the MPB if they had purchased or were contemplating the purchase of sound equipment. The MPB wanted to know the type and make of the equipment and promised to place those exhibitors on a special mailing list to include a sound-only catalogue in October 1932.[64] While I have no knowledge of a special sound-only catalogue, the catalogue for 1933–34 included 35mm sound films, suggesting that some exhibitors of non-theatrical genres remained committed to 35mm even in the face of significantly higher capital investment than 16mm. Moreover, 16mm and 35mm silent films were also distributed. While sound was ascending, silent movies did not go away quickly, suggesting that the 16mm non-theatrical context provided a technological supplement for the continued circulation of silent film beyond its use by classical Hollywood cinema.

Part of the service provided by the YMCA consisted of bundling films into a program. The Motion Picture Bureau claimed that the successful program would exhibit popular yet "appropriate" films for a school or church. The growing list of entertainment shorts and eventually re-purposed and re-cut feature films was not simply an alternative to the other genres provided by the MPB: these works represented parts of a whole, movies/reels to be assembled into a program. While speaking of a different exhibition context than the one described here, Steve Neale argues that structured programming is a method for generating an oppositional exhibition context other than the one offered by Hollywood.[65] The programming of films by the Motion Picture Bureau provides an insight into the use of films pastorally, regardless of whether a film might have had a Hollywood origin. Thus, the uses of films, whether initially imagined for educational or entertainment purposes, were affected by how those movies were attached to a mode of exhibition.

The catalogue for 1933–34 announced a change in the economics of the rental agreements between the MPB and its exhibitors. Noting the increase in postage rates and a reduction of income from American industries (a likely reference to fewer sponsored films) the MPB required "all exhibitors desiring to draw programs from our Free Film Section . . . to pay a registration fee of $2.00." This registration fee required each person to register, rather than simply the organization the person represented. Beyond the economic value, the pastoral value of such a registration process was to increase the contacts of the Y secretary. In light of the emerging film education movement, a new social need might have been taking hold, stimulating the 16mm network's control over the pastoral mode of exhibition. The Motion Picture Bureau was emphasizing the revenue stream of its rental business represented by ever more rental films, both silent and sound, in the catalogues after 1935–36. Moreover, the catalogue of 1935–36 marks the ascendancy of 16mm over 35mm rhetorically in the table of contents and economically with more 16mm than 35mm films being offered within the catalogue. Economically important, the conclusion of the 1935–36 season brought with it a budget surplus. The Motion Picture Bureau, set up on a non-profit basis, was making a profit.[66]

The rhetorical push for adopting sound began to register in the rise of sound films to the top of the table of contents in the catalogue for the 1936–37 season. While numerically there were still more silent films offered than sound (sound films represented twenty-three pages while silent films spread across fifty pages), the desire of the Y for its exhibitors to move toward sound was culturally represented by the vast majority of projector ads promoting 16mm sound. To economically support the transition in 1938, the YMCA set up special purchasing agreements between Y secretaries and technology companies. In a memorandum to all Y secretaries in March 1938, George Zehrung announced "an arrangement with sound projector manufacturers, whereby local associations can effect a saving of approximately $200.00 in purchasing sound equipment" through the National Council of the YMCA. The letter also indicated that the National Council is "recommending a more intensive use of motion pictures in connection with building and extension program work."[67] In a confidential memorandum attached to Zehrung's letter was another from Guy Harner, the director of purchasing for the National Council of the YMCA, with the prices for 16mm sound projectors, including the Victor (AC-25) for $254.16, the Bell and Howell (AC-138-F) for $256.67, the Ampro (AC-U) for $263.33, and the DeVry Challenger (CSL-AC) for $306.67.[68] Silent film was still represented on the cover of the MPB's promotional catalogues until 1945, and while economically and culturally ascendant in the catalogues after 1935, sound would not take top billing on the front cover until the 1939–40 season.

The third stage of the MPB's catalogue history is the return of the 16mm catalogue. As mentioned above, the catalogue of 1938–39 represents a consolidation of the 16mm network. References to 35mm films have been removed from the front cover. The table of contents makes no reference to 35mm films. The application form no longer has a 35mm preference and the only insurance an exhibitor can buy is associated with 16mm. The MPB could take for granted that its relationship with exhibitors was mediated by the distribution of 16mm. Fifteen years after its technological possibility a fully functioning 16mm network had emerged. One might ask: why did it take so long? Brian Winston suggests how we should proceed: "The state of the market, or better, of society is the crucial factor in enabling the development and diffusion of any communication technology or in hindering it."[69] Following this rule, we might approach non-theatrical cinema as the social context for the diffusion of 16mm. First, at least two types of filmmakers (industrial and educational) quickly emerged to promote 16mm. Arguably these new filmmakers also represented two significant social needs: advertising to promote and differentiate the mass production harnessed by the factories of modern capitalism and the continued relevance of non-theatrical cinema with regard to education. Second, technology companies were making cameras, projectors, and screens necessary for the transition. Third, as represented by the YMCA Motion Picture Bureau, distributors were willing to make the transition to 16mm faster than slower. Given all those social factors in favor of a faster diffusion of 16mm, why the delay?

The social actors averse to a faster transition seemed to be the exhibitors of non-theatrical cinema. Market uncertainties generated by the technological changes wrought by both 16mm and sound, especially in concert with the economic crisis of the Great Depression, may have contributed to their slow uptake. At the same time, key civic organizations like churches, schools, and YMCA buildings had made, and were continuing to make, significant investments in 35mm projectors. These capital investments may have affected the resilience of 35mm non-theatrical exhibition sites to the coming of 16mm. In contrast to my claim that educational and industrial movie makers might sustain a quick transition to 16mm, Brian Winston argues that no significant social necessity appeared to generate 16mm movie-making. Furthermore, even if the supply appeared, it did not guarantee demand. The long reach of silent cinema may also provide a clue. For even when non-theatrical cinema transitioned to 16mm it was often with silent projectors. The resilience of silent cinema, whether 35mm or 16mm, reminds us of the talking secretaries, teachers, and preachers who often lectured alongside, before, and after the program. This pastoral mode of exhibition may not have seen the need for a quick transition to 16mm because the latter failed to provide a unique social justification to distinguish it from the 35mm already available. What the pastoral mode of exhibition needs more than anything is the moral disposition of a cultural authority guiding how an audience might encounter the film. But, it also tends to work with other communicative techniques and technologies to promote interaction among the cultural authority and a group to create role models for imitation. The lack of a pastoral urgency to quickly reformat the mode of exhibition to the 16mm network may have slowed the installation of the network.

At the same time, while the orbit of the 16mm network may have been limited in comparison to its configuration after World War II, the Motion Picture Bureau points to a functioning network before World War II.[70] This network is partly configured by the YMCA's leadership pulling 16mm into a pastoral mode of exhibition while at the same time pushing exhibitors to replace 35mm exhibition technology with 16mm. Culturally, a host of advertisements grace the pages of the catalogue for 1938–39 all promoting the 16mm network. The catalogue's advertising of 16mm technology, such as screens and projectors, the value of "express mail" provided by Railway Express, corporate interests like the H. W. Wilson Company and Columbia Pictures, and the cultural authority of *Educational Screen* testify to how the Y's work as a distributor helped to create a functioning 16mm network of producers, distributors, exhibitors, and technological and educational interests. It was only due to its role in creating a 16mm network that the Y could declare on its application form: "Because of the saving involved in transportation and convenience, non-theatrical exhibitors are rapidly turning to the 16mm size film. For this reason the Bureau will discontinue the distribution of 35mm films after the 1938–1939 season. A list of available free 35mm films, silent and sound, will be sent on request."[71] The magnitude of the Y's reach is expressed by the print run of its silver anniversary issue: over forty thousand catalogues were in circulation. In 1939, fifty thousand copies of the catalogue were printed. First in Portland in 1937, and later in San Francisco in 1939, the Motion Picture Bureau nationalized its distribution exchange to make more efficient the movement of movies.

In closing, I wish to return to the modernization of pastoral power and what I have called pastoral exhibition. The mobility and versatility of 16mm provides pause. For Foucault, a key element of pastoral power is the shepherd's concern with the movement of the flock. In other words, the flock isn't tied to one physical place, but moves, and the shepherd is in charge of helping the flock make the journey. Thus, Foucault notes, "the shepherd's power is essentially exercised over a multiplicity in movement."[72] From its religious concern, this journey can be expressed spiritually as the movement of an individual: once lost, she or he is now found. From a governmental direction, the different movements of people made possible a concern about when and where they might congregate as modernity put populations in motion and attempted to reset the spatial and temporal dynamics of everyday life. The reconstitution of a pastoral mode of exhibition required not simply the management of a population's movement toward and away from the theatrical sites of classical Hollywood cinema, but also a new need to manage the mobility of

film, 16mm in particular. The mobile character of 16mm may have been difficult for the pastoral mode of exhibition because it proliferated in the sites and
genres of non-theatrical exhibition with or without the cultural authorities
deemed necessary to instill the proper moral disposition. The primary way in
which the YMCA Motion Picture Bureau exercised power over the movement
of 16mm was as a distributor of motion pictures. It attempted to serve as an ac-
celerator of the 16mm network. Yet, the pastoral exhibitors needed some distance from 16mm in order to better gauge how to use it and turn it toward pastoral purposes. To that end, the film education movement may have provided
a new social need for the exhibitors to bring 16mm within its educational contexts, and the development of group discussion techniques may have provided
a new way to blend the religious and governmental dimension of the 16mm
network. By 1939, the YMCA's pastoral mode of exhibition had provided the
infrastructure for 16mm to be called to duty in World War II.

NOTES

Portions of this chapter have been presented at the Useful Cinema Workshop, Concordia University, Montreal, August 2006, and the Society of Cinema and Media
Studies, Chicago, March 2007. I wish to thank the librarians at the Kautz Family
YMCA Archives at the University of Minnesota for their help in the production of
this chapter.

1   Antonio Gramsci, "Americanism and Fordism," 302.
2   Three things to note about the international dimensions of the YMCA: First the Inter-
    national Committee of the YMCA was an amalgam of the Ys of the United States and
    Canada. In 1923 the International Committee severed the two geographical interests
    into specific national councils. The YMCA Motion Picture Bureau was organization-
    ally maintained, first, by the Industrial Department of the International Committee
    and later by the National Council of the United States. It should be noted that the
    International Committee did not vanish; it became a holding company for many of
    the assets of the two different national councils. In point of fact, it was the Inter-
    national Committee that was the corporate owner of the Motion Picture Bureau.
    Second, due to the International Committee's role in providing aid and comfort to
    U.S. troops during World War I, key American representatives of the International
    Committee had extensive contacts in Europe, and they cultivated those relationships
    after the Great War. Third, during the first quarter of the twentieth century, Ameri-
    cans like John Raleigh Mott, the former secretary of the International Committee,
    led the worldwide YMCA movement.
3   Gramsci, "Americanism and Fordism," 285–86, 302.
4   It is possible that the Motion Picture Bureau was established in 1911: the archival

record seems ambiguous on this front. Earlier documents date the establishment as 1914, while later documents suggest 1911. After the Motion Picture Bureau was re-assigned to the National Council of the YMCA in the mid-1920s, the "Exhibits" was dropped from its name.

5   R. Greene, "Y Movies," 20.
6   "Moving Pictures," *Association Men* 37 (1912), 9.
7   R. Greene, "Y Movies," 21.
8   Waldman, "Toward a Harmony of Interests."
9   Ross, *Working Class Hollywood*, 224.
10 Slide, *Before Video*, 69.
11 Winston, *Technologies of Seeing*, 58.
12 R. Greene, "Y Movies," 30.
13 Foucault, "8 February 1978."
14 Bordwell, Thompson, and Staiger, *The Classical Hollywood Cinema*.
15 Hay, "Rethinking the Intersection of Cinema, Genre, and Youth" (accessed June 10, 2007).
16 "Women's Painting at Sale at Auction: National Association Will Exhibit Works of Art Beginning Thursday," *New York Times*, April 15, 1923, S4.
17 "Churches Helping in New Movie Body: Motion Picture Chamber of Commerce Aims to Unite Non-Theatrical Interests," *New York Times*, December 30, 1923, E2.
18 Ibid.
19 Ibid.
20 For a more thorough discussion of the interaction between Hollywood and non-theatrical exhibition, see Wasson, *Museum Movies*, 37–44.
21 Ibid., 32–37.
22 Dodge, "Motion Picture as a Force in Religious Education," 90.
23 Lindvall, *Sanctuary Cinema*.
24 "Who's Who: George J. Zehrung," *National Board of Review Magazine* 6 (January 1931), 3–4.
25 Grieveson, *Policing Cinema*, 31.
26 Zald and Denton, "From Evangelism to General Service," 215.
27 Hunter, *Culture and Government*, 39.
28 John 17:21 (New King James Version).
29 Winter, *Making Men, Making Class*, 136–37.
30 Hunter, *Culture and Government*, 47.
31 On the importance of imitation, see Winter, *Making Men, Making Class*, 136–37.
32 "Who's Who: George J. Zehrung," 4.
33 Acland, "Mapping the Serious and the Dangerous."
34 "Who's Who: George J. Zehrung," 4.
35 Acland, "The Film Council of America and the Ford Foundation."
36 Grieveson, *Policing Cinema*, 32.
37 The YMCA Motion Picture Bureau, *Selected Motion Pictures, 1928–1929 Season*, Box D, Association Films/Motion Picture Bureau, Folder: Association Films, Catalogues,

1920–32, 29, Kautz Family YMCA Archive, University Libraries, University of Minnesota, Minneapolis. All future citations from promotional catalogues will simply be referenced as *Selected Motion Pictures*, followed by the season date.

38 The Bureau of Motion Pictures and Exhibits, "Use of the Industrial and Educational Motion Pictures in the YMCA Practical Program: In and Out of the Association Building," Box 10, Industrial Records, Motion Picture Pamphlets, Kautz Family YMCA Archive.

39 *Selected Motion Pictures, Season 1928–29*, 4.

40 Ibid. The requirement to countersign would be lifted in 1939.

41 Smoodin, *Regarding Frank Capra*, 94.

42 Jacobs, "Reformers and Spectators."

43 It is beyond the scope of this essay, but the reworking of the pastoral value of groups in the ten years between the Industrial Department and the Boys' Divisions is partly due to the interface between Christian modes of moral improvement and progressive education. See C. Hopkins, *History of the YMCA in North America*, 550–52.

44 "Are You Made by Movies," *Christian Citizenship for Group Leaders* 12, no. 8 (1933), 1 (emphasis in original).

45 Wasson, *Museum Movies*, 57.

46 Winston, *Technologies of Seeing*, 60.

47 Ibid.

48 Wasson, *Museum Movies*, 46.

49 To the best of my knowledge, Haidee Wasson was the first to use the term "16mm network"; see Wasson, *Museum Movies*, 32–67.

50 Ibid., 49, 52–53.

51 Some comments about the methodology and archive underwriting this section: this part of the essay performs a discursive analysis of the extant promotional catalogues of the YMCA Motion Picture Bureau. These catalogues are available at the Kautz Family YMCA Archive, University Libraries, University of Minnesota, Minneapolis. The catalogues are grouped into four folders. The first folder, 1920–32, has four catalogues: what I take to be the first catalogue published in 1920, then seasonal catalogues for 1928–29 thru 1931–32, inclusive. The second folder, 1933–37, has catalogues starting with the 1933–34 season and ending with 1936–37, inclusive. The third folder, 1937–40, has three catalogues: 1937–38 thru 1939–40, inclusive. The fourth folder, 1940–44, has three catalogues: 1940–41, 1942–43, 1943–144. It is missing 1941–42. As noted above, all the catalogues can be found in Box D Association Films/Motion Picture Bureau. This section is primarily concerned with the first three folders. My discourse analysis is organized into three parts; the first is rhetorical, focusing on how certain textual features — for example, the arrangement of the table of contents and descriptions inviting exhibitors to rent films — orient the exhibitor toward one gauge or another. The second element includes references to the economics of distribution and exhibition. The economic elements include the cost of renting, shipping, and projecting 16mm and 35mm. Finally, a third element includes the film culture of 16mm and non-theatrical film: the ideas and practices surrounding the reception of 16mm films.

52 *Selected Motion Pictures, Season 1929–30, 6.*

53 Ibid., n.p.

54 I have yet to discover whether the YMCA received any revenue for placing these ads within its catalogue.

55 Will Whitmore, "What Are You Going to Do about Sound?," *Selected Motion Pictures, Season 1930–31,* 23–24.

56 Ibid., 23.

57 As I noted earlier, the nearness of the Y secretary was considered an important part of how the YMCA combined its desire to care for different populations with the use of film. My claim was informed by Acland, "Patterns of Cultural Authority."

58 *Selected Motion Pictures, Season 1930–31, 26.*

59 While cheaper, it would be a mistake to imagine the shift to 16mm as financially easy, especially during the Depression. We should not underestimate the cost for some exhibitors. The cost of 16mm would decline, but, in the early 1930s, the cost of projectors was still a significant impediment to adoption. See Wasson, *Museum Movies,* 48.

60 Way, "Growth of the Industrial Films," 300. My assumption is that the word "standard" in the quote refers to 35mm.

61 Winston, *Technologies of Seeing,* 63–74.

62 Ibid., 74.

63 *Selected Motion Pictures, Season 1931–32, 4.*

64 Ibid., 6.

65 Neale, "Oppositional Exhibition Notes and Problems," 49–51. It is worth noting that in the 1930s commercial cinema often packaged films together into "double bills," so, as Neale suggests, a program may need spaces for discussing the films and modes of documentation about the film to make the exhibition site oppositional.

66 "Report on Association Films," 1947, 3, Kautz Family YMCA Archives, YMCA of the USA, Box D, Association Films/Motion Picture Bureau, Folder: Association Films.

67 Sound memorandum, March 18, 1938, Kautz Family YMCA Archives, YMCA of the USA, Box D, Association Films/Motion Picture Bureau, Folder: Association Films.

68 "Confidential memorandum to Local General Secretaries," March 18, 1938, Kautz Family YMCA Archives, YMCA of the USA, Box D, Association Films/Motion Picture Bureau, Folder: Association Films.

69 Winston, *Technologies of Seeing,* 3.

70 On the chaotic nature of the 16mm network after World War II see Acland, "The Film Council of America and the Ford Foundation."

71 *Selected Motion Pictures, Season 1938–39.*

72 Foucault, "8 February 1978," 125.

"A MOVING PICTURE OF THE HEAVENS"

THE PLANETARIUM SPACE SHOW AS USEFUL CINEMA

Alison Griffiths

Unless you are a teacher, tourist, parent of a teenager, or ex-hippy looking for a retro psychedelic experience at a Laserium show, chances are you haven't set foot in a planetarium in years.[1] The reasons are hardly obscure: catering mostly to tourists or school groups, planetarium shows are often denigrated as both expensive and kitschy. Despite their use of state-of-the-art digital effects, planetariums inevitably evoke an earlier era where visitors sat with craned necks on uncomfortable chairs fighting off sleep. However, the planetarium show remains a long-lived and highly adaptable cultural form, drawing on ideas from popular culture since its inception in the late 1910s. On the surface, the usually brief planetarium space show might seem an unlikely analog of useful cinema; however, the contemporary planetarium show contains cinema-like representational images in frequently elaborate narrative designs. Furthermore, many modern space shows, such as the "all-digital" StarRider Theater at the Adler Planetarium in Chicago where audiences are invited to "take a thrilling ride to the center of a black hole," provide the quintessential phantom ride experience associated with both early cinema and contemporary 2-D and 3-D IMAX. But in the planetarium space show the cinematic image is also evoked in more prosaic ways, such as time-lapse video and animation. Planetarium shows are (and have always been) heavily intertextual multimedia performances deploying photographic and digital projected images and special effects drawn from popular culture, motion pictures, and apocalyptic narratives from science fiction. Indeed, the planetarium is an exemplary intermedial form for the ways in which it employs modalities lifted from theater, literature, film, radio, television, popular music, video games, and even liturgy. For the space show past and present, the notion of the screen performance as an "experience" is the semantic glue that binds these disparate amusements together.

Exactly how cinema becomes "useful" in the planetarium space show and how, historically, it has engaged with a cinematic discourse is the subject of this chapter. More specifically, my goal is to examine the planetarium as a neglected source of useful cinema, considering the emergence of the planetarium as both spatial and institutional phenomena (classic dome architecture that is a prerequisite for the performance) as well as a fascinating barometer of larger sociopolitical currents and trends in the mainstream culture of the time. Given that this chapter cannot possibly consider all the different ways in which cinema becomes "useful" in the planetarium or go into technical detail about how special effects are created and integrated into the actual show, it will nevertheless stimulate a productive debate about how we can begin to think about cinema's residual legacy in the planetarium and why, for example, cinema is considerably more useful in the planetarium today than it was at any other time in its history. Cinema's current utility in the high-tech digitized planetarium space show has certainly surpassed levels from previous moments in its history, an issue I shall address in more depth in the chapter's conclusion. In relation to the overall aims of this volume, this chapter brings an unusual — and for the most part overlooked — site of cinema to the table, to help us better understand how film can find a seat and service the twin goals of astronomy and popular culture.

The chapter examines the planetarium as useful cinema roughly chronologically, taking time at the outset to comment briefly on the planetarium's history before dealing more substantially with its phenomenological make-up, especially in relation to the overdetermined sign of the Zeiss projector, the industry standard since 1923. The subsequent sections take us from the origins of the planetarium through to the 1950s, the era we dwell on the most, since the cold war seems to offer us especially good traction on how popular astronomy could articulate or enunciate the hopes and anxieties of an era. We come full circle at the end of the chapter to reflect further on ways in which cinema became useful in the contemporary planetarium show.

A BRIEF HISTORY OF THE PLANETARIUM

Devices representing the movements of the planets and our moon in relation to the sun have been in use since the early days of Copernican astronomy, although the sixteenth century ushered in a number of key developments in tabletop planetarium designs, including the addition of moveable circles representing the sun, moon, and planets, and a stand showing the horizon.[2] In the orrery, "the planets of a model solar system could be made to move in circular paths around a central sun by turning a handle connected to an ingenious system of gears and spindles" as seen in the often reproduced painting by Joseph Wright in 1768 entitled *The Philosopher Reading a Lecture on the Orrery*.[3] The atmospheric candlelight on the faces of the members of the assembled lecture party, especially the two young children in the center of the painting, posits wonder as isomorphic with astronomy. The two adult male spectators cast their eyes toward the lecturer-philosopher, whose downward glance at his notes with pen in hand confirms his role as the eminent source of rational scientific knowledge. The three adolescent males and younger boy and girl in the middle ground lean forward into the device, satisfying a tactile desire to get closer to the apparatus through touching the hemispherical bars (the girl's arm around the boy underscores this). The dramatically lit faces of the center girl and boy who appear mesmerized by the orrery attract our attention the most, their wistful gazes a powerful symbol of human fascination with the cosmos. The light radiating from the apparatus makes it the terrestrial (and metaphorical) equivalent of a brightly shining sun or star glowing in the darkened room. A tension between the lecture as a serious astronomy lesson and as a magical, even supernatural event explaining astronomical forces that while scientific in nature are nevertheless evocative of metaphysical, transcendentalist ideas is powerfully inscribed in this painting. The scene is reminiscent in many respects of a séance, with the orrery substituting for the Ouija board; "presence"—suggesting both the literal sense of being "part of space within one's immediate vicinity" and the supernatural connotation of "something (as a spirit) felt or believed to be present"—is also quite palpable and a recurring theme in planetarium discourse.[4]

However, it was not until the seventeenth century that a device was in-

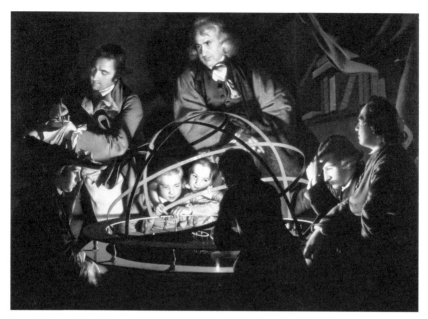

Joseph Wright, *The Philosopher Reading a Lecture on the Orrery* (1768), courtesy of the Derby Museum of Art, United Kingdom.

vented consisting of a "slowly turning sphere," in which holes were cut out for the stars and that accommodated observers on the inside of a celestial dome, as opposed to seated or standing around a tabletop apparatus. In 1654 Adam Oelschlager, a court mathematician and librarian to Duke Frederick of Holstein-Gottorp, designed a hollow globe large enough to accommodate several seated spectators: "Inside, a circular platform suspended from the axis of rotation held as many as ten people and as the globe rotated many stars and constellations drifted across the artificial sky in a way similar to that of the real sky."[5] Made of copper, the globe was eleven feet in diameter and on the inside showed gilded stars and constellation figures lit by two oil lamps. A map of the world was painted onto the outer surface, which could be examined in detail by spectators.[6] In 1660, the mathematician Erhard Weigel built a large celestial sphere on the roof of Duke Willhelm of Weimar's castle; made of iron it ended up damaging the roof and was dismantled in 1692.[7] A more sophisticated version of the "hollow sphere" type of planetarium that spectators entered was constructed between 1911 and 1913 by Wallace Atwood for the Chicago Academy of Sciences.[8] However, the prototype for today's planetarium projectors can be traced to the famous optical firm of Messrs.

Carl Zeiss of Jena, Germany, which between 1919 and 1922 worked on perfecting the technology for the opening of the Zeiss planetarium in Jena in 1924. Jointly conceived by Dr. Walther Bauersfeld and Werner Straubel of Zeiss, the projection planetarium received its first public demonstration on October 21, 1923 at the Deutsches Museum in Munich.[9] In Bauersfeld's words, the planetarium consisted of a "series of integrated projection lanterns by means of which the stars, sun, and planets are thrown upon the vaulted dome acting as a screen. The bulbous end of the instrument carry [sic] the slides for the fixed stars of the northern and southern firmaments respectively, while in the shank . . . the orbits of the sun, moon, and planets are arranged in tiers. Separate projectors are provided for the Milky Way, for Sirius, and for the brighter nebulae."[10] Zeiss projectors still dominate in space shows, and in 2000, the AMNH installed a Mark IX Zeiss projector for the Hayden Planetarium in the new Rose Center for Earth and Space.

Among the hurdles the Zeiss scientists had to overcome in the late 1910s and early 1920s was an opposition between the planetarium as a signifier of precision engineering and the planetarium as a device capable of unparalleled mimeticism. While we should tread with care when drawing too stark ontological comparisons between the planetarium and the motion picture, how each phenomenon was discursively constructed in the historical record as a superlative conveyor of illusion is worth briefly exploring. In contrast to the Zeiss planetarium, which German engineers initially thought was incapable of replicating the nighttime sky and astral configurations, the film projector was from its inception often referred to as nature's ally, a machine that could, in Tom Gunning's words, "serve as both tool of discovery and means of verification in a new worldview constructed on an investigation of actual entities explored through their visible aspects."[11] A "manufactured luminescence," a light that Antonia Lant argues was influenced by an Orientalist discourse, especially Egyptological referents, cinema was in no ways ontologically challenged in the task of conjuring up reality; in fact, cinema, like the sun, created light where previously there was none. Citing the early film theorist Vachel Lindsay, Lant sees valences in the metaphorical parallels he draws between cinema and the sun, a connection of especial interest to the subject of planetariums. According to Lant, Lindsay viewed film-going as akin to "sun-worshipping . . . a going to the sun" and considered cinema an instance of "our present ritual in the worship of light."[12] That Lindsey should be writing in 1924 at exactly the same time as the Zeiss planetarium opened to the public leads us to speculate on whether he was at all familiar with the experiments at Jena (trials open to

The Hayden Planetarium in an artist's rendition, looking like a giant egg from which a dinosaur has escaped. The audience lined out the door and people standing in the background present a serious challenge to the fire safety code (ca. 1935). Neg. no. 117195, courtesy of the Department of Library Services, AMNH.

the public took place in 1919) or was simply satisfying an intellectual curiosity for theories of light and projection.[13]

And yet cinema's positivism (and doppelganger, the uncanny) created a parallel universe and distinctly modernist subjectivity that while signifying reality did not pretend to represent it with the exact same perceptual coordinates as the human eye (the image, for one, is far larger than the corresponding reality, unless the vista on the screen is a distant landscape). The planetarium projector was thus charged with the engineering challenge of simulating vision into outer space, as if the roof of the dome had silently peeled back its covering to reveal the inky sky. Clyde Fisher, the director of the Hayden Planetarium, not only fell hook, line, and sinker for the illusionism when he visited Jena but was convinced that "due to some sub-conscious imagination . . . this artificial sky seems to possess the deep night blue seen in the real sky, and yet there is no blue color on the inside of the dome and none in the projection apparatus."[14]

But the Zeiss I model projector, capable of projecting forty-five hundred stars, was also charged with the task of representing what exceeded human vision, converting astronomical theory and projection into legible, visualizable images. However, in the minds of the scientists and engineers in Jena, early versions of the planetarium were too mechanical, too cumbersome, too terrestrial even to rise to the logistical and ontological challenge of replicating stargazing. And yet, we shouldn't lose sight of the fact that while these very early blueprints of the planetarium may seem at odds with cinema in relation to how reality was represented on the screen, the planetarium quickly turned to the world of popular culture for inspiration on how to transform the celestial heavens into an entertainment medium as well as an object lesson in astronomy. The repertoire of suitable planetarium topics quickly expanded, adding narrative, music, sound, special effects, and, starting in the 1960s, lasers. But not everyone was entirely happy about the planetarium's unproblematic descent from the "Wonder of Jena" show of 1923; Ian C. McLenna, the director of the Starsenburgh Planetarium in Rochester, New York argued at the meeting of the Middle Atlantic Planetarium Society in 1967 that he often wished that "invention of the planetarium were still a future event, and the inventor an astronomer rather than an engineer." In his opinion, the planetarium's geocentrism impeded its ability to present "conceptual or descriptive astronomy unless intricate, and sometimes expensive ancillary equipment" was added.[15] We therefore see an interesting binary between the "give them what they want" model of planetarium showmanship premised upon an Aristotelian/Ptolemaic view of the universe and a more scientifically ambitious approach proposed by McLenna. Writing roughly at the same time as McLenna, Dr. Henry Charles King thought that planetariums should be purged of gimmickry: in his words, "the modern sky, whether real or artificial, is not a sky to gape at but one to think about . . . You can almost hear the mental blinkers being removed. You know that every word is 'going home.'"[16]

INTERMEDIAL CROSSINGS:
SITUATING THE PLANETARIUM PHENOMENOLOGICALLY

> They see what is tantamount to a moving picture of the heavens—a picture portrayed with such realism that they feel they are sitting out of doors on the clearest night looking up at the canopy of stars overhead. —HENRY CHARLES KING, *The London Planetarium* (1958)

Like the nineteenth-century panorama, a 360-degree painting that surrounds spectators who enter and stand on a central viewing platform, the planetarium experience takes place inside a dome where a virtual reality is illusion-istically constructed.[17] However, unlike the panorama, spectators are seated rather than ambulatory, and the image is subject to considerable change as past, present, and future star constellations, galaxies, and universal phe-nomena such as black holes, asteroids, and meteors are projected onto the dome. The analogies are complex, though, with the similarities both vestigial and blatantly obvious. Each phenomenon takes place in a darkened audito-rium, although the panorama is packaged less as a performance and more as a fairground-type *trompe l'oeil*, where payment guarantees entry that in most in-stances is not timed but is contingent on spectators finally deciding they have seen enough and leaving the viewing platform in the rotunda. The insulated dome that entombs spectators for the duration of the performance is remi-niscent of the cinema auditorium, although in contrast to film, which requires spectators to look straight in front of them (or at a slight angle if they are seated on the wings), the planetarium requires an upward gaze, a look to the "celestial heavens." If in cinema the contiguity of time and space is provided by editing, in the planetarium, stars tend to dissolve from one configuration to the next rather than change suddenly, although this is by no means a hard and fast rule, since principles of editing are also to be found in planetarium shows and most of them today use motion pictures along with a range of spe-cial effects. Cinema's capacity for spatial and temporal manipulation was also realized in the planetarium, although with one difference: there were still the basic ingredients of one sun, one moon, five naked-eye planets, a Milky Way, and some three thousand stars. "Turn the planetarium sky back a thousand years more, move it forward in time a thousand years" and little would really change, hence the need, in King's words, "for additional dramatic material of a visual and mental nature."[18]

Configured something like a mathematical Venn diagram, where panora-mas, planetariums, and cinema share phenomenological properties found in the overlapping circles at the center, each must nevertheless be considered on its own terms in relation to spectatorship, mimesis, the exigencies of the exhibition space, and science and popular culture. Rather than belabor the similarities and differences between the three signifying practices, it is more productive to let their points of convergence and divergence become obvious to the reader. Any effort to articulate exactly what a planetarium experience is like, especially given the range of shows on offer in planetariums across the world (from hi-tech to low-tech), may end up being as elusive as the one written by an anonymous contributor to *Vogue* in 1935, who, in struggling to make sense of the planetarium's contradictory vectors, ended up embracing its paradoxes: "It is so far above the merely informative that it approaches the uplifting. And, ironically, it is also somewhat unearthly. It makes you feel successively, like an ancient philosopher, the weather man, and God."[19]

Notwithstanding the slipperiness of the planetarium as a signifier, a guidebook published by the United Nations Office for Outer Space Affairs in 2000 is surprisingly candid about the dos and don'ts of planetarium space shows (with some of the questions sounding a little like market research for the Playboy channel), especially the section entitled "Production Values for Planetariums," which begins with advice on the script and how to reach an audience: "What do people expect to see? How do they react to your shows now? What turns them off in a show? What turns them on in a show? It's important to know the answer to these questions." Recommending regular use of questionnaires, surveys, and even the posting of an "unmarked staff member/volunteer near the exit to gauge people's reactions," the authors aren't shy with their directives: "Listen to people as they leave. Are they animated and excited about the show? Are they shuffling out like zombies?"[20] Also on the list of recommendations are such issues as the need for accuracy, careful selection of narrator ("avoid the DJ/Voice of God/Newscaster narrator"), and music that "complements and enhances each new section or theme in the show" rather than a "'bed' of music that just lies there throughout the show." On the subject of visuals, the authors recommend including fewer of high quality over many of low quality, and varying the style such as mixing slides with video, slides with special effects, and varying the fade rates, screen locations, and use of animation and dissolve effects.[21] The chapter ends with a direct comparison to cinema: "We can't outdo movies, but we do have a unique theater which offers an experience a movie can't duplicate. Play up our strengths and minimize the weaknesses."[22]

That the UN document constructs the planetarium experience as a show requiring almost as much careful choreography as a Broadway musical should come as no surprise if we consider the historical interlacing of theater and science in the planetarium. Based on the sentiment in this document, what audiences encounter when they step inside the dome has to far exceed any old-fashioned notion of stars projected on a screen while an (obligatory) male narrator's solipsistic voice puts them to sleep.[23] This point is made clear in a chapter by J. E. Bishop in the same document in which we are told that auxiliary effects such as slides and audio aids must not only contribute to the realism but also promote an "aesthetic (peak) experience in the planetarium."[24]

Bishop's use of the word aesthetic here can be read in the Kierkegaardian sense of grasping the immediate impact of a phenomenon, what Alistair Hannay in his introduction to Kierkegaard's *Fear and Trembling* describes as something striking you in the here and now, of its tendency to attract or repel you through a sense of immediacy, as is found in a peak experience.[25] As described by Abraham Maslow a peak experience consists of emotions of "wonder, awe, reverence, humility, surrender, and even worship before the greatness of the experience."[26] Strange as it may seem, Kierkegaard's treatise on the subject of faith in *Fear and Trembling* resonates in intriguing ways with many of the themes and goals of the planetarium space show, such as the desire for higher knowledge and the struggle to articulate about such metaphysical and abstract concepts as faith and the universe. As the planetarium historian Jordan D. Marché II put it: "As purveyors of the modern understanding of space and time, Zeiss planetaria were deemed capable of imparting to audience members a profound sense of the magnificent structure and divine purpose of our universe."[27] Indeed, two of the most important American donors — Samuel Fels (Fels Planetarium, Philadelphia) and Charles Hayden (Hayden Planetarium, New York) — "were strongly attracted by the planetarium's purported affirmation of spiritual values," especially given the rise of anti-Semitism, which Fels and Hayden felt could be somehow mitigated; in Marché's words, each man shared an "optimism that planetaria might allow human differences to seem inconsequential by comparison to the immensity of the cosmos in which all Earth's inhabitants are enjoined."[28] Cinema it seemed, or at least the idea of projected images on the planetarium dome, could be harnessed to serve this cause.

Discourses of spirituality and faith crept into the planetarium space show like a hermit crab, especially from the 1930s through to the 1950s. For example, the idea of the planetarium performance as a "drama of the heavens" (a phrase used in 1938 by the authors of a *Cartoon Guide of New York City*),[29] or the notion that "the heavens can be brought to earth," serves as a refrain in planetarium reviews and promotional materials. In 1958, the popular author Billy Arthur argued that "the unique nature of the building makes it seem a spiritual as well as a cultural heaven," a sentiment echoed the same year in a Zeiss brochure pronouncing that "an hour in a Zeiss planetarium is like an hour in a mysterious temple, where we can leave the world and its everlasting rush far behind."[30] But if one was left in any doubt as to the quasi-religious nature of the planetarium, the show's content drove home the association, with many American planetariums, not surprisingly given their marketing game plans and desire to tap into audience interest, programming around the Christian calendar, with the Easter "Awakening" and "The Skies of Christmas Past"[31] attracting the biggest crowds.[32]

A staple of almost all planetariums in the United States in the 1950s and 1960s, the Christmas show not only underscored the non-secular proclivities of planetarium directors and curators, but also provided a golden opportunity to showcase special effects and to push the tone of the performance into the realm of the seriously kitsch, although for some spectators the religious content simply underscored the re-signification of the planetarium auditorium as a pseudo place of worship, not dissimilar to the transformation of movie theaters during the theatrical run of Mel Gibson's controversial hagio-flick *The Passion of the Christ* in the spring of 2004.[33] To quote Marché: "In the minds of several observers, planetarium lessons conveyed almost sacred experiences that placed them nearly on a level with churches or cathedrals."[34] Featuring a "very beautiful carousel . . . with all sorts of animals on it and sleighs and Christmas effects," the "Skies of Christmas Past" sounds more like a Radio City Hall extravaganza than a dignified Nativity.[35] In a poster for the "Star of Bethlehem" (ca. 1957), audience, projector, and star shore up the theatrical nature of the experience; as if appearing on a stage, the three wise men are cloaked in a spotlight while the projector protrudes into the sky like some medieval torture device. The representation of light in this image provides a fascinating meta-comment on the circulation of meaning, both secular and spiritual. Moreover, the layering of the biblical, the astronomical, and the commercial kitsch of Nativity iconography speaks volumes to the heterogeneous origins and valences of the planetarium show; the upward gaze of the spectators is an elegiac sign, affirming the neo-spiritualist undercurrent of the planetarium as a temple of worship, while the sky, star, and wise men look like they've been lifted from the cover of a Hallmark Christmas card.

Theatricality also functions as a metaphor not just for the planetarium show, but for the entire apparatus, as Armand Spitz, an American manufacturer of portable planetariums from the 1950s, argued in 1959: "'Planetarium' connotes an experience, and, in this light, must be differently planned and executed than any single facet of operation. It is more or less like 'theatre' as a general term, including every detail that goes to make the experience — theater building, stagecraft, playwriting, acting etc."[36] Waldemar Kaempffert collapsed theater with time travel, in this review of a space show at the Hayden Planetarium in 1928: "The lights are turned down gradually, just as in a theatre before the curtain rises on a play. Gradually your eyes accustom them-

Poster for "The Star of Bethlehem" at the Hayden Planetarium (ca. 1950). Neg. no. 322423, courtesy of the Department of Library Services, AMNH.

selves to the darkness. You lose all sense of confinement. In some incomprehensible optical way you have been transported into the open on a marvelously pellucid night."[37] However, while the planetarium is man-made, its chief concern is with representations that, while mediated, are *not* constructed in exactly the same way as other modes of popular culture, although in terms of iconography, the dividing line between the planetarium as astronomy and as pulpy, mass entertainment is increasingly hard to distinguish. Nevertheless, the idea of the planetarium as a performative space is signaled not only in the debate around the need to have a lecturer present, versus a "canned" show, but in the appropriation of theatrical terms: the stars are literally the *stars* of the show, the backdrop envisioned as one gigantic theatrical setting. Writing in the *New York Times* in 1928, Walter Kaempffert referred to the planetarium as a "playhouse in which the majestic drama of the firmament is unfolded." As the performance gets under way "a hush falls over the spectators. No *play* is ever more intently followed than this in which constellations, stars, planets, sun and moon enact their parts."[38] As a way of drawing a wide audience and staving off potential boredom, the planetarium show had to steer a careful path between astronomy and spectacle, as Franz Fieseler surmised in 1932: "Far too little attention is paid to the fact that the adult visitor does not as a rule, want to be instructed and only comes to look round; he merely wants to gaze and wonder and he ought not be prevented from doing so."[39] Interlacing striking visuals and special effects into a forty-minute planetarium show was considered vital in the war against waning spectator interest (although the battle against somnambulism, as I recently discovered in the Boston Charles Hayden Planetarium, can be hard fought).

CLOSE ENCOUNTERS OF THE CELESTIAL KIND:
THE DISCURSIVE EXCESS OF THE ZEISS PROJECTOR

> It is a school, theater and cinema in one, a school room under the vault of the heavens, a drama with the celestial bodies as actors.—PROFESSOR D. STROMGREN, 1928, quoted in Riesman, "The Zeiss Planetarium"

Prominent in the discourse on planetariums was a tension between expressions of wonder at the visual spectacle and the centripetal force of scientific rationalism; located literally and metaphorically at the epicenter of the performance is the Zeiss projector, an overdetermined and visually stunning icon, invested with fantasmatic meaning far exceeding the technological sum of its individual parts. The genre of science fiction writing is a ready referent in promotion stills from the Hayden Planetarium in which the dome itself becomes a spacecraft. Across time, and in a wide swath of professional and popular sources, the Zeiss projector is anthropomorphized into a cross between the Greek mythical monsters Typhon, a creature with many heads, and Argus, a monster with multiple sets of eyes. Kaempffert, for example, in 1928, called the projector a god-like machine that "makes the heavens do his bidding."[40] Gendered and invested with omniscient powers, although forever at the mercy of the all-powerful projectionist, whose role in the mid-1920s, as Marché points out, was nevertheless ill defined ("whether the individual should be considered a scientist, technician, educator, or entertainer was not yet clear"), the Zeiss projector is a highly adaptive technology capable of negotiating myriad tropes from rich intertextual sites, as well as projecting powerful beams of light from its bulbous eyes.[41] Capable of (literally) reflecting and refracting both Christian and classical Greek epistemes, the projector is summarily dismissed neither as a monster nor as a technological deity but as a fusion of the two. Writing in 1928, the journalist David Riesman described what he saw as a "grotesque looking instrument like a huge dumb-bell or a caterpillar with sprawling arms," while a *New York Times* reviewer in 1984 claimed that the spectacle had been projected by nothing less than "a graceful yet grotesque machine."[42]

Overinvestment in the projector as an anthropomorphized sign extraordinaire must also be read against the backdrop of the 1930s, an era suffering from the aftershock of the stock market crash of 1929 and a depression that left global economies on their knees. Not only could the Zeiss take us out of the world of unemployment, soup kitchens, and limited prosperity, as Marché points out, it could offer an alluring prescription to a world "laced with discord, animosity, and anxiety . . . a reassurance of supernatural purpose and design in the universe, to be fostered by attendance at the mechanized demonstrations of projection planetaria."[43] For Samuel Fels in particular, the stars could serve as a parable for ills of the era, harboring "'special meaning' for those beset with the uncertainties of a depression-ridden world." According to Marché, Fels urged men and women to "draw inspiration from the celestial pageantry as they repeatedly addressed the 'problems and promises of our changing world.'"[44] Indeed, the lectures of James Stockley, an astronomer at the Fels Planetarium, reflected "many of the broader social anxieties that swirled through a depression-ridden world poised on the brink of its second global conflict," in the process blurring the lines between projection booth, soap-box, and pulpit. (According to Marché, Stockley developed some of the most provocative and controversial planetarium programs of the prewar period, even fostering a rivalry of sorts with New York's Hayden Planetarium.)[45] Here we see the planetarium assuming a quasi-civic mission in diverting people's attention away from their plight (assuming they could afford to go to a planetarium) by offering intangible benefits: as Marché puts it, "as the 1930s drifted toward another global conflict, planetaria and their associated science museums were looked upon as emblems of American democracy, upholding and strengthening the values of free institutions and the freedom of inquiry that they embodied."[46]

TRIPS TO THE MOON AND POSTWAR AMERICA

One of the most creative ways that planetarium directors and educators leveraged public fascination in the science of astronomy while alleviating Depression-related anxiety was through the idea of space travel to the moon, which continued at least through the 1950s. The idea was not a new one, however. Georges Méliès's film of 1902, *Le voyage dans la lune*, was "not only the first science fiction film but also the first cinematic spoof of the genre," according to Elizabeth Ezra, a Méliès scholar. *Le voyage dans la lune* was also the title of a hugely popular illustrated lecture produced in New York by Garrett P. Erviss and also reproduced in Berlin in 1887.[47] In 1897, Albert A. Hopkins devoted a chapter of his *Magic: Stage Illusions and Scientific Diversions* to show how the illusion of witnessing the surface of the moon in the 1880s was created using two optical lanterns (magic lanterns) and foot, border, arc, and bunch lights.[48] The moon, as Ezra explains, had long been a "locus of narrative mystery and desire at least since the publication of Cyrano de Bergerac's *L'Autre monde* in the 17th century." (*Le voyage dans la lune* was based in part on a fantasy stage play adapted by Adolphe Dennery from Jules Verne.)[49] More recently, the Fels Planetarium began transforming the planetarium chamber into an imaginary space ship in 1936, taking its "visitors on imaginative trips to the moon, Mars, Saturn, and Jupiter."[50] Auxiliary projectors would show the landscape of these planets, and audiences would be primed for the hypothetical "Trip to the Moon" that would take place during the planetarium's centennial in the year 2033. The Fels even hired Dick Calkins, the creator of the Buck Rogers comic strip, who reportedly designed the control panel visible on the navigator's bridge.[51]

One of the most popular planetarium displays presented at the Hayden Planetarium in the summer of 1953 was described by Robert R. Coles, the chairman of the planetarium, as "a simulated trip on a rocket to the moon, in which spectators watching the planetarium's domed ceiling were *whisked* a quarter million miles through space for a landing at one of the moon's craters."[52] In the early 1950s, the Hayden Planetarium stretched the time travel analogy to its limits, when it mocked up a travel agency where children could "purchase" tickets to the moon.[53] Posters resembling package holiday ads touted the thrills of the excursion, inviting children (and adults) to mentally assimilate the idea of virtual travel via role-play (museum staff play-acted as travel agents). Ten years later, a virtually identical description of the planetarium show appeared in *Hart's Guide to New York City*: "Here's a fascinating way to take a trip to outer space. You sit in a comfortable chair in the Sky Theater and are *whisked* anywhere in the solar system. And, most surprisingly, you can travel in the past and in the future, as well as in the present."[54] Attend the Hayden Planetarium at the AMNH today, and you'll find that "whisking" has been replaced by a rather more prosaic "flying," although the theme of virtual travel is preserved: for a price of $24 ($14 for children), visitors are "sent into space using a Digital Dome System which flies audiences through a scientifically accurate virtual re-creation of our Milky Way Galaxy and beyond, to the 'edge' of the observable universe."[55]

When Apollo 11, commanded by Neil Armstrong and Edwin "Buzz" Aldrin, touched down on the moon in 1969 (three years after the Soviet Union made travel to the moon a reality), the Hayden Planetarium was quick to exploit the public's keen interest in this landmark event. Special coverage of the Apollo 11 splashdown at the Hayden included the use of ten American Airlines air stewards (all female) who served as "hostesses . . . dressed in space-travel costumes from the popular motion picture *2001: A Space Odyssey*." The soundtrack from the now cult classic film would "provide background music during the event." After a splashdown celebration luncheon, guests left with tray replicas of the plaque deposited on the moon and containers of space food.[56] Sponsored by Western Union International, the event is early evidence of the museum's unproblematic embrace of Edward Bernays's public relations techniques blended with Hollywood-style razzmatazz. That corporations (Western Union and American Airlines) celebrated this gargantuan achievement in U.S. space exploration suggests the ease with which the planetarium negotiated the worlds of business, astronomy, public relations, and popular culture. In fact, given the boost the Apollo 11 mission gave to planetarium attendance, it would have been shortsighted of the AMNH *not* to jump on the bandwagon. The AMNH's director, Dr. Franklyn Branley, delivered a lecture in the Hayden to honor the occasion and prior to splashdown a ten-minute film about the recovery ship the USS *Hornet* was screened. Entitled *The Right People at the Right Time*, it was sponsored by Western Union.

The postwar prosperity and culture of the cold war are also key informing contexts of the 1950s and should be taken into consideration when thinking about cinema's utility within the planetarium. Given that the 1950s were, as

Lynn Spigel reminds us, years in which society invested "an enormous amount of capital in the ability to form a family and live out a set of highly structured gender and generational roles," it should come as no surprise that popular astronomy and the planetarium space show were instrumental in this ideological task of consensus building.[57] With the planetarium competing against new forms of recreation targeting the entire family, such as television and theme parks, there was an added incentive to invest the show with a degree of relevancy that spoke to the zeitgeist, that alleviated anxieties about the present as the planetarium lecturer had done in the Depression-era talks of the 1930s, and that would hopefully lead to repeat visits. Disneyland, which opened in Anaheim, California in 1955, capitalized fully on the postwar interest in space travel and the belief that it would soon become a reality. The "Tomorrowland" exhibit depicted "simulated views from an earth-orbiting space station and a Rocket to the Moon ride," and Disney also produced a TV program entitled "Man in Space" which was broadcast on March 9, 1955.[58] This utopian vision of interplanetary travel was undercut, in the United States at least, by the dystopic shadow of the cold war, as Thomas Doherty explains in *Cold War, Cool Medium*: "The atomic bomb and, after 1952, the hydrogen bomb augured an apocalyptic payoff to the superpower face-off. For the first time in human history, the prospect of species annihilation, not just military defeat or cities laid to waste, loomed as a decided possibility."[59] There was even an ironic twist in the prospect of nuclear Armageddon serving as a backdrop to space travel; our own society on earth might vanish at the same time as other civilizations are discovered and humans can leave their planet for the first time.

Armand N. Spitz invented the portable pinhole planetarium, which, standing at three feet high and weighing thirty-five pounds, projected roughly one thousand stars down to the fourth magnitude. According to Marché it was "equipped with an electric motor that provided diurnal rotation in four minutes," it could be turned by hand, and its metal base was adjustable for a range of northern latitudes.[60] Seeing an opportunity to enter the market, especially when Zeiss suspended manufacture with the outbreak of war in 1939, Spitz unveiled his Model A projector in 1945.[61] Spitz attempted to ease the tensions of the cold war by appropriating a spiritualist discourse to promote universal humanism; in 1959 he wrote, "A Planetarium can inspire, almost to the point of being a semi-religious experience without being narrowed by sectarianism. It can be used to develop an appreciation of the abstract, and can give the most cynical members of the audience a sense of identity with other human beings who, like themselves, have the privilege of understanding something of the universe of which they are part."[62]

A piston in the engine of postwar prosperity and emergent consumerism, suburban living served as a backdrop for astronomy both ideologically in terms of space race propaganda and American idealism and literally as seen in an issue from the 1950s of the amateur magazine *Astronomy and You*, the front cover of which constructs astronomy as a highly social and bonding experience for both family and friends and is a useful indicator of what popular astronomy had become (and would go on to become).[63] Beneath the bright red title is an oval-shaped, matted drawing of a 1950s nuclear family standing in the yard of their house with a telescope on a tripod.[64] The bush in the foreground and the distant house in the left mid-ground are the only signs of life. Two-thirds of the image is taken up by the blue night sky full of twinkling stars. The representation of the family (with their backs to the camera) codes astronomy as a gendered pastime, with women and girls welcome additions providing they stand passively rather than actively participate. Reflecting Spigel's idea that "advice manuals and popular magazines also encouraged consumer-family lifestyles in private suburban homes,"[65] the cover shows an archetypal nuclear family, an image of the suburban family ideal, which Spigel claims was a "consensus ideology, promising practical benefits like security and stability to people who had witnessed the shocks and social dislocations of the previous two decades."[66] Looking carefully at the image, we notice that the son, who is clearly the older of the two children, is the only one actually using the telescope (the magazine, while appealing to boys, is not specifically targeting them), while his father—the "expert"—points out star constellations from behind. With their arms around one another (possibly because the temperature is cool), the mother and daughter are passive onlookers (the girl cannot even reach the eyepiece of the telescope unless the tripod legs are lowered or she is lifted up!).

Inside the planetarium dome, images of stargazers, especially children, served as calling cards for the space shows and journalistic reviews of shows. The photograph of five young schoolchildren attending a show at the Hayden Planetarium is no exception; the three children in the right-hand side of the image all crane their necks to gaze up at the ceiling, while the barely visible boy in the far left-hand side of the image has his hand up to his mouth and looks off to the right. The most enigmatic and memorable face in the photograph, however, belongs to the girl in the center who, rather than crane her

Front cover of *Astronomy and You* (ca. 1950s). Planetarium Ephemera Collection, courtesy of the Department of Library Services, AMNH.

neck upward, stares bug-eyed directly ahead with a look of bemusement on her face. Her transfixed expression is utterly captivating; staring directly ahead rather than up at the dome makes the girl a fascinating subject. While clearly enthralled at the ensuing show, she is nevertheless *not* responding in the same way as her classmates. And yet her look of wide-eyed wonder is disarmingly effective in conveying the rhapsodic nature of the experience. We might compare this image with the boy and the girl in Wright's painting *The Philosopher Reading a Lecture on the Orrery*. While also lost in thought, perhaps they long for a similarly visceral and embodied engagement with astronomy. These images of spectators' faces foreshadow the "wow effect" reaction shot that is ubiquitous in Imax film promotion, but they also tell stories of imaginations at work and somatic engagement, bodies and minds deeply affected by the sensory thrill of the planetarium space show. What is interesting about these images of spectators is that they could be looking at a movie screen, a correspondence that is perhaps the most evocative when we trace the cinematic in the planetarium show.

Rapturous wonder at the Hayden Planetarium space show (ca. 1950s). Neg. no. 2a1509, courtesy of the Department of Library Services, AMNH.

CINEMA IS/NOT THE PLANETARIUM: CONCLUDING REMARKS

The effect is overpowering; our flesh prickles and superlatives seem inadequate.

—"The Typical Performance and General Description of the Planetarium," in the

Special Collection of the American Museum of Natural History

The cinema certainly becomes "useful" in the space show, although exactly how it has been integrated into the performance, and how its status today has been largely replaced by the digital interface of the computer video game are issues that call for more research and theorizing. Comparisons to cinema have flowed freely throughout the planetarium's history; writing in the *World's Work* in 1927, O. D. Tolischus said that "this miracle of art and science is accomplished by the utilization of the moving picture principle. For the modern planetarium is really a moving picture of the sky," although Marché (who originally used the above quote), offers a quick corrective to the comparison, arguing that "apart from the optical projection of their images, there was little resemblance between a planetarium instrument and motion picture projector; no film of any kind was transported through the former."[67] Marché also cites Albert G. Ingalls's positive impression of the planetarium show from 1929 in which he enthused, "[it was] the best 'movie' I have ever seen." While Marché is quick to acknowledge that these journalists are speaking metaphorically, the fact that there is no engagement whatsoever with why journalists and audience members alike turned to cinema as a point of comparison is symptomatic I think of a more general reluctance to engage with how cinema becomes useful in the planetarium. Moreover, while Marché is correct that film was hardly ever projected in the planetarium dome, moving images did contribute to the overall planetarium experience and, with the invention of videotape in 1956, were projected on the domed ceiling. It is not so much cinema as projected film but the entire cinematic apparatus that is re-signified in the planetarium: discourses of virtual travel, escapism, mimesis, a temporary respite from the noise and frantic pace of the surging metropolis, and a place to achieve optimal viewing conditions that had been compromised by light pollution, fog, and haze. David Riesman, in his review of the Zeiss planetarium in 1928, lamented the unfavorable viewing conditions besetting urban dwellers: "Unfortunately, the majority of the inhabitants of our towns and cities seldom have an opportunity on account of the disturbing lights and the haze on the horizon of getting a good view of the heavens."[68] The ability to see clear skies above them was the prime reason multitudes visited the planetarium, "away from the fog and smoke of the city," in the words of Marian Lockwood, the former acting curator of the Adler Planetarium and one of the few women to achieve a directorship (in 1944).[69]

We may therefore need to rephrase the question about useful cinema and the planetarium, approaching it less as the literal inclusion of moving images in the show and more as a shared ontological desire to deliver unsurpassed illusionism. Reactions of wonderment accompanying the emergence of cinema in the 1890s that were directed as much — if not more — toward the apparatus as to the films resurface in the discourse surrounding the planetarium, when, as Marché, contends, "wonder and awe are expressed as human ingenuity in creating an exact, miniature replica of the heavens."[70] Not only does the planetarium space show provide optimal viewing conditions, but it also becomes an exemplar, an originary moment for star gazing, as King explained in 1958: "For forty minutes we sit enthralled as the age-old pageant of the skies is unfolded. In this time we see more than most of us can ever hope to see in a lifetime."[71] But cinema and the planetarium also line up on the subject of automation, which in the case of the planetarium mitigates the need for a live lecturer. Joseph Miles Chamberlain invested the tape recorder with not inconsiderable powers when he described a scenario in 1958 in which "if the lecturer is suddenly called away by some emergency, he can flick a switch and a tape recording will take over, giving the lecture, dimming the house lights, turning on the stars, putting the planets through their proper motions in perfect synchronization with the lecture, finally bringing the daybreak and sunrise, then turning on the house lights, thanking people for listening and inviting them to come again."[72] What the automated lecture gained in institutional convenience (and budget savings) it lost, in King's view, in its capacity for mental and visual imagery since for him, the speaker, "alive and compelling, is an integral part of the experience." For King, the speaker "identifies himself with his audience and with his presentation, and his voice is more than a 'soundtrack' on a film or reel of magnetized tape."[73]

That most large science and natural history museums contain both planetariums *and* Imax screens is testimony not only to their preeminent status as lucrative funding streams (the only source of admissions-based revenue in the case of the National Museum of Natural History in Washington, which is otherwise free), but also to their longstanding success in drawing audiences who are willing to pay for a programmed, thrilling, audiovisual experience that they feel they won't be exposed to if left to their own devices. Akin in some ways to the amusement park, where there are never any free rides, the experience bought will be far and beyond what one can find unassisted. For example, displaying (fetishizing even) the planetarium dome in a glass box at the AMNH as an object of beauty and wonder performs much of the show's ideological work even before the visitors reach the "departure lounge" (a feature of the dome and the projector that has long been exploited by museums). Not only does the Hayden Planetarium in the new Rose Center for Space and Earth go to lengths to connect the planetarium to its sister galleries, but also it openly acknowledges (exploits even) its close resemblance to cinema. The FAQ section of the Hayden Planetarium advises us to "keep in mind that the environment inside the theater is similar to a movie theater, in that it is dark, and the audience is surrounded by sounds and images."[74] The planetarium has in fact become a movie theater on occasions throughout its history, as evidenced by the "Cinema in the Sky" series jointly presented by the Franklin Institute and the Philadelphia Museum of Art in 1971. One of six films sponsored by the National Film Board of Canada's "Notes on a Triangle" was projected on the dome of the Fels Planetarium, representing what the *Franklin Institute News* called "new techniques in audiovisual communications by independent artists."[75] This is one of the few references to the planetarium dome literally becoming a movie theater; indeed, if the comments made by Ianis Arnoldovich Miezis, the curator of the Riga Planetarium, at the 5th International Planetarium Director's Conference in 1975 were in any way typical — "Under no circumstances should the visit to the Planetarium be reduced to the projection of a single film — for in this way the specific character of the equipment would be effaced" — then one can detect a proprietary claim on the planetarium experience as distinct from cinema, as a version of useful cinema with the emphasis on the *useful* rather than the *cinema*.[76]

Where then is cinema's utility in the contemporary planetarium space show? *Like* a movie but somehow different is how my pre-teen son described "Passport to the Universe" at the New York's Hayden Planetarium in 2006. Lacking the interactive dimension of the computer game that provides multiple points of entry and yet delivering on the immersive sensation that is a hallmark of both IMAX film and the graphical interface of computer games, the planetarium still needs the authority of astronomy in order to reign in these much needed but potentially contaminating popular culture influences. And yet the wonder of the Zeiss projector has been usurped by projected video, which now seems to take up much of the show. The Model IX Zeiss that uses fiber optics and forty-five integrated computers still relies upon projected video on the domed ceiling to expand the visual repertory of the program and to make shows appear more cinematic and similar in some ways to theme park dark rides that propel audiences into virtual spaces such as black holes.[77] However, as the art historian Damon Stanek observed at a show he attended in the fall of 2005, "Essentially the Hayden offered visitors big screen television, and not even high definition."[78] For fear that too much fantasy, as represented by the thrill ride connotations of the obligatory "entering a black hole" trope of high-tech planetarium space shows, might correspond too closely to Universal Studio type rides that Lauren Rabinovitz writes about,[79] the AMNH Web site and planetarium narrators point out the scientific credentials of such shows as "Passport to the Universe," which take visitors on an "exhilarating flight through a virtual recreation of our universe . . . [using] data on our solar system from NASA and the European Space Agency, and a statistical database of more than two billion stars developed by the Museum."[80]

While contemporary space shows rely increasingly on digital special effects, it would be misleading to assume that their intermedial status is by any means new. In many ways, much has changed but even more has stayed the same in the planetarium: its phenomenological infrastructure, like the steel and concrete skin stretched over its domed roof, still depends to a large extent on virtual travel, metaphysical contemplation of the nature of the universe, discourses of nationalist supremacy that first surfaced during the years of the space race, and, most significantly, sound effects, music, and narration. Without sound, the planetarium is a mute lecturer, a visual spectacle with little to bring that spectacle to life and yet, ironically, the world it represents is completely silent.

Untangling cinema's relationship to the planetarium is by no means an easy task; that the moving image has become a standard feature of re-vamped shows such as those at the swanky new Hayden is a given, although the galaxy itself is created by a Silicon Graphics Onyx2 InfiniteReality2 visual workstation, a supercomputer that generates a 3-D map of the galaxy. However, not all planetariums are as hi-tech as the Hayden Planetarium at the Rose Center for Earth and Space; the "Countdown to Supernova" at the Charles Hayden Planetarium at the Boston Museum of Science is far less kinetic than the New York Hayden's "Passport to the Universe," containing only short sequences of time-lapse video of the sun and a black hole. Irrespective of *how* the special effects audiences witness in the planetarium dome are created, the bottom line is that for most spectators these special effects are closely related to cinema, and for those Play Stationers and X-Boxers in the audience they resonate with the visual aesthetic of the video game save the missing tactile component. Pat Frendreis of the Adler Planetarium, who arranged for the transfer of the old Mark VI Zeiss from the Hayden, is not a fan of the newer planetarium shows whose effects are mostly accomplished using video projectors: "You're looking at a video image, so the stars are greenish and soft," he says, unlike the "*real* stars of the Zeiss [Mark VI]."[81] Not surprisingly, video takes up a significant proportion of contemporary space shows and carries a great deal of the space simulation sequences such as meteors, black holes, supernovas, and the like. For example, the script for "Countdown to Supernova," created by J. Kelly Beatty for the New York Hayden in December 2004, includes a time-lapse video showing a "seething sun . . . which zooms in and fills [the] southern sky,"[82] a sequence of a planetary nebula expanding, exploding stars, and a black hole consuming matter. Whether *most* planetarium space shows are shifting the emphasis away from Zeiss-dependent performances toward more digitally enhanced, computer-generated shows would require empirically based research on the content of planetarium shows in North American and, ideally, across the globe. Planetariums such as the Adler can satisfy the tastes of audiences accustomed to (and desirous of) more conventional shows with its traditional space show in the original dome while simultaneously drawing in newer (and presumably younger) audiences to the StarRider Theater. What we see taking place in the planetarium dome is a fascinating paradox of sorts, then; in its efforts to leverage the hyperkineticism and thrilling visuals of state-of-the-art special effects technology the planetarium space show has turned its back on the very technology that was the defining feature of the entire planetarium experience, the Zeiss projector. By abandoning the immersive simplicity of the Zeiss-created nighttime sky, the planetarium has ironically substituted an incredibly powerful simulacral effect with something that could not hold a candle to the original. Fiscally, though, it makes sense for some planetariums, which can charge visitors more for performances in both spaces or have visitors spend more money by buying discounted tickets to both shows as the Adler Planetarium does in Chicago. Cinema is not only useful in the planetarium, it would seem, but essential for its survival.

NOTES

My thanks go to Charles Acland and Haidee Wasson for their constructive feedback on an earlier version of this chapter. Parts of this work are drawn from chapter 4 of my book *Shivers Down Your Spine: Cinema, Museums, and the Immersive View* (New York: Columbia University Press, 2008), although this chapter was extensively rewritten for this anthology and incorporated new research conducted since the publication of *Shivers Down Your Spine*.

1 A co-production between the American Museum of Natural History (AMNH) and MTV2, Sonic Vision takes audiences on a "mind-warping musical roller-coaster ride through fantastical dreamspace," according to the Web site ("Sonic Vision," American Museum of Natural History, http://www.amnh.org/rose/dome/ [accessed December 28, 2009]).

2 Becklake, *The Official Planetarium Book*, 12. Copernicus's book challenged the theory of the earth's centrality in our solar system. Despite this radical discovery, Copernicus still wrongly believed that the planets moved in perfect circles (ibid.). While neither space nor the focus of this chapter permits in-depth analysis of the fascinating developments in tabletop planetariums throughout the course of the seventeenth, eighteenth, and nineteenth centuries, the gendering of globes as indispensable accessories for the proper gentleman is one of the more interesting discourses to consider. Before the mass production of globes made them a must for every late nineteenth-century schoolroom, they were considered the "necessary furnishings" of a gentleman, the perfect complement to one's library or country house.

These extremely ornate globes were useful objects to have at hand to illustrate one's travels on the "grand tour," the eighteenth-century right of passage for wealthy or merchant-class men (Middleton, "Globes of the Early 19th Century," 90). By the end of the nineteenth century, children were being targeted by toy and globe makers, who offered a wide array of globe and globe paraphernalia such as cut-out globes published on cards in magazines, inflatable balloon globes, umbrella globes, puzzle globes, building block globes, and so forth. Beginning in the 1930s, globes were the thematic inspiration of ladies' pendants and brooches (gold and silver) and even cocktail cabinets (Collins, "Educational, Ornamental, and Toy Globes," 98).

3   The painting is very often represented in the form of the famous mezzotint engraving by William Pether. The original painting can be seen in the Derby Museum and Art Gallery, United Kingdom (Collins, "Educational, Ornamental, and Toy Globes," 84).

4   Both definitions are from *Webster's New Collegiate Dictionary* (Springfield, Mass.: 1974).

5   "A Historical Survey," *The McLaughlin Planetarium*, Royal Ontario Museum, Toronto, 19. Clipping from planetarium ephemera files, Special Collections, American Museum of Natural History (hereafter abbreviated to SC-AMNH).

6   Ibid.

7   Cunningham, "The First Planetarium," 10.

8   Report by Higgins and Quadebarth for Polshek and Partners, AMNH *Planetarium and North Side Project*, Background Research Project commissioned by the AMNH, October 5, 1995, 24, SC-AMNH.

9   Marché, *Theaters of Time and Space*, 9. According to Marché, the first American-built projection planetarium was a little-known device constructed by Harvey Spencer Lewis, the imperator of the Ancient and Mystical Order of the Rosae Crucis (AMORC), in San Jose, California (ibid., 38).

10   Bauersfeld quoted in Riesman, "The Zeiss Planetarium," 238.

11   Gunning, "Phantom Images and Modern Manifestations," 42.

12   Lant, "Egypt in Early Cinema," 89–90.

13   The first planetarium program in Jena was presented unchanged for the first eight months when five hundred performances were witnessed by seventy-eight thousand people. Confident of the planetarium's ability to continue to draw audiences, David Riesman wrote in 1928 that "the program permits so many variations that there is no danger of exhausting popular interest" (Riesman, "The Zeiss Planetarium," 240).

14   Fisher, "The Hayden Planetarium," 251.

15   McLenna, "The Planetarium in Perspective," 3.

16   King, "The Planetarium and Adult Education," 38.

17   For more on the panorama, see chapter 2 of Griffiths, *Shivers Down Your Spine*; Oettermann, *The Panorama*; Hyde, *Panoramania!*; Altick, *The Shows of London*; Colligan, *Canvas Documentaries*; McDermott, *The Lost Panoramas of the Mississippi*; Miller, "The Panorama, the Cinema, and the Emergence of the Spectacular"; and Schwartz, *Spectacular Realities*, 149–76.

18 King, "The Planetarium and Adult Education," 38.

19 "Heavenly Adventures," *Vogue*, December 15, 1935, n.p.

20 Blankenbeckler, Kyro, and McColman, "Production Values for Planetariums," 97.

21 Ibid., 99–101.

22 Ibid., 102.

23 For more on gender and the staffing of American planetariums, see Marché, *Theaters of Time and Space*, 48–83. The Hayden Planetarium and the Adler Planetarium in Chicago were among the more progressive institutions in terms of their hiring policies in the 1930s, especially the Hayden, which employed the greatest number of women who published popular articles and textbooks on astronomy. The science journalist James Stokley, the first director of the Fels Planetarium, apparently refused to hire a woman lecturer. When the war effort drew some men from their roles as lecturers, women rarely broke through the glass ceiling. It would take until the adoption of Armand N. Spitz's inexpensive planetariums in the 1950s for women to gain acceptance (Marché, *Theaters of Time and Space*, 58).

24 Bishop, "The Educational Value of the Planetarium," 105.

25 Hanny, Introduction to *Fear and Trembling*, 9.

26 Maslow, *Religions, Values, and Peak Experiences*, 65.

27 Marché, *Theaters of Time and Space*, 34.

28 Ibid.

29 Hogner and Scott, "Hayden Planetarium," 31.

30 Arthur, "Please Fasten Your Seat Belt, Next Stop the Moon," 1; and "Genealogy of the Zeiss Planetarium," *The Zeiss Planetarium* brochure, 1959, SC-AMNH.

31 "The Star of Bethlehem" was one of the major crowd pullers for most planetariums; for example, in 1949 the Morehead Planetarium in Chapel Hill, North Carolina, recorded its highest attendance levels for the show, a total of 31,863.

32 In 1978, "The Star of Wonder" Christmas Show at the Hayden Planetarium was the second longest-running Christmas show in New York City after the Radio City Music Hall ("Department of Astronomy and the American Museum Hayden Planetarium," *Report of the Scientific and Education Departments*, AMNH, July 1977–June 1978, 7).

33 The film generated a great many instant books and more serious scholarly endeavors. See, for example, Beal and Linafelt, *Mel Gibson's Bible*; and Griffiths, "The Revered Gaze."

34 Marché, *Theaters of Time and Space*, 45.

35 Letter to Antoinette Gioudano from Gordon A. Atwater, October 27, 1948 in File #14 Correspondence October–December 1948 in Box 1 Guest Relations Bureau 1936–48, SC-AMNH. The first Christmas Show in Spanish was given at the Hayden Planetarium on December 16, 1970 with six hundred children in attendance. The idea was that of Tom Carey, a graduate astronomy student and intern who had served in the Peace Corps in Colombia. "Giggles, applause, and 'vivas'" were reportedly heard during the show (Meriemil Rodriguez, "Planetarium Tells the Story of la Navidad," *Daily News*, December 17, 1970, n.p. in File #2 News Clips, Box 2 News Clips 1968–84, SC-AMNH).

36   Armand N. Spitz, "Planetarium: An Analysis of Opportunities and Obligations," *The Griffith Observer*, June 1959, n.p. For a longer discussion of Spitz's business of manufactured miniature planetariums, see Spencer, "The Stars Are His Playthings," n.p.

37   Waldemar Kaempffert, "Now America Will Have a Planetarium," *New York Times Magazine*, June 23, 1928, 3.

38   Ibid., 11. Emphasis added.

39   Franz Fieseler, "A Layman's Views on Lectures in the Zeiss Planetarium," n.d., 8 pp., SC-AMNH, 3.

40   Kaempffert, "Now America Will Have a Planetarium," 11.

41   Marché, *Theaters of Time and Space*, 18.

42   Riesman, "The Zeiss Planetarium," 36; Richard F. Shepard, "Stellar Performance," *New York Times*, December 1, 1984, 13, clipping from Planetarium General Information File 1935–86, SC-AMNH.

43   Marché, *Theaters of Time and Space*, 35.

44   Samuel S. Fels, "Donation of the Planetarium to the Franklin Institute," *Journal of the Franklin Institute* 216 (July–December 1933), 791, cited in Marché, *Theaters of Time and Space*, 44.

45   Marché, *Theaters of Time and Space*, 75–76.

46   Ibid., 47.

47   Ezra, *Georges Méliès*, 120.

48   A. Hopkins, *Magic*, 348–53.

49   Ezra, *Georges Méliès*, 120.

50   Levitt, "The Planetarium," 2.

51   Marché, *Theaters of Time and Space*, 75.

52   Robert R. Coles, Untitled Document, American Museum of Natural History General Information File, 1935–1986, SC-AMNH. The Hayden has the unique distinction of being the only American planetarium to receive government/municipal funding for its construction; all the others relied on the support and backing of private businesses and foundations (Marché, *Theaters of Time and Space*, 25).

53   Joseph Kaselow, writing in the *World Journal Tribune* (February 19, 1967), quoted the National Aeronautics and Space Administration as predicting that commercial travel to the moon would not start until the year 2000 ("Selling Trips to the Moon," n.p.).

54   "Hayden Planetarium," *Hart's Guide to New York City*, 815.

55   Quote taken from "Hayden Planetarium," on the Web site for the Rose Center for Earth and Space at the American Museum of Natural History, http://www.amnh .org/rose/hayden-spacetheater.html (accessed December 28, 2009).

56   Press Release, "Special Event Coverage of Apollo Splashdown, 1969," Western Union International, New York, July 23, 1969, in General Information File 1935–86, 2, SC-AMNH.

57   Spigel, *Make Room for TV*, 2.

58   Marché, *Theaters of Time and Space*, 99–100.

59   Doherty, *Cold War, Cool Medium*, 8.

60   For more on Spitz's planetarium and his career, see Marché, *Theaters of Time and Space*, 87–115.

61   Spitz's Jr. projector, launched in 1954, was a toy planetarium that projected four hundred stars and retailed for $13.95 (Marché, *Theaters of Time and Space*, 93).

62   Spitz, "Planetarium," 81.

63   Martin J. Shannon, writing in *Wall Street Journal*, reported on the popularity of astronomy in 1967, arguing that "with imaginations fired by a decade of space achievements that make centuries of prior advances pale by comparison, businessmen, housewives, and other nonscientific types are taking up astronomy as a hobby." To support his claim Shannon referred to the doubling of subscriptions to *Sky and Telescope* in the past decade, from twenty thousand to forty thousand with 10 to 15 percent gains expected the following year (Shannon, "Gazing at the Stars: Hobby of Astronomy Lures More People," *Wall Street Journal*, October 23, 1967, n.p.).

64   We see a corollary of the social aspect of stargazing in an outdoor stargazing program developed by the Hayden Planetarium in conjunction with the New York City Department of Parks in 1969; called "Star Gazing—With or without Stars," it took place at 11:00 p.m. every other Wednesday on the Great Lawn in Central Park. In addition to an audio system and flashlight pointer that would help the lecturer address the crowd, a recommendation was also made to play soft background music to set the mood (Information in memo 4/4/68 in file 14 ["Stargazing in the Park, 1969, May–August"] in box 1, Special Events at the Planetarium, 1949–73), SC-AMNH.

65   Spigel, *Make Room for TV*, 27.

66   Ibid., 2.

67   Tolischus, "Seeing Stars," 98; and Marché, *Theaters of Time and Space*, 18.

68   Riesman, "The Zeiss Planetarium," 239. Henry Charles King, the director of the London Planetarium, addressed the issue of light pollution in his book of 1958 when he argued that in less than a minute in the planetarium we can "exchange the noise and bustle of London's busy streets for the silent beauty of the night, with a canopy of stars spread across a cloudless heaven" (King, *The London Planetarium*, 3).

69   Lockwood, "The Hayden Planetarium," 188.

70   Marché, *Theaters of Time and Space*, 71.

71   King, *The London Planetarium*, 3.

72   Chamberlain, "The Development of the Planetarium in the United States," 273. The years 1977–78 are something of a turning point with regard to the institutionalization of automation and the recorded lecture. An entry in the *Report of the Scientific and Education Departments* of the AMNH referred to the Hayden joining forces with the Morehead and the Charles Hayden Planetariums to contract with a consulting firm to study the feasibility of automation and to aid in the drawing up of a set of design and manufacturing specifications. The work would be partially funded by a conditional matching grant from the Charles Hayden Foundation ("Department of Astronomy and the American-Museum Hayden-Planetarium," *Report of the Scientific and Education Departments*, AMNH, July 1977–June 1978, 8). At the AMNH's Hayden, the live lecturer was replaced by recordings of actors such as Charlton Heston, Leonard Nimoy, and William Shatner (among others) narrating the scripts (Preston, "A Domeful of Stars").

73   King, "The Planetarium and Adult Education," 41.

74 "Frequently Asked Questions," on the Web site for the Rose Center for Earth and Space at the American Museum of Natural History, http://www.amnh.org/rose/faq.html (accessed December 28, 2009).

75 "By George! And lev and bob and oskars, Heavens!," *Franklin Institute News*, spring–summer 1971, 9. Atmospheriums, a subgenre of planetariums, are another source of useful cinema about which little has been written. The Desert Research Institute of the University of Nevada developed the idea in 1961. The daytime (as opposed to nighttime) sky is reproduced on the domed interior of the building: "special time-lapse motion picture cameras have been fitted with the new 'fish-eye' 180 degree lenses to produce fast motion films of the whole sky. The surface inch of the ⅝-inch diameter film image is enlarged approximately 400,000 times to cover the 30-ft diameter domed ceiling—the projection screen." In half an hour the audience can witness a day's worth of weather. The goal of the Atmospherium-Planetarium was to include films of all kinds of weather phenomena, including hurricanes, tornadoes, and many other dramatic weather events. For more information, see "The Fleischmann Atmospherium-Planetarium of the Desert Research Institute, University of Nevada," [untitled journal] 45, no. 7 (1964), 394–95.

76 Miezis, "Activity of the Planetarium in Riga," 62.

77 Glenn Collins, "Planetarium Introducing Updated City Star System," *New York Times*, August 11, 1999, B1.

78 Damon Stanek, "Immersion and Interactivity," paper submitted to a CUNY Graduate Center course entitled "Immersion and Interactivity in Film and the Related Arts," fall 2005, 4. My thanks to Damon for some of these references.

79 Rabinovitz, "More Than the Movies."

80 Quote from "Hayden Planetarium—Passport to the Universe," on the Web site for the Rose Center for Earth and Space at the American Museum of Natural History, http://www.amnh.org/rose/passport.html (accessed December 28, 2009).

81 Quoted in Fred Bernstein, "A Chicago Chop Shop Takes the Hayden Guts," *New Yorker*, November 4, 2001, emphasis in original.

82 "When Good Stars Go Bad" (version 3.0) / Countdown to Supernova / Original script by J. Kelly Beatty for the Charles Hayden Planetarium, 2004, SC-AMNH, 3.

DOUBLE VISION
WORLD WAR II, RACIAL UPLIFT, AND THE ALL-AMERICAN
NEWSREEL'S PEDAGOGICAL ADDRESS

Joseph Clark

Launched in November 1942, All-American News was a weekly newsreel entirely devoted to the activities and accomplishments of black Americans. The weekly series' first offering featured a selection of subjects typical of the issues to follow in the next decade, including, "Marion Anderson's christening of the new ship *Booker T. Washington*, the colored WAACS [Women's Auxiliary Army Corps], Satchel Paige's latest pitching and many other interesting events."[1] By combining coverage of African American celebrities with the details of the race's contributions to the war effort, the film's producers hoped race pride would make their upstart production a success. At a time when the newsreels produced by the major Hollywood studios all but ignored black America, All-American was able to fill a crucial niche in the American moving picture industry. Just as importantly, this new offering held out a promise to African Americans that the achievements and contributions of their race would finally be represented and acknowledged on film. Implicit in this promise was an unspoken faith in the power of representation. In the racial politics of the

1940s, the visual power and authority of the newsreel seemed to present a potent weapon in the battle for the uplift of the race. For the film's producers, its audience, and its critics, All-American had the potential to be far more than a simple chronicler of African American achievement. Indeed, many saw the newsreel as a crucial tool in achieving recognition and respect—by celebrating black accomplishment, but also by educating African American audiences. The newsreel adopted a specifically pedagogical address, aimed at promoting the values of hard work, discipline, and self-improvement. By looking at how All-American deployed this pedagogical address and the rhetoric of uplift in the context of wartime race relations and a Jim Crow motion picture industry, we will see how the newsreel contested racial inequality while accommodating segregation. All-American's images of achievement implicitly refuted racist portrayals of African Americans on film and encouraged its audience to advance the race through their own talents and diligence. Nevertheless, All-American News largely ignored the issue of racism itself, and critics and audiences began to question a politics of visibility that put the onus for change on the newsreel's black viewers rather than white America.

Founded by Emmanuel Glucksman, a film producer and veteran of the motion picture and theatrical entertainment businesses, All-American News made what were known at the time as race movies, films featuring African American casts made specifically to cater to black audiences.[2] Although Glucksman was a so-called white angel, he regularly employed African American talent behind the camera as well as in front of it. Charles Wilson was the voice of All-American, providing commentary in most of the reel's stories and William Alexander—who himself went on to produce films for African American audiences, including a documentary series called the By-Line Newsreel—worked as a cameraman, director, on-camera interviewer and, for a time, as All-American's Washington Bureau chief.[3] Glucksman also received important advice and support from Claude Barnett, the head of the Associated Negro Press, a wire service for black newspapers and magazines modeled on the Associated Press. This combination of white money and black talent was a common arrangement in the race-movie market of the late 1930s and the 1940s.[4]

Like other race movies of the era, All-American's audience was almost exclusively African American. The primary market for the All-American Newsreel was the black movie theater circuit—which included the segregated theaters of the South and black neighborhood houses in cities like New York,

Chicago, and Philadelphia. It is difficult to know exactly how widely the newsreel was exhibited, but, in November 1943, Glucksman boasted that 4 million people saw his product each week. He told the *American Cinematographer* that All-American was "seen regularly in 365 of the 452 civilian negro theatres" and added that the films were distributed to 70 military camps throughout the country.[5] With the help of Claude Barnett, Glucksman also distributed prints of the newsreel to several black colleges in the United States and even to Africa—screening the newsreel in Liberia and Nigeria.[6] Looking for ways to expand his audience further after the end of World War II, Glucksman planned to offer a version of the newsreel to television stations around the country. As Glucksman explained the situation to Barnett in a letter, segregation made it difficult to "put the accomplishments of the Negro race before the white theatre goers," while television could reach "the most influential class of people of all races."[7] By reaching a wider audience—in particular one that included white Americans—Barnett and Glucksman hoped that the series might extend All-American's ability to educate viewers about African American achievements.

The power and potential of the newsreel to educate viewers was an integral part of All-American's appeal from the outset. The black press praised the new offering and expressed hope that the series would help build black morale during the war, while contributing to the campaign for "Double Victory": a nationwide push to link African American support for the war effort with the struggle for civil rights on the home front.[8] Somewhat hyperbolically, a writer for the Scott Newspaper Syndicate called the newsreel "probably the most significant motion picture news item for negroes since the invention of the motion picture camera,"[9] while Ted Watson, a columnist for the *Atlanta Daily World*, expressed hope that, by reaching a white audience, the series could "mold national unity."[10] By offering visual evidence of the contributions African Americans were making to the war effort, All-American had the potential to be what another reviewer called a "Double V advancement!" "Now," he wrote, "we can 'see' the news as we read it in *The Pittsburgh Courier*."[11] At a time when the NAACP and others explicitly linked motion pictures to the struggle for equal rights, All-American seemed to offer both a powerful educational tool as well as a way to boost black morale. Despite the early optimism about All-American's potential to educate white audiences however, its limited viewership outside the black community would lead some to criticize the series and question its effectiveness in achieving the Double V.

In addition to its role in the wartime struggle for recognition, All-American's pedagogical address must also be seen in light of the general rhetoric of racial uplift. In the 1940s, the notion of racial uplift already had a long history in the political discourse of the African American community and it encompassed a complex set of popular and intellectual meanings. Historians like Evelyn Brooks Higginbotham and Kevin Gaines have charted the philosophy of racial uplift in the early twentieth century.[12] Although popular calls for racial uplift could be deployed in more or less democratic appeals for economic, political, and even spiritual betterment, these authors detail the ways in which middle-class black Americans and others took up the discourses of temperance, chastity, and social purity as a means to achieve a measure of social mobility and respect. Gaines points out that these discourses often had as much to do with class as they did race. For the black middle classes, respectability and individual achievement put the lie to notions of innate racial inferiority in favor of a philosophy of cultural difference and social evolution. Nevertheless, as middle-class blacks stressed the adoption of bourgeois mores as key to racial uplift, they "implicitly faulted African Americans for their lowly status, echoing judgmental dominant characterizations of 'the Negro problem.'"[13] All-American's pedagogical address blurred the lines between the social struggle for racial progress and the bourgeois values of self-help and respectability.

Finally, although All-American was a part of these wartime debates over racial uplift and the Double V, the visual potency of the newsreel form made the series somewhat unusual. What Higginbotham calls the "politics of respectability" was deeply invested in countering racist stereotypes of black Americans.[14] For All-American and others, the politics of vision, visibility, and appearance were key ways to achieve this goal. Given its ostensibly documentary authority, the newsreel was uniquely placed to counter negative images of African Americans in the media. At times, All-American would explicitly instruct its audience in the importance of appearance and good conduct. More often, by showing the patriotic actions of prominent and regular black Americans, the newsreel simply displayed a model for respectability while urging its viewers to do their part for the war effort. As important as these efforts to encourage patriotism were, many hoped All-American would provide something more than a boost to black morale. They hoped that the newsreel would not only help to promote wartime contributions, but would ensure that the black community was *seen* to be making these contributions. As we shall see, the visibility of the African American war effort became a key axis along which the struggle for Double Victory was fought.

The last half of this essay will focus on the content of thirty-nine issues of the All-American Newsreel released between 1944 and 1945.[15] Practically all that remains of the newsreel's decade-long weekly output, these films reveal a company negotiating the politics of visibility and the rhetoric of racial uplift during World War II. All-American's pedagogical address proved to be a critical component of these efforts. Before examining these issues, however, it is first necessary to situate the newsreel more fully in the context of a Jim Crow film industry and the debates within the African American community over civil rights in the 1940s.

A JIM CROW CINEMA

American cinema was a segregated world in 1942. African Americans were marginalized behind the camera, on screen, and in movie theater audiences. But segregation did not prevent African Americans from being eager participants in the production and consumption of American films. Indeed, at the outset of World War II the relationship between the movies and the black community had become an important economic, social, and political issue. Academic publications like the *Journal of Negro Education* repeatedly discussed the educational uses of motion pictures as well as the effects of movies on race relations and black morale.[16] African Americans were also a growing market for moviemakers, as independent race-movie producers capitalized on the segregation of movie theaters to find a willing if not always eager audience. But by the early 1940s black audiences were becoming increasingly dissatisfied with race movies and groups like the NAACP were pushing for better roles for black actors in mainstream Hollywood films. This push branded race movies as Jim Crow films. Instead, the NAACP looked for (and in some cases won) support in Hollywood and Washington toward improving the representations of blacks in mainstream film. New Deal liberalism and the wartime push for national solidarity finally made racial integration on screen a possibility. But even while the war paved the way for better roles for black actors, the reality of war—on screen and off—remained segregated. The U.S. military was not officially integrated until 1948 and the newsreels produced by Hollywood's big five all but ignored the contributions of black regiments and of African Americans on the home front. Just as it had created the conditions for the race moviemakers of the 1930s, segregation provided the possibility and the demand for an all-black newsreel in the 1940s. The fact of segregation gave All-American both a captive audience and plenty of racially homogenous footage.

Thus, while Hollywood moved toward a degree of racial integration and the representation of blacks on screen improved, the reality of the war for African Americans — filmic and otherwise — remained a Jim Crow affair.

When All-American made its debut, it found a home in the legally segregated theaters of the South and the culturally and geographically segregated black neighborhood cinemas of the North. Large centers in the North and the South supported these "negro theaters" and, as black Americans migrated from the rural South to these cities, their numbers grew rapidly.[17] According to the *Motion Picture Herald* the number of black movie houses in the United States rose from 232 in 1937 to 430 in 1942 and then to 684 in 1947.[18] As a result, in major urban centers African Americans often enjoyed a relatively wide selection of movie houses. For example, according to the *Negro Handbook 1944*, by that year, 13 of the 65 cinemas in Washington, D.C. were "Negro theaters."[19] But despite the growing number of all-black cinemas in larger cities, most African Americans in 1942 still watched movies from the balconies of white theaters.[20] By law in the South and by custom in the North, black moviegoers were relegated to the cramped quarters of the "peanut galleries," where patrons would suffer the heat, few if any refreshments, and sometimes a restricted view of the screen itself. When they weren't segregated spatially — and sometimes even when they were — many southern theaters chose to segregate their audiences by time. Midnight screenings for black audiences became common in the 1930s and 1940s.[21] These late night offerings added to the so-called race circuit of black theaters and provided another potential outlet for the All-American Newsreel.

The race circuit had only limited options when it came to films for and about African Americans in the 1930s and 1940s. While black independent producers had found some success in the silent era, they were all but wiped out by the Depression and the rising cost of moviemaking brought on by the advent of the "talkies." The limited number of theaters willing to show all-Negro productions, the ad hoc distribution networks needed to reach them, and the lower ticket prices they charged made it difficult for African American production companies to overcome the new challenges posed by sound and a black public disproportionately affected by the economic turmoil of the early 1930s. The void left by the collapse of the black independents was filled by a host of white entrepreneurs seeking to capitalize on the African American market. Indeed, black filmmakers like Oscar Micheaux continued to make films in the 1930s and 1940s, but did so with the financial backing of so-called white angels.[22] These independent producers mostly made low budget genre films but distinguished themselves by using exclusively black casts. While these films offered much needed work to African American actors, and gave audiences a chance to see people like themselves represented on screen, they were far from a "black cinema" and did little to confront racism and inequality. In fact these films were often curiously devoid of racial content. As Thomas Cripps, a historian of black film, points out, "to 'inject race' would have spoiled the premise of all-black casts, caused 'trouble' in Southern markets, and closed off 'extra juice' from white patrons."[23] For its part, Hollywood made some limited efforts to cater to black audiences—and capitalize on the vogue for all things Negro in the late 1920s—with crossover films such as Fox's *Hearts in Dixie* (1929) and MGM's all-black musical *Hallelujah!* (1929). Disappointing box office results discouraged any further such forays, however, and African Americans in Hollywood were limited for the most part to the peripheral roles of porters and maids.

As war spread from Europe to the Pacific, attitudes in and about Hollywood began to change. The rhetoric of war called on Americans to unite and fight for democracy. Government propaganda denounced Hitler's notions of racial superiority as abhorrent, and in doing so brought America's own racial problems into focus. The Double Victory campaign and similar arguments seized on official pronouncements against fascism and sought to apply them to the situation of African Americans in the United States. In addition to the federal government, Hollywood and the motion picture industry became prime targets for these campaigns.[24] Pushing for more and better representation for African Americans on film, the NAACP held its annual meeting of 1942 in Los Angeles. Executive Secretary Walter White spoke at a special luncheon hosted by Walter Wagner and Darryl F. Zanuck of 20th Century Fox and attended by over seventy well-placed representatives of the film industry. White told the gathering that the "restriction of Negroes to roles with rolling eyes, chattering teeth, always scared of ghosts, or to portrayals of none-too bright servants perpetuates a stereotype which is doing the Negro infinite harm" and contributing to "low morale."[25] In a second trip to California the following year White explicitly tied the country's war aims to film portrayals of African Americans, arguing that the United States needed to use the "media to build a world free of racial and religious hatred" in order "to insure a durable peace."[26] By linking race harmony on screen to victory in the war, the NAACP and others implicitly rejected all-black race movies in favor of a more tolerant Hollywood. The low quality and limited distribution of race movies meant that they would never have the universal power of Hollywood fare. More importantly, the films, with their all-black casts, did not depict the integrated America of U.S. propaganda. In an article in the *Journal of Negro Education* that detailed the ways in which the federal government should boost African American morale during the war, Mary Morton rejected the creation of "all-Negro films" in favor of integrated motion pictures. "Negroes must be portrayed as self-respecting citizens integrated into a cross-section of American life," she argued. "Their likeness to other Americans — not their real or imagined differences — must be emphasized if harmful stereotypes of long standing are to be destroyed."[27] For Morton and White, motion pictures represented a medium not necessarily for black cultural expression, but one through which mainstream America could come to appreciate and acknowledge the role of African Americans in the nation as a whole. In the context of these efforts and a war whose aims ostensibly included the fight for self-determination and racial harmony, race movies had become an anachronism.[28] But while the NAACP and others pushed for integration in the fictional films of Hollywood, similar pressure could not be applied so easily to the production of non-fiction motion pictures.

It was difficult for factual films to represent an integrated war effort simply because the war effort itself was not integrated. While fictional scenarios could be imagined where blacks and whites found themselves together, the armed forces remained segregated until 1948 and much of American society was similarly divided. As Thomas Doherty points out, most of the wartime movies that showed blacks and whites interacting on screen — such as *Casablanca* (1942), *Bataan* (1943), and *Sahara* (1943) — did so in exotic locales far removed from the realities of segregation at home.[29] Unable to manufacture integrated settings, newsreels and other documentary films were left to cover the segregated reality of war. The Department of Defense and the Office of War Information (OWI) did produce a few documentaries showing blacks and whites working together, but these could only go so far. Films from the OWI such as *Manpower* (1942) and *Colleges at War* (1942) featured only token mention of the role of the black community in the war effort, while movies focusing on the contributions of African Americans, such as *The Negro Soldier* (1944) and *Negro Colleges in War Time* (1943), had virtually all-black casts, making them poor models of integration and limiting their distribution to white audiences.

Meanwhile, the commercial newsreels simply ignored African Americans. The Hollywood Writers' War Board pointed out in 1944 that out of the previous year's newsreels it had found only three items featuring Negro troops: "one showing a Negro soldier guarding a hen coop, another concerning a jitterbug contest in Australia. Only the third was of a serious nature, depicting the 99th Pursuit Squadron."[30] There was considerable ongoing pressure on the newsreels to exclude material relating to the African American war effort from their releases. Exhibitors and municipal censors in the South routinely cut out material from fiction and non-fiction films showing blacks in situations of "social equality" with whites. According to *Variety*, "local censors [would] eliminate such scenes, regardless of the effect on the artistic side or the continuity of the film."[31] Such editing not only made the onscreen product "patched up" and "confusing" but also made the print unusable for further circulation. With only eight to ten minutes per newsreel the effects of censorship could often be felt more dramatically than in a feature-length drama. It is perhaps not surprising then that Hollywood newsreel producers were unwilling to risk the artistic and economic damage of carrying black material.

The reluctance of the mainstream newsreels to represent African Americans in general and the war effort in particular created a growing resentment, and in January 1944 the issue became headline news in the black press. Front-page stories in the *Atlanta Daily World* and *New York Amsterdam News* accused the government and Hollywood of a "blackout" and of "cutting" scenes of black soldiers from the major newsreels.[32] Specifically, the press charged the major newsreel companies with deliberately omitting scenes showing President Roosevelt reviewing black troops in his recent trip overseas. The omission was discovered after these scenes subsequently appeared in the All-American Newsreel, which, along with the five studio newsreels, had access to the Army's Signal Corps footage of the events in question. According to the *New York Amsterdam News*, in their zeal to delete the African American troops, the newsreels "sacrificed the best shot of the president and General Eisenhower chatting in the jeep, merely because a Negro furnished the background."[33] The NAACP and others vigorously protested this apparently Jim Crow policy. In a letter to the major studios the organization pointed out that about seven hundred thousand African Americans worked in various branches of the armed services. Their omission from the newsreels was, according to the NAACP, "a serious blow at the morale of Negro Americans and justifies them in feeling that their sacrifices are being disparaged, discounted, and concealed."[34] Meanwhile, the editors of *Crisis* saw a deliberate attempt to give white people "the impression Negroes are doing little if anything to win the victory," arguing that "this scheme to keep from white America the news that the minority is doing its part in the war is a dastardly trick, as mean as any perpetuated against the race."[35] These protests show how critical visibility was to achieving the goals of the Double V campaign. How could the war effort be used to push for civil rights gains if African American sacrifices were being "concealed" from the American public?

Both the major studio newsreel companies and the War Department denied there was any policy excluding African Americans from their films. Walton Ament, the chairman of the newsreel pool and editor at Pathé News, said the studios were not discriminating against black soldiers. He told the press that there was "no effort made along the line by the War Department or the newsreel cutters to make deletions except those based on pure pictorial judgment."[36] Likewise, Major General A. D. Surles of the War Department denied any policy restricting the distribution of black subjects, insisting that the department provided all companies with the same footage each week. In a letter responding to the concerns of the NAACP, Surles wrote, "Beyond including, wherever available, footage which shows Negro troops in action, the War Department can exercise no supervision over the editorial choices of the newsreel companies."[37]

Despite these denials, this episode raised the question of All-American's complicity in keeping the newsreels segregated. The newsreel relied heavily on the footage it received from the War Department. Beyond providing engaging and high-quality pictures, the Signal Corps films allowed All-American to cover international and war stories with an African American angle on the company's limited budget. Critics, however, questioned whether All-American's access to footage featuring black soldiers was part of an arrangement that prevented this footage from being used by the other newsreels.[38] The OWI denied the existence of any exclusivity deal, but there remained a growing feeling that All-American may not have been serving the best interests of the African American community.[39] The NAACP's assistant secretary, Roy Wilkins, pointed out that while All-American did provide a valuable service, it could not achieve the proper recognition of African Americans in white society. "Of course," said Wilkins, "it is beneficial for Negroes who go to all-colored houses to see pictures of their men, but it is just as necessary that white Americans also see pictures of our fighting men."[40] In his "Watchtower" column for the *New York Amsterdam News*, Wilkins argued that any benefit All-American offered to maintaining African American morale and encouraging further contributions to the war effort was overshadowed if it was preventing white Americans from seeing these contributions. If that were the case, he stated, the All-American Newsreel was "making profits at the expense of the future status of Negroes as Americans [and] should be forced out of business."[41] For Wilkins and the NAACP, white acknowledgment of African American sacrifices was crucial to the struggle for equality. The motion picture industry, and the newsreel in particular, could play a key role in ensuring this visibility, but not if the news itself was segregated.

All-American was not forced out of business, but following the public outcry, the studio newsreels did make some concessions to placate their critics. A story on the all-black 99th Pursuit Squadron appeared in RKO-Pathé's newsreel and Paramount carried shots of Negro members of the Women's Auxiliary Corps parading on Staten Island. This was seen as a sign of progress for the NAACP and the black press that had pushed the issue. New York's left wing *People's Voice* called the Pathé item "a major victory in the battle waged by the Negro for fair and representative treatment of the Negro soldier's contribution to the war."[42] But the victory was fleeting. The mainstream newsreels did not dramatically change the way they covered the war and there remained a place for an all-black newsreel in the segregated world of American motion pictures.

Although the NAACP and others grew increasingly hostile toward All-American and its race movie cousins, the fact remained that the newsreel offered black audiences a chance to see footage they would not see anywhere else. While the mainstream newsreels portrayed the war as a nearly lilywhite affair, All-American offered its viewers a very different image of war's reality. Even if the newsreel failed to reach white Americans, its supporters believed the series could be a strong instrument of visual education for its black audience. Moreover, despite being circumscribed by the system within which it operated, the newsreel did provide an important, if conflicted and contested, venue for the message of racial uplift. The next part of this essay looks specifically at All-American's content to see how its pedagogical address worked to disrupt as well as confirm the racial status quo. For all its faults, the segregated nature of the All-American Newsreel meant that it acknowledged a reality that the integrationist films supported by the NAACP elided. In this way its point of view was radically different from anything else available to audiences, black or white. All-American may have been a Jim Crow company, offering a Jim Crow product, for exhibition in Jim Crow cinemas, but for the vast majority of African Americans in the 1940s, Jim Crow was their reality.

ALL-AMERICAN'S PEDAGOGICAL ADDRESS:
RACIAL UPLIFT AND THE POLITICS OF VISIBILITY

All-American announced its pedagogical intent right from its opening title sequence. The sequence featured a fanfare of horns playing a march accompanied by the company's logo—an eye with a globe as its pupil. The globe dissolved to reveal the stars and stripes followed by a succession of scenes typical of the series, including various African American military personnel on parade and several sports scenes featuring black athletes. The music, the globe, the shots of marching and sporting events were all typical features of the major studio newsreels in the United States in the 1930s and 1940s, but a voice-over declaring, "All-American News brings you our people's contribution to America and freedom," along with the prominent display of black faces, clearly marked the newsreel's difference. The slogan directly addressed the spectator and pointed to the film's efforts to represent the African American community as patriotic and industrious. These representations were deployed both as evidence of accomplishment and as instructive examples for the film's audience. The visual nature of the didactic elements to come was underlined by the use of the eye motif. The superimposition of footage within that eye further highlighted the ways in which the visual qualities of the newsreel itself were crucial to the pedagogical aims of All-American. Trajectories of looking literally framed the content of the film. By applying the visual rhetoric of the newsreel in a unique way, All-American hoped to promote race pride and offer a model for behavior and self-improvement to its African American audience, while ostensibly providing white viewers with evidence of the black community's participation in the war effort. But, as we shall see, the politics of visibility were by no means straightforward. In the context of Jim Crow America, the struggle for racial uplift was as much about maintaining appearances as it was about white recognition. All-American's pedagogical mode reveals a company and a community negotiating the complex and sometimes contradictory politics of race and visibility during World War II.

The slogan in All-American's title sequence—with its use of the second-person pronoun and its emphasis on the word "our"—defined the newsreel's distinctive point of view. By referring to "our people's contribution to America and freedom," All-American clearly identified itself with the black community. In doing so, the slogan implied the newsreel would provide a corrective to its mainstream cousins and framed the stories to come as instructional as well as informational. All-American's use of the second-person "you" was

All-American News opening sequence.

more equivocal. The second-person address was not unique to All-American, but its deployment by the newsreel took on added resonance given its segregated audience. While the mainstream newsreels used the direct address as a way to draw the audience in and collapse the distance between the action on screen and the audience in the theater, All-American's use of the second person also posed an important question in the context of the newsreel's pedagogical mode: to whom was the newsreel's instruction directed? As we have seen, despite the efforts of Glucksman and Barnett, All-American's audience was overwhelmingly black. Nevertheless, the title sequence was ambiguous. The phrasing, "bringing you our people's contribution to America and freedom," left open the possibility that All-American also aimed to address a white American spectator. After all, the almost complete absence of black faces from the major studio newsreels made the notion of "bringing" the news of the African American war effort to white audiences an important element of the Double Victory campaign. Indeed, it was All-American's potential to do just this that garnered the newsreel many of its early positive reviews from the black press. So, while some of the newsreel's items explicitly addressed an African American audience, the newsreel's slogan worked both ways. This ambiguity allowed All-American to identify its pedagogical mode with the politics of visibility as well as the philosophy of racial uplift.

The potential doubleness of the second-person address in All-American's title sequence draws attention to the equally undetermined identity of the disembodied eye that frames the footage of these "contributions to America and freedom." Whose eye was this? No doubt, it implicitly belonged to the newsreel's black audience, able to witness the accomplishments of the race onscreen for the first time. But it might also be understood as standing in for the critical eye of white America. In this sense, the eye recalls the state of African American self-surveillance that W. E. B. Du Bois famously described as double consciousness. In *The Souls of Black Folk*, Du Bois refers to that "sense of always looking at one's self through the eyes of others, of measuring one's soul by the tape of a world that looks on in amused contempt and pity."[43] This visual metaphor, describing the conflicted nature of African American identity at the beginning of the last century, was echoed in All-American's pedagogical address. While its evidence of achievement and patriotism could inspire race pride, the newsreel's examples carried with them an implicit, and sometimes explicit, exhortation to its African American audience to understand the importance of maintaining appearances. In this context, the newsreel's cameras provided the lens through which African Americans could look, in order to see themselves through the eyes of white America. Jane Gaines has pointed out in her work on the race movies of the 1920s and 1930s that Du Bois's analysis takes on new meaning when thinking about race in the context of black film spectatorship. "Suddenly," she writes, "one of the foundational statements in race theory appears as film theory, addressing the question of the execution of power through the trajectory of the eye."[44] But, while Gaines extends this theorization to argue that race movies offered black audiences a chance to look at themselves through something other than the "distorted lens" of white America, All-American's pedagogical address could not fully escape the dilemma described by Du Bois. Even as the newsreel sought to inspire race pride and overcome the distortions of mainstream representations of African Americans, it reinscribed the self-surveillance logic of double consciousness.

All-American's pedagogy was most evident when the newsreel addressed the viewer directly and offered explicit instruction. Officials, instructors, and authority figures regularly spoke straight to the camera and the viewing audience. Instruction on filing proper tax returns, information on the benefits available through the Veteran's Administration, and repeated exhortations to maintain good conduct were among the straightforwardly didactic messages to be found in the All-American Newsreel.

In 1944 and 1945 good conduct was a frequent feature of All-American's pedagogy. The newsreel carried several stories on the importance of proper etiquette and courtesy and, in 1944, it joined with the *Pittsburgh Courier* to promote the newspaper's "Better Conduct Crusade."[45] The campaign featured prominent citizens, such as Bishop Gregg, who lectured All-American's audience on the value of manners and refinement, as well as the perils of "vulgarity," including "loud talk"[46] that might make others uncomfortable. These lessons in good conduct neatly encapsulated the black middle-class philosophy of racial uplift and what Evelyn Brooks Higginbotham has called the "politics of respectability." According to Higginbotham, in order to counter racist stereotypes, "respectability demanded that every individual in the black community assume responsibility for behavioral self-regulation and self-improvement along moral, educational, and economic lines."[47] A vivid example of this notion of self-regulation came in issue 123 of the All-American News, when Dorothy Rogers and the teenagers of Parkway Community Center modeled good conduct for the newsreel cameras.[48] Speaking directly to the audience, Rogers introduced the item by saying, "We are so often judged by the little things in life. If we stop to think, we realize that it is as easy, often easier, to do things the right way instead of the wrong way." What followed was a series of vignettes illustrating proper manners as well as what not to do in social situations. After showing a pair of teenagers dancing sloppily—he with his hat on and she chewing gum demonstratively, the camera turned to a young man politely asking his date to dance and leading her to the dance floor. Rogers's accompanying commentary explicitly linked self-respect to respectability. She told the audience that "this young couple having respect for themselves and for each other command like respect from everyone," adding, "now don't you suppose they're having a good time, and yet they're not offensive to good taste." Although Rogers did not reference white Americans as those who might judge the black teenagers onscreen as well as those in the newsreel audience, she didn't have to. Implicit in the notions of good conduct presented in these frankly didactic segments was the assumption that, for the black race as well as for individual black Americans, self-respect and respectability went hand in hand. In this context, how whites perceived African Americans became crucially important. Indeed, Rogers concluded the item by saying, "This has been a good chance to see ourselves as others see us. To which group do you belong? Let's make good conduct a habit, a good habit from now on." Rogers's invitation to her viewers—"[Let us] see ourselves as others see us"—implicitly aligned the gaze of the camera with the gaze of white America. As a visual medium, the All-American Newsreel could counter racist stereotypes by celebrating black achievement, but it also offered a lens through which African Americans might be able to look at themselves. In doing so, it vividly recalled the self-surveillance raised by Du Bois in his definition of double consciousness. If racial uplift was premised on changing white perceptions of the

"This has been a good chance to see ourselves as others see us." Dorothy Rogers addresses the audience directly. *All-American News*, 123 (1945).

race, the didacticism of the good conduct campaigns put the onus on individual black Americans to do so by adopting bourgeois mores. In cases like this one, the politics of respectability and the newsreel's pedagogical address appear to have reinforced rather than to have countered what Jane Gaines described as the "execution of power through the trajectory of the eye."

In addition to its straightforwardly didactic use of the direct address, All-American's pedagogical mode was evident in the newsreel's many stories of black achievement, which comprised the vast majority of the reel's content. The celebration of extraordinary accomplishments and the glorification of outstanding individuals were commonplace in the mainstream newsreels of the 1930s and 1940s. From presidential inaugurations, sporting events, and the ubiquitous ticker tape parade, the mainstream newsreels represented the honoring of celebrity achievement as much as the achievements themselves. In contrast to these public displays of adoration, the All-American Newsreel focused its cameras on more quotidian—although, in the context of the politics of respectability, no less important—successes. These achievements were lessons in hard work and perseverance. Stories of people like Flournoy English, who was awarded one hundred dollars by the quartermaster for making an efficiency suggestion, or two firemen promoted to the rank of lieutenant, "the first negro firemen thus promoted in New York City," celebrated the achievements of regular black Americans.[49] Items like these gave All-American the supportive feel of a community newsletter and suggested that members of the audience might be able to see themselves or people they knew celebrated onscreen. A letter to Marcus Bruce Christian, a poet in New Orleans, from his wife, Ruth, in Chicago illustrated this sense of community at work in the newsreel's audience. Ruth described seeing an old friend, Dr. Buggs, in the All-American Newsreel. Buggs was apparently "the only Negro at Wayne University."[50] Rather than stress the differences between the audience and the personality in the news, these stories implicitly, and sometimes explicitly, stressed their sameness. Even those African American celebrities who might command public shows of admiration—such as Joe Louis—were typically featured in private settings. Louis, for example, was shown with his daughter as she demonstrated her abilities on the piano. Stories like this one humanized black celebrities, while reflecting the pride many African Americans felt in the achievements of their racial brethren. Charles Wilson's voice-over commentary expressed this sense of pride: "The baby is mighty proud of her daddy, and aren't we all?"[51] While the studio newsreels displayed celebrity with the effect of marking the distance between the outstanding individual and the audience, stories like this one showed African American celebrities as regular people. As such, they were models of racial uplift as well as race pride. The achievements of Joe Louis were, like those of Flournoy English, exemplary and implicitly pedagogical—for All-American, achievement was something to emulate not simply contemplate.

All-American's stories of achievement reflected the philosophy of racial uplift—that through hard work and dedication individual African Americans could overcome many of the obstacles that American society put in their path. Unlike the civil rights discourse promoted by the NAACP and others, this philosophy placed the onus for change on African Americans. This faith in self-help was dramatically reinforced by stories in All-American News dedicated to black Americans who had overcome physical challenges. One such story profiled a blind man who had "beaten his handicap" to become an accomplished student.[52] Another told the story of Clifford Blount, a man born without arms who became a successful stenographer with his own letter writing business. All-American showed Blount brushing his teeth, shaving, and tying his tie with his feet, while the commentator remarked that he "did everything except ask for help" and called him a "shining example of courage."[53] It is difficult to read these stories of individual triumph in the face of huge impediments as anything but lessons in the politics of racial uplift. Overcoming racism and inequality was implicitly aligned with the challenges of physical disabilities. But instead of challenging America to remove the obstacles to equality, this alignment suggested that black Americans themselves could overcome their situations. Moreover, such stories implied that one's race—as opposed to white racism—was the handicap to be overcome. By celebrating the achievements of men like Blount, All-American offered its viewers a lesson in perseverance and courage, but by failing to question a deeply unjust America, it also gave a lesson in accommodation.

Given the almost complete absence of African American news and personalities in the mainstream newsreels, one of the key pedagogical functions of All-American News was to provide evidence of the presence of black men and women in the war effort and beyond. This evidentiary role was crucial to the mission of the newsreel as it related to the politics of uplift — African American "contributions to America and freedom" needed to be recorded and exhibited in order for them to be used in the struggle for dignity and respect. Nowhere was the importance of the evidentiary function of the newsreel more apparent than in All-American's use of Signal Corps footage. Not only did these films offer a morale-boosting lesson in patriotism for African American audiences, they also provided proof of African American participation in the military and vivid evidence of the sacrifices black Americans were making in the war effort. The films of the 92nd Infantry Division were particularly important in this task as the "Fighting 92nd" was the only African American unit to see combat in Europe during World War II. All-American featured several items on the 92nd Infantry Division in 1944 and 1945. These stories stressed the presence of black troops in the field of battle. In one item covering the 92nd in Italy, All-American's voice-over declared that the division was "making history" and that "whenever the Signal Corps [made] a movie of a battle, the 92nd [would] be in the middle of it."[54] Later stories further served to underscore the sacrifice these troops were making. The division was shown advancing under fire in Italy, with images of shelling and wounded African American soldiers.[55] And, after victory in Europe had been won, an item showed the 92nd honoring its dead. A somber musical score accompanied these scenes, and All-American's commentator noted that "tribute [was] paid to those who gave their lives for liberty."[56] These records of sacrifice made visible the contributions African Americans were making to the war effort — providing the dramatic evidence that ought to have been decisive in the struggle for Double Victory.

As we have seen, the use of Signal Corps films became a topic of heated debate in the black press in 1944 as critics began to view All-American's apparently exclusive prerogative to show footage of black soldiers with suspicion. Indeed, given the way in which these images dramatically demonstrated the African American community's wartime sacrifice, it is easy to see why many lamented the fact that they were not reaching white audiences. Nevertheless, All-American proudly used the footage and made a habit of noting the source

U.S. Signal Corps footage of the
92nd infantry Division in Italy
provided visual evidence of the
presence of African Americans in
the military. *All-American News*,
131 (1945).

of those scenes in its intertitles. At times, the newsreel went further, explicitly noting the presence of Signal Corps photographers in its voice-over commentary. On one occasion, when the Signal Corps recorded scenes of General
Clark hosting several newly promoted black officers, All-American noted that
these were "scenes the Signal Corps was proud to record."[57] These references
to the Signal Corps suggested that the army itself did acknowledge the participation and sacrifices of African American soldiers, even if the mainstream
newsreels did not. All-American's emphasis on the Signal Corps' willingness
to film African American soldiers seemed to argue that black audiences could
be proud that their community's efforts were being witnessed by the U.S. government. Such pride points to the complicated relationship between pedagogy, visibility, and racial uplift at work in the All-American Newsreel. The
films may have been lessons in race pride and models for uplift, but these lessons placed heavy emphasis on the white gaze of the Signal Corps cameras.
Once again, in its use of this footage, All-American seemed to reinforce as
much as it countered that "sense of always looking at one's self through the
eyes of others."

Visibility was key to All-American's pedagogical mode and its message of
racial uplift, but there were clear limits to this politics of looking. As we saw,
black middle-class notions of respectability as represented in the newsreel
were so much about the crucial trajectories of power inherent in looking at
race. Not only was the pedagogical address a way to offer models of behavior and bolster race pride, it was a way to address the "race problem" in visual
terms. The celebration of African American achievement and black contributions to the war effort, however, could not obscure the realities of Jim Crow.

As black audiences watched the All-American Newsreel in segregated theaters they must have been acutely aware of this reality. The company portrayed the world of which it was a product: segregation. In the films of All-American, black troops, black celebrities, and black middle-class bond buyers appeared in a virtually monochromatic world. But while the newsreel showed the fact of segregation it failed to probe that reality. Racism, poverty, and social and political marginalization were simply not discussed. Indeed, racism worked like a "structuring absence" in the films of All-American News. It—like the eye of the newsreel's opening credits—framed the achievements of black Americans.

Given the segregated nature of the United States military, stories about black soldiers inevitably confronted—if only obliquely—the question of racism in America. Despite their sacrifices, African American military personnel remained second-class citizens and the All-American newsreel could not help but represent this fact. Thus, even stories that celebrated African American wartime sacrifice were often freighted with the unspoken irony of segregation and inequality. A vivid example of this appeared in a story about a celebrated athlete turned naval enlistee.[58] In this story, Buddy Young, a star halfback for the University of Illinois football team, was shown in training at the Great Lakes naval base in Michigan. The commentary declared Young to be "on Uncle Sam's team now." The piece went on to show Young in lessons and at work on the base. But while the story ostensibly applauded Young for doing his patriotic duty and implicitly called on its audience to do the same, the story was tinged with irony. Despite Young's physical abilities, his talents were applied to apparently mundane tasks, such as laundry and delivering the mail. As the voice-over stated: "Those muscles Buddy developed throwing forward passes come in pretty useful now—sailor whites get plenty dirty," and "The general needs to send a message. Who gets the job? Buddy Young, the fastest guy on the base." Instead of showing African Americans in a heroic light, this story cast black naval enlistees—even those with exceptional talents—as the errand boys and laundry workers of a segregated military. It was scenes like this that pointed to the limits of the All-American Newsreel. In the context of a Jim Crow military and a Jim Crow motion picture industry, All-American was left to try and put a positive spin on some uncomfortable facts.

Stories such as this one raise the question of how audiences responded to the All-American Newsreel. It is hard to believe that audiences would have easily accepted the demotion of a star athlete to errand boy as a model of achievement and object of race pride. Thomas Cripps notes that, by the 1940s,

"Those muscles Buddy developed throwing forward passes come in pretty useful now — sailor whites get plenty dirty." *All-American News*, 125 (1944).

race-movie audiences were growing increasingly critically aware of the genre's failures and limits. Cripps describes black audiences watching race movies and "calculatedly laughing in all the wrong places." He argues that this laughter was "politically purposeful, a way of telling each other that they *knew* not only the absurdity of racism but the absurdity of making movies to accommodate it."[59] Indeed, laughter became a critical way in which All-American's audience members expressed their opinion on the newsreel. Although black audiences may have appreciated seeing their prominent citizens on screen and hearing about the achievements of regular African Americans, they resisted the series when they saw it as condescending. Audience members voiced their disapproval by laughing inappropriately or by refusing to laugh when the newsreel made its own lame attempts at comedy. Letters to the editors of the black press indicate that some audience members were particularly uncomfortable with the comedy duo, "Butterbeans and Susie," a broad vaudeville type skit that ran for some time at the end of the newsreel. Sergeant Melvin Williamson wrote to the *Chicago Defender* to call these comedic interludes "tiresome and worn out." He pointed out that such comedy detracted from the newsreel and created the "impression that any serious news concerning the Negro would be utterly ridiculous."[60] Another letter sent to the *New York Amsterdam News* and signed only A. Private registered a similar complaint. In an otherwise positive review of the newsreel, the author said that to him these scenes were not "funny or comical at all."[61] But at times, All-American's audience was ready to laugh at the absurdity of racial inequality. Indeed, All-American's pedagogical address could underline such ironies and, in so doing, raise the ire of audiences. In one scene, designed to instruct veterans on their benefits,

George Hollan of the Veteran's Administration staged an interview with a newly returned black soldier.[62] The wooden dialogue began with the GI saying, "I'm a regular vet, what can you do for me?" The answers Hollan gave did not please all audiences. According to Alfred E. Smith, the author of the "Adventures in Race Relations" column for the *Chicago Defender*, "when these 'benefits' boiled down to the fact [that the veteran was] entitled to free burial in a national cemetery, the all-Negro audience practically laughed the news reel out of the theater, and it was sarcastic laughter."[63] In cases like this one, All-American's attempts to promote race pride and the philosophy of uplift ran up against the realities of racism and inequality. Audience laughter in the face of All-American's pedagogical address suggests that African Americans understood the implicated nature of the newsreel's relationship to segregation and accommodation.

Unlike the mainstream newsreels that all but ignored black America, All-American News acknowledged—if only implicitly—the fact of segregation. The struggle for racial uplift necessarily took place in the context of a racist society. It is in this context that we must view All-American's pedagogical address. Instead of ignoring Jim Crow America, the newsreel offered instruction on how to better oneself within it. By displaying African American achievement and evidence of the community's contribution to the war effort, the newsreel aimed to show the path to racial uplift—a path that put the onus on individuals to rise above the obstacles of racism rather than confront an unjust society. As we have seen, visibility was crucial to the newsreel's pedagogy. From All-American's opening credits, the film's lessons in respectability, patriotism, and courage were framed by the newsreel's watchful eye—an eye that could stand in for the proud eyes of the black community as well as the critical eyes of white America. Ironically, in a series premised so much on the politics of the visible, it was what went unrepresented that may have overshadowed the newsreel's own message. The reality of racism cast doubt on the value of All-American's pedagogical address.

CONCLUSION

As the war came to an end, the All-American Newsreel struggled to remain relevant. Glucksman and Barnett worked to keep the newsreel alive and to make sure African Americans and others had the opportunity to see the accomplishments of their community on screen. Forays into television and sponsored film kept All-American going into the 1950s, but never again did All-American regain the relevance that it had during wartime. The growing consciousness of the civil rights movement made the politics of racial uplift increasingly out of place in postwar America, while changes in Hollywood made an all-black newsreel seem like a relic of an accommodationist era now past. But it is too simple to dismiss the All-American Newsreel as simply an agent of accommodation and of the Jim Crow society that it reflected. As Edward Wheeler points out in his work on racial uplift in the South, accommodation and uplift were far from an endorsement of the racial status quo. Wheeler argues that accommodation "had a subversive quality." While uplift reflected bourgeois notions of respectability and white standards of achievement, it was also "a denial of what white society meant by accommodation, for it spoke of a possibility to move beyond the limits prescribed by the dominant society.[64] By celebrating the achievements of African Americans who overcame racism and inequality as well as by urging and instructing others to do the same, All-American did offer the possibility of progress, however incremental. Indeed, All-American's pedagogical address was premised on the idea that black Americans could and should achieve a better life in the United States. Moreover, by representing a segregated America, All-American News did what no other film was able to do during World War II. It reflected the reality of race relations in the United States. Unlike its mainstream cousins, which simply whitewashed over the question of race, or fictional race movies that posited surreal all-black worlds, All-American represented a Jim Crow America. Although it failed to confront the question of racism inherent in its own images, All-American made an uncomfortable reality visible.

NOTES

1   "Fletcher Henderson at Apollo; All-Negro Newsreel on Screen," *People's Voice*, November 7, 1942 in Tuskegee Institute News Clipping File, Tuskegee Institute, Ala.: Division of Behavioral Science Research, Carver Research Foundation (Sanford, N.C.: Microfilming Corporation of America, 1981), reel 81, 268.
2   In addition to producing films and theatrical revues, Glucksman wrote a guide for theater managers: Glucksman, *General Instructions Manual for Theatre Managers*.
3   Bowser, "Pioneers of Black Documentary Film."
4   See Rhines, *Black Film / White Money*; Cripps, *Slow Fade to Black*, and *Making Movies Black*.
5   "Negro Newsreel Seen by 4,000,000," *American Cinematographer*, November 1943, 408.

6　Letter from Claude Barnett to All-American News, August 14, 1948, in Meier and Rudwick, *The Claude Barnett Papers Microform*, part 2, series D, roll 4.

7　Letter from Emmanuel Glucksman to Claude Barnett, April 5, 1949, in Meier and Rudwick, *The Claude Barnett Papers Microform*, part 2, series D, roll 4. Although this plan never materialized, Glucksman partnered with Barnett to produce a series of documentaries, sponsored by Liggett and Myers, the makers of Chesterfield Cigarettes. The six part "Negro America" series featured episodes on "The Negro in . . ." education, sports, entertainment, science, industry, and national affairs (Scripts for "The Negro in Education," and "The Negro in Industry" can be found in ibid., part 2, series D, roll 5). Using footage from All-American newsreels as well as original material, the series aimed to highlight black achievement in various areas of American life. Having secured sponsorship for the films, Glucksman also made prints available at low cost to "interested social and fraternal organizations, trade unions, colleges and educational groups." ("Six Dramatic Movies to Portray Negro America in Nation's Motion Picture Theatres," press release in ibid., part 2, series D, roll 3.)

8　"The Courier's Double 'V' for Double Victory Campaign Gets Country-Wide Support," *Pittsburgh Courier*, February 14, 1942.

9　"Negro Newsreel to Be Produced Weekly in U.S.," *Atlanta Daily World*, October 19, 1942, 2. "1st Newsreel for Negroes Now Ready," *New York Amsterdam Star-News*, October 31, 1942, 16.

10　Ted Watson, "Says Negro Newsreel Will Explain Race to Whites," *Atlanta Daily World*, November 16, 1942, 2.

11　Frank White, "'All-American News': A Negro Newsreel," *Pittsburgh Courier*, April 10, 1943, 17.

12　E. Wheeler, *Uplifting the Race*; Higginbotham, *Righteous Discontent*; and K. Gaines, *Uplifting the Race*.

13　K. Gaines, *Uplifting the Race*, 4.

14　Higginbotham, *Righteous Discontent*.

15　These thirty-nine issues were among forty-five reportedly discovered in a New York City garage by Ephraim Horowitz in the early 1990s. The CBS News Archive purchased the 35mm originals and an uncatalogued viewing copy is available at the Schomburg Center for Research in Black Culture in New York City (Cf. R. Wheeler, "News for All Americans"). Fred MacDonald, of MacDonald and Associates, a private historical film archive based in Chicago, claims he owns the rights to these same films. In correspondence with me, MacDonald claims he purchased a collection of All-American Newsreels from a retired ABC News technician. MacDonald received a Beta master of these films—an almost identical collection as that held by the CBS News Archive—but was told that before they could be delivered to him the film originals were lost.

　　The CBS News Archive provided viewing copies of the films in its collection to me. Subsequent references to items in these newsreels will be cited according to year and issue number per the CBS News Archive's cataloguing information.

16　See Logan, "Negro Youth and the Influence of the Press, Radio, and Cinema"; Barnett, "The Role of the Press, Radio, and Motion Picture and Negro Morale"; Morton, "The Federal Government and Negro Morale"; Reddick, "Educational Programs for the Improvement of Race Relations."

17 Stewart, *Migrating to the Movies.*
18 Cited in Stones, *America Goes to the Movies*, 212.
19 Cited in Noble, *The Negro in Films*, 99.
20 Ibid.
21 Stones, *America Goes to the Movies*, 211.
22 Cripps, *Slow Fade to Black.*
23 Ibid., 329.
24 Reddick, "Educational Programs for the Improvement of Race Relations," 367.
25 Herman Hill, "Walter White Is Winning His Fight for Better Roles," *Pittsburgh Courier*, August 8, 1942, in Tuskegee Institute News Clipping File, reel 81, 275.
26 "Distorted Roles of Negro on Screen Must Go, Says White," *Atlanta Daily World*, October 13, 1943, in Tuskegee Institute News Clipping File, reel 86, 234.
27 Morton, "The Federal Government and Negro Morale," 357.
28 Cripps, *Making Movies Black*, 129.
29 Doherty, *Projections of War*, rev. ed., 210.
30 "Negroes' War Efforts Get H'wood Brushoff: Writers Complaining," *Variety*, March 15, 1944, 32.
31 "More Negro Scenes Cut Out in Dixie Set New Problems for Pix Producers," *Variety*, July 12, 1944, 32.
32 "Newsreels Blackout Race Troops," *Atlanta Daily World*, January 9, 1944, 1; "Newsreels 'Cut' Negro Fighters," *New York Amsterdam News*, January 8, 1944, A1; "Newsreels and the Negro in the War," *Journal and Guide*, January 15, 1944, in Tuskegee Institute News Clipping File, reel 90, 539.
33 "Newsreels 'Cut' Negro Fighters," A1–2.
34 "Newsreels Blackout Race Troops," 1.
35 "Omissions from Newsreels," *Crisis*, February, 1944, 39.
36 "Newsreels 'Cut' Negro Fighters," A2.
37 "No Agreement with Newsreels, NAACP Is Assured by War Dep't," *Atlanta Daily World*, February 2, 1944, 1.
38 Letter from Truman K. Gibson Jr. to Claude Barnett, December 14, 1942, in Meier and Rudwick, The Claude Barnett Papers Microform, part 2, series D, roll 4. Harry McAlpin, "OWI Deal Bars Negro in Major Newsreels," *Chicago Defender*, January 2, 1943.
39 Harry McAlpin, "Silver Lining," *Chicago Defender*, February 13, 1943, 13.
40 "No Agreement with Newsreels, NAACP Is Assured by War Dep't, 1.
41 Roy Wilkins, "The Watchtower," *New York Amsterdam News*, January 15, 1944, 7A.
42 "99th Fliers in Newsreels on Broadway," *People's Voice*, February 12, 1944, in Tuskegee Institute News Clipping File, reel 90, 543.
43 Du Bois, *The Souls of Black Folk*, 3.
44 J. Gaines, *Fire and Desire*, 12.
45 Luther Hill, "Newsreel to Back 'Good Conduct' Campaign," *Pittsburgh Courier*, May 13, 1944, 13.

46 "Churchman Makes Good Conduct Plea," *All-American News,* 113 (1944) in CBS News Archive.

47 Higginbotham, *Righteous Discontent,* 196.

48 "Teenagers Show 'Good' Conduct," *All-American News,* 123 (1945) in CBS News Archive.

49 "Flournoy English Wins Award for Efficiency," *All-American News,* 116 (1944), "Firemen Promoted in New York City," *All-American News,* 120 (1945) in CBS News Archive.

50 Letter to Marcus Bruce Christian from Ruth, June 1, 1945 in Letters from the online archives of Marcus Bruce Christian, "Chickenbones: A Journal of Literary and Artistic African American Themes." http://www.nathanielturner.com/ruthenjoysnegro lifechicago.htm (accessed August 5, 2008).

51 "Champs Baby Punches Ivories," *All-American News,* 117 (1945), in CBS News Archive.

52 "Blind Man Fine Student," *All-American News,* 221 (1945), in CBS News Archive.

53 "Armless, He Is a Success," *All-American News,* 140 (1945), in CBS News Archive.

54 "92nd in Italy Rout Nazis," *All-American News,* 108 (1944), in CBS News Archive.

55 "92nd Infantry in Italy," *All-American News,* 131 (1945), in CBS News Archive.

56 "92nd Honors Its Dead," *All-American News,* 138 (1945), in CBS News Archive.

57 "Gen. Clark Host to New Officers," *All-American News,* 115 (1944), in CBS News Archive.

58 "Buddy Young Now a 'GOB,'" *All-American News,* 125 (1944), in CBS News Archive.

59 Cripps, *Making Movies Black,* 150.

60 Melvin R. Williamson, "Soldiers Criticize All-American News," *Chicago Defender,* August 26, 1944, 12.

61 A. Private, "Likes 'All American News'," *New York Amsterdam News,* May 27, 1944, 6A.

62 "Hollan Explains Vet Policy," *All-American News,* 142 (1945), in CBS News Archive.

63 Alfred E. Smith, "Adventures in Race Relations," *Chicago Defender,* August 11, 1945.

64 E. Wheeler, *Uplifting the Race,* xvii.

MECHANICAL CRAFTSMANSHIP
AMATEURS MAKING PRACTICAL FILMS

Charles Tepperman

> As yet we are very self-conscious about expressing the industrial and
> economic forces that surround us. . . . Our minds have found the new
> world, but our deeper life of feeling and emotion lags behind. . . .
> If we ever succeed in making an adequate adjustment to the city and
> the laboratory, if we ever turn our dread and dislike into an active faith,
> we shall not need a host of reasoned artistic theories. We shall find
> creative insight spontaneous and natural, and who knows but imagina-
> tion will raise mechanical craftsmanship to the level of fine art?
> —JOHN HERMAN RANDALL, *Our Changing Civilization*

In 1929, when the philosopher John Herman Randall penned these remarks, critics, artists, and scholars were still struggling with the question of how to balance the "deeper life of feeling" with a modern industrial world. Though Randall, like many thinkers of the moment, believed that industrial design was one place where modern craftsmanship might be found, scholars since the 1930s have also identified motion pictures as a quintessential locus for joining together modern technology, culture, and "creative insight." Pointing to the Hollywood movie studios as a model of efficient factory production, and to Hollywood commercial films as the cultural products most tailored to mass consumption, more recent historians of film and American culture have argued that popular cinema is important to our understanding of twentieth-century American life because it reproduced in aesthetic form the mass technological experience of modern life.[1] In a slightly different way, the encounter between modern life and motion pictures has been traced in specialized and non-theatrical film circuits, including educational, agricultural, and community contexts. Scholarship in this area has shown that many institutions understood movies as an instrument capable of extending and reinforcing various modern discourses of citizenship, efficiency, and the rationalization of work.[2]

But while film scholarship has tended to see moviegoing as an experience of mass entertainment that played important roles in representing and negotiating social discourses on a large scale, Randall's comments suggest a creative collaboration between modern life and an individual's imagination. And if recent scholarly accounts have emphasized the instrumental use of motion pictures in non-theatrical contexts, Randall's interest in balancing modern life with a "deeper life of feeling" represents a different kind of encounter with technology.[3] Amateur filmmakers were one group that explored the nature of this encounter from the standpoint of artistic production. During the 1930s, many amateurs brought creativity into dialogue with questions of modern industry, education, and spirituality. They called this broad category of moviemaking "practical films," and it is here that we find a direct intersection between modern work and individual creativity.

It was a related notion of the "film amateur" as both technically oriented and creative that Hiram Percy Maxim hoped to advance when he founded the Amateur Cinema League (ACL) in 1926.[4] The ACL promoted the growth of amateur film culture through publications (such as its magazine *Movie Makers*),[5] alternative distribution circuits, and annual movie competitions, attracting thousands of amateur filmmakers to its membership over the course of its three-decade lifespan. Members of the ACL often moved far beyond the "point-and-shoot" aesthetic of home movies, and distinguished their work through attention to the planning and finishing (pre- and post-production) of their films.[6] Originally the domain of affluent hobbyists, amateur moviemaking expanded during the 1930s to include a more diverse, if still predominantly middle-class, constituency of individual moviemakers and local amateur clubs. Echoing the pragmatic tradition of Randall's mentor, John Dewey, amateur discourse eschewed theoretical approaches to filmmaking and instead promoted practical, experimental, and individual engagements with motion picture technology, creativity, and everyday life. Even though we might think of amateur filmmaking as an activity in which people made films primarily for recreation, during the 1930s amateurs also became involved in other kinds of film production, including industrial and educational moviemaking. The ACL even included sponsored and commercial non-theatrical films in a special category of its annual competitions between 1936 and 1947, a provision that might seem to contradict a basic tenet of amateurism — not receiving compensation.[7] Clearly, amateur film occupied a more complex social and aesthetic terrain than the image of the hapless home moviemaker suggests.

This essay explores the overlapping worlds of amateur and practical film production. In particular, it considers how amateurs responded to Randall's aspiration for an individual and creative engagement with modern life and technology. The ACL's *Movie Makers* magazine regularly reported on its members' production of educational, religious, industrial, and social problem films, eventually, in 1932, collecting this news into a regular monthly column called "Practical Films." The ACL's discursive construction of this genre in order to describe the "use of personal films in serious fields" provides us with an avenue for examining a specific area of amateur filmmaking.[8] In contrast to both popular cinema, which addressed spectators as part of a mass audience, and documentary film, which quickly came to designate a specific kind of government or institutional propaganda, amateur films generally reflected a personal and independent attitude toward practical filmmaking.[9] In fact, rather than presenting an anomaly in amateur filmmaking, this creative engagement with the practical conditions and activities of modern life stood at the center of the ACL's mission. During the 1930s, amateur activities expressed a utopian aspiration to move cinema making and watching beyond its theatrical settings and into non-theatrical contexts, in order to explore, in imaginative ways, the motion picture's relationship to working life and social problems. While other groups, such as the Worker's Film and Photo League, responded to the dire conditions of the Great Depression by politicizing practical filmmaking, the ACL opposed calls, from both right and left, to channel the diverse activities of its members into coherent political action. Certainly, this did not prevent some individual amateur filmmakers from producing films that supported particular social or political causes. As an organization of amateurs, however, the ACL actively resisted being subsumed into the political currents that swept through the 1930s, taking a position that seems at once blithely apolitical and naïvely optimistic about the creative pleasure and social potential for a new mode of expression: personal motion pictures.[10] All of this changed with the onset of World War II, an event that marked both the peak of practical filmmaking and the beginning of its decline as an amateur genre.

The ACL defined and encouraged the production of four different subcategories of the amateur practical film: educational, industrial, social problem, and religious.[11] While these are all categories of filmmaking that predate the ACL's founding, in 1926, they occupied an important place in amateur film publications and contests.[12] The discourses around these practical films show that amateurs understood the "use of personal films in serious fields" to be part of an earnest, if idealistic, attempt to repair the fissure between modern experience and creative insight that Randall had identified. Understood in this way, amateur practical films can be seen as more than impersonally "useful" texts; they can also be seen as works that shed light on the complex negotiations taking place between art and technology, as well as mass culture and individual experience, in American society.

AMATEUR EDUCATIONAL FILMMAKING

> To itemize the applications of amateur or semi-professional cinematography, means to go on indefinitely. With each thought and each possibility other avenues of usage appear until one actually wonders how civilization has progressed without the cine-camera. —J. H. MCNABB, "The Amateur Turns a Penny"

Movies were touted as an educational tool almost immediately after their invention. Indeed, early film pioneers like Thomas Edison and Charles Urban promised a future in which motion pictures would quickly replace textbooks. But it was not until the late 1910s, and the introduction of non-flammable safety film that could safely be shown in classrooms, that the widespread use of films for educational purposes seemed likely to become a reality. By the early 1920s, a number of national organizations and publications had been established to address the burgeoning topic of visual education.[13] But even with the introduction of 16mm film in 1923, the supply of reliable educational films lagged far behind the demand suggested by this discourse. So it is not surprising that when the Amateur Cinema League was established in 1926, educators saw a way of resolving the problem of unreliable supply: they could make their own films. Accordingly, articles in the ACL's *Movie Makers* magazine often addressed how amateurs might use their new 16mm equipment for educational or scientific purposes. "The motion picture field," wrote one contributor, "hitherto confined to the realm of professionalism, is now being invaded by an insistent and ever increasing demand of amateur desire, made possible through amateur genius."[14]

By May 1927, *Movie Makers* had a regular column that addressed educational and applied uses of amateur film. This column kept amateurs apprised of developments in educational, scientific, social, and industrial filmmaking, much as readers of visual education magazines were becoming aware of amateur filmmaking. An editorial in 1928 by Roy Winton, the ACL's managing director, cemented this relationship: "Amateur cameras and projectors have released the potency of motion pictures into an immensely larger field than existed four years ago. As film entertainment spread from theatres into homes, so film education has spread from school into homes. . . . We believe that schools and homes can better carry on their educational processes by using this great force of personalized movies, and we feel we have a clear mission to foster this use as far as we can."[15] So for Winton the amateur field offered two ways of expanding educational film: the first used amateur exhibition equipment to allow educational films into the home (though they also spread to many other locations), and the second promoted the production of "personalized movies," which meant instilling practical films with something of the personal, or amateur, "desire and genius." One frequent justification for amateur practical films was that by "join[ing] their filming experience to the exact knowledge of the field" amateurs could infuse a film related to their professional work with a personalized quality, thus amplifying its subject matter with a kind of personal authority.[16] Articles in *Educational Screen* from the 1930s made a similar claim, as one educator wrote that his amateur educational films were "a happy union of my vocational and avocational interests."[17]

The pages of *Movie Makers* reported on a wide range of amateur educational films about biology, math, geography, and other subjects, which were made for use in classrooms and other non-theatrical venues. But beyond these fairly conventional films, there were also educational works that exceeded the informational requirements of the genre and appeared interested in developing creative and aesthetic expressions of their subject matter. John Grierson's first film, *Drifters* (1929), is an excellent example of this combination. His "solid adventure of the herring fishery" is in one sense a process film that illustrates the herring's journey from the depths of the sea to the family dinner table. But it is also a poetic interpretation of this process and, according to Grierson, a film with all the "crescendo in energies, images, atmospherics and all that make up the substance of the cinema."[18] In its annual "Ten Best Amateur Films" competitions, the ACL awarded works that displayed a similar interest in aesthetically shaping their educational material. For example, the ACL named *Ceramics*, a silent film made by Kenneth Bloomer and Elizabeth Sansom of the Mount Kisco Cinémats, one of the "Ten Best Amateur Films of 1933," for this reason.[19] Stylistically, *Ceramics* has a familiar actuality film structure that shows the process by which the potter Leon Volkmar produced his ceramic works. But like *Drifters*, *Ceramics* is also a visually complex work that explores the aesthetic dimensions of an educational topic.

Industrial processes are common among silent educational films because they are both visually striking and they share with cinema a kind of temporal and mechanical linearity. The most interesting process films are those that recognize moments of visual affinity between process and camera; these produce an effect that some amateurs vaguely referred to as visual "interest" and are reminiscent of what French critics of the previous decade had called "*photogénie*." [20] In *Ceramics*, such an affinity is evident in the extended sequences of Volkmar working his clay at the potter's wheel. Shown in medium long shots from several different angles, the clay's shifting shapes, height, and depth take on a dance-like quality (not unlike the undulating waves in *Drifters*) that is representable only with motion pictures. The idea of a dance is further suggested by an intertitle at the beginning of this sequence that announces: "The Potter's Wheel — coordinating the brain, the hands, and the feet." Occasional shots of Volkmar's feet turning the wheel reinforce the dance motif even further, as they provide a counterpoint to the undulations of the clay itself. Finally, the spinning action of the wheel offers a visual synecdoche of a film spool turning in the camera. So even as the film presents an informational record of the potter at work, it also traces a kind of creative and visual movement across three different media: dance, pottery, and film.

While these aesthetic qualities might seem to be secondary in importance to the film's presentation of practical information — it shows how a clay pot is made — writers in *Movie Makers* suggested an important link between these two aspects: "*Ceramics*," they wrote,

> . . . is probably the most ambitious amateur film ever attempted on this particular subject and perhaps stands alone in its field. The makers of the film were fortunate in having the cooperation of a famous ceramic artist, Leon Volkmar, who maintains his atelier at Bedford Village, N.Y. It was here that the entire film was produced, its makers having imbibed the spirit of the artist craftsmen so thoroughly that every deft touch, every careful step in the process of making a lovely vase are recorded. . . . Such a film might be described as a "glorified industrial" but, more than that, it is an educational film in the best sense of the word. [21]

But what is an "educational film" in the best sense of the word? For Roy Winton, this meant amateur films that "have to do with the complex problems of human relations in industry, in education, in recreation, in religion,

Ceramics (Kenneth Bloomer and Elizabeth Sansom, 1933), National Archives, Washington.

Ceramics.

and in daily life as a whole," with amateur filmmaking technology providing "a new factor which they can use with all the variations suitable to their personal desires."[22] In *Ceramics*, we can see the amateur's attempt to work out these "human relations in industry" aesthetically, and in doing so the film compares an old kind of craftsman (Volkmar) with a new one (the filmmakers). What we find here is not just the recording of a process for educational purposes, but also a situation in which the amateur filmmakers' sensitivity to creativity and imagination primed them to "imbibe the spirit of the artist craftsman" and reinterpret it in light of the cinema's mechanical visual craft.

Ceramics also evokes the idea of the "practical artist," a figure that appeared a number of times in ACL publications, and was perhaps best exemplified by the advertising and artistic photographer Edward Steichen. "[Steichen] can best be described as a man of contradictions," wrote one amateur. "He is an artist and a dreamer. Yet he is a hard worker, a shrewd craftsman, and a firm believer that there is nothing on earth without interest if you are attracted to it."[23] This mix of creativity and hard work appealed, no doubt, to the editors of *Movie Makers*, and informed some of their promotion of the practical use of amateur films. This is particularly evident in articles about the use of films to create a broader understanding of classroom learning; although some saw educational films as effective instruments for conveying the practical—rather than the theoretical or abstract—substance of lessons, educators also experimented with the production of motion pictures. Some made their own films so they could unite "vocational and avocational" interests, while others experimented with film production as a classroom activity in which students could gain firsthand experience of both the subject being filmed and the craft required to film it.[24] In this way, filmmaking became a pragmatic way of reinforcing the union between artistic and practical work.

AMATEUR INDUSTRIAL FILMMAKING

Early industrial films, such as *A Visit to Peek Frean and Co.'s Biscuit Works* (Cricks and Martin, 1906), exploited the cinema's ability to record and display the fascinating complexity of modern factories for purposes of both advertising and visual spectacle. Thus it is not surprising that the industrial application of amateur movies and movie technology was also evident from the early years of the ACL. In 1930, Arthur Gale, the editor of *Movie Makers*, reported that amateurs were "generally awakening to the fact that the universal applicability of the motion picture extends to business and industry as well as fields of recreation." While acknowledging that professional publicity firms were necessary for more extensive production and use of industrial film, Gale pointed to the personal appeal of such films to amateurs: "every movie maker wants the personal satisfaction of himself recording one of the most important of his interests—his business or vocation."[25] While it might be tempting to dismiss Gale's editorializing as merely an effort to expand amateur filmmaking into new areas of activity, the regularity with which specific practical films made by amateurs were discussed in *Movie Makers* in the 1930s is quite surprising. These works approached industrial topics in a variety of different ways, and, like the amateur educational films, they often explored aesthetic or personal dimensions of the subject matter that pushed industrial filmmaking beyond its familiar coordinates.

To promote its relationship to industrial works, the Amateur Cinema League offered a consultation service to help amateurs make practical films, which left us with statistics on amateur industrial filmmaking. In 1931 Gale noted, "More than one hundred and twenty seven first rate industrial films have been made by amateur movie makers. Almost an equal number are now in the process of production."[26] He went on to categorize amateur industrial film projects as follows:

> First, there is the industrial film made by an amateur for his own satisfaction and pleasure, in much the same spirit that he would make a film record of a vacation. Such films are more entertaining than one might realize and they offer a great deal of satisfaction in the making. Second, there is the industrial film record, the purpose of which is to analyze the operation of machines, scientific apparatus or perhaps the movements of a workman. Such films are most often made in order to secure increased efficiency.... Third, there are films made for the purpose of publicizing or advertising products or for direct sales appeal.[27]

This delineation of categories is illuminating. It shows that what was seen as productive about amateur industrial filming included three possible applications: a satisfying personal chronicle, an analytic tool that produced a commercial advantage, and a relatively inexpensive form of publicity. Writers also commented on amateur industrial film's ability to reveal overlooked aspects of a business, as well as the value of the amateur's "personal touch" in their own industrial films; some writers even suggested that the amateur industrial film's quality of personal sincerity more than made up for its technical shortcomings.[28]

Dent Harrison's incomplete films—*Building a Bakery 1930, Harvesting and Baking*—about his own Pride of Montreal (POM) bakery illustrate some of the personal and aesthetic qualities that characterized amateur industrial work.[29] Though missing its head titles and clearly out of sequence at certain moments, the silent footage on these reels nevertheless features moments of surprising complexity and departs from our usual expectations of industrial films in its creative playfulness. The films show the construction of the filmmaker's new bakery, and later, the process of bread-making more broadly, from harvesting grain to the delivery of the freshly baked bread. The footage of the bakery's construction appears at first very rough in technique, employing unsteady panning shots and choppy in-camera editing. But if Harrison's film initially seems like little more than a point-and-shoot, personal chronicle of the construction project, it soon becomes clear that the film has some logic as a construction project in its own right. Beginning with roughly taken images of mechanical shovels and men pouring a foundation, the footage gradually assumes greater technical proficiency as it shows bricklayers working on a nearly completed exterior and other, more advanced stages of the bakery's construction. Intertitles narrate the footage throughout this process, and one title in particular would seem to confirm the relationship between style and content in the film, announcing, "order comes out of the chaos," at just the moment when both building and film style are beginning to assume a coherent form. Evidently, Harrison crafted the earlier footage to mimic in style the rough and embryonic stage of the building's construction; in doing so he gave aesthetic shape to personal chronicle footage. The film's second reel shows the bakery at work and advertises its products. Much like the *Peak Frean* film, made more than two decades earlier, we see bakers and machinery at work, as well as shots of cakes and loaves. Finally, an intertitle foregrounds the publicizing function of this film: "When you want the best say POM."

Harrison's two reels about his bakery mark the intersection of his personal interests (in cinema *and* in business) and the commercial application of amateur work. Harrison's film has a number of elements in common with Gale's itemization of amateur industrial works, functioning as both a chronicle and a personalized advertisement. But it is also important to make a distinction between these amateur films and professional advertising work. As Jackson Lears argues in his history of advertising, *Fables of Abundance*, professional advertisers address themselves to the masses; they have a managerial project that sees the masses as impersonal markets to be organized and exploited. Amateurs, in contrast, were interested in resisting this kind of assimilation into mass society. Even in films that advertised a business, amateur industrials were, in a certain sense, a kind of personal advertising, earnestly seeking a bond with the viewer/customer, rather than trying to dupe him or her. These films depart from our expectations of industrial impersonality by proudly showing off images related to the filmmaker's own business or profession, much as one would show off images of one's children in more typical home movies. The exhibition context enhanced the intimacy of this kind of film. Harrison likely showed his films of the POM bakery in person and at amateur cinema club meetings, or to other small groups, but probably didn't intend them to be distributed widely and impersonally. These exhibition strategies also tended to shore up the social and economic status that Harrison's playful and creative films spoke from: they insulated Harrison's position of privilege from the democratizing effects of mass popular culture and established —

between the domesticity of home movies and the impersonality of modern advertising—a reassuring middle space for personal industrial films.[30]

We find a different kind of industrial film, one that pushes the conventional model toward a radical visual experiment, in *The Eyes of Science* by J. S. Watson and Melville Webber.[31] Produced in 1931, and named one of the "Ten Best Amateur Films" of that year by the ACL, *The Eyes of Science* was commissioned by Bausch and Lomb to illustrate the production of lenses and optical instruments at its factory. Though in certain respects a polished industrial film, *The Eyes of Science* is perhaps better characterized as a hybrid work that reveals the aesthetic interests of Watson and Webber, and recalls aspects of their experimental amateur films *Fall of the House of Usher* (1928) and *Lot in Sodom* (1932). These aspects of experimentation are particularly evident in the filmmakers' efforts to complement content with aesthetic style in *The Eyes of Science*, which they do by foregrounding experiences of self-conscious and distorted vision.

The Eyes of Science begins with a shot of scientists working in a laboratory, accompanied by voice-over narration that announces man as a "scientific animal." But the conventionality of this introduction is quickly, and literally, dissolved when a distorting lens intervenes, obstructing our clear view of the scientists. As this distortion gives way to an extreme close-up of a human eye, the narrator tells us that man "has constructed new eyes with which to extend the range and acuity of his vision." The enormous eye fills the screen and looks straight out, confronting us with a gaze that is both human and mechanically mediated, mirroring our own spectatorship through the visual prosthesis of the cinema. *The Eyes of Science* later presents images of a movie camera and projector, each upside down with spinning shutters, at once revealing and estranging our own encounter with moving pictures. Tracing vision to its constituent elements, the film presents a study of prisms, in which the camera follows rays of light as they travel down from the heavens, through clouds, a cathedral, and a glass prism, as if to offer a short journey of light from divine origin to scientific instrument. Notably, this stylized sequence of clouds and refracted light foreshadows the relationship developed between light, prisms, and divinity in Watson and Webber's *Lot in Sodom* the following year. Elsewhere, the film proceeds more conventionally by depicting the process of making glass and lenses, but again, lessons in tempering glass are made visually stunning through slow motion photography and repetition.

As this description suggests, even though *The Eyes of Science* is an industrial film, it is one that reveals the insistent influence of amateur experimentation. Since Watson and Webber's own amateur experimental films made extensive use of prisms like those manufactured by Bausch and Lomb, there is something appropriate about such aesthetic flourishes in their industrial film.[32] For amateurs such as Harrison, or Watson and Webber, machinery and industry were like the movie camera itself, presenting new modern tools and landscapes with which—and *through* which—individuals could produce creative interpretations of the world. *Movie Makers* praised both the aesthetic and industrial aspects of *The Eyes of Science*, noting, "The combination of cinematic art and skill with which this film is composed places it well in the front rank of all existing industrials regardless of the source of their production."[33] During the 1930s, the ACL further promoted this blending of art and industry, renaming its annual competition the "Ten Best Non-Theatrical [not just amateur] Films" in 1935, and creating a new category of awards for sponsored or commissioned films in 1936. Though amateurs responded to industrial filmmaking with varying degrees of personalization and aesthetic experimentation, the ACL consistently rewarded these aspects of practical filmmaking.

AMATEUR SOCIAL PROBLEM FILMMAKING

Non-professional uses of the cinema for social causes long predate the history of organized amateur film activities, first becoming prominent as a tool of progressive causes in the 1910s and 1920s. From Jane Addams's exhibition of films in Hull House to the production of independent films about child labor, white slavery, and temperance, and to the adoption of film in schools and other practical training contexts, reformers of the progressive era were quick to take up film for their causes.[34] For these reformers, however, film was a double-edged sword. The popularity of commercial films, they argued, posed a danger to the supposedly impressionable minds of the young, the working class, and recent immigrants; but if the popularity of film could be harnessed to productive ends, film stood to become a powerful instrument for behavioral and social change. Consequently, blending entertainment with instruction became a hallmark of progressive appropriations of the cinema. This could take place at the level of the program, where Chaplin's comedies brought in the crowds and then didactic reform films drove the message home. Or, entertainment and instruction could be blended at the level of the film text itself, such as in *Traffic in Souls* (IMP/Universal 1913), where a dramatic narrative animates the reformer's lesson. These examples shared with later amateur films a desire to re-contextualize the subject matter and exhibition spaces of motion pictures away from commercial entertainment. But at the same time, it is important to make a distinction between these two modes; while reformers saw movies as an instrument that could be put to work on many impressionable minds, amateurs were more likely to see the medium as a tool for the personalized expression — and localized promotion — of their commitments and causes. In 1930, the very first year of the "Ten Best Amateur Films" announcements in *Movie Makers*, social problem films were already represented among the notables. Listed among the year's "Special Mentions" was Marvin Breckinridge's epic amateur film, *The Forgotten Frontier*. In its commendation of this film, *Movie Makers* observed:

> *The Forgotten Frontier*, filmed by Miss Marvin Breckinridge, is the most ambitious amateur made welfare film yet recorded. To show the operation of the Kentucky Nursing Service, Miss Breckinridge spent several months filming in the mountain districts reached by that organization. With the cooperation of the mountain folk, she staged several short dramas, each demonstrating the usefulness of one of the centers or some phase of their work. The completed picture runs 6000 ft., 35mm, and in spite of the numerous technical difficulties, it is excellently photographed.[35]

This brief comment notes the film's extraordinary ambition as an amateur production, including its length and use of 35mm film, as well as its blend of fictional and factual elements. And although the article does not mention it, the ACL deserved some credit for the structure and execution of this film; Marvin Breckinridge's diaries reveal that after deciding to make a film about the nursing service, she sought out training from the Amateur Cinema League and received several lessons in cinematography and editing from Arthur Gale, the editor of *Movie Makers*. Also unacknowledged here is Breckinridge's personal connection to the film's subject. The Frontier Nursing Service had been founded just a few years before by her cousin Mary Breckinridge, who appears in the film. As a rare silent film directed by a woman, and as a work that has since been named to the Library of Congress's National Film Registry (in 1996), it is surprising how little *The Forgotten Frontier* has been seen or discussed.[36]

The Forgotten Frontier pays careful attention to the rules of continuity editing, and makes extensive use of both "working in" and shot-reverse-shot structures. But the film also contains a number of elements that seem to exceed any social or narrative motivation. On the one hand, the film has a clearly established narrative structure, made up of a series of five docudrama episodes and

The Forgotten Frontier (Marvin Breckinridge, 1930), National Library of Medicine, Bethesda, Md.

framed by a conversation with some visitors to Kentucky. But on the other hand, *The Forgotten Frontier* employs a set of recurring images and visual motifs that mark it as a more complex aesthetic object than its structure and social purpose might suggest. The images that stand out most memorably in *The Forgotten Frontier* are recurring long shots of nurses and doctors fording rivers on horseback: these occur five different times over the course of the film, appearing in four of the episodes, and at the film's conclusion. In a film that otherwise makes consistent, if sometimes clumsy, use of continuity editing, these exceptionally long takes of medical personnel battling their way across strong river currents seem particularly strange; their lengthy duration — the longest one clocks in at slightly more than a minute — marks these shots as important, yet they are not necessarily informational. One way to interpret these scenes is to see them as emblematic of the Frontier Nursing Service's heroic struggles to reach its patients in remote Appalachia under any circumstances. And while this may be the principal purpose of such images, it is hard to overlook the aesthetic qualities of the shots themselves. These images are carefully composed, placing small figures on horseback against a background of rough riverside terrain as they move slowly through the swift-moving and reflective surface of the water. In other words, if these are emblematic shots, they do not simply foreground the nurses' heroism; they are also emblematic of the aesthetic possibilities of the cinema, its ability to capture such dramas and to reframe the grueling work of social hygiene as a heroic, and even epic, struggle.

Indeed, *The Forgotten Frontier* produces a number of similar aesthetic emblems that both augment and exceed the film's narrative and practical dimen-

The Forgotten Frontier.

sions, revealing the potential for practical films to give amateurs a momentary glimpse of their lives reframed as aesthetic and dramatic experiences. For example, in several sequences that follow closely from the fording scenes, the nurses are shown transforming their identities through changes in clothing and uniform. From western-hero stars that have just braved the Kentucky wilderness, the women become modern and professional as they remove outer coats to reveal their crisp white shirts, trousers, and black neckties. Though practically concerned with depicting different aspects of the nursing service, such as midwifery, home visits, inoculations, and emergency medical treatment, the film also serves as a visual expression of the shifting—but always professional—identities that these women have taken on. The film's dramatization of scientific hygiene in a "forgotten frontier" is what marks it most clearly as a progressive-influenced film. But even though it presents a staging of this struggle for good health, *The Forgotten Frontier* doesn't seem intended solely as an instrument of social propaganda. Rather, the film's framing narrative, which depicts "visitors who have come to observe the work," implies an intended spectator from Breckinridge's own peer group of urban philanthropists and activists; to these like-minded viewers, the film presented a creative and personal engagement with practical social problems.[37] Ultimately, *The Forgotten Frontier* embodies a range of both aesthetic and historical tensions. It blends fact with fictional elements; it interrupts narrative episodes with these emblematic sequences of shifting identity and costume; and it offers an epic portrayal of life on the "forgotten frontier"—a historical contradiction some three decades after the American frontier was declared closed. And, notably, it does all of this through the contradictory medium of 35mm amateur cinema, a mode that is neither professional in quality nor a rough home movie. In fact, as a modern application of motion picture technology, with an already fading form of silent cinema, *The Forgotten Frontier* offers a potent symbol of the aesthetic and historical contradictions of practical amateur cinema itself.

No doubt, some amateurs continued to address progressive causes in their practical filmmaking, and the pages of *Movie Makers* reported on many films about social causes and local charities, particularly as social conditions during the Depression worsened.[38] Over the course of the 1930s, however, the meaning of social filmmaking shifted and became the principal terrain of the documentary film. Some (primarily non-amateur) organizations, like the Workers' Film and Photo League, redefined their filmmakers as artist-workers so as to narrow the gap between themselves and the subjects they filmed. But there were other key distinctions between amateur and progressive or documentary works. Whereas the progressive tradition hoped to harness the cinema's powers to indoctrinate spectators (even as it transmuted these powers into the rhetorics of documentary film), practical amateurs more often claimed a fair-minded, rational communication with their spectators. Indeed, the editors of *Movie Makers* repeatedly asserted the amateur filmmaker's special claim to free expression. In an editorial in 1934 called "A Free Art," the anonymous author contrasts "the harsh, negative and forbidding picture of experiments in social regimentation" against the amateur film where there is "either expression or nothing." Praising the inevitable democratization of filmmaking as equipment became less expensive, the editorial presents an image of amateurs who were engaged in an individual activity with aggregate significance: "Personal filmers are so absorbed in the practical phases of their hobby that they would be surprised, not to say embarrassed, if they were told that they are trusted guardians of one of the world's great social values, the right of free, individual self expression."[39] We might conclude from this editorial that in contrast to Grierson, who, following Walter Lippmann, saw the cinema as a means of conveying mass propaganda that could reduce the complexity of modern social issues and thus shape public opinion, amateurs were more likely to echo John Dewey's call for "free and enriching communication" as a way of negotiating social problems in a modern democracy.[40] In this liberal-democratic vein, the amateur's goal was not to indoctrinate using the medium's instrumentality so much as it was to employ his or her movies as a tool for just the kind of informed and personalized—not mass, not propagandistic—inter-communication that Dewey had promoted.

Religious filmmaking is a subgenre of amateur work that marks an even more challenging negotiation of the instrumental and the artistic—as well as the personal and the practical—poles of moviemaking in this history. Religious films had appeared in non-theatrical contexts since at least the 1910s when passion play films were distributed among churches and Chautauqua meetings. But churches, like schools, often had difficulty finding suitable materials to exhibit well into the 1920s and 1930s. One writer suggests that amateur religious works were prompted by exactly this shortage of professionally made religious films: "Into this 'problem situation,'" he writes, "came the amateur movie photographer with his intense 'mother love' for every picture he took, whether it was good or bad."[41] *Movie Makers* commented on such productions from time to time, such as in the article, "Motion Pictures and the Minister" of 1931. This article recounts the efforts of a number of different churches in their use of amateur films as a way of "raising funds, stimulating membership, holding attention of the congregation, widening [their] educational interests and providing palatable and, at the same time, suitable entertainment."[42] Thus amateur film equipment allowed for the possibility of even more numerous and smaller-scale productions about specialized topics, questions of quality notwithstanding.

One of the most acclaimed amateur religious films of the 1930s was also a film that drew on experimental montage techniques in order to present an aesthetic interpretation of Christianity. *Movie Makers* named *In the Beginning* (Fred C. Ells, 1935) one of the "Ten Best Nontheatrical Films for 1935." That magazine's anonymous writer offered even higher praise, calling it one of the best films (amateur or professional) ever made: "*In the Beginning*, although far from being a perfect picture, is nevertheless one of the few truly great films thus far to come from a motion picture camera—either theatrical or amateur. Here, the magnificent beauty and awesome strangeness of the natural world have been seen in their fundamental and ultimate meanings. As an interpretation of the epic story of creation, *In the Beginning* follows directly in the noble tradition of Homer, Dante and Milton."[43] Such high praise sheds light on the critical assumptions of the Amateur Cinema League at this moment. Though the aesthetic tradition evoked here—of transcendental beauty and Homer, Dante, and Milton—long predates the movies, Ells's accomplishment lay in joining this tradition with the mechanical craftsmanship of amateur moviemaking.

Composed almost exclusively of non-continuous shots, placed in graphic and associational montage sequences, *In the Beginning* illustrates the first verses of the Book of Genesis. The film's carefully controlled structure alternates between intertitles that narrate the biblical creation story and montage sequences of increasing duration and cutting rate. Ells's film begins with slow, contemplative images, suggesting "the face of the deep"; it reaches its most complex point when it visualizes the diversity of the animal kingdom through montage, in a sequence that combines twenty-eight shots over two and a half minutes. The film's rapid cutting tempo subsequently drops off and presents human figures for just a single shot, drawing in fishing nets on a beach. Many of the film's individual images are visually striking in their own right. Shots of dramatic skies that open and close the film recall paintings by the old masters; shots of the complex patterns formed by droplets on water are reminiscent of abstract films by Joris Ivens and Ralph Steiner; and plants and animals take on strange shapes when presented in extreme close-up, recalling the abstraction of earlier science films. Ells composes his shots to emphasize light objects, details, and backlit silhouettes against otherwise dark backgrounds; in this way, the images sustain a great deal of their graphic and estranging qualities, rather than functioning merely as a representation.

While this kind of religious film evidently differs from the practical movies that recorded histories of local churches, or the story of the Catholic mass, writers for *Movie Makers* praised *In the Beginning* for its creative evocation of religious materials:

> One is left stilled and humble before the simple purity of imagination which conceived it. To this superb document of nature F. C. Ells, ACL, the producer, has brought a technical skill and sensitive craftsmanship more than equal to the demands of his subject.... Somber and stunning scenes of the heaving waters, the new born earth and bursting streams in the first reel are followed in the second, by flawlessly executed telephoto and macroscopic studies of the earth's myriad creatures. Integrating the entire production is a musical accompaniment of stately church music, recorded on disc by the Sistine Choir. Mr. Ells, who has looked upon the earth and found it is good, has produced a sincere and beautiful film, great even as it falls short of perfection.

While praising the "sensitive craftsmanship" and technical skill evinced by Ells's film, these remarks again allude to some slight, though unspecified, shortcoming. The glowing review suggests that any discernable imperfection

In the Beginning (Fred C. Ells, 1935),
National Archives, Washington.

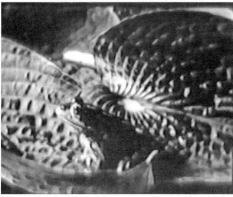

In the Beginning.

is less a measure of the film's inadequacy than a mark of the filmmaker's broad imaginative scope and his willingness to experiment with film form and technique in new and innovative ways. But if this inclines us to see this film as primarily an artistic work, archival papers and program notes related to its exhibition emphasize the ways in which it could be seen as practical as well.[44] An exhibitor's guide contains detailed suggestions for the film's use in religious and educational programming in different venues, such as a college or high school class in English literature; a book club, in connection with Bible study; at YMCAS, YWCAS, YMHAS, and YWHAS; in Sunday school class; and at an outdoor showing of a youth conference, to name just a few. The guide also includes discussion notes, "observation tests," and a cue sheet for music to be played live, or with specified Victor phonograph records.[45] Though these materials suggest an extensive educational apparatus, one letter from the film's production file suggests a limit to the educational practicality of this film. In a note from the Library Bureau, a correspondent indicates: "I feel that as it stands, IN THE BEGINNING is beautiful but not educational. Public school authorities, I think properly, generally shy away from presenting religion in any form, and for that reason, the present treatment would be taboo." So even though there were clear restrictions on its practical application, the film presents a union of practical, spiritual, and aesthetic qualities.

Although there is a great distance between the practical use of amateur films for church history and the more creative works made by Fred Ells, these films hint at a broad terrain of amateur works concerning religious themes.[46] These works have different degrees of creative experimentation and artistry — and therefore somewhat different interpretations of the relationship between religion and film—but were still produced by amateurs to have a practical effect on religious education and experience. This encounter between spectator and film could take the form of a religious lesson, or, like *In the Beginning*, it might employ aesthetic means to elicit spiritual wonder. In each of these cases, amateurs produced films that attempted to balance practical and spiritual value with mechanical and aesthetic means; in these ways, amateurs aligned religious belief with an "active faith" in the modern, technological medium of cinema.

CONCLUSION

The different films presented in this essay—from classroom films and industrials to social problem films and spiritual reflections—stand as a microcosm of the amateurs who made them. The filmmakers display an effort to resist many of the conventions and dominant practices that characterized the mass, commercially produced versions of these genres. But in the discussions that constituted amateur movie discourse during the 1930s, these films occupied a space in which motion pictures could creatively animate practical aspects of daily life. To illuminate this intersection of imagination and mechanical craftsmanship still further, we might look to John Dewey, who expressed a similar interest in expanding the relationship between everyday work and artistic experience. In his writings about *art*, understood distinctly as a kind of purposeful and reflective *experience*, Dewey explored the necessary balance between "instrumental" (useful) and "consummatory" (delightful) aspects in artworks. "For arts that are merely useful," he wrote, "are not arts but routines; and arts that are merely final are not arts but passive amusements and distractions, different from other indulgent dissipations only in dependence upon a certain acquired refinement or 'civilization.'"[47] Ultimately, Dewey argued that art (and artful experience) occurred when useful and pleasurable activities were brought into dialogue, and "when activity is productive of an object that affords continuously renewed delight." It is hard to think of a more precise distillation of the amateur filmmaker's ethos than this formulation of the practical and pleasurable working together to produce "continuously renewed delight."

World War II offered an opportunity for amateurs to bring the practical aspects of their filmmaking to the forefront of their activities, but it also shifted the terms of this practical engagement away from its pleasurable associations. The war demonstrated the usefulness of amateur movie technology in propaganda and institutional uses far beyond amateur circles; but with its conclusion came a re-evaluation of the relationships between creativity and practicality that had developed among amateurs during the 1930s. In 1948 the ACL revised its rules for the ten best films of the year, renaming them the "Ten Best Amateur Films" (no longer "non-theatrical" films) and eliminating the special categories for sponsored films. An editorial called "All Amateur" explained the change: "Few, if any, amateur filmers are now interested in making pictures for gain—even non-professionally. The production of such films is now big business, carried on by elaborately equipped, highly trained and well paid professionals. Their product, for better or for worse, has lost the amateur touch. As such, it no longer belongs in competition with true amateur movies."[48] This editorial speaks to the emergence of a professional industry of 16mm moviemakers who had displaced the role of amateurs, and with it the "amateur touch." In addition to this factor, a growing number of postwar moviemakers understood 8mm film (first introduced in 1932) as the "true" amateur moviemaking format. Given the experience of World War II, when so many aspects of life at the "home front" had become practical, it is perhaps unsurprising that the postwar years should show a turn in the opposite direction, reconfiguring amateur filmmaking as a strictly leisure activity. The "Ten Best" competitions between 1948 (when the categories were revised) and 1954 (when the ACL ceased operations) were populated primarily by short fictional and chronicle films. Practical filmmaking had been central to the first two decades of amateur moviemaking but found itself displaced in the 1940s and 1950s by more family-oriented production.

Amateur practical films grew out of pre-existing traditions of silent non-fiction works, but they also employed aesthetic experimentation and mechanical craftsmanship to link work and creativity. Though this specific configuration of mechanical, imaginative, and practical experience diminished in importance in amateur circles after World War II, it is possible that aspects of this impulse persisted in postwar developments of the independent documentary and experimental film, as well as more recent digital media production. But amateur practical films of the 1930s, in particular, help us to discern certain utopian impulses in American culture. First, they reveal the prospect of a democratized art making that was rooted in free personal expression; and second, and perhaps more pertinently, these films present the possibility that art itself could be joined to the practical aspects of everyday life in meaningful ways. Through this union, art could begin to repair some of the damage that industrial mass society had imposed on both work (its alienation and dehumanizing danger) and leisure (its depersonalization and reduction to consumption). Cautious of top-down mass cultural reformations, amateurs resisted submergence into mass culture and instead sought to productively reconfigure practical, personal, and aesthetic aspects of life. For amateurs in the 1930s, it seemed as though nothing could achieve Randall's dream of "raising mechanical craftsmanship to the level of high art" better than the movie camera, a device that joined so many of these warring factions of life — the mechanical and the creative, the informative and the imaginative, work and play — into a single field of vision.

NOTES

1   For general versions of this historical approach see Sussman, *Culture as History*; Sklar, *Movie-Made America*; and L. May, *Screening Out the Past*. More recently, Miriam Hansen has provided an important reconsideration of these ideas in her essay "The Mass Production of the Senses."

2   Chapters by Gregory Waller and Ronald Greene in this volume contribute in important ways to this work.

3   A similar pairing of craftsmanship and film technology is highlighted in Dana Polan's work on the history of film studies: see Polan, *Scenes of Instruction*.

4   Maxim had previously been instrumental in the founding of a similar organization, the American Radio Relay League, in 1914.

5   The ACL publication *Amateur Movie Makers* first appeared in 1926 and shortened its name to *Movie Makers* in 1928.

6   Film scholarship has primarily approached amateur moviemaking as home movies; see Patricia R. Zimmermann, *Reel Families*. Recent work has started to examine the work of more serious amateurs: see Stone and Streible, Special issue on "Amateur Cinema." In my study of work by serious amateurs, I identify four principal modes of production that were common during the ACL era; aside from "practical films," they are experimental, chronicle (travelogue and family), and fictional narrative films.

7   By "sponsored and commercial non-theatrical films" I mean films that were com-
    missioned or produced for profit, generally either for industrial promotion or for
    presentation to another kind of specialized audience—instructional, religious, and
    fundraising—in a non-theatrical venue (that is, not commercial movie theaters).

8   The "Practical Films" section began to appear regularly in *Movie Makers* (hereafter
    referred to as *MM*) beginning with the issue of July 1932. The section was often ac-
    companied by a subtitle, such as "Business, civic, medical, school and other uses";
    the subtitle "Reporting the use of personal films in serious fields" appeared in the
    issue of January 1936.

9   In both Britain (with John Grierson) and the United States (with Pare Lorenz), most
    significant work in documentary film during the 1930s was government-sponsored or
    politically motivated.

10 Many years later, the ACL's managing editor, Roy Winton, recalled the organiza-
    tion's position to the political currents of the 1930s: "Many times in the past twenty
    years, when something has been proposed by zealous but remorseless idealists, we at
    headquarters have had to reject the project because it would not, as far as we could
    see, bring about any increase of pleasure. . . . In the full swing of the late Fascist era
    in Europe, some Italians and, soon afterward, some Spaniards developed most am-
    bitious projects for systematizing and controlling personal filming internationally.
    Because of its world standing, the League was asked to become a part of these totali-
    tarian efforts. When we gave a blunt negative, we were assailed bitterly." (Winton,
    "Twenty Years of the ACL," 300.)

11 These are categories that recur in *Movie Makers* through the 1930s; to these we might
    add the sub-category of surgical films, which are like educational films in some ways,
    but also had their own specific production and exhibition contexts, and, starting in
    1934, their own separate ACL film exchange. The exhibition and distribution contexts
    of amateur practical films, more generally, are hard to pinpoint; the films discussed
    in this essay were likely screened privately by the filmmaker, at local movie clubs,
    business or trade associations, schools, and churches, and were distributed privately,
    commercially, and through the ACL film library or other institutional libraries.

12 My work here draws heavily on the ACL monthly magazine *Movie Makers*, but it is
    supplemented by other related periodicals, including *Educational Screen*, *Photoplay*,
    and *American Cinematographer*, all of which published regularly about amateur film-
    making. Because these publications relied on commercial film and film equipment
    companies for advertising revenue, we should not be surprised to find in them favor-
    able attitudes toward these industries. But none of them were in-house publications
    (like Bell and Howell's *Filmo Topics*, or *Kodakery*), and *Movie Makers*, in particular,
    foregrounded its editorial independence from the industry.

13 Most prominent among the organizations were the National Education Associa-
    tion's Department of Visual Education, and the Society for Visual Education; impor-
    tant publications included *Moving Picture Age*, *Educational Screen*, and *Visual Educa-
    tion*. For the early history of educational film see Slide, *Before Video*; Arthur Edwin
    Krows, "Motion Pictures: Not for Theatres," serial publication in *Educational Screen*,

1938–44; Mebold and Tepperman, "Resurrecting the Lost History of 28mm Film in North America"; and Wiatr, "Between Word, Image, and the Machine."

14 McNabb, "The Amateur Turns a Penny," 19.

15 Winton, "Editorials: A Clear Mission," 219.

16 Bailey, "Educational Films," 728.

17 "Making an Educational Movie," *Educational Screen*, February 1934, 41.

18 Grierson, *Grierson on Documentary*, 135. The question of whether we should consider Grierson an amateur filmmaker is an interesting one; his lack of technical film training and his interest in exploring the relationships between practical life and experimental film aesthetics suggest some commonalities with amateurs. But *Drifters* was produced for a British government agency, the Empire Marketing Board, and Grierson's ideas about institutional filmmaking might be seen as the result of his many years studying the field of mass communication; ultimately, Grierson's later writings reflected his interest in being understood as a professional propagandist, a position that placed him at odds with amateur (or at least ACL) discourse.

19 A copy of *Ceramics* is now held at the U.S. National Archives 2 (NARA), College Park, Md.

20 Developed by Louis Delluc and Jean Epstein, the concept of *photogénie* describes ways in which particular movements and aspects of the real world are "enhanced by filmic reproduction." See J. Epstein, "On Certain Characteristics of *Photogénie*," 314.

21 "The Ten Best," MM, December 1933, 499–500. It is also worth noting that most amateur practical films during the 1930s were silent works, due to the expense and unreliability of early amateur sound technologies. It was not until the arrival of magnetic sound equipment after World War II that amateur sound films became a widespread reality. The complete filmography of "The Ten Best" is published in Kattelle, "The Amateur Cinema League and Its Films."

22 Winton, "The Amateur Cinema Camera Man," 37.

23 Tazelaar, "Portrait of a Pioneer," 18–19.

24 See, for example, Filut, "Fractions," 70; Eldridge, "High School Films without Subsidy," 541, and "Practical Films," 296.

25 Gale, "Note: Tabloid Industrial Scenarios," 540.

26 Gale, "Continuity of Amateur Industrials," 256. *Movie Makers* also published occasional articles specifically about distributing practical films, such as Parmenter, "Distributing Industrial Films," 436.

27 Gale, "Continuity of Amateur Industrials," 256–57.

28 Kenneth Space wrote, "The most common fault of all is the lack of personal touch which is necessary to arouse and keep the interest of spectators who are not familiar with the plant itself"; Space, "Amateur Industrial Films," 706; see also Hugon, "Dramatizing Industrials," 793.

29 Harrison was an active member of the ACL and amateur movie clubs in Montreal; his better-known completed film, *The Highway of Tomorrow, or How One Makes Two* (1930) marks him as a technically sophisticated and gifted amateur filmmaker. His films are now held by the National Archives of Canada, in Ottawa.

30 In a related vein, Neil Harris develops the idea of a "culture of reassurance" in rela-

tion to John Phillip Sousa's bridging of the gap between classical and popular music, as well as art and commerce; Harris, "John Philip Sousa and the Culture of Reassurance."

31 A copy of *The Eyes of Science* is held at George Eastman House, Rochester.

32 Some amateurs delved even further into modernist abstractions of machinery and industrial processes, and displayed a fascination that was at times closely related to avant-garde film. See, for example, Potamkin, "The Magic of Machine Films," 722. The late 1920s and the early 1930s saw growing interest in both photography (Charles Sheeler and Margaret Bourke-White) and films (such as Ralph Steiner's *Mechanical Principals* [1930]) that focused on machinery and industrial processes as objects of aesthetic fascination in their own right.

33 "The Ten Best," MM, December 1931, 657.

34 For comprehensive and detailed histories of progressive reformers and the movies, see Grieveson, *Policing Cinema*; Stokes and Maltby, *American Movie Audiences*; and Jowett, Jarvie, and Fuller, *Children and the Movies*.

35 "The Ten Best Amateur Films of 1930," MM, December 1930, 788.

36 A copy of Marvin Breckinridge's diaries are held in the Motion Picture Reading Room of the Library of Congress, Washington; copies of *The Forgotten Frontier* are held by the Library of Congress and the National Library of Medicine, Bethesda, Md.

37 The film's exhibition history would seem to confirm the film's intended audience of potential donors. According to Mary Breckinridge, the film drew a full house at its fundraiser premier in New York; it was subsequently shown "hundreds of times . . . sometimes to drawing room groups (in 16mm size) and sometimes (in 35mm size) at regular motion picture theatres and in large halls." Breckinridge, *Wide Neighborhoods*, 278–79.

38 For example, a film about "agricultural despotism and destitution" was produced in 1937 by Alan S. Hacker, a member of the ACL. The proceeds were to aid southern sharecroppers ("Practical Films," MM, March 1937, 128).

39 "A Free Art," MM, May 1934, 185.

40 Dewey wrote, "[Democracy] will have its consummation when free social inquiry is indissolubly wedded to the art of full and moving communication." Dewey, *The Public and Its Problems*, 184. The imagery Dewey uses here of course brings motion pictures poetically (if coincidentally) to mind. Grierson remarks upon his debt to Lippman in his writing, most notably in *Grierson on Documentary*, 207. For a succinct account of documentary film in the United States during the 1930s, see Wolfe, "The Poetics and Politics of Nonfiction."

41 Rogers and Veith, *Visual Aids in the Church*, 14. For a general history of religious filmmaking during this period, see Slide, *Before Video*; and Krows, "Motion Pictures: Not for Theatres."

42 Bailey, "Motion Pictures and the Minister," 134.

43 "The Ten Best for 1935," MM, December 1935, 550. The copy of *In the Beginning* held by NARA doesn't correspond exactly to this description.

44 RG 200-HF-138, Harmon Foundation Files, NARA. *In the Beginning*, *Ceramics*, and

about a dozen other winners of ACL "Ten Best" recognition during the 1930s and early 1940s were distributed by the Harmon Foundation, whose collection of films and film documentation is now held at NARA. The Harmon Foundation was a philanthropic organization that supported a range of activities, including school playgrounds and awards for African American artists. This organization entered the world of motion pictures by establishing the Religious Motion Picture Foundation in 1925, which, by the mid-1930s, had developed into a "Division of Visual Experiment" that distributed and sometimes produced films on religion, social progress, education, and artistic instruction. Despite employing a staff cinematographer in this division, the Harmon Foundation sometimes commissioned or partially funded amateur filmmakers to work with a specialist and produce a film in their fields of expertise.

45 Ibid. Materials in the file include the following discussion topics: "The source of the Story; What Creation Means; Steps in Creation; The Purpose of Creation; Does Creation Continue?; Observation Test (and discussion); Project Activity Suggestions: Creation through the ages; The variety of creation; various creation stories."

46 An additional and interesting point of comparison would be the amateur religious films produced outside of the ACL or organized activities, such as *Hell Bound Train* (1930) and *Verdict: Not Guilty at the Judgment Day* (1933) (also known as simply *Verdict: Not Guilty*), religious films produced by African American amateurs Eloyce and James Gist.

47 Dewey, "Experience, Nature and Art."

48 "Editorial: All Amateur," MM, August 1948, 358.

EXPERIMENTAL FILM AS USELESS CINEMA

Michael Zryd

The film begins in long shot of the interior of a large room.[1] There's some wild street noise—trucks accelerating, cars honking their horns—rising from the space visible through the windows at the far wall. A woman directs two people moving a large bookshelf into the room. A long pause. Then the woman appears again with a friend and they listen to the radio. Then nothing happens.[2] And nothing happens for a long time. An optical zoom starts to narrow the visual field. Slowly. When the zoom begins, so too does a sine wave that very gradually increases in pitch. At long last, the zoom comes to rest on a close-up of a photograph. It's a picture of waves. What is this movie? What are we doing in this classroom watching it?

One of the most influential—and notorious—so-called structural films of North American experimental cinema in the years after World War II is Michael Snow's *Wavelength* (1967).[3] The overall shape or "structure" of the film seems simple enough: the film slowly zooms through the interior of a New York loft, coming to rest on a photograph. The apparent simplicity of the trajectory of the film, however, belies its actual variety, complexity, and density. Indeed, *Wavelength* is a film that has suffered from simplistic descriptions — starting with Snow's own program note, which reduces the densely textured film to its apparent "structure," a "continuous zoom" of "45 minutes," which hardly does justice to just how much is going on in the film.[4] The zoom is slow and intermittent. Filming over the course of a week in December 1966, Snow shifts the camera position and films the loft during the day and night. The quality of light in the image changes radically, shifting from black and white to color to negative, with added layers of color filters, reel flares, different film stocks, and a final section that includes multiple superimpositions. Although the soundtrack is dominated by the sine wave, it also includes dialogue, music, and ambient street noise.[5] Embedded in the film is a four-scene micro-narrative, which is swept aside, almost literally (and comically) as the zoom passes over an apparently dead body. As the inexorable zoom traverses the three-dimensional space of the loft to get to the paradoxically infinite space of the two-dimensional photograph of waves, and the fade to white at the film's end, the film takes on an almost metaphysical grandeur. The film's durational strategy (this action takes a full forty-five minutes but can feel even longer) is finally what makes it a challenging but rewarding teaching film.

Wavelength has confronted and confounded audiences since its celebrated premiere at the Fourth International Experimental Film Festival at Knokke-le-Zoute, Belgium, 1968.[6] Since then, it has become canonical, and has been screened as widely as any experimental film can be in the festivals and museums that form experimental cinema's most prestigious exhibition sites. But in North America, since the brief moment when experimental film attained a modicum of popularity in the late 1960s, the place where the overwhelming majority of experimental film screenings has taken place has been the college and university classroom. From the 1970s through the 1990s, 70–80 percent of film rentals at the three major North American experimental film distributors, Film-Makers' Cooperative (New York), Canyon Cinema (San Francisco), and Canadian Filmmakers Distribution Centre (Toronto), went to colleges and universities.[7] *Wavelength* has been a canonical teaching film in advanced cinema studies curricula since the 1970s. It is also one of a series of North American experimental or avant-garde films[8] of the late 1960s and the 1970s that challenge and complicate — but ultimately affirm — the possibilities for pedagogical cinema. At first glance, these films seem to be a useless waste of time, and they are unpopular with a majority of students. Certainly, compared with engaging narrative film, or even informative documentary and edu-

Frame enlargement, *Wavelength* (Michael Snow, 1967). Courtesy of the Canadian Filmmakers Distribution Centre.

cational films, experimental cinema presents a challenge to both students and faculty. Surprisingly, once initial resistance has been processed through discussion—indeed, precisely through this processing—these films often prove to be remarkably useful films, especially in the classroom, their dominant exhibition site.[9]

Ultimately, these films become useful by being anti-useful, by opposing utilitarian, instrumental pedagogy in favor of an approach that invites open, complex, and sometimes discomfiting experience. Many experimental films expressly reject the dominant mode of cinema spectatorship—that is, consumption, embodied in commercial Hollywood cinema. Instead, experimental filmmakers construct a cinema that addresses viewers in radical ways, ambitiously offering new forms of experience and invitations for reflection. And it is precisely the classroom, a very different kind of movie theater, that affords reflective space and time. *Wavelength*, like much experimental cinema, performs a particular kind of pedagogical work, forcing students to reflect on their activities as viewers. How do expectation and anticipation dilate time? How do the spaces of the film—the loft, the screen, and the space in which the film is being projected—interplay? How does the film balance what Snow calls "illusion" and "fact"?[10] (Just reflecting upon the title of the film gets students to think about how it resonates with the materiality of light and sound as waves.) How do the film's optical and sonic trajectories conjure the very act of concentration demanded in the encounter with this film?

In my experience, verified by others who have taught this film, postscreening discussions that draw out students' experience find expressions of frustration, even anger with the film. This frustration emerges partly from the mismatch between *Wavelength* and conventional cinema. As Scott Mac-Donald points out, *Wavelength* creates a crisis for the viewer: "For nearly all viewers, the idea of structuring a film around a zoom across a New York loft and rising sine wave is nearly untenable; such a principle could not be the foundation for a real movie."[11] As students grapple with this "useless" film, one that does not provide standard pleasures of narrative, spectacle, or even ennobling theme, they wrestle with the very definition of what cinema is and might be. Grappling with this film allows them to break through to insights about how cinema, and indeed any challenging artwork, works perceptually, ontologically, and culturally. *Wavelength* brilliantly foregrounds cinematic protocols (form, material, temporality, exhibition) such that students do not need to like it to learn from it.[12] Importantly, this lesson about pedagogical pleasure and anti-pleasure also makes apparent the mismatch between the experience of this film and conventional educational experience, which is supposed to be about gaining useful knowledge and skills. Experimental cinema is integrally linked to experimental pedagogy.

In this essay, I will sketch the parameters of how certain forms of experimental film have functioned as pedagogical cinema. While experimental film has been examined in aesthetic, theoretical, and cultural terms, its relation to education, its primary institutional exhibition site, has been largely unexamined. I argue that the aspirations of certain forms of post-1950s North American experimental cinema and progressive or experiential education dovetail in interesting ways, especially in the late 1960s and the 1970s when experimental film as a conceptual practice found a home in the classroom. I examine how experimental film's constructive but critical approach to both film and pedagogy parallels tensions in educational theory characterized by debates in the 1950s and 1960s between programmed instruction and experiential education. Indeed, there is a subgenre of experimental films that parody programmed instruction. Other films, like *Wavelength*, dramatize the open and critical nature of experiential education. I conclude by looking at two case studies of particularly influential and complex examples of experimental film pedagogy: Ken Jacobs's *Tom, Tom the Piper's Son* (1969) and Hollis Frampton's *Zorns Lemma* (1970). Both of these films, along with *Wavelength* and other experimental cinema, embody the highest ambitions of both cinema and education: transforming consciousness.

The very difficulty and complexity of these films makes them a limit case for the notion of "use" in cinema and education. Cinema of varying kinds of "usefulness"—whether in the tradition of programmed instruction, as with the conventional Encyclopedia Britannica teaching film, or the practice of experiential education, as with experimental film and its formal alterity and required openness on the part of the viewer/student—has long been conscripted into varying projects, each of which has been institutionalized in different cinematic and educational contexts. Experimental pedagogical cinema is invested in, and even presumes, a complexity of cinematic construction and spectatorial engagement. It thus rejects the very explanatory clarity that the educational training films work so hard to achieve. In so doing, it shifts the classroom from a place where knowledge is theoretically hypodermically inserted to one where the very forms and limits of knowledge are ideally debated and contested.

EXPERIMENTAL FILM IN THE CLASSROOM

The 1960s was a radical period of experimentation in both filmmaking and education. During this period, when film courses were the most rapidly growing area in the arts on American campuses, film instruction on campus offered students the opportunity to make personal, expressive, and improvisational forms (in addition to more conventional cinema).[13] Filmmakers like Jonas Mekas, D. A. Pennebaker and other direct cinema filmmakers, Stan Brakhage, Kenneth Anger, and other "underground" filmmakers, inspired students to make diary, documentary, personal narrative, and vaguely "surrealist" forms of film. These popular genres of student filmmaking paralleled a contemporaneous emphasis on student-centered learning.

So-called structural films like *Wavelength* emerged slightly later in the late 1960s and early 1970s and were more interested in foregrounding qualities of the medium than in direct authorial expression. In one way, they can be seen partly as a modernist reaction against the loosely expressive forms that dominated both underground and amateur student film genres. Structural film favored minimalist and conceptual strategies to call attention to the materiality of film and the language of cinema. Although less often recognized, they also foreground aspects of the exhibition, perception, and reception of cinema. As Owen Land puts it in one of his films, "This film is about you, not about its maker."[14]

Structural film of the early 1970s was particularly suited to the classroom for some purely practical reasons. First, unlike most other forms of experimental cinema, structural film enjoyed a limited embrace by the art world that, if nothing else, created a body of academic writing and criticism. Essays in art catalogues and articles in *Artforum* and later *October* magazine provided readings for course syllabi. Second, structural film benefited from the relative formality of the classroom, which allowed these films to be analyzed, critiqued, and contextualized before a captive audience that was, unlike the theatrical audience, not allowed to leave the screening room or classroom.

If the classroom was a privileged space for structural film screenings, it was not without a price. One consequence of structural films being taken up in the classroom was that the films' pedagogical function reduced them to the formal characteristic they demonstrated. Thus, Snow's *Wavelength* (1967) was said to be "about" the zoom and his ↔*(Back and Forth)* (1969), which was actually set in a classroom, was "about" the pan; Ernie Gehr's *Reverberation* (1969) was "about" photographic grain; and Gehr's *Serene Velocity* (1970) was "about" focal length. Of course, these films were also about much more, including their wit and playfulness, and the dynamic pleasures and challenges of watching them; they were "about" much more than the formal qualities of the medium. Being painted with the pedagogical brush took a lot of the fun out of these films — for, if the severity of the films was sometimes daunting, they often contained a wry humor reminiscent of the wit evident in the work of Samuel Beckett, Yoko Ono, or Gertrude Stein. The reductive nature of this use and thus the conceptualization of the avant-garde film dramatize two clear institutionally imposed limits: on the one hand, the concept of pedagogical utility rises to the fore with a common focus on clarity and transparency, and on the other, we can see an educational paradigm that reduces an artwork to a kind of demonstration exhibit. Any film — whether experimental, documentary, or narrative — is subject to being used reductively in the classroom. This is one of the consequences that any teaching film faces, and one perhaps inherent in the critical act of analysis: only a few aspects of a film tend to get highlighted in the classroom as the film is used to illustrate, allegorize, or embody an idea being taught.

Many of these films, along with earlier films by Maya Deren, Brakhage, Anger, and others, became canonical teaching films in the 1970s, occupying an important place in a new discipline, cinema studies, that was also engaged with defining itself and its limits. In 1967 were the first screenings of *Wavelength*, as well as the publication of the English translation of the first volume of André Bazin's writings, *What Is Cinema?* — whose title announced the formative question for the discipline in the 1960s and 1970s. As Bill Simon put it, the intellectual excitement of the formation of film studies as a discipline in the early 1970s lay in the modernist investigation of the nature of the medium, a project with which the avant-garde was explicitly engaged.[15] Much of that investigation took as its crucial figure the filmmaker-theorist. These artist-writers both made films and wrote texts—and sometimes made films that functioned as texts—usually around the modernist impulse to define cinematic specificity.[16] As David James describes Frampton's *Zorns Lemma*, "it is at once a film and a theory of film."[17] The inherently pedagogical and often manifesto-like quality of the writing of these artists is a crucial complement to their filmmaking. In the case of almost every one of these figures (Frampton, Deren, Brakhage), their work, like *Wavelength* above, seeks to re-define cinema, working against a conventional commercial or instructional standard of what constitutes a film. Their films and writing thus complemented broader scholarly and disciplinary developments across the university.

Another potential context for understanding the pedagogical function of structural film is in relation to the political critiques generated by avant-garde forms of modernism (for example, Brecht, Adorno).[18] Certainly, there is a long tradition of filmmakers who engage in the paradoxically productive avant-garde strategy of negation, whether through modernist strategies of defamiliarization (making strange the text or unlearning patterns of seeing and comprehension) or more radically destructive programs (ranging from Duchamp to punk). While an element of this avant-garde agenda underlies North American experimental film, I would argue that most of this cinema ultimately has a constructive, even earnestly utopian approach to art making that is rooted in a desire to heighten the consciousness of its viewers through challenge and amelioration. Despite acknowledging, and indeed insisting on the difficulty of their films, most experimental filmmakers during the late 1960s and early 1970s sought a public. Despite the obscurity of many of the films and artists, American experimental cinema was not elitist. The films require work and sometimes context, but the fundamental impulse was to create opportunities for new ways of seeing, what P. Adams Sitney calls the specifically American visionary tradition in the wake of Emerson and Whitman.[19] The democratic ethos of the experimental film world invited anyone to watch the films providing he or she was willing to work and to open his or her mind to a transformative experience. In so doing, these films implicitly construct the viewer as student—most often in an actual classroom, but elsewhere as well—simultaneously and paradoxically wanting the viewer to have both an immediate experience of the film and a profound reflection on the film through multiple viewings, historical and aesthetic contextualization, and, crucially, the convention of post-screening discussion.[20]

Clockwise from top left: Gerald O'Grady, the founder of the Center for Media Study, SUNY Buffalo; Sharon Ruppert, student; the filmmaker Stan Brakhage, University of Colorado, Boulder; and in the foreground, the filmmaker Hollis Frampton, SUNY Buffalo. Courtesy of Anthology Film Archives. Photo: Robert Haller, 1972.

The urge to open film viewers' eyes and minds to new possibilities in cinema is an important impulse in Stan Brakhage's famous manifesto *Metaphors on Vision*, perhaps the most frequently assigned text in North American experimental film teaching. It begins with an instruction: "Imagine an eye unruled by man-made laws of perspective, an eye unprejudiced by compositional logic, an eye which does not respond to the name of everything but which must know each object encountered in life through an adventure of perception. How many colors are there in a field of grass to the crawling baby unaware of 'Green'?" But Brakhage is simultaneously suspicious of the very notion of learning, seeking an ideal, natural, "untutored eye."[21] Such an eye is unattainable given the power of culturally familiar conventions, not only in film but also in painting and other forms of visual composition. Much of *Metaphors on Vision* is an attack on Hollywood, but Brakhage's notorious logophobia sought further to free vision from the constraints of language and social symbolic systems in general.[22] Despite the desire for a kind of direct, natural vision, both his films and his writings articulate a paradoxical injunction to be "unruled." We must be unruled because vision is so ordinarily dominated by conventional, rule-bound seeing.

EDUCATION: THEORY AND PARODY

The paradox of an educational approach that compels freedom of thought goes to the heart of central debates in educational theory. At the risk of cartooning a complex history, two main approaches have dominated educational theory during the twentieth century in the United States. The first approach is highly structured and directs students to knowledge and skills using test-oriented rote learning and behavioral training. A good example is B. F. Skinner's "Teaching Machines" (1958), which proposes applied behavior analysis, curriculum-based measurement, and direct instruction. This systematization of education as training culminated in the evocatively named "programmed instruction movement" during the mid-1950s through the mid-1960s.[23] The second approach emphasizes students constructing new meaning and knowledge, and emerges from constructivist approaches, including experiential education, "progressive education" (Dewey), and the pedagogies of Jean Piaget, Lev Vygotsky, Paulo Freire, Maria Montessori, and Rudolph Steiner.[24] These two contesting approaches — programmed instruction versus experiential education — have often coexisted in the same historical period, although with varying popularity in different contexts. These approaches have also been adapted to audiovisual media in different ways. During World War II, the need for intensive military and industrial training led to extensive use of instructional films, whose effectiveness led educational researchers to carry over this paradigm into public education.[25] Robert A. Reiser, in his survey of instructional media technology and design, notes that subsequent attempts to mobilize "television as a medium for delivering instruction" in the 1950s lost steam in the mid-1960s.[26] "Immediately after World War II, many of the psychologists responsible for the success of the military training programs continued to work on solving instructional problems. . . . During the late 1940s and throughout the 1950s, psychologists working for such organizations started viewing training as a system, and developed a number of innovative analysis, design, and evaluation procedures."[27] Reiser notes that the behavioral psychologist B. F. Skinner proposed that programmed instruction "should present information in small steps, require overt responses to frequent questions, provide immediate feedback, and allow for learner self-pacing."[28] Ultimately, programmed instruction was labeled "a technology of instruction."[29]

These "technologies of instruction" were deliberately satirized by the subgenre of experimental films in the late 1960s and the early 1970s that responded to pedagogies like programmed instruction, attempting to short circuit the rational instrumentality that dominated the conventional educational paradigms of highly structured rote education. Some of these paradigms are used in educational films, themselves a pure example of a "technology of instruction," which became the specific objects of parody. Where educational films seek to be useful, these experimental films sought to be anti-useful by satirizing a utilitarian pedagogy that seemed dedicated to simplifying intellectual problems. Experimental filmmakers were interested in exploring other forms of text-viewer interaction, and insisted upon complexity.

Standish Lawder's *Dangling Participle* (1970) takes on sexual and social education films from the 1940s and 1950s, capturing the presumptive logic of these films by creating a looped refrain from a repeated phrase from the soundtrack of one of the films, a prim voice intoning, "perfectly normal." Like many found footage filmmakers, Lawder hyperbolizes the literally normalizing cultural logic of the original films, here by using repetition, a favored technique of instrumental education, now as a technique of defamiliarization. Christie Milliken points out how Lawder's use of experimental film techniques ("sound looping and strategic sound-image juxtapositions"), by foregrounding the conventionality of educational films of the 1940s and 1950s, also foregrounds the larger educational paradigm: "the utilitarian approach of sex education is exaggerated by the ways in which Lawder combines sound and image."[30] Robert Nelson's *Bleu Shut* (1971) satirizes activities like standardized testing and multiple-choice exams. The film asks the audience to respond to the questions voiced on the soundtrack, performing a rhetoric of interactivity that the linear and univocal form of the film medium does not permit. Nelson's film seems to suggest that the rhetoric of interactivity is structurally limited by the fact that there is always just one correct answer to a multiple-choice question: the choice is itself a fiction. Owen Land's *Institutional Quality* (1969), "remade" as *New Improved Institutional Quality: In the Environment of Liquids and Nasals a Parasitic Vowel Sometimes Develops* (1976), uses a found soundtrack tape that Land received from a retired schoolteacher that directs listeners through a remarkably didactic multiple-choice type quiz. Land's *Remedial Reading Comprehension* (1970) includes images of a large college lecture audience and a simulated speed-reading exercise. His *What's Wrong with This Picture 1 and 2* (1971–72) incorporates found instructional film.[31] In all of these films, the paradigm of programmed instruction is held up to ridicule by exploring the complexity of the film-viewer relationship.

These parodies reflected a larger critique of programmed instruction as exponents of experiential education gained ground in the 1960s, helping to shape and modify pedagogy. Marshall McLuhan was enormously influential in relation to media education, specifically, but also to artists interested in exploring the relationships among media, experience, and environments.[32] Most media and fine arts teaching adopted some version of the experiential learning model, moving away from rote instruction, although a tension continues to exist between emphasis on craft and professional skills development on the one hand, and expression, freedom, and experimentation on the other.

Two films that move beyond parody to engage in experiential education are Ken Jacobs's *Tom, Tom the Piper's Son* and Hollis Frampton's *Zorns Lemma*. Both filmmakers had already begun to teach at colleges and universities to supplement their incomes — no North American experimental filmmaker has ever made a living strictly from film purchases or rentals — although when these films were made they had not yet taken positions in the experimental-film-focused programs with which they were subsequently associated (SUNY Binghamton in the case of Jacobs, and SUNY Buffalo in the case of Frampton).[33] While *Tom, Tom the Piper's Son* enacts a perverse form of (de-) programmed instruction, *Zorns Lemma* allegorically strips away language — the dominant medium of instruction — to reveal the fullness of the image world.

TOM, TOM THE PIPER'S SON

Tom, Tom the Piper's Son is perhaps the most celebrated example of pedagogical experimental film. Its form literalizes a standard way in which educators teach films in a classroom: show a film, discuss and analyze it, and then watch it again (or at least clips) to see how analysis reveals new qualities about the film.[34] As Jacobs himself avers: "*Tom, Tom, the Piper's Son* exemplifies my teaching. A film is shown usually without any introduction. Instead of promiscuously going on to the next, we work at it. Finally, it's shown again straight; there's now a wild rush of newly familiar subtleties. Students learn what it is to know a film."[35]

Jacobs's film begins by showing the original early film from 1905, *Tom, Tom the Piper's Son*, then proceeds to the equivalent of a modernist discussion ses-

Frame enlargement, *Tom, Tom, the Piper's Son* (Ken Jacobs, 1969). Courtesy of Ken Jacobs.

sion, as the original film undergoes a veritable catalogue of formal manipulations of the image (backward motion, step-frames, slip-frame, magnification of objects, grain, and print damage, showing the projection screen) that allow the viewer to isolate visual details, slow down the action, and revisualize the screen. After one hundred minutes of formal manipulation, the film concludes by showing the complete film of 1905 a second time. The effect is remarkable, as the film is transformed—but now, not on screen by Jacobs, but by spectators. Showing the original a second time foregrounds how we have learned to see the film anew through analysis to learn our lesson. Re-viewing the original foregrounds how analysis and education itself have transformed the student's viewing. Teaching is here a form of transformation, or even stronger, a form of conversion. Indeed, when Jacobs faced his straight-laced students at his first academic teaching job as a lecturer at St. John's University in Jamaica, Queens, in 1968–69, he declared his mission: "I was to undo their upbringing."[36] His course at St. John's was officially titled "Films and Film-making," but subtitled "The Evils of Andy Hardy," and described as "Cinematic Mind-Breaking and Mind-Making."[37] The process of transformation he demanded was difficult and full of conflict, but ultimately oriented toward a utopian sense of value in learning "to recognize and cherish the life that is art."[38]

In another text, "Essential Filmmaking," Jacobs extols a cinema that would be "an instrument of thought," that "would prompt thought, hesitation, unpredictable individual response." He rejects the use of cinema as a "device of power," equating that function with the instrumentality of advertising.

Rather, the creative filmmaker must discover authenticity through hard work and by grappling with complexity: "Freedom will make things difficult. The supremely difficult task for each student as it remains for the accomplished artist is to work from necessity, to discover what is personally important and keep at it (it calls for brains, heart, courage and luck, 'the luck,' Stan Brakhage says, 'that comes to those that work hard')."[39] The ethic of hard work applies as much to the film viewer as it does to the filmmaker.

Jacobs's educational approach, while idiosyncratic, was nevertheless in line with the anti-utilitarian educational philosophy ascendant in the arts and humanities in the 1960s and 1970s. An educational model based on skills-based training is temperamentally incompatible with an approach that sought to elevate individual consciousness in a mode of radical critique. For instance, a statement from 1975 on the goals of the Binghamton Cinema program (the program where Jacobs and other filmmakers taught) states, "Specific skills of analysis and production, including those of video, are taught, but not as ends in themselves. The major program aims to produce not narrow specialists in lighting, cinematography, or film editing, but rather broadly trained artists and thinkers sensitive to a whole range of cinematic values."[40] Students are "broadly trained" to be artists and thinkers rather than trained to be technicians. The pedagogy for this approach would necessarily be expansive and experimental.

The tension that subtends the goal of teaching people to unlearn what they know in order to be free, observed above in Brakhage's invocation that we must see things anew, also undergirds Jacobs's pedagogy. "Personality, who you are, is what's really important. There's a great statement by Picasso that genius is 10% talent and 90% personality. So just come into your personhood."[41] The meaning of personality oscillates between a kind of essential character ("who you are") and a notion of potential that needed to be activated through the transformative pedagogical experience ("come into your personhood").[42] The transformative element of his development of personality lies in seeing it in a capacious sense as "conscious life," and thereby as a form of resistance, and indeed a pre-condition for resistance, against the enormous suffering and injustice that he observes in the world. This is an important context pointing to what Jacobs feels is at stake in pedagogy: "If tragedy is taking place in the world, it is because something really valuable is being destroyed. I'm thinking, conscious life is valuable, and that's what this work should be: it should be a concentration of conscious life — of human, passionate intelligence. That's something. That's making something. That's salvaging something from these stupid societies we've created, okay?"[43] Art, life, and teaching come together under pressure of "human, passionate intelligence."

A crucial element of *Tom, Tom the Piper's Son* is its debunking of the standard teleology of film history that privileges narrative as the master cinematic form. Decades before Tom Gunning's and André Gaudreault's cinema of attractions model became a standard frame of understanding for early cinema — in which narration exists in tension with monstration/spectacle — Jacobs and other experimental filmmakers like Frampton and Gehr had heralded the radical possibilities for cinema evident in early film.[44] Early film became a historical template for experimental filmmakers' exploration of the limits and possibilities of the medium. Moreover, early cinema was a model for the creation of a visual field that could be excessive compared to the narrative economy that would come to drive classical Hollywood forms. Jacobs's film revels in the detail and strangeness of the mise-en-scène of the early film, both undermining the presumption of narrative and directing the viewer to see more in the image than the narrative imperative would encourage.[45]

Teaching this cinema is parallel to an English class encountering James Joyce's *Finnegans Wake*: Jacobs presents a modernist cinema that is self-conscious about training its spectator how to see itself (and to unlearn patterns of learning and seeing).[46] Avant-garde filmmakers are pedagogues of a particular type. They critique established institutions yet invest in the idea of exploring education within institutional settings using experimental film language.

ZORNS LEMMA

While *Tom, Tom the Piper's Son* enacts and demonstrates the transformation of consciousness through visual analysis, Hollis Frampton's *Zorns Lemma* functions as an allegory for pedagogy itself and as a commentary on film pedagogy's use of language — the dominant medium of instruction — to attempt to understand image — the medium of film, the material object under study. David James describes the film: "As a meta-filmic demonstration of the points of articulation between verbal and film language and as a systematized meditation on film-as-language, *Zorns Lemma* raises the reflexive project of structural film to its highest abstraction."[47] The film uses a repetitive serial structure that teaches its spectator how to watch it, and how to play the game of the film's meditation on the interpenetration of language and image.

James notes that, "In the tradition of the great pedagogical primers, Framp-

Frame enlargement, *Zorns Lemma* (Hollis Frampton, 1970). Courtesy of Anthology Film Archives.

ton's *Zorns Lemma* is divided into three parts."[48] The film begins with an explicit reference to education, a voice-over taken from a Puritan children's instructional rhyme, "The Bay State Primer," which teaches the alphabet: "In Adam's Fall, we sinneth all; My life to mend, this *Book* attend," and so forth. We hear this text over images of massive letters of the alphabet (actually, magnified typewriter letters struck on tin foil), and the primer is clearly set up as a paradigm to be critiqued. Like many others, Frampton recognized language as the "master code" of our culture. Starting the film—recalling Genesis's "In the beginning was the word"—with a text drenched in biblical disapprobation foregrounds how language is associated with law and convention.

The film gradually moves from the master code of language to a poetics of light. The second section of the film is a highly rhythmic series of one-second shots of what Frampton calls "word images"—alphabetically arranged words filmed largely in urban locations in Manhattan. The first three shots are "A," "baby," "cabinet," and so on until "zenith," after which a new cycle of "word images" ("abbey," "back," "cable," and so on) starts up. We literally read the film (and in silence)—but the act of reading two-dimensional words is complicated by their location in the rich three-dimensional urban space of the city. The language code learned in the first part of *Zorns Lemma* becomes embedded in a fascinating, polymorphous space characterized by play and puzzle. Gradually, the "word images" are taken over by what Frampton called "replacement images" featuring a number of human and natural phenomena. "A raging fire" replaces "X" while "hands tying shoes" replaces "P."[49] After the viewer learns the alphabet, "A," "B," and "C" are transformed into "turning pages of a book," "frying an egg," and "red ibis flapping its wings," an absurd and poetic encyclopedia of the world in the tradition of Frampton's idol, Jorge Luis Borges.[50]

The third section shifts from metrically edited images to an apparent long take of a couple walking into the deep space of a snowy landscape. Instead of silence, the soundtrack is dominated by a staccato reading of a Latin treatise on the relation of light to matter. The reading, by a round of six female speakers offering one word per second (paralleling the image per second pace of the second section) is almost impossible to follow aurally: in the end, language dissolves into sound, subsumed to the plenitude of the image. The film ends as the camera roll fades to white, dissolving from the snow in the world to the pure white light of the projector beam. Both language and image become, depending on your perspective, purely abstract, or fully replete.[51]

The treatise embedded in the film becomes explicit only through the viewer's thought and reflection, which develops understanding of the formal and cultural valences of light, language, and consciousness. The film rejects a clear expository format. Frampton refuses to explain the treatise; as he once said, sarcastically, "We are told the explanation is simple; all explanations are."[52] Frampton, like other experimental filmmakers of this moment, prefers complexity to simple explanation—and if explanation is to be affiliated with useful educational cinema, then Frampton desires an anti-useful cinema. Frampton embeds the treatise in a cinematic experience that a viewer must go through to encounter, on both a cognitive and physical level, watching the film for its full sixty-minute length, its meditation on the production of meaning requiring duration. In this sense, the film's experimental and experiential form is finally useful, indeed crucial in embodying the film's lesson.

Frampton has articulated a justification for his experimental cinema:

As one era slowly dissolves into the next, some individuals metabolize the former means for physical survival into new means for psychic survival. These latter we call art. They promote the life of human consciousness by nourishing our affections, by reincarnating our perceptual substance, by affirming, imitating, reifying the process of consciousness.

What I am suggesting, to put it quite simply, is that no activity can become an art until its proper epoch has ended, and it has dwindled, as an aid to gut survival, into total obsolescence.[53]

Perhaps the greatest challenge that experimental film makes to the paradigm of utilitarian educational cinema lies in inhabiting a Kantian domain of disinterested aesthetic activity wherein its very capacity to be defined as art derives from its proclaimed lack of usefulness. Cinema can serve this function because according to Frampton film is a relic of what he calls the "Age of Machines," superseded in utility by electronic arts, whose advent he dates back, not to video, but to the invention of radar in 1941. Nonetheless, he insists that cinema continued to possess a certain kind of utility, a connection to the lived world.[54] He points to the uses that cinema serves: "The cinema . . . performed prize-worthy functions: it taught and reminded us (after what then seemed a bearable delay) how things looked, how things worked, how we do things . . . and, of course (by example), how to feel and think."[55]

The photograph and home movie, though lacking the immediate gratification that video camera playback and digital camera screens provide, had long showed people memories and acted as social record. Film's mimetic qualities maintained instructional and educational functions, showing how things work. Educational cinema (and of course Hollywood) modeled "how to feel and think." To these brute uses, Frampton implicitly contrasts art's capacity to nurture humanity's "psychic" survival by promoting "the life of human consciousness." Art "nourishes our affections," our ability to make connections, see relationships, and deepen our emotions. By the phrase "reincarnating our perceptual substance," Frampton means that, in a phenomenological sense, art takes what we see and hear and otherwise perceive, and re-presents or embodies that work of human consciousness in the medium of the artwork. This is the root of aesthetics, the interaction of human perception with the object, that which is outside us but always mediated by consciousness. Finally, art has a fundamentally reflexive function, "by affirming, imitating, reifying the process of consciousness." By making the process of consciousness into concrete, iconic form and simply affirming that act of reflection, art contributes to humanity's ability to understand and mobilize the work of consciousness for our "psychic survival."

CONCLUSION

During the 1960s and 1970s, North American experimental filmmakers working in what I am calling a pedagogical mode grappled with the paradox of
seeking radically to transform consciousness while refraining from dictating, didactically, the parameters of that transformed consciousness. Whether
through parody, analysis, or allegory, the films they made rejected instrumental models of education and thought while simultaneously encouraging forms
of experiential education that often, through the simple instrument of duration, refined for most spectators—whether they liked it or not—what the experience of cinema could be. This rejection of the instrumental mode signals
the rejection of a certain kind of "useful cinema." But, of course, the project
of these films was ultimately one that embraced a "useful" function—and earnestly so—precisely in challenging the parameters of "use" in pedagogy and
proposing an alternative whose difficult, even utopian aspirations for the exploration of consciousness was transformative—for Jacobs, in search of "vital,
interesting, amusing, crazy-making stuff,"[56] and for Frampton, "film art as a
model for human consciousness."[57] Together these two examples show that
the concept of utility requires careful consideration. Here we can see that
being useful can, at least occasionally, be institutionally complex, aesthetically
rich, pedagogically experimental, and dialectically tethered to its opposite.

NOTES

My thanks to Charles Acland, Haidee Wasson, and anonymous referees for numerous and invaluable editorial comments; to Michele Pierson and William Rose for
sharing rare documents; and to the critical support of colleagues who have read
earlier versions of this text, Janine Marchessault, Michael Prokopow, and Tess Taka-
hashi. I presented an early version of this material and benefited from feedback from
the ARTHEMIS group (Advanced Research Team in History and Epistemology of
Moving Image Study) at Concordia University, especially Martin Lefebvre and Eric
Prince. The research was funded in part by a Faculty of Fine Arts Minor Research
grant from York University.

1   There are brief credits typed on lined paper that appear for a few frames at the very
    beginning of the film, but they are barely perceptible.

2   *Nothing Happens* is the title of Ivone Margulies's volume on Chantal Akerman. Aker-
    man was highly influenced by Snow and structural film.

3   P. Adams Sitney coined the term "structural film" in his influential essay, "Structural
    Film." Although the term has been controversial—and was often disavowed by the
    filmmakers included under its umbrella—its usage is sufficiently widespread that I

shall retain it for the purposes of this text. See B. Jenkins, "A Case Against 'Structural Film,'" for one early critique.

4   Snow, "A Statement on *Wavelength* for the Experimental Film Festival of Knokke-le-Zoute."

5   Although *Wavelength* is often described in schematic terms as a film about space, it is also rooted in place, bearing the markers of its New York location and late-1960s time period. Snow makes the film in a loft, an industrial space converted to artists' use, which is eclectically and minimally furnished, and populated with bohemian types dressed in the fashion of the period. On the soundtrack, we hear a strong New Yawk accent and the Beatles's "Strawberry Fields Forever" while the street noise outside the windows is location recording from Canal Street, a busy industrial route between Soho and Tribeca, the neighborhoods where the first generation of industrial/artist space conversions occurred in New York in the 1960s.

6   MacDonald, *Avant-Garde Film*, 31.

7   For a fuller discussion, see Zryd, "The Academy and the Avant-Garde"; and Kreul, "New York, New Cinema." During the 1990s, film rentals to colleges and universities gradually waned as 16mm projection facilities vanished, film rental budgets were cut, and the availability of (some) experimental films on DVD increased.

8   The terms "experimental film" and "avant-garde film" have complex, contested, and ultimately intertwined legacies. Avant-garde is often used in relation to specific film movements and tends to connote films with a political critique or a celebration of the new. Experimental film is a more general term whose openness and permeability accurately reflects its eclectic usage. In English-language film criticism, the terms are often used interchangeably and are still rarely applied rigorously. In this essay, I will retain the general term experimental.

9   It must be acknowledged that for some students, experimental films are the most popular and engaging, even entertaining, cinema in the curriculum.

10 Snow, "A Statement on *Wavelength* for the Experimental Film Festival of Knokke-le-Zoute," 1.

11 MacDonald, *Avant-Garde Film*, 31.

12 See Zryd, "Avant-Garde Films." Several excellent essays on the film provide strong interpretive frameworks: MacDonald, *Avant-Garde Film*; Farber, *Negative Space*, 250–58; Michelson, "Toward Snow"; and Elder, *Image and Identity*.

13 See Zryd, "Experimental Film and the Development of Film Study in America."

14 *Remedial Reading Comprehension* (1970).

15 Personal interview with Bill Simon, September 5, 2003, New York.

16 Examples include Germaine Dulac, Jean Epstein, Sergei Eisenstein, Vsevolod Pudovkin, Lev Kuleshov, Dziga Vertov, John Grierson, Maya Deren, Stan Brakhage, Jean-Luc Godard, Hollis Frampton, Laura Mulvey, Peter Wollen, and Trinh T. Minh-ha.

17 James, *Allegories of Cinema*, 259.

18 The most influential essay in experimental film criticism in this regard is Wollen, "The Two Avant-Gardes." A rich recent account is James, *Allegories of Cinema*.

19 Sitney, *Visionary Film*, 3rd edn., and *Eyes Upside Down*.

20 There is a long tradition, at least since Germaine Dulac and Maya Deren, of experi-

mental filmmakers appearing in person to screen and discuss their work. In the 1960s and 1970s in North America, college campuses were the dominant site for these informal circuits of filmmaker appearances. Sitney argues that "among the most important achievements of the American avant-garde cinema has been the continuation of a serious level of theoretical discourse by filmmakers. The lecture circuit is one essential locus of that exchange." Sitney, "Letter," 70.

21 Brakhage, "From *Metaphors on Vision*," 228. Brakhage's text and an essay by Maya Deren are anthologized in this major textbook and are likely the most widely read primary texts on American experimental film in basic introductory film course syllabi.

22 Brakhage's suspicion of language is manifested in his films and the content of his writings. He was nevertheless enormously articulate, a master storyteller, teacher, and writer whose sense of language was as poetic as his filmmaking.

23 Reiser, "A History of Instructional Design and Technology: Part I," 59.

24 For a sampling of texts see Lawson and Petersen, *Progressive Education*; Dewey, *Democracy and Education*; Piaget, *Science of Education and the Psychology of the Child*; Vygotsky, *Thought and Language*; Freire, *Pedagogy of the Oppressed*; Montessori, *The Montessori Method*; and Steiner, *The Foundations of Human Experience*.

25 Reiser, "A History of Instructional Design and Technology: Part I," 57.

26 Ibid., 58.

27 Reiser, "A History of Instructional Design and Technology: Part II," 58.

28 Ibid.

29 R. Heinrich, quoted in ibid., 59.

30 Milliken, *Generation Sex*, MS p. 6. *Dangling Participle*, Milliken suggests, through its interrogation of "larger social scripts" and "sexual behavior," anticipates queer and postmodern approaches to sexuality and gender: "The film's structure . . . encourages us to see all of this behavior and scripting as unabashed odd. In a curiously portentous way, this eighteen minute avant-garde film of the early 1970s reflects the breakdown of clear and stable sex and gender categories and a loss of faith in any 'grand narrative' of sexuality which is, precisely, what queer theory begins to do twenty years later via sexed and gendered reworkings of poststructuralism and postmodernism" (ms7–8).

31 For more on Owen Land, see Mellencamp, "Receivable Texts"; Mellencamp, *Indiscretions*; and Sitney, *Modernist Montage*.

32 McLuhan, *Understanding Media*.

33 Jacobs began teaching at Binghamton in 1969–70, just after *Tom, Tom the Piper's Son* was released, while Frampton began teaching in Buffalo in 1973. A useful brief history of the Department of Cinema at Binghamton is Hawkins, "Binghamton University—Cinema Department and Artists Lab at School for Advanced Technology." A recent exhibition on the remarkable Center for Media Study at SUNY Buffalo took place in 2006–7 at ZKM in Germany, with an exhibition catalogue that includes a substantial chapter on Frampton. See Vasulka and Weibel, *Buffalo Heads*.

34 An influential essay on the film by Bill Simon and Lois Mendelson, published in the special issue of *Artforum* that put experimental film on the radar of the art world, ex-

plicitly notes the "didactic" nature of *Tom, Tom the Piper's Son*. Simon and Mendelson, "*Tom, Tom the Piper's Son*."

35   Alessio Galbiati and Paola Catò, "Ken Jacobs: The Demiurgo of the Moving Image [Interview]," *Digimag*, March 2008, http://www.digicult.it/digimag/article.asp?id=1155.

36   Michael Zryd, interview with Ken and Flo Jacobs, New York, October 3, 2008.

37   "Films and Film-Making," Course Advertisement, St. John's University, 1968. Thanks to William Ball for sharing this document. This pattern of large-class teaching that explicitly stated its intention to subvert normal expectations would be repeated throughout his career as a teacher.

38   This quotation is from Ken Jacobs's syllabus for his course Cinema 121: Experience, History and Analysis of Cinema (spring 1991). A program note for a Jacobs show at the Collective for Living Cinema in 1983 proposes the same analytic procedure applied to Frank Capra's *Meet John Doe* (1941) over several weeks: "First we'll screen the film. Then talk. The second and third sessions we'll inch through it (no mind can protect itself against 24 frames per second), stop and comment, replay. We will marvel at the extraordinary number of masks Capra shifts over the Cooper bones. The last session should include a reseeing of the film in its rhythmically precise entirety." Ken Jacobs, "Sick of Movies? Join MOVIEFANS ANONYMOUS," program note, Collective for Living Cinema, ca. 1983. My thanks to Michele Pierson for providing me with this program note.

39   Ken Jacobs, "Essential Filmmaking," unpublished poster for Summer Film-Making Class, 1978.

40   Quoted in Minkowsky, "Survey."

41   Kreisler, "Film and the Creation of Mind."

42   Asked in an interview what important message Jacobs would leave to students of film, he replied, "Film is, and you're really studying existence, film is mysterious as much as anything else is. Break away from being an expert in your life. Forget about being an expert. Forage. Struggle to do with it. And don't have a premature idea of who you are. You are in a state of becoming. You don't know what your actual potentials are. Don't buy a personality off the rack. Don't be allured by the latest fashion in interesting celebrities. Take your time, don't define yourself too early." Kreisler, "Film and the Creation of Mind."

43   Price and Dent, "An Interview with Ken Jacobs [2003]."

44   Indeed, it was Tom Gunning's knowledge of experimental cinema, and Jacobs's film specifically, that facilitated his influential formulation; see Gunning, "The Cinema of Attractions."

45   The original film is also sophisticated, not "primitive," containing, in its opening tableau a reference to William Hogarth's painting *Southwark Fair* (1733). Jacobs himself has returned to this opening tableau for subsequent "remakes" of his own film, including its most recent incarnation, *Anaglyph Tom: Tom with Puffy Cheeks* (2008), which incorporates experiments in 3-D reimaging.

46   Thanks to Eric Smoodin for this comparison.

47   James, *Allegories of Cinema*, 259.

48 Ibid., 255.

49 Frampton's production notes are reproduced in Vasulka and Weibel, *Buffalo Heads*, 198–202.

50 Frampton states, "The encyclopedia does a rather odd thing: namely it proposes to arrange all areas of human knowledge according to the first letters of their names. . . . The encyclopedia takes many disparate, disjunct things and groups them together, not even as they are related in language, but as they are related to the precedence of the graphic signs that constitute their names." MacDonald, "Hollis Frampton," 50–51.

51 On his production notes, Frampton wrote, "I wanted Lumière's static camera — for which *all* cinematographic images were NUMINOUS and *replete*." Vasulka and Weibel, *Buffalo Heads*, 199, Frampton's emphasis.

52 Frampton, *Circles of Confusion*, 196.

53 Ibid., 112.

54 Ibid.

55 Ibid., 112–13.

56 Kreisler, "Film and the Creation of Mind."

57 Frampton, "Statement of Plans for *Magellan*," 228.

FILMOGRAPHY

Accuracy First (Western Union, 1927)
After Vacation There Is a Job to Be Done
    (Willys-Overland Motor Co., 1930)
Alexander Hamilton (Kenneth S. Webb, 1924)
Alibi Racket (George B. Seitz, 1935)
Alice Adams (George Stevens, 1935)
Alice in Wonderland (Norman Z. McLeod, 1933)
All Quiet on the Western Front (Lewis Milestone, 1930)
The American Wing (Metropolitan Museum of Art, 1925)
Anaglyph Tom: Tom with Puffy Cheeks (Ken Jacobs, 2008)
Another to Conquer (National Tuberculosis Association, 1941)
Armless, He Is a Success (All-American News, 1945)
Aseptic Resection of Stomach for Carcinoma and Ulcer
    (Emile Homan, 1940)
↔*(Back and Forth)* (Michael Snow, 1969)
Bataan (Tay Garnett, 1943)
Behind the Scenes at the Museum
    (Metropolitan Museum of Art, 1928)
Berkeley Square (Frank Lloyd, 1933)
Black Legion (Archie Mayo, 1937)
Bleu Shut (Robert Nelson, 1971)
Blind Man Fine Student (All-American News, 1945)
Body Defenses against Disease (ERPI Classroom Films, 1937)

The Body Fights Bacteria (Audio Productions / McGraw-Hill Text-Films, 1948)

Bring Them to the Salesroom (Willys-Overland Motor Co., 1927)

Buddy Young Now a "GOB" (All-American News, 1944)

Casablanca (Michael Curtiz, 1942)

Ceramics (Kenneth Bloomer and Elizabeth Sansom, 1933)

Champs Baby Punches Ivories (All-American News, 1945)

Choose to Live (U.S. Public Health Service and American Society for
   the Control of Cancer, 1940)

Churchman Makes Good Conduct Plea (All-American News, 1944)

City of Wax (Educational Films Corp of America, 1934)

Cloud in the Sky (National Tuberculosis Association, 1940)

Colleges at War (Office of War Information, 1942)

Columbus (Edwin L. Hollywood, 1923)

The Criminal Code (Howard Hawks, 1931)

The Daily Life of the Egyptian — Ancient and Modern
   (Metropolitan Museum of Art, ca. 1930s)

Dangling Participle (Standish Lawder, 1970)

Defense against Invasion (Walt Disney, 1943)

Diagnostic Procedures in Tuberculosis (National Tuberculosis Association, 1938)

Digging into the Past (Metropolitan Museum of Art, ca. 1930s)

Drifters (John Grierson, 1929)

Elements of the Automobile (U.S. Armed Forces, ca. 1910–20)

The Emperor Jones (Dudley Murphy, 1933)

Enemy X (U.S. Public Health Service, 1942)

The Eternal Fight (United Nations Film Board / Madeline Carroll Films, 1948)

Eyes for Tomorrow (Coordinator of Inter-American Affairs, 1943)

The Eyes of Science (J. S. Watson and Melville Webber, 1931)

Fall of the House of Usher (J. S. Watson and Melville Webber, 1928)

The Fight against the Communicable Diseases (U.S. Public Health Service, 1950)

Fight Syphilis (U.S. Public Health Service, 1943)

Firearms of Our Forefathers (Metropolitan Museum of Art, 1923)

Firemen Promoted in New York City (All-American News, 1945)

Flournoy English Wins Award for Efficiency (All-American News, 1944)

The Forgotten Frontier (Marvin Breckinridge, 1930)

For the Nation's Health (Communicable Disease Center, 1952)

The Frontier Woman (Webster Campbell, 1924)

Fury (Fritz Lang, 1936)

Gen. Clark Host to New Officers (All-American News, 1944)

The Gorgon's Head (Metropolitan Museum of Art, 1925)

Greed (Erich von Stroheim, 1924)

Gumming (Western Union, 1930)

Hallelujah! (King Vidor, 1929)

Health Is a Victory (American Social Hygiene Association, 1942)

Heart and Circulation (ERPI Classroom Films, 1937)

Hearts in Dixie (Paul Sloane, 1929)

Hell Bound Train (Eloyce and James Gist, 1930)

Help Wanted (Johnson and Johnson, 1940)

Hernioplasty for Direct Inguinal Hernia (Lawrence S. Fallis, 1941)

The Hidden Talisman (Metropolitan Museum of Art, 1928)

The High Cost of Loving (José Ferrer, 1958)

The Highway of Tomorrow, or How One Makes Two (Dent Harrison, 1930)

Hollan Explains Vet Policy (All-American News, 1945)

In Defense of the Nation (U.S. Public Health Service, 1941)

Institutional Quality (Owen Land, 1969)

Intelligent Bullying Is as Important as Intelligent Selling
    (Willys-Overland Motor Co., 1928)

In the Beginning (Fred C. Ells, 1935)

The Italian Straw Hat (René Clair, 1928)

Keep 'em Out (U.S. Public Health Service, 1942)

Keyboard Errors (Western Union, 1929)

Know for Sure (U.S. Public Health Service, ca. 1941)

Little Women (George Cukor, 1933)

Local Health Problems in War Industry Areas
    (New York State Department of Health, 1942)

Lot in Sodom (J. S. Watson and Melville Webber, 1932)

Magic Bullets (U.S. Public Health Service, 1940)

Maid of Salem (Frank Lloyd, 1937)

Making Your Demonstrations as Impressive as Your Products
    (Willys-Overland Motor Co., 1929)

Manpower (Office of War Information, 1942)

Marine Circus (James A. FitzPatrick, 1939)

Mechanical Call Distribution System for Receiving Telegrams by Telephone from
    Patrons of the Western Union (Western Union, 1930)

Mechanical Principals (Ralph Steiner, 1930)

The Mechanism of the Heart Beat and Electrocardiography (Lewis M. Hurxthal, 1932)

Meet John Doe (Frank Capra, 1941)

Middletown Goes to War (National Tuberculosis Association, 1942)

Military Sanitation: Disposal of Human Waste (War Department /
    U.S. Army Signal Corps, 1943)

A Modern Oliver Twist, or The Life of a Pickpocket (J. Stuart Blackton, 1906)

The Mosquito (U.S. Army Air Forces, 1945)

Negro Colleges in War Time (Office of War Information, 1943)

The Negro Soldier (Office of War Information, 1944)

New Improved Institutional Quality: In the Environment of Liquids and
    Nasals a Parasitic Vowel Sometimes Develops (Owen Land, 1976)

92nd Honors Its Dead (All-American News, 1945)

92nd Infantry in Italy (All-American News, 1945)

92nd in Italy Rout Nazis (All-American News, 1944)

Nursing the Americas (Coordinator of Inter-American Affairs, 1943)

Oliver Twist (J. Stuart Blackton, 1909)

On the Firing Line: A Travel-Tour to Scenes of the Fight against Tuberculosis (National Tuberculosis Association, 1939)

The Oxbow Incident (William Wellman, 1943)

Pagodas of Peiping (Fox Films, 1933)

The Passion of the Christ (Mel Gibson, 2004)

The Pilgrims (Edwin L. Hollywood, 1924)

Plane Crazy (Walt Disney, 1928)

Prevention of the Introduction of Diseases from Abroad (U.S. Public Health Service / Bray Studios, 1946)

The Puritans (Frank Tuttle, 1924)

Quality Street (George Stevens, 1937)

Reconstruction of Cleft Lips (James Barrett Brown, 1940)

Remedial Reading Comprehension (Owen Land, 1970)

Reverberation (Ernie Gehr, 1969)

Reward Unlimited (U.S. Public Health Service / Office of War Information, 1944)

The Right People at the Right Time (Western Union, 1969)

Romeo and Juliet (George Cukor, 1936)

Sahara (Zoltan Korda, 1943)

Save a Day! (Federal Security Agency / U.S. Public Health Service, 1941)

The School of the Soldier (U.S. Armed Forces, ca. 1910–20)

Selling to Women (Audiovision for Plymouth Motor Co., 1936)

Serene Velocity (Ernie Gehr, 1970)

Service That Sells (Audiovision for Delaware Lackawanna and Western Coal, 1936)

The Silent Invader (U.S. Public Health Service, 1957)

Something of Value (Richard Brooks, 1957)

Song of Love (Clarence Brown, 1950)

Son of the Gods (Frank Lloyd, 1930)

Speed Killers (Western Union, 1930)

Standard Presentation (Willys-Overland Motor Co., 1927)

The Story of a Country Doctor (Castle Films for Lockwedge Shoe Corp. of America, ca. 1934)

A Tale of Two Cities (Jack Conway, 1935)

Tapestries and How They Are Made (Metropolitan Museum of Art, 1933)

Teenagers Show "Good" Conduct (All-American News, 1945)

The Temples and Tombs of Egypt (Metropolitan Museum of Art, ca. 1930s)

They Do Come Back (National Tuberculosis Association, 1940)

The Three Little Pigs (Burt Gillett, 1933)

Tom, Tom, the Piper's Son (Billy Blitzer, 1905)

Tom, Tom, the Piper's Son (Ken Jacobs, 1969)

To the People of the United States (U.S. Public Health Service, 1944)

Traffic in Souls (IMP/Universal, 1913)

Transfusion of Unmodified Blood (Demonstrating Transfusion Needles and Continuous Flow Instrument) (Michael E. DeBakey, 1938)

Tsutsugamushi: Prevention (U.S. Navy, 1945)

2001: A Space Odyssey (Stanley Kubrick, 1968)

Vasantasena (Metropolitan Museum of Art, ca. 1924)

Verdict: Not Guilty (Eloyce and James Gist, 1933)

A Visit to the Armor Galleries of the Metropolitan Museum of Art (Metropolitan Museum of Art, 1922)

A Visit to Peek Frean and Co.'s Biscuit Works (Cricks and Martin, 1906)

Le voyage dans la lune (Georges Méliès, 1902)

Washington at Valley Forge (Gene Gauthier, 1908)

Water—Friend or Enemy (Walt Disney, 1943)

Wavelength (Michael Snow, 1967)

What's Wrong with This Picture 1 (Owen Land, 1971)

What's Wrong with This Picture 2 (Owen Land, 1972)

The Winged Scourge (Walt Disney, 1943)

With These Weapons: The Story of Syphilis (American Social Hygiene Association, 1939)

Work Your Work Sheet (Willys-Overland Motor Co., 1927)

World without End (Paul Ratha and Basil Wright, 1953)

X Messages (Western Union, 1927)

Your Health Department (National Motion Pictures Co., 1941)

Zorns Lemma (Hollis Frampton, 1970)

BIBLIOGRAPHY

ARCHIVES AND COLLECTIONS

American College of Surgeons Archives, Chicago
American Museum of Natural History Special Collections,
    New York City
CBS News Archive, New York City
Cleveland Public Library Archives, Cleveland
George Eastman House, Rochester, N.Y.
Kautz Family YMCA Archives at the University of Minnesota,
    Minneapolis
Library of Congress, Washington
Margaret Herrick Library, Academy of Motion Picture Arts
    and Sciences, Beverly Hills
Metropolitan Museum of Art Library, New York City
National Archives, Washington
National Archives of Canada, Ottawa
National Board of Review of Motion Pictures Collection,
    New York Public Library, New York City
National Library of Medicine, Bethesda, Md.
National Museum of American History Archives Center,
    Washington
Rockefeller Archive Center, Sleepy Hollow, N.Y.
Schomburg Center for Research in Black Culture, New York City
UNESCO Archives, Paris

United States National Archives and Records Administration (NARA),
College Park, Md.

BOOKS, ARTICLES, PAPERS, AND DISSERTATIONS

Abel, Richard. *Americanizing the Movies and "Movie-Mad" Audiences, 1910–1914.*
Berkeley: University of California Press, 2006.

———. "The 'Backbone' of the Business: Scanning Signs of U.S. Film Distribution in
the Newspapers, 1911–1914." *Networks of Entertainment: Early Film Distribution 1895–*
1915, ed. Frank Kessler and Nanna Verhoeff, 85–93. Eastleigh: John Libbey, 2007.

Acland, Charles R. "Classrooms, Clubs, and Community Circuits: Cultural Authority
and the Film Council Movement, 1946–1957." *Inventing Film Studies,* ed. Lee
Grieveson and Haidee Wasson, 149–81. Durham: Duke University Press, 2008.

———. "Curtains, Carts, and the Mobile Screen." *Screen* 50, no. 1 (2009), 148–66.

———. "The Film Council of America and the Ford Foundation: Screen Technology,
Mobilization, and Adult Education in the 1950s." *Patronizing the Public: American*
Philanthropy's Transformation of Culture, Communication, and the Humanities in the
Twentieth Century, ed. William J. Buxton, 261–80. Lanham, Md.: Lexington, 2009.

———. "Mapping the Serious and the Dangerous: Film and the National Council of
Education, 1920–1939." *Cinémas: Revue d'Études Cinématographiques* 6, no. 1 (1995),
101–18.

———. "Patterns of Cultural Authority: The National Film Society of Canada and the
Institutionalization of Film Education, 1938–1941." *Canadian Journal of Film Studies*
10, no. 1 (2001), 2–27.

———, ed. *Residual Media.* Minneapolis: University of Minnesota Press, 2007.

Adam, T. R. *Motion Pictures in Adult Education.* New York: American Association for
Adult Education, 1940.

Addams, Jane. *The Spirit of Youth and the City Streets.* New York: Macmillan, 1909.

Allen, Robert C. "Manhattan Myopia; or, Oh! Iowa!" *Cinema Journal* 35, no. 3 (1996),
75–103.

Altick, Richard. *The Shows of London.* Cambridge: Harvard University Press, 1978.

Altman, Rick. *Silent Film Sound.* New York: Columbia University Press, 2004.

Anderson, Mark Lynn. "Taking Liberties: The Payne Fund Studies and the Creation
of the Media Expert." *Inventing Film Studies,* ed. Lee Grieveson and Haidee Wasson,
38–65. Durham: Duke University Press, 2008.

Andrews, J. Frederic. "The Visual Program: Its Equipment and Cost." *Educational Screen*
13, no. 4 (1934), 93–94.

Annas, George J. "Reframing the Debate on Health Care Reform by Replacing Our
Metaphors." *New England Journal of Medicine* 332 (1995), 745–48.

Armes, Roy. *Third World Filmmaking and the West.* Berkeley: University of California
Press, 1987.

Arthur, Billy. "Please Fasten Your Seat Belt, Next Stop the Moon." *Tarheel Wheels* 15,
no. 2 (1958), 1, 3, 5.

Augst, Thomas. "Faith in Reading: Public Libraries, Liberalism, and the Civil Religion."

Institutions of Reading: The Social Life of Libraries in the United States, ed. Thomas Augst and Kenneth Carpenter, 148–83. Amherst: University of Massachusetts Press, 2007.

Bailey, Louis M. "Educational Films: Film Progress in School, Medical, Civic, Welfare and Related Fields." *Movie Makers*, November 1929, 728, 743.

———. "Motion Pictures and the Minister." *Movie Makers*, March 1931, 134, 163.

Barnett, Claude A. "The Role of the Press, Radio, and Motion Picture and Negro Morale." *Journal of Negro Education* 12, no. 3 (1943), 474–89.

Beal, Timothy K., and Tod Linafelt, eds. *Mel Gibson's Bible*. Chicago: University of Chicago Press, 2006.

Becklake, Sue. *The Official Planetarium Book*. Rocklin, Calif.: Prima, 1994.

Beebe, Leo C. "Industry." *Sixty Years of 16mm Film, 1923–1983: A Symposium*, 88–98. Evanston: Film Council of America, 1954.

Benjamin, Walter. "The Work of Art in the Age of Mechanical Reproduction." *Illuminations: Essays and Reflections*, ed. Hannah Arendt, 217–51. New York: Schocken, 1968.

Bennett, Tony. "Useful Culture." *Cultural Studies* 6, no. 3 (1992), 395–408.

Bishop, J. E. "The Educational Value of the Planetarium." *Planetarium: A Challenge for Educators*, 103–8. New York: United Nations, 1992.

Blair, Patricia. "Films in Public Libraries." *Ideas on Film*, ed. Cecile Starr, 112–16. Freeport, N.Y.: Funk and Wagnalls, 1951.

———. "*The Information Film* by Gloria Waldron." *A Forum on the Public Library Inquiry*, ed. Lester Asheim, 146–56. New York: Columbia University Press, 1950.

Blankenbeckler, W., L. Kyro, and R. McColman. "Production Values for Planetariums." *Planetarium: A Challenge for Educators*, 97–102. New York: United Nations, 1992.

Bloom, Peter. *French Colonial Documentary: Mythologies of Humanitarianism*. Minneapolis: University of Minnesota Press, 2008.

Bobinski, George S. *Carnegie Libraries: Their History and Impact on American Public Library Development*. Chicago: American Library Association, 1969.

Bordwell, David, Kristin Thompson, and Janet Staiger. *The Classical Hollywood Cinema: Film Style and Mode of Production to 1960*. New York: Columbia University Press, 1985.

Bottomore, Stephen. "The Panicking Audience? Early Cinema and the 'Train Effect.'" *Historical Journal of Film, Radio and Television* 19, no. 2 (1999), 177–216.

Boule, Michelle Anne. "Hot Rods, Shy Guys, and Sex Kittens: Social Guidance Films and the American High School, 1947–1957." Ph.D. diss., New York University, 2004.

Bowser, Pearl. "Pioneers of Black Documentary Film." *Struggles for Representation: African American Documentary Film and Video*, ed. Phyllis R. Klotman and Janet K. Cutler, 1–33. Bloomington: Indiana University Press, 1999.

Brakhage, Stan. "From *Metaphors on Vision*." *Film Theory and Criticism*, 5th edn., ed. Leo Braudy and Marshall Cohen, 228–34. New York: Oxford University Press, 1999.

Breckinridge, Mary. *Wide Neighborhoods: A Story of the Frontier Nursing Service*. New York: Harper and Row, 1952.

Brown, Simon. "Coming Soon to a Hall Near You: Some Notes on 16mm Road-Show

Distribution in the 1930s." *Journal of British Cinema and Television* 2, no. 2 (2005), 299–309.

Budd, Mike. "The National Board of Review and the Early Art Cinema in New York: *The Cabinet of Dr. Caligari* as Affirmative Culture." *Cinema Journal* 26, no. 1 (1986), 3–18.

Burns, J. M. *Flickering Shadows: Cinema and Identity in Colonial Zimbabwe*. Athens: Ohio Center for International Studies, 2002.

Burts, S. L. "Operating Supervision: Cooperative Measures Necessary for Efficiency." *Western Union News* 1, no. 7 (January 1915), 4.

Caldwell, Gladys. *The Public Library and the Motion Picture Studio*. Chicago: American Library Association, 1926.

Carlton, Newcomb. "Introducing the News." *Western Union News* 1, no. 1 (July 1914), 1.

Cartwright, Lisa. *Screening the Body: Tracing Medicine's Visual Culture*. Minneapolis: University of Minnesota Press, 1995.

Cartwright, Lisa, and Brian Goldfarb. "Cultural Contagion: On Disney's Health Education Films for Latin America." *Disney Discourse: Producing the Magic Kingdom*, ed. Eric Smoodin, 169–80. New York: Routledge, 1994.

Chamberlain, Joseph Miles. "The Development of the Planetarium in the United States." *Smithsonian Report for 1957*, 261–77. Washington: Smithsonian Institution, 1958.

Charney, Leo, and Vanessa R. Schwartz, eds. *Cinema and the Invention of Modern Life*. Berkeley: University of California Press, 1995.

Cocks, Orrin G. "Libraries and Motion Pictures: An Ignored Educational Agency." *Library Journal* 39, no. 9 (1914), 666–68.

———. "Motion Pictures and Reading Habits." *Library Journal* 43, no. 2 (1918), 67–70.

Colligan, Mimi. *Canvas Documentaries: Panoramic Entertainments in Nineteenth-Century Australia and New Zealand*. Victoria: Melbourne University Press, 2002.

Collins, Jeremy. "Educational, Ornamental, and Toy Globes." *The World in Your Hands: An Exhibition of Globes and Planetaria*, ed. Tom Lamb and Jeremy Collins, 98–107. London: Christie's, 1994.

Cornwell, Regina. "Maya Deren and Germaine Dulac: Activists of the Avant-Garde." *Film Library Quarterly* 5, no. 1 (1971–72), 29–38.

Cramer, C. H. *Open Shelves and Open Minds: A History of the Cleveland Public Library*. Cleveland: Case Western Reserve University Press, 1972.

Crary, Jonathan. *Suspensions of Perception: Attention, Spectacle, and Modern Culture*. Cambridge: MIT Press, 1999.

———. *Techniques of the Observer: On Vision and Modernity in the Nineteenth Century*. Cambridge: MIT Press, 1990.

Cremin, Lawrence A. *The Transformation of the School: Progressivism in American Education, 1867–1957*. New York: Alfred A. Knopf, 1962.

Cripps, Thomas. *Making Movies Black: The Hollywood Message Movie from World War II to the Civil Rights Era*. New York: Oxford University Press, 1993.

———. *Slow Fade to Black: The Negro in American Film, 1900–1942*. New York: Oxford University Press, 1977.

Cunningham, Clifford J. "The First Planetarium: The Desire to Simulate the Night Sky Has Been Around for Centuries." *Mercury* 34, no. 5 (2005), 10.

Curtis, Scott. "Still/Moving: Digital Imaging and Medical Hermeneutics." *Memory Bytes: History, Technology, and Digital Culture*, ed. Lauren Rabinovitz and Abraham Geil, 218–54. Durham: Duke University Press, 2004.

Dale, Edgar. "A Comprehensive Program for the Teaching of Motion Picture Appreciation." *Educational Screen* 7 (1934), 125–28.

———. *How to Appreciate Motion Pictures: A Manual of Motion-Picture Criticism Prepared for High-School Students*. New York: Macmillan, 1938.

Dana, John Cotton. *The Gloom of the Museum*. Woodstock, Vt.: Elm Tree, 1917.

———. "The Library in 1912." *Newarker* 2, no. 3 (1913), 240–47.

Dawson, Jonathan. "The Grierson Tradition." *The Documentary Film in Australia*, ed. Ross Lansell and Peter Beilby, 139–41. North Melbourne: Cinema Papers, 1982.

deCordova, Richard. "Ethnography and Exhibition: The Child Audience, the Hays Office, and Saturday Matinees." *Looking Past the Screen: Case Studies in American Film History and Method*, ed. Jon Lewis and Eric Smoodin, 229–45. Durham: Duke University Press, 2007.

Demos, T. J. *The Exiles of Marcel Duchamp*. Cambridge: MIT Press, 2007.

Dennis, Jonathan, ed. *"The Tin Shed": The Origins of the National Film Unit*. Wellington: New Zealand Film Archive, 1981.

Dewey, John. *Democracy and Education*. New York: Macmillan, 1922.

———. "Experience, Nature and Art." Excerpt from *Experience and Nature* (1925) in *Pragmatism*, ed. Louis Menand, 238–41. New York: Vintage, 1997.

———. *The Public and Its Problems*. New York: Henry Holt, 1927.

Dickinson, Margaret, and Sarah Street. *Cinema and State: The Film Industry and the Government, 1927–84*. London: British Film Institute, 1985.

Diehl, Harold S. *Healthful Living*. 3rd edn. New York: McGraw-Hill, 1949.

———. *Textbook of Healthful Living*. 5th edn. New York: McGraw-Hill, 1955.

Doane, Mary Anne. *The Emergence of Cinematic Time: Modernity, Contingency, the Archive*. Cambridge: Harvard University Press, 2002.

Dodge, H. E. "Motion Picture as a Force in Religious Education." *Association Seminar* 22 (December 1914), 90.

Doherty, Thomas. *Cold War, Cool Medium: Television, McCarthyism, and American Culture*. New York: Columbia University Press, 2003.

———. *Projections of War: Hollywood, American Culture, and World War II*. New York: Columbia University Press, 1993.

———. *Projections of War: Hollywood, American Culture, and World War II*. Rev. ed. New York: Columbia University Press, 1999.

Dollard, John. *Caste and Class in a Southern Town*. 3rd edn. Garden City, N.Y.: Doubleday Anchor, 1957.

Dorris, Anna Verona. *Visual Instruction in the Public Schools*. Boston: Ginn, 1928.

Downing, John D. H., ed. *Film and Politics in the Third World*. Brooklyn: Autonomedia, 1987.

Druick, Zoë. "Mobile Cinema in Canada in Relation to British Mobile Film Practices."

Screening Canadians: Cross-cultural Perspectives on Canadian Film, ed. Wolfram R. Keller and Gene Walz, 13–34. Marburg: Universitätsbibliothek Marburg, 2008.

———. *Projecting Canada: Government Policy and Documentary Film at the National Film Board*. Montreal: McGill-Queen's University Press, 2007.

———. "'Reaching the Multimillions': Liberal Internationalism and the Establishment of Documentary Film." *Inventing Film Studies*, ed. Lee Grieveson and Haidee Wasson, 66–92. Durham: Duke University Press, 2008.

———. "*World without End*: International Development in the Global Village." Conference paper delivered at the Orphan Film Symposium 6, New York University, March 28, 2008.

Du Bois, W. E. B. *The Souls of Black Folk*, ed. David W. Blight and Robert Gooding-Williams. Boston: Bedford, 1997.

Duncan, Carol. "Museums and Department Stores: Close Encounters." *High-Pop: Making Culture into Popular Entertainment*, ed. Jim Collins, 129–54. London: British Film Institute, 2002.

Duncan, Carol, and Alan Wallach. "The Universal Survey Museum." *Art History* 3, no. 4 (1980), 448–69.

Dykyj, Oksana. "Cinema Collections: Academic Libraries." *Video Collection Development in Multi-Type Libraries*, ed. Gary P. Handman, 199–223. Westport.: Greenwood, 2002.

Dysinger, Walter S., and Christian A. Ruckmick. *The Emotional Responses of Children to the Motion Picture Situation*. New York: Macmillan, 1935.

Eberwein, Robert. *Sex Ed: Film, Video, and the Framework of Desire*. New Brunswick, N.J.: Rutgers University Press, 1999.

Eisenstein, Sarah. *Give Us Bread but Give Us Roses: Working Women's Consciousness in the United States, 1890 to the First World War*. Boston: Routledge and Kegan Paul, 1983.

Elder, R. Bruce. *Image and Identity: Reflections on Canadian Film and Culture*. Waterloo, Ont.: Wilfrid Laurier University Press, 1989.

Eldridge, Donald A. "High School Films without Subsidy." *Movie Makers*, November 1937, 541.

———. "Motion-Picture Appreciation in the New Haven Schools." *Journal of Educational Sociology* 11, no. 3 (1937), 175–83.

———. "Practical Films." *Movie Makers*, June 1938, 296.

Elliot, Huger. "The Museum's Cinema Films." *Metropolitan Museum of Art Bulletin* 21, no. 9 (1926), 216.

Ellis, Don Carlos, and Laura Thornborough. *Motion Pictures in Education: A Practical Handbook for Users of Visual Aids*. New York: Thomas Y. Crowell, 1923.

Ellis, Jack C. *John Grierson: Life, Contributions, Influence*. Carbondale: Southern Illinois University Press, 2000.

Emirbayer, Mustafa. "Beyond Structuralism and Voluntarism: The Politics and Discourse of Progressive School Reform, 1890–1930." *Theory and Society* 21, no. 5 (1992), 621–64.

Epstein, Jean. "On Certain Characteristics of *Photogénie*," trans. Tom Milne. Repr. in *French Film Theory and Criticism*, vol. 1, *1907–1929*, ed. Richard Abel, 314–20. Princeton: Princeton University Press, 1988.

Epstein, Steven. *Impure Science: AIDS, Activism, and the Politics of Knowledge.* Berkeley: University of California Press, 1996.

Evans, Gary. *In the National Interest: A Chronicle of the National Film Board of Canada from 1949 to 1989.* Toronto: University of Toronto Press, 1991.

Ezra, Elizabeth. *Georges Méliès.* Manchester: Manchester University Press, 2000.

Fagelson, William Friedman. "Fighting Films: The Everyday Tactics of World War II Soldiers." *Cinema Journal* 40, no. 3 (2001), 94–112.

Farber, Manny. *Negative Space.* New York: Praeger, 1971.

Farr, Henry L. "The CCC: A Rich Field for Visual Education." *Educational Screen* 13, no. 9 (1934), 236.

Fein, Seth. "From Collaboration to Containment: Hollywood and the International Political Economy of Mexican Cinema after the Second World War." *Mexico's Cinema: A Century of Film and Filmmakers,* ed. Joanne Hershfield and David R. Maciel, 123–64. Wilmington, Del.: Scholarly Resources, 1999.

Film Council of America. *Sixty Years of 16mm Film, 1923–1983: A Symposium.* Evanston, Ill.: Film Council of America, 1954.

Filut, Ann M. "Fractions: How One School Has Dramatized Them on Substandard Film." *Movie Makers,* February 1936, 70.

Fisher, Clyde. "The Hayden Planetarium." *Natural History* 34, no. 3 (1935), 187–258.

Forman, Henry James. "Molded by Movies." *McCall's,* November 1932, 17, 54.

———. "Movie Madness." *McCall's,* October 1932, 14, 28, 30.

———. *Our Movie Made Children.* New York: Macmillan, 1933.

———. "To the Movies—But Not to Sleep!" *McCall's,* September 1932, 12, 13, 58–59.

Foucault, Michel. "8 February 1978." *Security, Territory, Population: Lectures at the Collège de France, 1977–1978,* ed. Michel Senellart, trans. Graham Burchell, 115–34. New York: Palgrave Macmillan, 2007.

Fox, Susannah, and Sydney Jones. *The Social Life of Health Information: Americans' Pursuit of Health Takes Place within a Widening Network of Both Online and Offline Sources.* Washington: Pew Internet and American Life Project, 2009.

Frampton, Hollis. *Circles of Confusion: Film, Photography, Video: Texts, 1968–1980.* Rochester: Visual Studies Workshop Press, 1983.

———. "Statement of Plans for *Magellan.*" *On the Camera Arts and Consecutive Matters: The Writings of Hollis Frampton,* ed. Bruce Jenkins, 226–29. Cambridge: MIT Press, 2009.

Frederking, Brian. *The United States and the Security Council: Collective Security since the Cold War.* London: Routledge, 2007.

Freire, Paulo. *Pedagogy of the Oppressed.* New York: Herder and Herder, 1970.

Friedberg, Anne. *The Virtual Window: From Alberti to Microsoft.* Cambridge: MIT Press, 2006.

———. *Window Shopping: Cinema and the Postmodern.* Berkeley: University of California Press, 1993.

Frutchey, F. P. "Can Youth's Appreciation of Motion Pictures Be Improved." *Educational Research Bulletin* 16, no. 4 (1937), 97–102.

Frutchey, F. P., and Edgar Dale. "Testing Some Objectives of Motion-Picture Appreciation." *Educational Research Bulletin* 14, no. 2 (1935), 34–37.

Gaines, Jane. *Fire and Desire: Mixed-Race Movies in the Silent Era.* Chicago: University of Chicago Press, 2001.

Gaines, Jane, and Michael Renov, eds. *Collecting Visible Evidence.* Minneapolis: University of Minnesota Press, 1999.

Gaines, Kevin K. *Uplifting the Race: Black Leadership, Politics, and Culture in the Twentieth Century.* Chapel Hill: University of North Carolina Press, 1996.

Galbiati, Alessio, and Paola Catò. "Ken Jacobs: The Demiurgo of the Moving Image [Interview]." *Digimag,* March 2008, http://www.digicult.it/digimag/article.asp?id=1155.

Gale, Arthur. "Continuity of Amateur Industrials." *Movie Makers,* May 1931, 256–57.

———. "Note: Tabloid Industrial Scenarios." *Movie Makers,* September 1930, 540.

Galvin, Hoyt R. *Films in Public Libraries.* Chicago: American Library Association, 1947.

Geller, Evelyn. *Forbidden Books in American Public Libraries, 1876–1939: A Study in Cultural Change.* Westport: Greenwood, 1984.

Gill, Brian, and Steven Schlossman. "'A Sin Against Childhood': Progressive Education and the Crusade to Abolish Homework, 1897–1941." *American Journal of Education* 105, no. 1 (1996), 27–66.

Gitelman, Lisa, and Geoffrey B. Pingree. *New Media, 1740–1915.* Cambridge: MIT Press, 2003.

Glander, Timothy. *Origins of Mass Communications Research during the American Cold War: Educational Effects and Contemporary Implications.* Mahwah, N.J.: Lawrence Erlbaum, 2000.

Glucksman, E. M. *General Instructions Manual for Theatre Managers.* Chicago: Chicago Show, 1930.

Goldfarb, Brian. *Visual Pedagogy: Media Cultures in and beyond the Classroom.* Durham: Duke University Press, 2002.

Gomery, Douglas. *Shared Pleasures: A History of Movie Presentation in the United States.* Madison: University of Wisconsin Press, 1992.

Goodman, Cynthia. "Frederick Kiesler: Designs for Peggy Guggenheim's Art of This Century Gallery." *Arts Magazine* 51, no. 10 (1977), 90–95.

Gramsci, Antonio. "Americanism and Fordism." *Selections from the Prison Notebooks of Antonio Gramsci,* ed. and trans. Quintin Hoare and Geoffrey Nowell-Smith, 277–318. New York: International, 1971.

Gray, Howard A. "Can Educators Profit from Industry's Experience with the Motion Picture?" *Educational Screen* 12, no. 4 (1933), 101–2; 12, no. 5 (1933), 123–25, 131.

Greene, Nelson L. Editorial. *Educational Screen,* March 1934, 64.

———. Editorial. *Educational Screen,* June 1934, 149.

Greene, Ronald Walter. "Selling Reputation: The Economic and Cultural Value of the YMCA's Film Business, 1946–1949." Paper presented at the Society for Cinema and Media Studies, London, March 2005.

———. "Y Movies: Film and the Modernization of Pastoral Power." *Communication and Critical/Cultural Studies* 2, no. 1 (2005), 20–36.

Grierson, John. "The Film and Primitive Peoples." *The Film in Colonial Development*, 9–15. London: British Film Institute, 1948.

———. *Grierson on Documentary*, ed. Forsyth Hardy. New York: Praeger, 1971.

Grieveson, Lee. *Policing Cinema: Movies and Censorship in Early Twentieth Century America*. Berkeley: University of California Press, 2004.

Grieveson, Lee, and Haidee Wasson, eds. *Inventing Film Studies*. Durham: Duke University Press, 2008.

Griffiths, Alison. "The Revered Gaze: The Medieval Imaginary of Mel Gibson's *The Passion of the Christ*." *Cinema Journal* 46, no. 2 (2007), 3–39.

———. *Shivers Down Your Spine: Cinema, Museums, and the Immersive View*. New York: Columbia University Press, 2008.

———. *Wondrous Difference: Cinema, Anthropology and Turn-of-the-Century Visual Culture*. New York: Columbia University Press, 2002.

Guggenheim, Peggy, ed. *Art of This Century: Objects, Drawings, Photographs, Paintings, Sculpture, Collages, 1910 to 1942*. New York: Guggenheim, 1942.

Gunning, Tom. "An Aesthetic of Astonishment: Early Film, and the (In)credulous Spectator." *Art and Text* 34 (1989), 31–45.

———. "The Cinema of Attractions: Early Film, Its Spectators and the Avant-Garde." *Wide Angle* 8, nos. 3–4 (1986), 63–70.

———. "Phantom Images and Modern Manifestations: Spirit Photography, Magic Theater, Trick Films, and Photography's Uncanny." *Fugitive Images: From Photography to Video*, ed. Patrice Petro, 42–71. Bloomington: Indiana University Press, 1995.

Hanny, Alistair. Introduction. *Fear and Trembling*, by Søren Kierkegaard, trans. Alistair Hanny, 7–37. London: Penguin, 1985.

Hansen, Miriam. *Babel and Babylon: Spectatorship in American Silent Film*. Cambridge: Harvard University Press, 1991.

———. "Early Cinema, Late Cinema: Transformations of the Public Sphere." *Viewing Positions: Ways of Seeing Film*, ed. Linda Williams, 134–52. New Brunswick, N.J.: Rutgers University Press, 1997.

———. "The Mass Production of the Senses: Classical Cinema as Vernacular Modernism." *Modernism/Modernity* 6, no. 2 (1999), 59–77.

Harris, Neil. "John Philip Sousa and the Culture of Reassurance." *Perspectives on John Philip Sousa*, ed. John Newsom, 11–40. Washington: Library of Congress, 1983.

———. "Museums, Merchandising and Popular Taste: The Struggle for Influence." *Cultural Excursions: Marketing Appetites and Cultural Tastes in Modern America*, 56–81. Chicago: University of Chicago Press, 1990.

Hartshorne, Hugh, Mark A. May, and Julius B. Maller. *Studies in the Nature of Character, II: Studies in Service and Self-Control*. New York: Macmillan, 1929.

Hawkins, Pamela Susan. "Binghamton University—Cinema Department and Artists Lab at School for Advanced Technology." *Video History Project*, http://www.experimentaltvcenter.org/history/, 1998.

Hay, James. "Rethinking the Intersection of Cinema, Genre, and Youth." *21st Century Films Studies: A Scope Reader*, ed. James Burton, http://www.scope.nottingham.ac.uk/reader/chapter.php?id=5, February (2011).

"Hayden Planetarium." *Hart's Guide to New York City*, 815. New York: Hart, 1964.

Hediger, Vinzenz, and Patrick Vonderau, eds. *Films That Work: Industrial Film and the Productivity of Media*. Amsterdam: University of Amsterdam Press, 2009.

Hendershot, Heather, ed. "In Focus: 16mm." *Cinema Journal* 45, no. 3 (2006), 109–40.

Higginbotham, Evelyn Brooks. *Righteous Discontent: The Women's Movement in the Black Baptist Church, 1880–1920*. Cambridge: Harvard University Press, 1993.

Hogner, Nils, and Guy Scott. "Hayden Planetarium." *Cartoon Guide of New York City*, 30–31. New York: J. J. Augustin, 1938.

Hopkins, Albert A. *Magic: Stage Illusions and Scientific Diversions*. New York: Benjamin Blom, 1967 [1897].

Hopkins, C. Howard. *History of the YMCA in North America*. New York: Association Press, 1951.

Horníček, Jiří. "The Institutionalization of Classroom Films in Czechoslovakia between the Wars." *Film History* 19, no. 4 (2007), 384–91.

How, When, Where to Show 16mm Victory Loan Film. Washington: U.S. Department of the Treasury, 1945.

Howe, Winifred. *A History of the Metropolitan Museum of Art, 1905–1941*. New York: Columbia University Press, 1946.

Hubbard, Elbert. "The Law of Wages." *Western Union News* 1, no. 4 (October 1914), 6.

Hugon, Paul D. "Dramatizing Industrials: Suggestions on How to Film Your Business Effectively." *Movie Makers*, December 1929, 793.

Hunter, Ian. *Culture and Government: The Emergence of Literary Education*. London: Macmillan, 1988.

Hyde, Ralph. *Panoramania! The Art and Entertainment of the "All-Embracing" View*. London: Trefoil / Barbican Art Gallery, 1988.

Industrial Relations: Final Report and Testimony Submitted to Congress by the Commission on Industrial Relations. Washington: U.S. Government Printing Office, 1916.

Inglis, Ruth A. *Freedom of the Movies*. Chicago: University of Chicago Press, 1947.

Ishikuza, Karen, and Patricia R. Zimmermann, eds. *Mining the Home Movie: Excavations in Histories and Memories*. Berkeley: University of California Press, 2008.

Jacobs, Lea. "Reformers and Spectators: The Film Education Movement in the Thirties." *Camera Obscura* 22 (1990), 29–49.

Jacoby, Sanford M. *Employing Bureaucracy: Managers, Unions, and the Transformation of Work in American Industry, 1900–1945*. New York: Columbia University Press, 1985.

James, David. *Allegories of Cinema: American Film in the Sixties*. Princeton: Princeton University Press, 1989.

Jarvie, Ian. "Free Trade as Cultural Threat: American Film and TV Exports in the Post-War Period." *Hollywood and Europe*, ed. Geoffrey Nowell-Smith and Steven Ricci, 34–46. London: British Film Institute, 1998.

———. *Hollywood's Overseas Campaign: The North Atlantic Movie Trade, 1920–1950*. London: Cambridge University Press, 1992.

Jenkins, Bruce. "A Case Against 'Structural Film.'" *UFA Journal* 33 (spring 1981), 9–14.

Jenkins, Henry. *Convergence Culture: Where Old and New Media Collide*. New York: New York University Press, 2006.

Jessup, Lynda. "Moving Pictures and Costume Songs at the 1927 'Exhibition of Canadian West Coast Art, Native and Modern.'" *Canadian Journal of Film Studies* 11, no. 1 (2002), 2–39.

Jowett, Garth. *Film: The Democratic Art*. Boston: Little, Brown, 1976.

Jowett, Garth S., Ian C. Jarvie, and Kathryn H. Fuller. *Children and the Movies: Media Influence and the Payne Fund Controversy*. Cambridge: Cambridge University Press, 1996.

Juhasz, Alexandra. *AIDS TV: Identity, Community, and Alternative Video*. Durham: Duke University Press, 1995.

Kahana, Jonathan. *Intelligence Work: The Politics of American Documentary*. New York: Columbia University Press, 2008.

Kattelle, Alan D. "The Amateur Cinema League and Its Films." *Film History* 15, no. 2 (2003), 238–51.

———. *Home Movies: A History of the American Industry, 1897–1979*. Nashua, N.H.: Transition, 2000.

Katz, Elihu, and George Wedell, with Michael Pilsworth and Dov Shinar. *Broadcasting in the Third World: Promise and Performance*. Cambridge: Harvard University Press, 1977.

Kessler, Frank, and Nanna Verhoeff, eds. *Networks of Entertainment: Early Film Distribution 1895–1915*. Eastleigh: John Libbey, 2007.

Kierkegaard, Søren. *Fear and Trembling*, trans. Alistair Hanny. London: Penguin, 1985.

King, Henry Charles. *The London Planetarium*. London: London Planetarium, 1958.

———. "The Planetarium and Adult Education." *Proceedings from the Second International Planetarium Directors Conference*, ed. H. Kaminiski. Boechum, Germany, 1966.

Klinger, Barbara. *Beyond the Multiplex: Cinema, New Technologies, and the Home*. Berkeley: University of California Press, 2006.

———. "Cinema's Shadow: Reconsidering Non-Theatrical Exhibition." *Going to the Movies: Hollywood and the Social Experience of Cinema*, ed. Richard Maltby, Melvyn Stokes, and Robert C. Allen, 273–90. Exeter: University of Exeter Press, 2007.

Koppes, Clayton R., and Gregory D. Black. *Hollywood Goes to War: How Politics, Profits and Propaganda Shaped World War II Movies*. Berkeley: University of California Press, 1990.

Koszarski, Richard. *An Evening's Entertainment: The Age of the Silent Feature Picture, 1915–1928*. New York: Charles Scribner's Sons, 1990.

Kreisler, Harry. "Film and the Creation of Mind: Conversation with Ken Jacobs, Film Artist." *Conversations with History*, Institute of International Studies, University of California, Berkeley, 1999, http://globetrotter.berkeley.edu/people/Jacobs/jacobs-cono.html.

Kreul, James. "New York, New Cinema: The Independent Film Community and the Underground Crossover, 1950–1970." Ph.D. diss., University of Wisconsin, 2004.

Kridel, Craig. "Educational Film Projects of the 1930s: Secrets of Success and the Human Relations Series." *Learning with the Lights Off: Educational Film in the United*

States, ed. Dan Streible, Devin Orgeron, and Marsha Orgeron. Oxford: Oxford University Press, forthcoming.

Lamb, Tom, and Jeremy Collins, eds. *The World in Your Hands: An Exhibition of Globes and Planetaria*. London: Christie's, 1994.

Lant, Antonia. "Egypt in Early Cinema." *Images across Borders: 1896–1918*, ed. Roland Cosandey and François Albera, 73–94. Zurich: Nuit Blanche / Payot, 1996.

Lant, Antonia, and Ingrid Periz, eds. *Red Velvet Seat: Women's Writing on the First Fifty Years of Cinema*. New York: Verso, 2006.

Lawson, M. D., and R. C. Petersen. *Progressive Education: An Introduction*. Sydney: Angus and Robertson, 1972.

Learned, William S. *The American Public Library and the Diffusion of Knowledge*. New York: Harcourt, Brace, 1924.

Lears, T. Jackson. *Fables of Abundance*. New York: Basic Books, 1994.

Lerner, Daniel. *The Passing of Traditional Society: Modernizing the Middle East*. Glencoe, Ill.: Free Press, 1958.

Lerner, Frederick Andrew. *The Story of Libraries: From the Invention of Writing to the Computer Age*. New York: Continuum, 1998.

Lester, Peter. "'The Perilous Gauge: Canadian Independent Film Exhibition and the 16mm Mobile Menace." *Cinema and Technology: Cultures, Theories, Practices*, ed. Marc Furstenau, Adrian Mackenzie, and Bruce Bennett, 23–36. New York: Palgrave Macmillan, 2009.

Levitan, Stuart D. *Madison: The Illustrated Sesquicentennial History*. Madison: University of Wisconsin Press, 2006.

Levitt, I. M. "The Planetarium." *The Planetarium: A Special Edition Commemorating the Dedication of the New Fels Planetarium of the Franklin Institute (September 18, 1962)*, 1–16. Philadelphia: Franklin Institute, 1962.

Lewis, Justin, and Toby Miller, eds. *Critical Cultural Policy Studies: A Reader*. Oxford: Blackwell, 2003.

Lindvall, Terry. *Sanctuary Cinema: Origins of the Christian Film Industry*. New York: New York University Press, 2007.

Lockwood, Marian. "The Hayden Planetarium." *The Book of the Hayden Planetarium, the American Museum of Natural History*, 188–90. New York: American Museum of Natural History, 1935.

Logan, Rayford W. "Negro Youth and the Influence of the Press, Radio, and Cinema." *Journal of Negro Education* 9, no. 3 (1940), 425–34.

Loukopoulou, Katerina. "'Films Bring Art to the People': The Art Film Tour in Britain (1950–1980)." *Film History* 19, no. 4 (2007), 414–22.

Low, Theodore L. *The Museum as a Social Instrument*. New York: Metropolitan Museum of Art for the American Association of Museums, 1942.

MacBride, Sean, and Colleen Roach. "The New International Information Order." *The Global Media Debate: Its Rise, Fall, and Renewal*, ed. G. Gerbner, H. Mowlana, and K. Nordenstreng, 3–11. Norwood, N.J.: Ablex, 1993.

MacCann, Richard Dyer. *The People's Films: A Political History of U.S. Government Motion Pictures*. New York: Hastings House, 1973.

MacDonald, Scott. *Avant-Garde Film: Motion Studies.* Cambridge: Cambridge University Press, 1993.

———. "Hollis Frampton" [interview]. *A Critical Cinema*, 21–77. Berkeley: University of California Press, 1988.

Maltby, Richard. "The Genesis of the Production Code." *Quarterly Review of Film and Video* 15, no. 4 (1995), 5–32.

Maltby, Richard, Melvyn Stokes, and Robert C. Allen, eds. *Going to the Movies: Hollywood and the Social Experience of Cinema.* Exeter: University of Exeter Press, 2007.

Manlove, Ruth Thorpe. "The Educational Motion Picture Film in Public Library Service." Master's thesis, Columbia University, 1942.

Manovich, Lev. *The Language of New Media.* Cambridge: MIT Press, 2001.

Marché, Jordan D., II. *Theaters of Time and Space: American Planetaria, 1930–1970.* New Brunswick, N.J.: Rutgers University Press, 2005.

Marchessault, Janine, and Susan Lord, eds. *Fluid Screens, Expanded Cinema.* Toronto: University of Toronto Press, 2007.

Margulies, Ivone. *Nothing Happens.* Durham: Duke University Press, 1996.

Martin, Emily. *Flexible Bodies: The Role of Immunity in American Culture from the Days of Polio to the Age of AIDS.* Boston: Beacon, 1994.

Martin, Reinhold. *The Organizational Complex: Architecture, Media, and Corporate Space.* Cambridge: MIT Press, 2005.

Maslow, Abraham H. *Religions, Values, and Peak Experiences.* New York: Penguin Arkana, 1994.

Masson, Eef. "Celluloid Teaching Tools: Classroom Films in the Netherlands (1941–1953)." *Film History* 19, no. 4 (2007), 392–400.

May, Lary. *Screening Out the Past.* Chicago: University of Chicago Press, 1983.

May, Mark A. *Education in a World of Fear.* Cambridge: Harvard University Press, 1941.

———. "Educational Possibilities of Motion Pictures." *Journal of Educational Sociology* 11, no. 3 (1937), 148–60.

———. "Educational Projects." *Educational Screen*, April 1947, 200–201, 232.

———. "Films and Teaching Functions." *Educational Screen*, October 1945, 339, 340, 345.

———. *Planning Films for Schools: Final Report of the Commission on Motion Pictures.* Washington: American Council on Education, 1949.

———. "Psychological Warfare." *Science News Letter*, March 21, 1953, 191.

———. "What Is Character Education?" *Parents' Magazine*, April 1957, 21, 58, 60.

———. "What Should the New Administration Do about Psychological Warfare?" *Foreign Policy Bulletin*, March 15, 1953, 4, 6.

May, Mark A., and Arthur A. Lumsdaine. *Learning from Films.* New Haven: Yale University Press, 1958.

May, William F. *The Physician's Covenant: Images of the Healer in Medical Ethics.* Philadelphia: Westminster, 1983.

McCarthy, Anna. "From the Ordinary to the Concrete: Cultural Studies and the Politics of Scale." *Questions of Method in Cultural Studies*, ed. Mimi White and James Schwoch, 21–53. Malden, Mass.: Blackwell, 2006.

McCullough, Constance. "A Preview of an Investigation of Motion-Picture Class and Club Activities." *English Journal* 28, no. 2 (1939), 120–29.

McDermott, John Francis. *The Lost Panoramas of the Mississippi*. Chicago: University of Chicago Press, 1958.

McGuire, Laura M. "A Movie House in Space and Time: Frederick Kiesler's Film Arts Guild Cinema, New York, 1929." *Studies in the Decorative Arts* 14, no. 2 (2007), 45–78.

McIntire, George. "Visual Instruction in Indiana." *Educational Screen* 11, no. 5 (1932), 139–40, 149.

McKay, Herbert C. *Motion Picture Photography for the Amateur*. New York: Falk, 1924.

McLenna, Ian C. "The Planetarium in Perspective." Paper presented at meeting of the Middle Atlantic Planetarium Society, Frederick, Md., May 12, 1967.

McLuhan, Marshall. *Understanding Media: The Extensions of Man*. New York: McGraw-Hill, 1964.

McNabb, J. H. "The Amateur Turns a Penny." *Amateur Movie Makers*, December 1926, 19.

Mead, Margaret, and Rhoda Métraux, eds. *The Study of Culture at a Distance*. Chicago: University of Chicago Press, 1953.

Mebold, Anke. "'Just Like a Public Library Maintained for Public Welfare.'" *Networks of Entertainment: Early Film Distribution 1895–1915*, ed. Frank Kessler and Nanna Verhoeff, 260–74. Eastleigh: John Libbey, 2007.

Mebold, Anke, and Charles Tepperman. "Resurrecting the Lost History of 28mm Film in North America." *Film History* 15, no. 2 (2003), 137–51.

Meier, August, and Elliott Rudwick, eds. *The Claude Barnett Papers Microform*. Frederick, Md.: University Publications of America, 1985.

Mellencamp, Patricia. *Indiscretions: Avant-Garde Film, Video, and Feminism*. Bloomington: Indiana University Press, 1990.

———. "Receivable Texts: U.S. Avant-Garde Cinema, 1960–1980." *Wide Angle* 7, nos. 1–2 (1985), 74–91.

Messaris, Paul. *Visual Literacy: Image, Mind, and Reality*. Boulder: Westview, 1994.

Metropolitan Museum of Art. *Cinema Films: A List of Museum Films and Others with the Conditions under Which They Are Distributed*. New York: Metropolitan Museum of Art, 1938.

Mettler, Suzanne. *Soldiers to Citizens: The G.I. Bill and the Making of the Greatest Generation*. New York: Oxford University Press, 2005.

Michelson, Annette. "Toward Snow: Part 1." *Artforum* 9, no. 10 (1971), 30–37.

Middleton, Arthur. "Globes of the Early 19th Century." *The World in Your Hands: An Exhibition of Globes and Planetaria*, ed. Tom Lamb and Jeremy Collins, 90–97. London: Christie's, 1994.

Miezis, Ianis Arnoldovich. "Activity of the Planetarium in Riga." Paper presented at the 5th International Planetarium Director's Conference, Prague, 1975.

Miller, Angela. "The Panorama, the Cinema, and the Emergence of the Spectacular." *Wide Angle* 18, no. 2 (1996), 34–69.

Miller, Toby, Nitin Govil, John McMurria, Richard Maxwell, and Ting Wang. *Global Hollywood 2*. London: British Film Institute, 2005.

Milliken, Christie. *Generation Sex: Reconfiguring Sexual Citizenship in Educational Film and Video*. Minneapolis: University of Minnesota Press, forthcoming.

Minkowsky, John. "Survey of Film/Television/Video/Still Photography/Electronic Music Activity at State University of New York Campuses, [1977]." "Binghamton University: Cinema Department and Artists Lab at School for Advanced Technology." Video History Project, http://www.experimentaltvcenter.org/history.

Mongoven, Ann. "The War on Disease and the War on Terror: A Dangerous Metaphorical Nexus?" *Cambridge Quarterly of Healthcare Ethics* 15 (2006), 403–16.

Montessori, Maria. *The Montessori Method*. New York: Schocken, 1964.

Moore, Paul S. *Now Playing: Early Moviegoing and the Regulation of Fun*. Albany: SUNY Press, 2008.

Morey, Anne. *Hollywood Outsiders: The Adaptation of the Film Industry, 1913–1934*. Minneapolis: University of Minnesota Press, 2003.

Morton, Mary A. "The Federal Government and Negro Morale." *Journal of Negro Education* 12, no. 3 (1943), 452–63.

Mullen, Sarah McLean. *How to Judge Motion Pictures: A Pamphlet for High School Students*. New York: Scholastic, 1935.

Münsterberg, Hugo. "Public Library in America" [1921]. *The Library and Society: Reprints of Papers and Addresses*, ed. Arthur E. Bostwick, 79–86. Freeport, N.Y.: Books for Libraries, 1968.

Neale, Steve. "Oppositional Exhibition Notes and Problems." *Screen* 21, no. 3 (1980), 45–56.

Noble, Peter. *The Negro in Films*. London: Skelton Robinson, 1948.

Notcutt, L. A., and G. C. Latham. *The African and the Cinema*. London: Edinburgh House, 1937.

Oettermann, Stephan. *The Panorama: History of a Mass Medium*. New York: Zone, 1997.

O'Grady, Gerald. "The Preparation of Teachers of Media." *Journal of Aesthetic Education* 3, no. 3 (1969), 113–34.

1000 and One: The Blue Book of Non-theatrical Films. 4th ed. Chicago: Educational Screen, 1926.

Ostherr, Kirsten. *Cinematic Prophylaxis: Globalization and Contagion in the Discourse of World Health*. Durham: Duke University Press, 2005.

———. *Medical Visions: Producing the Patient through Film, Television, and Imaging Technologies*. New York: Oxford University Press, forthcoming.

Parascandola, John. "Syphilis at the Cinema: Medicine and Morals in VD Films of the U.S. Public Health Service in World War II." *Medicine's Moving Pictures: Medicine, Health, and Bodies in American Film and Television*, ed. Leslie J. Reagan, Nancy Tomes, and Paula Treichler, 71–92. Rochester, N.Y.: University of Rochester Press, 2007.

Parmenter, Ross. "Distributing Industrial Films." *Movie Makers*, September 1938, 436, 459–61.

Patterson, James. *Grand Expectations: The United States, 1945–1974*. New York: Oxford University Press, 1997.

———. *Restless Giant: The United States from Watergate to Bush v. Gore*. New York: Oxford University Press, 2007.

Perry, Everett. "Aims and Methods of Library Publicity." *Library Journal* 39, no. 4 (1914), 259–66.

Peterson, Mark Allan. *Anthropology and Mass Communication: Media and Myth in the New Millennium*. New York: Berghahn, 2003.

Peterson, Ruth C., and L. L. Thurstone. *Motion Pictures and the Social Attitudes of Children*. New York: Macmillan, 1933.

Piaget, Jean. *Science of Education and the Psychology of the Child*. New York: Grossman, 1970.

Pines, Jim, and Paul Willemen, eds. *Questions of Third Cinema*. London: British Film Institute, 1989.

Polan, Dana. *Scenes of Instruction: The Beginnings of the U.S. Study of Film*. Berkeley: University of California Press, 2007.

Potamkin, Harry Alan. "The Magic of Machine Films." *Movie Makers*, November 1929, 722–23, 744.

Prelinger, Rick. *The Field Guide to Sponsored Films*. San Francisco: National Film Preservation Foundation, 2006.

Preston, Douglas J. "A Domeful of Stars." *Natural History* (1985), 92–101.

Preston, William Jr., Edward S. Herman, and Herbert Schiller. *Hope and Folly: The United States and UNESCO, 1945–1985*. Minneapolis: University of Minnesota Press, 1989.

Price, Brian, and Michelle Dent. "An Interview with Ken Jacobs [2003]." *Cultural Society* (2004), www.culturalsociety.org/kjinterview.html.

Quigley, Martin. "Public Opinion and the Motion Picture." *Public Opinion Quarterly* 1, no. 2 (1937), 129–33.

Rabinovitz, Lauren. *For the Love of Pleasure: Women, Movies, and Culture in Turn-of-the-Century Chicago*. New Brunswick, N.J.: Rutgers University Press, 1998.

———. "More Than the Movies: A History of Somatic Visual Culture through Hale's Tours, IMAX, and Motion Simulation Rides." *Memory Bytes: History, Technology, and Digital Culture*, ed. Lauren Rabinovitz and Abraham Geil, 99–125. Durham: Duke University Press, 2004.

Rabinovitz, Lauren, and Abraham Geil. *Memory Bytes: History, Technology, and Digital Culture*. Durham: Duke University Press, 2004.

Randall, John Herman. *Our Changing Civilization: How Science and the Machine Age Are Reconstructing Modern Life*. New York: Frederic A. Stokes, 1929.

Reagan, Leslie J., Nancy Tomes, and Paula Treichler, eds. *Medicine's Moving Pictures: Medicine, Health, and Bodies in American Film and Television*. Rochester, N.Y.: University of Rochester Press, 2007.

Reddick, L. D. "Educational Programs for the Improvement of Race Relations: Motion Pictures, Radio, the Press and Libraries." *Journal of Negro Education* 13, no. 3 (1944), 361–66.

Reiser, Robert A. "A History of Instructional Design and Technology, Part I: A History of Instructional Media." *Educational Technology Research and Development* 49, no. 1 (2001), 53–64.

———. "A History of Instructional Design and Technology, Part II: A History of

Instructional Design." *Educational Technology Research and Development* 49, no. 2 (2001), 57–67.

Renshaw, Samuel, Vernon L. Miller, and Dorothy P. Marquis. *Children's Sleep.* New York: Macmillan, 1933.

Ress, Etta Schneider. "The Literature in Audio-Visual Instruction." *Educational Screen,* October 1949, 358–59.

Rhines, Jesse Algernon. *Black Film / White Money.* New Brunswick, N.J.: Rutgers University Press, 1996.

Riesman, David. "The Zeiss Planetarium." *General Magazine and Historical Chronicle* 31 (1928), 236–41.

Robinson, Edward S. *The Behavior of the Museum Visitor.* Washington: American Association of Museums, 1929.

Rogers, William, and Paul Veith. *Visual Aids in the Church.* Philadelphia: Christian Education Press, 1946.

Ross, Steven J. *Working-Class Hollywood: Silent Film and the Shaping of Class in America.* Princeton: Princeton University Press, 1998.

Rossi-Snook, Elena. "Persistence of Vision: Public Library 16mm Film Collections in America." *Moving Image* 5, no. 1 (2005), 1–27.

Rothman, David. "Ethics and Human Experimentation: Henry Beecher Revisited." *New England Journal of Medicine* 317 (1987), 1195–99.

Ruoff, Jeffery, ed. *Virtual Voyages: Cinema and Travel.* Durham: Duke University Press, 2006.

Samarajiwa, Rohan. "The Murky Beginnings of the Communication and Development Field." *Rethinking Development Communication,* ed. Neville Jayaweera and Sarath Amunugama, 3–19. Singapore: Asian Mass Communication Research and Information Centre, 1987.

Sammond, Nicholas. *Babes in Tomorrowland: Walt Disney and the Making of the American Child.* Durham: Duke University Press, 2005.

Sandberg, Mark B. *Living Pictures, Missing Persons: Mannequins, Museums, and Modernity.* Princeton: Princeton University Press, 2003.

Scandiffio, Theresa. "'Better'n Any Circus That Ever Come to Town': Cinema, Visual Culture and Educational Programming at Chicago's Field Museum of Natural History, 1921–35." Ph.D. diss., University of Chicago, 2008.

Schaefer, Eric. *"Bold! Daring! Shocking! True!": A History of Exploitation Films, 1919–1959.* Durham: Duke University Press, 1999.

———. "Gauging a Revolution: 16mm Film and the Rise of the Pornographic Feature." *Cinema Journal* 41, no. 3 (2002), 3–26.

Schatz, Thomas. *Boom and Bust: American Cinema in the 1940s.* Berkeley: University of California Press, 1999.

Schiller, Herbert. "Genesis of the Free Flow of Information Principles." *Communication and Class Struggle,* vol. 1, *Capitalism, Imperialism,* ed. Armand Mattelart and Seth Siegelaub, 345–53. New York: International General, 1979.

Schivelbusch, Wolfgang. *The Railway Journey: The Industrialization of Time and Space in the 19th Century.* Berkeley: University of California Press, 1986.

Schramm, Wilbur, ed. *Mass Communications*. Urbana: University of Illinois Press, 1949.
———. *Mass Media and National Development: The Role of Information in Developing Countries*. Stanford: Stanford University Press, 1964.

Schramm, Wilbur, P. H. Coombs, F. Kahnert, and J. Lyle, eds. *The New Media: Memo to Educational Planners*. Paris: UNESCO International Institute for Educational Planning, 1967.

Schwartz, Vanessa R. *Spectacular Realities: Early Mass Culture in Fin-de-Siècle France*. Berkeley: University of California Press, 1998.

Scott, Mary G. H. "Woman's Affairs." *Telegraph World* 3, no. 5 (May 1921), 199–200.

Seal, Ethel Davis. "The American Wing of the Metropolitan Museum." *Ladies' Home Journal*, May 1925, 20, 21, 188, 191.

Sellers, William. "Making Films in and for the Colonies." *Journal of the Royal Society of the Arts* 101 (1953), 828–37.

Sharits, Paul. "A Cinematics Model for Film Studies in Higher Education: Center for Media Study/State University of New York at Buffalo." *Film Study in the Undergraduate Curriculum*, ed. Barry Keith Grant, 28–38. New York: Modern Language Association, 1983.

Sherman, Clarence E. "Relations between Libraries and Moving Pictures." *ALA Bulletin* 19 (1925), 210.

Shuttleworth, Frank K., and Mark A. May. *The Social Conduct and Attitudes of Movie Fans*. New York: Macmillan, 1933.

Siebert, Fred S., Theodore Peterson, and Wilbur Schramm. *Four Theories of the Press: The Authoritarian, Libertarian, Social Responsibility, and Soviet Communist Concepts of What the Press Should Be and Do*. Urbana: University of Illinois Press, 1956.

Simmel, Georg. "The Metropolis and Mental Life." *On Individuality and Social Forms*, ed. Donald N. Levine, 324–39. Chicago: University of Chicago Press, 1971.

Simon, Bill, and Lois Mendelson. "*Tom, Tom, the Piper's Son*." *Artforum* 10, no. 1 (1969), 46–52.

Simpson, Christopher. *Science of Coercion: Communication Research and Psychological Warfare 1945–1960*. New York: Oxford University Press, 1994.

Singer, Ben. "New York, Just Like I Pictured It . . ." *Cinema Journal* 35, no. 3 (1996), 104–28.

Sitney, P. Adams. *Eyes Upside Down: Visionary Filmmakers and the Heritage of Emerson*. Oxford: Oxford University Press, 2008.
———. "Letter." *Film Comment* 15, no. 1 (1979), 70.
———. *Modernist Montage: The Obscurity of Vision in Cinema and Literature*. New York: Columbia University Press, 1990.
———. "Structural Film." *Film Culture* 47 (summer 1969), 1–10.
———. *Visionary Film*. New York: Oxford University Press, 1974.
———. *Visionary Film: The American Avant-Garde, 1943–2000*. 3rd edn. New York: Oxford University Press, 2002.

Skinner, B. F. "Teaching Machines." *Classic Writings on Instructional Technology*, ed. Donald P. Ely and Tjeerd Plomp, 211–27. Englewood, Colo.: Libraries Unlimited, 1996.

Sklar, Robert. *Movie-Made America*. New York: Vintage, 1994 [1974].

Slide, Anthony. *Before Video: A History of the Non-Theatrical Film*. Westport: Greenwood, 1992.

Smoodin, Eric. *Regarding Frank Capra: Audience, Celebrity and American Film Studies, 1930–1960*. Durham: Duke University Press, 2004.

Smyth, Rosaleen. "The Development of British Colonial Film Policy, 1927–1939, with Special Reference to East and Central Africa." *Journal of African History* 20, no. 3 (1979), 437–40.

———. "Movies and Mandarins: The Official Film and British Colonial Africa." *British Cinema History*, ed. James Curran and Vincent Porter, 129–43. London: Weidenfeld and Nicholson, 1983.

Snook, Vera. "Getting Pictures for Small Children." *Library Journal* 43, no. 3 (1919), 157–58.

Snow, Michael. "A Statement on *Wavelength* for the Experimental Film Festival of Knokke-le-Zoute." *Film Culture* 46 (autumn 1967), 1.

Sobchack, Vivian, ed. *The Persistence of History: Cinema, Television, and the Modern Event*. New York: Routledge, 1996.

Sontag, Susan. *Illness as Metaphor*. New York: Farrar, Straus and Giroux, 1978.

Space, Kenneth. "Amateur Industrial Films: Suggestions for Making Them Interesting." *Movie Makers*, November 1929, 706–7, 738–39.

Spencer, Steven M. "The Stars Are His Playthings." *Saturday Evening Post*, April 24, 1954, 42–43.

Spigel, Lynn. *Make Room for TV: Television and the Family Idea in Postwar America*. Chicago: University of Chicago Press, 1992.

Stadtlander, Elizabeth L. "Relative Importance of Placement of Motion Pictures in Class-Room Instruction." *Elementary School Journal* 40, no. 4 (1939), 284–90.

Stamp, Shelley. *Movie-Struck Girls: Women and Motion Picture Culture after the Nickelodeon*. Princeton: Princeton University Press, 2000.

Staniszewski, Mary Anne. *The Power of Display: A History of Exhibition Installations at the Museum of Modern Art*. Cambridge: MIT Press, 1998.

Staples, Amy. "Safari Adventure: Forgotten Cinematic Journeys in Africa." *Film History* 18, no. 4 (2006), 392–411.

State of California Education Bulletin, Number 9: Motion Picture Appreciation in the Elementary School. Sacramento: California State Department of Education, 1934.

Steiner, Rudolf. *The Foundations of Human Experience*. Foundations of Waldorf Education, vol. 1. Hudson, N.Y.: Anthroposophic, 1996.

Stephenson, George. *American College of Surgeons at 75*. Chicago: American College of Surgeons, 1994.

———. "Visual Education in Surgery: Contributions of the American College of Surgeons in the Past Fifty Years." *Bulletin of the American College of Surgeons* 61 (May 1976), 8–18.

Stewart, Jacqueline Najuma. *Migrating to the Movies: Cinema and Black Urban Modernity*. Berkeley: University of California Press, 2005.

Stokes, Melvyn, and Richard Maltby, eds. *American Movie Audiences*. London: British Film Institute, 1999.

———. *Hollywood Abroad: Audiences and Cultural Exchange*. London: British Film Institute, 2004.

Stone, Melinda, and Dan Streible, eds. Special issue on "Amateur Cinema." *Film History* 15, no. 2 (2003).

Stones, Barbara. *America Goes to the Movies: 100 Years of Motion Picture Exhibition*. Hollywood: National Association of Theatre Owners, 1993.

Streible, Dan, Marsha Orgeron, and Devin Orgeron, eds. *Learning with the Lights Off: Educational Film in the United States*. Oxford: Oxford University Press, forthcoming.

Susman, Warren. *Culture as History*. New York: Pantheon, 1984.

Tazelaar, Marguerite. "Portrait of a Pioneer." *Amateur Movie Makers*, July 1927, 18–19.

Teaching Film Custodians. "The TFC Story." New York: TFC, 1952.

Thompson, E. P. "Time, Work-Discipline, and Industrial Capitalism." *Past and Present* 38 (1967), 56–97.

Thorburn, David, and Henry Jenkins, eds. *Rethinking Media Change: The Aesthetics of Transition*. Cambridge: MIT Press, 2003.

Thorp, Margaret Farrand. *America at the Movies*. New Haven: Yale University Press, 1939.

Tolischus, O. D. "Seeing Stars: How an Intricate German Machine Reveals the Heavens." *World's Work*, November 1927, 96–100.

Tompkins, Calvin. *Merchants and Masterpieces: The Story of the Metropolitan Museum of Art*. New York: Henry Holt, 1989.

Trumpbour, John. *Selling Hollywood to the World: U.S. and European Struggles for Mastery of the Global Film Industry, 1920–1950*. New York: Cambridge University Press, 2002.

Tuchman, Mitch. "The Mekas Bros. Brakhage and Baillie Traveling Circus." *Film Comment* 14, no. 2 (1978), 9–18.

Ulrikkson, Vidkunn. *The Telegraphers, Their Craft and Their Unions*. Washington: Public Affairs, 1953.

UNESCO. *A Chronology of UNESCO, 1945–1987*. Paris: UNESCO, 1987.

———. *A New World Information and Communication Order: Towards a Wider and Better Balanced Flow of Information*. Paris: UNESCO, 1979–81.

———. *Report of the Commission on Technical Needs: Press, Radio, Film*. Paris: UNESCO, 1948.

———. *Universal Declaration on Cultural Diversity*. Paris: UNESCO, 2001.

———. *World Communications: Press, Radio, Film*. 3rd edn. Paris: UNESCO, 1956.

United Nations, ed. *Planetarium: A Challenge for Educators*. New York: United Nations, 1992.

Van Slyck, Abigail. *Free to All: Carnegie Libraries and American Culture 1890–1920*. Chicago: University of Chicago Press, 1995.

Vasulka, Woody, and Peter Weibel, eds. *Buffalo Heads: Media Study, Media Practice, Media Pioneers 1973–1990*. Cambridge: MIT Press, 2008.

Vygotsky, Lev. *Thought and Language*. Cambridge: MIT Press, 1962.

Waldman, Diane. "'Towards a Harmony of Interests': Rockefeller, the YMCA and the Company Movie Theater." *Wide Angle* 8, no. 1 (1986), 41–51.

Waldman, Diane, and Janet Walker, eds. *Feminism and Documentary*. Minneapolis: University of Minnesota Press, 1999.

Waldron, Gloria. *The Information Film: A Report of the Public Library Inquiry*. New York: Columbia University Press, 1949.

Waller, Gregory A. "Distributing 16mm: The Midwest and Beyond." Paper presented at the Society for Cinema and Media Studies, Chicago, March 2007.

————. "Free Talking Picture: Every Farmer Is Welcome: Non-theatrical Film and Everyday Life in Rural America during the 1930s." *Going to the Movies: Hollywood and the Social Experience of Cinema*, ed. Richard Maltby, Melvyn Stokes, and Robert C. Allen, 248–72. Exeter: University of Exeter Press, 2007.

Wasson, Haidee. "Electric Homes! Automatic Movies! Efficient Entertainment!: Domesticity and the 16mm Projector in the 1920s." *Cinema Journal* 48, no. 4 (2009), 1–21.

————. "Every Home an Art Museum: Towards a Genealogy of the Museum Gift Shop." *Residual Media*, ed. Charles Acland, 301–44. Minneapolis: University of Minnesota Press, 2006.

————. *Museum Movies: The Museum of Modern Art and the Birth of Art Cinema*. Berkeley: University of California Press, 2005.

————. "The Reel of the Month Club: 16mm Projectors, Home Theaters and Film Libraries in the 1920s." *Going to the Movies: Hollywood and the Social Experience of Cinema*, ed. Richard Maltby, Melvyn Stokes, and Robert C. Allen, 217–34. Exeter: University of Exeter Press, 2007.

Way, E. I. "Growth of the Industrial Films." *Congressional Digest*, November 1928, 299–301.

Wheeler, Edward L. *Uplifting the Race: The Black Minister in the New South, 1865–1902*. Lanham, Md.: University Press of America, 1986.

Wheeler, Robyn E. "News for All Americans: History of All-American News, a Series of 45 Newsreels about Blacks Made in the 1940s." *American Visions* 8, no. 1 (1993), 40–41.

Whitehill, Walter Muir. *Boston Public Library: A Centennial History*. Cambridge: Harvard University Press, 1956.

Whiting, Frederic Allen. "Isolation of Museum Objects for Emphasis." *Museum Work* 1, no. 3 (1918), 85–86.

Wiatr, Elizabeth. "Between Word, Image, and the Machine: Visual Education and Films of Industrial Process." *Historical Journal of Film, Radio and Television* 22, no. 3 (2002), 333–51.

Willemen, Paul. "The Third Cinema Question: Notes and Reflections." *Questions of Third Cinema*, ed. Jim Pines and Paul Willemen, 1–29. London: British Film Institute, 1989.

Wilson, Elizabeth. "A Short History of a Border War: Social Science, School Reform, and the Study of Literature." *Poetics Today* 9, no. 4 (1988), 711–35.

Winston, Brian. *Technologies of Seeing: Photography, Cinematography and Television.* London: British Film Institute, 1996.

Winter, Thomas. *Making Men, Making Class: The YMCA and the Workingmen, 1877–1920.* Chicago: University of Chicago Press, 2002.

Winton, Roy. "The Amateur Cinema Camera Man — Before the 1927 Meeting of the National Board of Review of Motion Pictures." *Amateur Movie Makers*, March 1927, 28, 37.

———. "Editorials: A Clear Mission." *Movie Makers*, April 1928, 219.

———. "Twenty Years of the ACL: How an Assignment Has Been Carried Out." *Movie Makers*, August 1946, 300–301, 312, 314.

Witt, Paul W. F. "How Hollywood Serves Education through TFC." *Educational Screen and Audiovisual Guide*, December 1961, 644–47.

Wolfe, Charles. "The Poetics and Politics of Nonfiction: Documentary Film." *Grand Design*, ed. Tino Balio, 351–86. Berkeley: University of California Press, 1995.

Wollen, Peter. "The Two Avant-Gardes." *Studio International* 190, no. 978 (November–December 1975), 171–75.

Zald, Mayer N., and Patricia Denton. "From Evangelism to General Service: The Transformation of the YMCA." *Administrative Science Quarterly* 8, no. 2 (1963), 214–34.

Zimmermann, Patricia R. *Reel Families: A Social History of Amateur Film.* Bloomington: Indiana University Press, 1995.

Zryd, Michael. "The Academy and the Avant-Garde: A Relationship of Dependence and Resistance." *Cinema Journal* 45, no. 2 (2006), 17–42.

———. "Avant-Garde Films: Teaching *Wavelength*." *Cinema Journal* 47, no. 1 (2007), 109–12.

———. "Experimental Film and the Development of Film Study in America." *Inventing Film Studies*, ed. Lee Grieveson and Haidee Wasson, 182–216. Durham: Duke University Press, 2008.

ABOUT THE CONTRIBUTORS

CHARLES R. ACLAND is a professor and Concordia University Research Chair in Communication Studies. His books include *Screen Traffic: Movies, Multiplexes, and Global Culture* and the edited collection *Residual Media*. His newest book on the history of ideas about media manipulation, *Swift Viewing: The Popular Life of Subliminal Influence*, will be published by Duke University Press.

JOSEPH CLARK is the development director at DOXA Documentary Film Festival in Vancouver, British Columbia. In 2011 he graduated with a Ph.D. in American Civilization from Brown University. His dissertation, "Canned History: The American Newsreel and the Commodification of Reality, 1927–1950," examines the history of the sound newsreel — its modes of production, distribution, exhibition, and representation.

ZOË DRUICK is an associate professor in the School of Communication at Simon Fraser University. She has written widely on educational and media history. Her book *Projecting Canada: Government Policy and Documentary Film at the National Film Board* was published in 2007.

RONALD WALTER GREENE is an associate professor in the Department of Communication Studies at the University of Minnesota. His publications include the monograph *Malthusian Worlds: U.S.*

Leadership and the Governing of the Population Crisis (1999). He is currently researching the YMCA Motion Picture Bureau.

ALISON GRIFFITHS is a professor in the Department of Communication Studies at Baruch College, City University of New York. Her research has appeared in such journals as *Cinema Journal*, *Screen*, and *Film History*, and she was the recipient of numerous awards for her monograph *Wondrous Difference: Cinema, Anthropology and Turn of the Century Visual Culture* (2002).

STEPHEN GROENING is an assistant professor of film and media studies at George Mason University. He has published articles on the connections between media, mobility, and transportation in *Velvet Light Trap*, *New Media and Society*, and *Visual Studies*. His current book project, *Cinema beyond Territory*, traces the linked histories of in-flight entertainment, globalization, and transnational Hollywood.

JENNIFER HORNE is an assistant professor of media studies at the Catholic University of America in Washington. Her publications have appeared in *Afterimage*, the *Moving Image*, and the *Historical Journal of Film, Radio and Television*. She is currently writing a book about the history of motion picture use by social reformers, educators, cultural institutions, and civic associations.

KIRSTEN OSTHERR is an associate professor in the Department of English at Rice University. She is the author of *Cinematic Prophylaxis: Globalization and Contagion in the Discourse of World Health*.

ERIC SMOODIN is a professor of American studies at the University of California, Davis. His most recent book is *Regarding Frank Capra: Audience, Celebrity and American Film Studies, 1930–1960*. He has published widely in the field of American film history, and his current research project involves the study of motion pictures in a variety of educational settings from 1920 to 1960.

CHARLES TEPPERMAN is an assistant professor of film studies in the Faculty of Communication and Culture at the University of Calgary. He received his Ph.D. from the University of Chicago and has published in such journals as *Film History* and the *Canadian Journal of Film Studies*. His dissertation won the Katherine Singer Kovacs Award, granted by the Society for Cinema and Media Studies, in 2008. His book on the history of amateur film will be published by the University of California Press.

GREGORY A. WALLER is a professor in the Department of Communication and Culture at Indiana University. He has published widely on rural and regional film exhibition, including his works *Main Street Amusements: Movies and Commercial Entertainment in a Southern City, 1896–1930* and *Moviegoing in America: A Sourcebook in the History of Film Exhibition*.

HAIDEE WASSON is an associate professor in the Mel Hoppenheim School of Cinema at Concordia University. Her book *Museum Movies: The Museum of Modern Art and the Birth of Art Cinema* was named an "outstanding academic title" by the American Library

Association. She is a co-editor of *Inventing Film Studies* and is currently writing a history of portable film projectors.

MICHAEL ZRYD is an associate professor in the Department of Film at York University. He has published various articles on the avant-garde and the academy, and he is currently writing *Exploring the Infinite Cinema: Hollis Frampton and the Magellan Cycle*.

INDEX

Page numbers in *italics* refer to illustrations.

Abel, Richard, 39, 176 nn. 37–38

Accuracy First, 34, 49–50

Acland, Charles, 8, 212, 213

Addams, Jane, 300; "Civic Housekeeping," 48; *Spirit of Youth and the City Streets, The*, 20

Adler, Mortimer, 60

Adler Planetarium, 230–31, 250, 253, 254, 256 n. 23

Advisory Commission on Information, 76

Advisory Committee on the Use of Motion Pictures in Education, 66–69. *See also* Teaching Film Custodians

African Americans: achievements of, 265, 278–80, 285; as actors, 264, 267, 269, 270; All-American News and, 11–12, 263–64, 273, 275, 283–84; as audience, 264, 267, 269, 273, 275, 283–84; commercial news-reels and, 270–72, 273, 276, 278, 280; as filmmakers, 264, 268–69; Hollywood and, 263, 269; movie theaters and, 268; portrayal in films of, 269; respectability and, 266, 276–77, 278, 281, 285; self-surveillance by, 276, 281; social classes and, 266, 277; visibility of, 275, 281, 284; white perceptions of, 277–78; World War II and, 263, 265, 266, 269–73, 274, 280–82. *See also* racial uplift

Akeley Camera company, 199 n. 8

Albright, Roger, 72

Alexander, William, 264

Alibi Racket, 24

Alice Adams, 66

Alice in Wonderland, 29

All-American Newsreel, 11–12, 263; African Americans in World War II and, 271–72, 280–82; audiences for, 264–65, 275, 282–84; on black achievement, 278–80; black movie theater circuit and, 264–65; commercial newsreels vs., 274–75; didacticism of, 276; educational function of, 264, 265; on good conduct, 276–78; opening title sequence of, 274–76; postwar, 284–85; racial uplift and, 264, 266, 267, 274; racism and, 264, 282, 284; segregation and, 264, 267–68, 272–73, 282, 285; television and, 265

All Quiet on the Western Front, 20

Altman, Rick, 5–6

amateur cinema, 12; amateur exhibition equipment and, 293; as creative encounter with modernity, 290, 291, 292; educational, 290, 291–92, 292–96; expansion of, 291; Great Depression and, 291, 304; as home movies, 310 n. 6; industrial, 290, 291–92, 296–300; industrial processes in, 294; as leisure activity, 309; personalized movies and, 293; practical artist and, 295–96; practical films and, 291; religion and, 291–92, 305–8; 16mm, 125, 292; of social problems, 291–92, 300–304; World War II and, 291, 309

Amateur Cinema League (ACL), 12, 290–92, 296–97; "Ten Best Amateur Films," 293, 300, 309; "Ten Best Non-Theatrical Films," 300, 305

Ament, Walton, 272

America at the Movies (Thorp), 166

American College of Surgeons (ACS), 104; Committee on Approval and Development of Motion Picture Films, 105, 107; Committee on Medical Motion Pictures, 117–18; Committees on Video-Based Education and Informatics, 117; Division of

Education, 117–18; E-Learning Resource Center, 118; film program, 116–17; "Films for the Laity," 108–9; "Foreign Distribution of Approved Medical Motion Picture Films," 107; "Guiding Principles in Evaluating Medical Motion Picture Films," 106; medical films, 105–10; "Medical Modeling and Simulation Database," 118; Medical Motion Picture Committee, 109; "Medical Motion Picture Films," 107–8, 110; Motion Picture Program, 105; MPPDA and, 119 n. 5

American Council on Education (ACE), 61, 67; Commission on Motion Pictures, 72–73

American Film Center (AFC), 67, 71

American Library Annual, 167–68

American Library Association (ALA), 152, 155, 162; Committee on Relations Between Libraries and Moving Pictures, 172–73

American Museum of Natural History (AMNH), 234

American Projectoscope, 127

American Wing, The (Metropolitan Museum of Art), 192, 194–95, 200 n. 10

Americans, The (Münsterberg), 150

Ampro, 132, 133–34, 138, 139–40, 143–44, 223

Amprosound projectors, 139, 143

Anderson, Mark Lynn, 64

Anger, Kenneth, 319, 320

Animatographs, 143

Animatophone projectors, 135, 138, 143, 144

Another to Conquer, 109

anti-censorship movement, 22, 32 n. 14, 168–70

Apollo 11, 245

Appleton's Journal of Literature, Science and Art, 149–50

Are We Movie Made? (Morley), 60

Armes, Roy, 90

Army Overseas Motion Picture Service, 137

Arnold, Matthew, 150

Art and Prudence (Adler), 60

Artforum, 320

Arthur, Billy, 239

Aseptic Resection of Stomach for Carcinoma and Ulcer, 109
Associated Negro Press, 264
Association Films, Inc., 207
Association Men (YMCA), 206, 220
Association of School Film Libraries, 67
Association Seminar, 210
astronomy, 247
atmospheriums, 259 n. 75
atomic bombs, 112, *113*, 246
Atwood, Wallace, 233
audiences: of ACS medical films, 108; African American, 264, 267, 269, 273, 275, 283–84; of All-American Newsreel, 264–65, 267, 275, 282–84; captive, 36; children and, 38–39; cultural authority and, 213, 214; films in museums and, 196; Hollywood and, 38–39; of medical films, 116; Metropolitan Museum of Art films and, 183; of non-theatrical cinema, 209–10; of pastoral exhibitions, 208; pastoral relationships and, 211–12; at planetariums, 238, 251; for postwar educational films, 104; of race movies, 264–65; segregation of, 268; silent vs. sound movies and, 219; training films and, 36, 43; women and, 38–39. *See also* spectatorship
Audio Productions, Inc., 111
Augst, Thomas, 151
avant-garde cinema, 12–13; defined, 333 n. 8. *See also* experimental cinema

Babel and Babylon (Hansen), 42
Babes in Tomorrowland (Sammond), 60
↔ . . . *Back and Forth*, 320
Barnett, Claude, 264, 265, 275, 284
Barrell, Charles, 221
Barrett, Wilton, 221
Bataan, 270
Bauersfeld, Walther, 234
Bauhaus, 187
Bausch and Lomb, 299, 300
Bayer, Herbert, 185
Bazin, André, 320

Beatty, J. Kelly, 253
Beckett, Samuel, 320
"Behavior of the Museum Visitor, The" (Robinson), 188, 190
Behind the Scenes at the Museum, 195
Bell and Howell: Filmo projector, 130, *131*; Filmosound projector, 138; projectors, 129, 138, 142–43, 144, 223
Benjamin, Walter, 55–56 n. 14
Bennett, Tony, 3, 183
Bernays, Edward, 245
Billboard, 136
Binghamton cinema program, 327
Bishop, J. E., 238–39
Black Legion, 66
black movie theaters, 268
Bleu Shut, 324
block-booking, 27, 209
Bloomer, Kenneth, 293
Blount, Clifford, 279
Bobinski, George, 153
Body Care and Grooming, 111
Body Defenses against Disease, 108
Body Fights Bacteria, The, 9, 105, 107, 111–16, 117, 118
Boîte-en-Valise, La (Duchamp), 187
Borges, Jorge Luis, 330
Boston Public Library, 149–50
Bostwick, Arthur E., 155
Brakhage, Stan, 319, 320, 321, 327; *Metaphors on Vision*, 322–23
Branley, Franklyn, 245
Breckinridge, Marvin, 301–4
Breckinridge, Mary, 301
Britain: colonial film, 83, 90, 92; documentary film tradition in, 95, 97; UNESCO and, 83, 84
Building a Bakery, 297–99
Bureau of Motion Pictures, 137
Burns, J. M., 90, 92
Bush, W. Stephen, 38
Business Screen, 132, 133
"Butterbeans and Susie," 283
By-Line Newsreel, 264

Caldwell, Gladys, 173
California Education Department, 28–30
California State Library, 167–68
Calkins, Dick, 244
Canadian Filmmakers Distribution Centre, 316
Canyon Cinema, 316
Capra, Frank, 335 n. 38
Carlton, Newcomb, 37
Carroll, T. W., 58 n. 41
Cartwright, Lisa, 109
Casablanca, 270
Caste and Class in a Southern Town (Dollard), 63
Castle Films, 136
"Cavalcade of America," 75
Centers for Disease Control and Prevention, 118
Century of Progress International Exposition, 126
Ceramics, 293–94, 295–96
Chamberlain, Joseph Miles, 251
Chaplin, Charlie, 300
character education, 62–64, 65, 75–76
Charles Hayden Planetarium (Boston), 242; "Countdown to Supernova," 253
Charters, W. W., 59
Chicago, 126
children: as captive audience, 36; film education and, 20; in libraries, 156–58, *160,* 161, 162–64; matinees and, 163–64, 169; motion pictures and, 60, 62–63; movie theaters and, 38–39, 163; Payne Fund Studies and, 20, 60–61, 215; in planetariums, 247–49; progressivism and, 27–28; spectatorship and, 162–64
Children and the Movies (Jowett; Jarvie; Fuller), 60–61
China, 82
Choose to Live, 108
Christian, Marcus Bruce, 278–79
Christian, Ruth, 278–79
Christian Citizenship (YMCA), 215
Chronicles of America Photoplays, The, 199 n. 3

cinema: education and, 18; film vs., 158–59; modernity and, 19; museums and, 183, 190–91; planetariums and, 11, 231, 234, 236, 237, 238, 245–46, 249–54; public libraries and, 174; segregation and, 267; sun and, 234; usefulness of, 2–4, 6–7, 318–19, 330–31, 332
"Cinema as Art, The" (MOMA), 24
"Cinema in the Sky" series, 251
City of Wax, 70
Civilian Conservation Corps (CCC), 126
Clark, Joseph, 11–12
Clement, Ina, 171–72
Cleveland Public Library, 159, *160,* 161–62, 166, *168*
Cloud in the Sky, 109
Cocks, Orrin G., 169–70, 171
cold war, 81; culture and, 110; "domination" model of communication and, 88; planetariums and, 231–32, 245–46; UNESCO and, 86–87
Cold War, Cool Medium (Doherty), 246
Coles, Robert R., 244
Colleges at War, 270
colonialism, decolonization: film and, 82; films resisting, 96–97; literacy and, 90, 92; UN resolution on decolonization, 97; UNESCO and, 97
Columbia Pictures, 219
commercial cinema: experimental film and, 318; museums and, 203 n. 40; non-theatrical, 290–91; non-theatrical cinema vs., 2, 13; progressivism and, 300–301; understanding of American life and, 289. *See also* Hollywood
Commercial Telegrapher's Union, 56 n. 16
Commission on Human Relations, 65–66, 71
Commission on Motion Pictures, 72–73
Commission Permanente Interafricaine du cinéma, 97
Committee on Social Values in Motion Pictures, 65, 67
communication studies, 81, 86–87

Conquest Pictures series, 163
Copernicus, 232, 254 n. 2
"Countdown to Supernova," 253
Counts, George, 19
Cressey, Paul, 59
"Crime Doesn't Pay" series, 70
Criminal Code, The, 20
Cripps, Thomas, 269, 282–83
Crisis, 271
culture: cinema and, 8; cold war and, 110;
    national, 82, 84–85; politics and, 96–97;
    usefulness of, 3

Dale, Edgar, 21, 22, 59, 62; How to Appreciate
    Motion Pictures, 23, 26, 215
Dana, John Cotton, 164–65, 175 n. 32
Dangling Participle, 324
Day, Edmund E., 72
deCordova, Richard, 164, 169
Defense against Invasion, 108
democracy: literacy and, 87–89; public
    libraries and, 151
Department of Audio-Visual Instruction
    (DAVI), 74–75
Deren, Maya, 320, 321
de Sica, Vittorio, 95–96
DeVry, 138, 217; Challenger projector, 134,
    223; 16mm projector, 132; 35mm projec-
    tor, 127–29
DeVry, H. A., 221
Dewey, John, 19, 20, 61, 290, 304, 308–9, 323
Diagnostic Procedures in Tuberculosis, 109
Diehl, Harold S., 111–12
Diseases of the Heart and Circulatory System,
    111
Disney, Walt, 30
Disney company, 246
distribution: films in public libraries and,
    170, 173; of films to schools, 69–70, 71–72
documentary films, 304; British, 95, 97;
    UNESCO and, 86
Dodge, H. E., 210
Doherty, Thomas, 270; Cold War, Cool
    Medium, 246

Dollard, John, 64; Caste and Class in a South-
    ern Town, 63
Dorris, Anna Verona, 146 n. 15
Dots and Dashes, 42, 51
double bills, 27, 229 n. 65
Double Victory campaign, 265, 266, 269, 271,
    275, 280
Drifters, 293
Druick, Zoë, 8–9
Du Bois, W. E. B., 276
Duchamp, Marcel, 187
Dudgeon, Matthew S., 158–59
Due Process of the Law Denied, 72

Earl, Edward P., 209
Eastman, 69; Teaching Films, Inc., 107
Eastman, George, 9, 105
Edgewater (N.J.) public library, 166
Edison, Thomas, 292; Vitascope, 154
Edison studios, 163
education: All-American News and, 265;
    anti-utilitarian, 327; cinema and, 18, 82,
    210, 292; civic, 150; constructivist ap-
    proaches to, 323–24; cultural artifacts of
    leisure and, 23; experiential, 318, 319, 323,
    325, 332; film industry and, 64; Hollywood
    and, 62, 71; mass, 21; motion pictures and,
    18–19, 67–75; MPPDA and, 64, 65; pastoral
    power and, 207, 211; programmed instruc-
    tion and, 323–25; reform of, 61; religious,
    210, 211, 212; screen, 75, 76; theory of,
    323–24; UNESCO and, 82; YMCA Motion
    Picture Bureau and, 210. See also film edu-
    cation
educational films, 35–36; amateur, 290,
    291–92, 292–96; audience for, 104; captive
    audience and, 36; classification system
    for, 170–71; criteria for quality of, 294–95;
    exhibition sites of, 18, 104; feature films
    vs., 103–4; film industry and, 66, 67; free
    flow of, 92; Hollywood and, 67–69; inter-
    changeability of, 118; literacy and, 89–90;
    politics of, 9; in public libraries, 156–57,
    170; reading and, 88–89; screening loca-

educational films (*continued*)

tions for, 103–4; 16mm, 36, 125, 292; 16mm vs. 35mm, 107; sound vs. silent, 218–19; spectatorship and, 9; UNESCO and, 86, 94; World War II and, 111, 115, 323. *See also* film education; short films; training films

"Educational Possibilities of Motion Pictures" (May), 18–19

Educational Screen, 18, 36, 43, 293; on films for military use, 136; on schools changing from 35mm to 16mm, 126; on school vs. church, 22; screening sites and, 133; on 16mm film during World War II, 137; 16mm projectors advertised in, 131, 132, 138, 140; 35mm projectors advertised in, 127–28; *Visual Education* merger with, 35

Education in a World of Fear (May), 76

efficiency, in workplace: labor-management relations and, 37–38; mechanization and, 53; self-regulation and, 41

8mm film, 127, 309

Eisenstein, Sarah, 43

Elementary School Journal, 18

Elliot, Huger, 192, 203 n. 40

Ells, Fred C., 305–8

Elton, Arthur, 94

Emirbayer, Mustafa, 19

Emotional Health, 111

Enemy X, 111

English, Flournoy, 278, 279

English Journal, 18

ERPI, 69, 70

ethnographic films, 93

Exceptional Photoplay, 169

Executive Interview, The, 72

exhibition sites: of educational films, 18, 104; schools as, 208–9; types of, 2. *See also* movie theaters; non-theatrical exhibition sites

experiential education, 318, 319, 323, 325, 332

experimental cinema: American visionary tradition and, 321; avant-garde forms of modernism and, 321; cinematic protocols and, 318; in colleges and universities,

12–13, 316–17; distributors of, 316; early film and, 328; experimental pedagogy and, 318; narrative and, 328; new ways of seeing and, 321–23; pedagogical cinema and, 318; post-screening discussions and, 317–18; programmed instruction and, 324–25; spectatorship and, 317; structural films vs., 319; transformative, 321, 326, 332; usefulness of, 4

Eyes for Tomorrow, 108

Eyes of Science, The, 299–300

Ezra, Elizabeth, 244

Fables of Abundance (Lears), 298

Fair Play, 157

Fall of the House of Usher, 299

Famous Players–Lasky Corporation, 209

Fear and Trembling (Kierkegaard), 239

feature films: educational films vs., 103–4; excerpting of, 65, 66, 71–72, 222; films for schools and, 71–72; Hollywood-centered, 208; World War II and, 136–37. *See also* motion pictures

Fein, Seth, 109

Fels, Samuel, 239, 243

Fels Planetarium, 239, 244, 252, 256 n. 23

Ferguson, Ida May, 163

Fieseler, Franz, 242

Fight Syphilis, 109, 111

film: cinema vs., 158–59; as didactic medium, 39–40, 181; educational uses, 75, 82; genres, 2, 5, 170–71; political use of, 96–97; social reality and, 53; teaching role of, 65; as teaching tools, 35–36; in underdeveloped regions, 83; war imagery in, 111–14

Film Daily, 69

film education: block-booking and, 27; clubs in schools, 26–28; Depression and, 31; double bills and, 27; in elementary school, 28–30; film industry and, 23, 31; film production in, 30; free dramatic expression in, 30; image of child and, 20; improved film consumption and, 24–26; intermedia and, 24; language and, 328–30; leisure

and, 31; literature on, 18–19; mass education and, 21; motion picture councils, 23,
24, 26; movie theaters and, 27; in New
Haven, 22–28; personality and, 327–28;
progressivism and, 19–20; quality of consumer choice and, 22, 28, 29; in schools,
7; school-theater relationship and, 26;
skills teaching and, 327; structural film
and, 320–21; symposia and, 24; TFC and,
75; YMCA and, 215–16. *See also* educational
films; short films
"Film in Colonial Development, The" (conference), 94
film industry: anti-censorship and, 32 n. 14;
education and, 64; educational film and,
66, 67; film education and, 23, 31; public
libraries and, 169–70; TFC and, 75. *See also*
Hollywood
Film-Makers' Cooperative, 316
Filmo projectors, 130, *131*
Filmosound projector, 138
Films for Classroom Use (TFC), 70
Films on Art (UNESCO), 93, 95
Films That Work (Hediger andVonderau), 3
film studies, 5–6, 18, 20–21, 31, 319, 320–21
Film World, 137, 138, 144
Finnegans Wake (Joyce), 328
Fisher, Clyde, 235
Ford Foundation, 96; UNESCO and, 83
Ford Motor Company, 35
Fordism, 206
Forgotten Frontier, The, 301–4
Forman, Henry James, 59, 61; *Our Movie
Made Children*, 60, 215
Foucault, Michel, 3, 207, 225
Four Theories of the Press (Schramm), 87
Frampton, Hollis, 318, 321, 325, 328–31
Freeman, Marilla, 175 n. 32
Freire, Paulo, 323
French Colonial Documentary (Bloom), 3
Frendreis, Pat, 253
Freud, Sigmund, 64
Frick Museum, 202 n. 32
Friedberg, Anna, 5–6, 181–82

Fuller, Kathryn, 62; *Children and the Movies*,
60–61
Fury, 66

Gaines, Jane, 276, 278
Gaines, Kevin, 266
Gale, Arthur, 296, 297, 301
Gaudreault, André, 328
Gaumont-British, 69
Gehr, Ernie, 320, 328
gender: film studies and, 28; globes and,
254–55 n. 2; museum fatigue and, 203
n. 34; planetarium staffing and, 256 n. 23;
portable projector and, 132; projectors
and, 129; Western Union and, 7
German Ideology, The (Marx), 43
Gessner, Robert, 21
Gibson, Mel, 240
Gilbert, Cass, 155
Gilman, Charlotte Perkins, 172
Glander, Timothy, 87
Glucksman, Emmanuel, 264, 265, 275, 284
Golden Laurel awards, 95–96
Goldfarb, Brian, 109
Gramsci, Antonio, 205–6
Great Depression: amateur filmmaking and,
291, 304; film education and, 31; motion
pictures and, 18; planetariums and, 243
Greene, Ronald, 10–11, 115
Gregg, Able, 215
Gregg, Bishop, 276–77
Grierson, John, 94, 95, 304; *Drifters*, 293, 294
Grieveson, Lee, 5–6, 152, 210
Griffith, D. W., 29–30
Griffiths, Alison, 11, 180
Groening, Stephen, 7–8
Guggenheim, Peggy, 185–86
Gumming, 34, 40, 48–49
Gunning, Tom, 5–6, 234, 328
Gutlohn, 69

Hall, G. Stanley, 19, 20
Hallelujah!, 269
Hannay, Alistair, 239

Hansen, Miriam, 156; *Babel and Babylon*, 42

Harner, Guy, 223

Harris, Neil, 183–84

Harrison, Dent, 297–99

Hartshorne, Hugh, 62

Harvesting and Baking, 297–99

Hay, James, 208

Hayden, Charles, 239

Hayden Planetarium (New York), 235, 239; children in, 247–49; Christmas show at, *241*; moon travel in, 244–45; moving images at, 253; "Passport to the Universe," 252, 253; sister galleries and, 251; as spacecraft, 242; stargazing program at, 258 n. 64; time travel and, 240–41, 244–45; women employed at, 256 n. 23; Zeiss projector at, 234, 242

Hays, Will, 9, 64, 66, 68, 70, 105

Haze, Joseph, 71

health films, 9; medical films, 105–10, 310 n. 11; propaganda and, 103; replacement of, 118

Health Is a Victory, 111

Heart and Circulation, 108

Hearts in Dixie, 269

Hediger, Vincent, 3

Help Wanted, 109

Hernioplasty for Direct Inguinal Hernia, 109

Higginbotham, Evelyn Brooks, 266, 277

High Cost of Loving, The, 72

Hiroshima, 112, *113*, 114

Hode, Hal, 24

Hollan, George, 284

Hollywood: African Americans and, 263, 267, 269; audience and, 38–39; classical cinema and, 4, 208, 209; education and, 62, 67–69, 71; non-theatrical cinema viewed by, 219; studies of films and, 18; World War II and, 269. *See also* commercial cinema; film industry

Hollywood Writers' War Board, 270–71

Home Movies, 138, 140, *141*, 142–43

Hopkins, Albert A., 244

Hormones and the Endocrine Glands, 111

Horne, Jennifer, 9–10

How to Appreciate Motion Pictures (Dale), 23, 26, 215

Human Relations project, 64, 65–66, 67, 68, 71

Human Reproduction, 111

Hunter, Ian, 211, 212

hydrogen bombs, 246

illiteracy and literacy: free flow of information and, 86–87; media and, 90, 92; UNESCO and, 82; visual media and, 89–90

IMAX, 231, 248, 251, 252

Imhoff, Harriet, 157

India, 86

Indiana University, 137

industrial films, 290, 291–92, 294, 296–300

Ingalls, Albert G., 250

installations, 185–87

Institute of Human Relations, 73

Institutional Quality, 324

instructional films. *See* educational films

Instructional Films, Inc., 69

intermedia: exhibition sites and, 2; film education and, 24; planetariums and, 11, 231, 252–53

In the Beginning, 305–8

Ivens, Joris, 306

Ivins, Clinton, 221

Jacobs, Ken, 318, 325–28, 331

Jacobs, Lea, 215

James, Arthur, 209

James, David, 321, 328–29

Japan, 86

Jarvie, Ian, 62; *Children and the Movies*, 60–61

Johnston, Eric, 72, 73, 74

Journal of Educational Sociology, 18

Journal of Negro Education, 267

Jowett, Garth, 62; *Children and the Movies*, 60–61

Joyce, James, 328

Kaempffert, Waldemar, 240–41, 242

Keliher, Alice, 66, 71

Kelly, William R., 209

Kentucky Nursing Service, 301–4

Keyboard Errors, 34, 40, 50

Kierkegaard, Søren, 239

Kiesler, Frederick, 185–86

King, Henry Charles, 236, 237, 250–51, 258 n. 68

Klee, Paul, 186

Kleine, George, 163

Know for Sure, 109

Kodak, 127

Konenkamp, Sylvester, 57–58 n. 41

Korda, Alexander, 95–96

Koszarski, Richard, 38

Lake Okoboji Leadership Conferences, 74–75

Land, Owen, 319, 324–25

Lant, Antonia, 176–77, 234

Latin America, 108–10

Lawder, Standish, 324

Lazarsfeld, Paul, 59

League of Nations Intellectual Cooperation Committee, 83

Learning from Films (Motion Picture Research Project), 73

Lears, Jackson, 298

Legion of Decency, 60

leisure: amateur cinema and, 309; education and cultural artifacts of, 23; film education and, 28, 31; modernity and, 22; as moral education, 9; public libraries and, 155–56; schools and, 22

Lerner, Daniel, 96; *Passing of Traditional Society, The*, 89

Lerner, Fred, 157

LeSourd, Howard, 65

"Let's Make a Movie" (USDA Visual Information Section), 107

libraries: civic education and, 150; qualities of, 150–51; social mixing in, 149–50. *See also* public libraries

Library Journal, 157, 163, 165, 169, 171

Library of Congress, National Film Registry, 301

library profession: film in libraries and, 157, 159, 164–65; motion pictures and, 172; movie theaters and, 165; MPPDA and, 173; professional autonomy in, 159

Lindsay, Vachel, 234

Lindvall, Terry, 210

Lippmann, Walter, 304

Lissitzky, El, 185

literacy, illiteracy: colonialism, neocolonialism, and, 90, 92; free flow of information and, 86–87; media and, 90, 92; UNESCO and, 82; visual media and, 89–90

Lockwood, Marian, 250

Lot in Sodom, 299

Louis, Joe, 279

MacCann, Richard Dyer, 115, 135

MacDonald, Scott, 318

Macy's, 18

Madison Free Library, 157–58, 161

Magic: Stage Illusions and Scientific Diversions (Hopkins), 244

Maid of Salem, 28

Maller, Julius B., 62

Maltby, Richard, 152

"Man in Space" (TV program), 246

Manpower, 270

Marché, Jordan D., II, 239, 240, 243–44, 246, 249–50

Marine Circus, 70

Marshall, John, 60, 66, 71

Marx, Karl, 43

Maslow, Abraham, 239

Mass Communication series (UNESCO), 93

Massey, Vincent, 94–95

mass media: literacy and, 88–89; UNESCO and, 90; World War II and, 81

Mass Media and National Development (UNESCO), 87

matinees, 163–64, 169

Maxim, Hiram Pervy, 290

May, Mark A., 8: Advisory Committee on the Use of Motion Pictures in Education and, 66–67; character education and,

May, Mark A. (*continued*)
  62–64, 75; Commission on Motion Pictures and, 72–73; contribution of, 76–77;
  "Educational Possibilities of Motion Pic-
  tures," 18–19; *Education in a World of Fear*,
  76; films in education and, 73–74; on "life
  studies" and film, 69; Motion Picture
  Research Project and, 73; MPPDA and,
  64–65, 66; *Social Conduct and Attitudes of
  Movie Fans, The*, 63; *Studies in the Nature of
  Character*, 62–63; TFC and, 69, 72, 74, 76;
  U.S. Advisory Commission on Informa-
  tion and, 76; Yale University Institute of
  Human Relations and, 63–64
Mayer, Arthur, 73
McCarthy, Anna, 198
McClusky, Frederick Dean, 36
McGraw-Hill Text-Films, 111
McLaren, Norman, 94
McLean, Ross, 84, 94–96
McLenna, Ian C., 236
McLuhan, Marshall, 325
McMillan, G. N., 221
*Mechanical Call Distribution System for Re-
  ceiving Telegrams by Telephone from Patrons
  of the Western Union*, 34
*Mechanism of the Heart Beat and Electrocardi-
  ography*, 109
media: indigenous, 82; literacy and, 90, 92;
  UNESCO and, 82; varied, 2, 11, 24, 231,
  252–53. *See also* film; television
medical films, 105–10, 310 n. 11; health films,
  9, 103, 118
"Medical Modeling and Simulation Data-
  base" (ACS), 118
"Medical Motion Picture Films" (ACS),
  107–8, 110
Meet John Doe, 335 n. 38
Mekas, Jonas, 319
Méliès, Georges, 244
Metaphors on Vision (Brakhage), 322–23
Metropolitan Museum of Art: American
  Wing, 192, 194–95, 200 n. 10; architec-

ture of, 178; attendance at, 184; *Behind
  the Scenes at the Museum*, 195; collection
  of, 178; Committee on Cinema, 198 n. 3;
  educational extensions program of, 200
  n. 18; Education Department, 183; expedition films at, 199–200 n. 10; film and, 179;
  film and institutional goals of, 182–83; film
  at, 10, 191–96; Great Hall, *182*; Lecture
  Hall, 179, *189*; media used by, 184; Moving
  Picture Projection Room, *186*; new technologies and, 179–80; projector at, 179–80;
  screens in, 181–82, 196; subjects of movies
  made by, 180; tours of collections and
  wings, 180; as universal survey museum,
  178; uses of cinema, 180–81; *Vasantasena*,
  203 n. 39; *Visit to the Armor Galleries of the
  Metropolitan Museum of Art*, 193–94
MGM, 70
Micheaux, Oscar, 268–69
Miezis, Ianis Arnoldovich, 252
Milam, Carl H., 172–73
Miller, Marion, 196
Milliken, Carl, 71
Milliken, Christie, 324
Milwaukee, South Side Library, 166
Minneapolis Public Library, 163
Modern Language Association, 75
modernity: amateur cinema and, 290, 291,
  292; cinema and, 19; leisure and, 22; media
  and, 89; motion pictures and, 289–90
modernization: literacy and, 88; of pastoral
  relationships, 207, 208, 213, 214, 218, 225–
  26; public libraries and, 154; of schools, 7;
  UNESCO and, 8, 82, 90, 99; visual media
  and, 90, 92
Moholy-Nagy, László, 185; "Room of Our
  Time, The," 201 n. 25
Montessori, Maria, 323
moon landings, 244–49
Morley, Raymond, 60
Morton, Mary, 270
motion, movement: meaning and, 187; museums and, 10, 183–87, 188, 190, 194

Motion Picture and the Family, The, 21

Motion Picture Appreciation in the Elementary School (California Education Department), 28–31

Motion Picture Association of America (MPAA), 72–73

Motion Picture Board of Trade, 125

Motion Picture Chamber of Commerce, 209

motion picture councils, 23, 24, 26

Motion Picture Herald, 125, 268

Motion Picture Producers and Distributors Association of America (MPPDA), 66, 152; ACS and, 119 n. 5; American Library Association and, 162, 172; Committee on Social Values in Motion Pictures, 65, 67; Division of Educational Services, 72; education and, 64, 65; Human Relations film project and, 65–66, 67; library profession and, 172, 173; May and, 64–65, 66; as Motion Picture Association of America (MPAA), 72; Motion Picture Chamber of Commerce and, 209; New Haven project and, 23; public libraries and, 169; Studio Relations Committee, 152; TFC and, 69, 71, 72

Motion Picture Production Code, 22

Motion Picture Research Project, 73

motion pictures: books vs., 158, 161, 164–65, 166; children and, 60, 62–63; "civic," 171; as collective commodity, 171–72; community education and, 171–72; education and, 18–19, 67–75; equal rights and, 265; functions of, 2; Great Depression and, 18; national betterment and, 107; public libraries and, 152–53, 157–74; technology, culture, and creative insight joined by, 289; World War II and, 107, 135, 136–37. *See also* feature films; short films

Motion Pictures Available and Suitable for Use Abroad (State Department), 95

Motion Picture Theatre Owners of America, 209

Mount Kisko Cinémats, 293

Movie Makers, 290, 291, 292–93, 294, 296, 300, 304; "Motion Pictures and the Minister," 305

Movie Supply Co., 145–46 n. 11

movie theaters: African-American, 264–65; children and, 163–64; educational spaces and, 23–24, 36; expansion of, 154; film education and, 27; library profession and, 165; New Haven project and, 23; non-theatrical cinema and, 209; progressivism and, 154; public libraries and, 153, 154, 156; schools and, 23, 26; segregation of, 268; social interactions within, 42

Moviemaker, 218

Moving Picture World, 38

Mullen, Sarah McLean, 21

Münsterberg, Hugo, 150

Museum of Modern Art (MOMA), 20, 21, 191; "Cinema as Art, The," 24

museums: cinema and, 183, 190–91; commercial cinema and, 203 n. 40; density of visual field at, 194; dispersed, 184; exhibitions of paintings in, 191; "fatigue," 190–91, 195; film and, 10, 180, 187, 194, 196; IMAX in, 251; motion and, 183–87, 194; other attractions vs., 183–84; planetariums in, 251; scale and, 187, 197–98; visitors' movement through, 10, 188, 190, 194

NAACP: African American representation on film and, 267, 269; civil rights discourse and, 279; integration in Hollywood films and, 270; motion pictures and equal rights linked by, 265; race harmony for victory and, 269; race movies and, 273; white acknowledgment of African American sacrifices and, 273; whitewashing of newsreel footage and, 271, 272

National Board of Censorship, 152, 169, 170

National Board of Review (NBR), 32 n. 14, 152, 162, 168–69, 170

National Board of Review Magazine, 169, 218

National Committee for Better Films, 169, 170–71

National Council of Teachers of English, 23

National Education Association (NEA), 64, 69; Department of Visual Education, 310 n. 13

National Film Board of Canada (NFB), 94, 95, 96; "Notes on a Triangle," 251–52

National Museum of Natural History, 251

National University Extension Association, 70

Neale, Steve, 222

"Negro America" series, 286 n. 7

Negro Colleges in War Time, 270

Negro Soldier, The, 270

Nelson, Robert, 324

New Haven, Conn., 22–28

New Institutional Quality (Land), 324

New World Information and Communication Order (UNESCO), 84

New York University (NYU), 20, 21

nickelodeons, 156

9.5mm film, 127

Non-Aligned Movement, 97

non-theatrical cinema: audiences of, 209–10; commercial, 290–91; commercial cinema vs., 2, 13; exhibition sites for, 209; Hollywood reaction to, 219; movie theaters and, 209; silent films and, 224; 16mm film and, 126, 219–24; YMCA and, 206–7, 209–10

non-theatrical exhibition sites, 209; amateur educational films and, 293; Ampro and, 133–34; 16mm film and, 126, 133

Nose, Throat, and Ears, The, 111

"Notes on a Triangle" (National Film Board of Canada), 251–52

Nursing the Americas, 108

October, 320

Oelschlager, Adam, 233

Office of Inter-American Affairs (OIAA), 108, 109–10

Oliver Twist, 157–58

Ono, Yoko, 320

orreries, 232

Ostherr, Kirsten, 9

Our Movie Made Children, 60, 215

Oxbow Incident, The, 72

Pagodas of Peiping, 70

panoramas, 236–37

Parkway Community Center, 277

Passing of Traditional Society, The (Lerner), 89

Passion of the Christ, The, 240

"Passport to the Universe" (Hayden Planetarium), 252, 253

pastoral exhibition, 208, 214–15, 225–26; 16mm film and, 217

pastoral relationships: audience and, 211–12; cultural authority in, 213; educational, 208, 212; modernization of, 207, 208, 213, 214, 218, 225–26; power, 11, 207, 212–13, 225; social control and, 212

Pathé, 127; RKO-Pathé, 273

Pathescope Company of America, 154

Patten, Simon N., 156

Payne Fund Studies, 8, 20, 21, 59–62, 74, 75, 215

Pearl Harbor, 134

Pennebaker, D. A., 319

People's Voice, 273

Perry, Everett, 165

Peterson, Mark, 88

Philadelphia Museum of Art, 201–2 n. 28, 251

Philosopher Reading a Lecture on the Orrery, The (Wright), 232, 233, 248

Piaget, Jean, 323

Pittsburgh Courier, 276–77

planetariums: audiences at, 238, 251; automation and, 251; Christmas shows at, 240; cinema and, 11, 231, 234, 236, 237, 238, 245–46, 249–54; Depression and, 243; as dramas of heavens, 239; experience of, 236–40; features of, 231; history of, 232–36; illusionism of, 250; intermedial, 11, 231, 252–53; in museums, 251; panoramas vs., 236–37; pinhole, 246; popular culture and, 236, 241–42; projectors at, 233–34, 235, 242–44, 246, 253, 254; social relevancy and, 246; space and, 237; as space ships,

242, 244; special effects at, 231, 252–54; spectatorship in, 11, 237, 242, 247–49, 250–51; spirituality of, 239–40; theater and science in, 238–39; theatricality of, 240–42; time and, 237, 240–41; videotape and, 250

Power's Projectors, 145 n. 11

practical films, 12, 290, 291

Pratt, George, 198 n. 3

Prelinger, Rick, 5

Press, Film, and Radio in the World Today (UNESCO), 92–93

Pride of Montreal (POM) bakery, 297

Production Code, 60

productivity: labor-management relations and, 37–38; mechanization and, 53; self-regulation and, 41

progressive education, 19–20; children and, 27–28; constructivist, 323; educational reform and, 61; experimental cinema and, 318; New Haven project and, 26; YMCA and, 211

Progressive Education Association, 65–66, 196

progressivism, 149–50, 154–55, 300

projectors: adaptability of, 4–5; advertising for, 138–45; in museums, 196; as nature's allies, 234; planetarium, 233–34, 235, 242–44, 246, 253, 254; portable, 127–32; in schools, 67, 70–71, 129–30, 132–33; 16mm, 125–26, 127, 129–32; Spitz, 246; 35mm, 127–29, 224; video, 253; Zeiss, 234, 242–44

propaganda: ACS medical films and, 110; films and, 103; health films and, 9; World War II, 81, 104, 110, 111, 115, 117, 118

public libraries: accessibility and, 155; architecture of, 151, 155; Carnegie, 153, 175 n. 17; cinema and, 174; educational film in, 156–57; film exhibitors and, 165–66, 168; film selection in, 159; growth in numbers of, 154; history of, 153; immigrants and, 164; leisure industry and, 155–56; media in, 9–10, 151–52, 165; modernization and, 154; motion pictures and, 10, 152–53, 157–74; movie theaters and, 153, 154, 156; perfor-

mance in, 157; progressivism and, 154–55; public film libraries and, 171–72; as public utility, 151, 152, 168; public values and, 153; reading and, 151; recreation vs., 165; reform movement and, 154–56; scholarship and, 151; social functions of, 149–50, 151; spectatorship and, 10

Public Libraries, 157, 158

Quigley, Martin, 115–16, 152

Rabinovitz, Lauren, 252

race movies, 264, 267, 268–70

racial uplift, 266; All-American News and, 11–12, 264, 267, 275, 276–78, 281, 284; civil rights movement and, 285; maintenance of appearances and, 274; philosophy of, 279–80

racism: All-American News and, 264, 282, 284; race movies and, 269; racial uplift vs., 279–80

Randall, John Herman, 289, 290, 291, 292, 310

Rathvon, N. Peter, 71, 73

RCA, 129, 132

reading: decline of, 170; educational media and, 21, 88–89; libraries and, 150; literacy and, 87–89; public libraries and, 151

Reconstruction of Cleft Lips, 109

Reddick Library (Ottawa, Ill.), 162

Reiser, Robert A., 323–24

religion: amateur filmmaking and, 291–92, 305–8; YMCA and, 210–11, 212, 214

Remedial Reading Comprehension, 324–25

Renaud, André, 93

Renshaw, Samuel, 61, 62

respectability, 266, 276–77, 278, 281, 285

Reverberation, 320

Rhem, I. R., 221

Riesman, David, 243, 250, 255 n. 13

Right People at the Right Time, The, 245

RKO-Pathé, 273

Robinson, Edward S., 188, 190

Rochemont, Louis de, 73

Rockefeller Foundation, 66, 71

Rogers, Dorothy, 277, 278

Romeo and Juliet, 24–26

"Room of Our Time, The" (Moholy-Nagy), 201 n. 25

Roosevelt, Franklin, 126, 271

Ross, Steven, 206

Rossi-Snook, Elena, 154–55, 168

Rotha, Paul, 94

Rubin, J. Robert, 71

Rubin, Sanford, 143

Sahara, 270

Sammond, Nicholas, 61; *Babes in Tomorrowland*, 60

Sansom, Elizabeth, 293

Sapir, Edward, 64

Scandiffio, Theresa, 180

Schatz, Thomas, 136

Schiller, Herbert, 92

schools: amateur educational films in, 293; catalogue of films for, 69–70; as exhibition sites, 208–9; film education in, 7; leisure and, 22; modernization of, 7; movie theaters and, 23, 26; progressivism and, 19; projectors in, 67, 70–71, 129–30, 132–33; public libraries and, 153, 154; "Secrets of Success" series and, 65

Schramm, Wilbur, 92; *Four Theories of the Press*, 87

Schumann Story, The, 72

Schwartz, Vanessa, 5–6

Science of Coercion (Simpson), 86–87

screening locations. *See* exhibition sites

screens: at Metropolitan Museum of Art, 181–82, 196; at museums, 196; windows and, 181–82

Seattle Public Library, 166–67

"Secrets of Success" series, 65, 66, 71

segregation: All-American News and, 264, 267–68, 272–73, 282, 285; of armed forces, 270–71; of cinema, 267; of movie theaters, 268; newsreels and, 12; race movies and, 267; during World War II, 267–68

Sellers, William, 93, 94

Selznick, David, 95–96

Sembene, Ousmane, 97

Serene Velocity, 320

Sherwood, J. E., 157

short films: ACL and, 309; educational films as, 104; for educational use, 68–72; on health, 103; Metropolitan Museum of Art and, 203 n. 41; military use of, 137; MPPDA and, 64, 68–70; in museums, 181, 193, 194, 197; public libraries and, 159, 166, 168; "Secrets of Success" series and, 65; YMCA and, 222

Shuttleworth, Frank, 63

silent films: African American filmmakers and, 268; amateur cinema and, 312 n. 21; industrial processes in, 294; non-theatrical cinema and, 224; sound vs., 218–19; YMCA and, 207, 208, 224

Silicon Graphics Onyx2 Infinite Reality2, 253

Simon, Bill, 320–21

Simplex projectors, 128, 166

Simpson, Christopher, 88; *Science of Coercion*, 86–87

Sitney, P. Adams, 321, 332 n. 3

16mm film: advent of, 125; amateur filmmaking and, 292; cost of shift to, 229 n. 59; dominance of, 9; educational films and, 36, 107, 125, 292; foreign and foreign-language films in, 135; globalization of, 135, 140–41; importance of, 6, 10–11; in libraries, 173; Metropolitan Museum of Art and, 179; mobility of, 226; network, 217, 225; non-theatrical cinema and, 126, 219–24; non-theatrical sites and, 126, 133; pastoral exhibition and, 216–17; projectors, 125–26, 127, 129–32; propaganda and, 117; screening locations and, 125, 132–35; 35mm vs., 36, 126, 127, 129, 217, 218, 219–22, 223–24; utopianism of, 9; videotape and, 117; World War II and, 115, 117, 134, 135–45, 226; YMCA and, 207, 217, 218, 219–24, 225

Skinner, B. F., 324; "Teaching Machines," 323

Sklar, Robert, 156

Slide, Anthony, 207

Smith, Alfred E., 284

Smoodin, Eric, 7, 75–76, 215

Snook, Vera, 162

Snow, Michael, 315–18, 320

Social Conduct and Attitudes of Movie Fans, The (May and Shuttleworth), 63

social control: libraries and, 150–51; pastoral relationships and, 212, 214–15

social problems, 291–92, 300–304

Society for the Promotion of Scientific Management, 35

Society for Visual Education, 310 n. 13

Something of Value, 72

Song of Love, 72

Son of the Gods, 20

Souls of Black Folk, The (Du Bois), 276

sound films, 218–19, 268, 312 n. 21

Soviet Union, 82, 85

space: Metropolitan Museum of Art films and, 10, 181, 183, 197; museums and, 194; planetariums and, 237; worker consciousness and, 43

space ships, 242, 244

space travel, 244–49

spectatorship: children and, 162–64; educational films and, 9; experimental films and, 317; modes of, 42; museums and, 181; orreries and, 232; of planetariums, 11, 237, 242, 247–49, 250–51; public libraries and, 10; work ethic and, 42. *See also* audiences

Speed Killers, 34, 40, 51–52

Spigel, Lynn, 246, 247

Spirit of Youth and the City Streets, The (Addams), 20

Spitz, Armand N., 240, 246–47

Spurr, Norman, 93, 94

Stamp, Shelley, 39, 40, 42, 48

Stanek, Damon, 252

Staniszewski, Mary Anne, 185

StarRider Theater, 254

State Department: ACS and, 108, 109; intelligence reports, 87; Lerner's study and, 89; *Motion Pictures Available and Suitable for Use Abroad*, 95; UNESCO and, 83

State University of New York, 12–13

Steichen, Edward, 295–96

Stein, Gertrude, 320

Steiner, Ralph, 306

Steiner, Rudolph, 323

Stockley, James, 243, 256 n. 23

Story of a Country Doctor, The, 18

Straubel, Werner, 234

Streible, Dan, 5

structural films, 315, 319–21

student filmmaking, 319

Studies in the Nature of Character (May), 62–63

Surles, A. D., 272

Tale of Two Cities, A, 17

talkies, 218–19, 268, 312 n. 21

Taylorism, 43

Taylor Society, 35

teaching, films and, 35–36, 65. *See also* educational films

Teaching Film Custodians (TFC), 8, 69–76

"Teaching Machines" (Skinner), 323

Telegraph World, 38, 39, 40, 42, 44–48, 51, 53

telegraphy, 37, 42–44. *See also* Western Union

television: All-American News and, 265; health information and, 118; TFC and, 74; in UNESCO's survey of national media, 86

Tepperman, Charles, 12

Textbook of Healthful Living (Diehl), 111–12

TFC Story, The, 74

Thackeray, William, 158

"Theatre in a Suitcase," 129, 132

Third Cinema, 83–84, 96–97

Third World Filmmaking and the West (Armes), 90

35mm film: ACS and, 107; educational films and, 107; Metropolitan Museum of Art and, 179, 180; pastoral exhibition and, 216; projectors, 127–29, 224; 16mm vs., 36, 126, 127, 129, 217, 218, 219–22, 223–24

Thompson, E. P., 50

Thorndike, E. L., 62

Thorp, Margaret Farrand, 166

Thrasher, Frederic M., 18, 59

Three Little Pigs, The, 30

Thurstone, L. L., 21

time: Metropolitan Museum of Art films and, 10, 181, 183, 197; museums and, 194; planetariums and, 237, 240–41; travel, 244–45; Western Union and, 50–52; women workers and, 50–51; worker consciousness and, 43

Tolischus, O. D., 249

Tom, Tom the Piper's Son, 318, 325–328

Traffic in Souls, 300

training films: ACS and, 116; communication skills and, 55 n. 4; corporate use of, 35; digital video and, 117–18; disciplining of audience and, 43; exteriorization and, 40–41; fictional films vs., 40; origins of, 55 n. 4; point-of-view shots in, 40–41; as proxy managers and supervisors, 35; self-regulation and, 54; site-specific, 36; Western Union and, 7–8, 34–35, 36–37, 39–42, 53–54; women and, 48–49; work supervisors in, 41–42. *See also* educational films

Transfusion of Unmodified Blood, 109

28mm film, 127, 173

2001: A Space Odyssey, 245

underdeveloped regions, 83

UNESCO (United Nations Educational, Scientific and Cultural Organization), 8–9; Britain and, 83; cold war and, 86–87; colonialism, decolonization, and, 97; Commission Permanente Interafricaine du cinéma and, 97; conferences and workshops of, 93–94; developed vs. underdeveloped worlds and, 83, 99; educational film and, 83, 94; ethnographic films and, 93; film activities of, 96; *Films on Art*, 93, 95; Film Sub-Commission, 89–90, 95; free flow of information and, 8, 82, 87, 92; Hollywood films and, 83; illiteracy and, 82; indigenous media and, 84; League of Nations Intellectual Cooperation Committee and, 83; mass communication division, 83; *Mass Communication* series, 93; *Mass Media and National Development*, 87; mediated international communication and, 81; modernization and, 8, 82, 90, 99; national cinemas and, 84–85; national media and, 85–87; *New World Information and Communication Order*, 84; objectives of, 82; peace and, 81–82; policies of, 83–84; *Press, Film, and Radio in the World Today*, 92–93; U.S. and, 8, 82, 83–84, 87, 88, 97; visual media and, 82, 89; the West and, 82–83; *World Communications: Press, Radio, Film*, 85–86, 92; *World without End* and, 94

unionization: in telegraphy, 55 n. 13; Western Union and, 37–38; women workers and, 47

United Nations (UN): American and Western bias of, 82; Office for Out of Space Affairs, 238; Security Council, 82–83

United States: Department of Audio-Visual Instruction (DAVI), 74–75; Department of Defense, 270; health care in, 118; Office of War Information (OWI), 110, 137, 270, 272; Treasury Department, 137; UNESCO and, 8, 83–84, 87, 88, 97; War Department, 272. *See also* State Department

United World Films, 73

Universal Pictures Corporation, 219

Universal projector, 129

Urban, Charles, 292

Van Halen Productions, 138

Vanity Fair (Thackeray), 158

Variety, 271

Vasantasena, 203 n. 39

Verne, Jules, 244

Victor: AC-25, 223; Animatograph, 125–26, 129; Animatophone, 135, 138, 143, 144; projectors, 129, 132, 134–35, 138, 140, 141–42, 144

Victor, Alexander F., 141

Visit to Peak Frean and Co.'s Biscuit Works, A, 296, 298

Visit to the Armor Galleries of the Metropolitan Museum of Art, 193–94

Visual Education, 35, 127

Visual Education Institute, 35

Visual Instruction (McClusky), 36

Visual Instruction in the Public Schools (Dorris), 146 n. 15

Visual Review, 138

Volkmar, Leon, 293–94, 295

Vonderau, Patrick, 3

Voyage dans la lune, 244

Vygotsky, Lev, 323

Wagner, Walter, 269

Waldman, Diane, 37, 206

Waller, Gregory, 9, 115

War Activities Committee, 137

Wasson, Haidee, 10, 125, 132, 209–10, 216–17

Water—Friend or Enemy, 109

Watson, J. S., 299–300

Watson, Ted, 265

Wavelength, 315–18, 319, 320, 321

Way, E. I., 220

Webber, Melville, 299–300

Weigel, Erhard, 233

Weil, Marion, 157

Western Electric projector, 129

Western Union, 7–8; labor-management relations at, 37–38; speed of work and, 51; telegraph technology and, 37, 42–43; time and, 50–52; training films at, 34–35, 36–37, 39–42, 48–49, 53–54; unionization and, 37–38; on women as moviegoers, 39; women employees of, 7–8, 37, 38, 39, 43–44, 46–47

Western Union News, 37–38

"What Are You Going to Do about Sound?" (Whitmore), 218–19

What Is Cinema? (Bazin), 320

What's Wrong with This Picture 1 and 2, 325

Wheeler, Edward, 285

White, Walter, 269, 270

white people: African Americans in World War II and, 273; All-American News and, 264, 265, 280; racial uplift and, 277–78

Whitmore, Will, 218–19

Whitney Museum, 202 n. 32

Why We Fight, 121 n. 33

Wilkins, Roy, 272–73

Willemen, Paul, 97

William H. Dudley Visual Education Service, 132

Williamson, Melvin, 283

Willys-Overland Motor Company, 35

Wilson, Charles, 264, 279

Wilson, Howard, 70

Winged Scourge, The, 108

Winston, Brian, 207, 216, 220, 223–24

Winter, Thomas, 211–12

Winton, Roy, 293, 294–95, 310 n. 10

Wisconsin Library Bulletin, 157, 158–59

With These Weapons, 108

women: domestic and workplace behavior of, 49–50; films and, 39; home and, 47–48; in movie-going audience, 38–39; private vs. public sphere and, 47–48

women workers: advantages of, 38; in comic strips, 46–47; home and, 43, 47–49, 54; male resentment of, 47; as separate category of worker, 44, 54; space-time and, 43; supervisors of, 41–42; in *Telegraph World*, 44–48; time and, 50–51; training films and, 39–40; Western Union and, 7–8, 37, 38, 43–44, 46–47

"Work of Art in the Age of Mechanical Reproduction, The" (Benjamin), 55–56 n. 14

workers: mechanical technology and, 52–53; regulated behavior of, 35

Workers' Film and Photo League, 291, 304

World Communications: Press, Radio, Film (UNESCO), 85–86, 92

World War II: ACS medical films and, 107–8, 110; African Americans and, 263, 265, 266, 269–73, 274, 280–82; amateur cinema and, 291, 309; educational cinema and, 111, 115, 323; Hollywood and, 269; integration and, 269–70; mass media and, 81; motion pictures and, 107, 135, 136–37; propaganda, 81, 104, 110, 111, 115, 117, 118; segregation dur-

World War II (*continued*)
ing, 267–68; 16mm film and, 115, 117, 134, 135–45, 226
World without End, 94
Wright, Basil, 94
Wright, Joseph, 232, *233*, 248
Wythe, F. S., 209

X Messages, 34, 40, 52

Yale University, Institute of Human Relations, 63–64, 199 n. 3
Yale University Press, 199 n. 3
YMCA (Young Men's Christian Association): Americanism and, 205; changing concerns of, 210–11; Christian Citizenship Program, 215; film education and, 215–16; ideology of films program, 206–7; Industrial Department, 205, 207, 211–12, 215; industrial welfare programs, 206; International Committee, 69, 205, 207; international dimensions of, 226 n. 2; National Council, 223; as non-theatrical distributor and exhibitor, 206–7, 209–10; pastoral exhibition and, 214–15; Payne Fund Studies and, 215;

progressive education and, 211; religious education and, 210–11, 214; youth discussion of films and, 215–16
YMCA Motion Picture Bureau, 11; educational film and, 210; establishment of, 206; Hollywood and, 219; moral alliance of cultural authorities and, 216; non-theatrical cinema and, 207, 209, 213–15; pastoral exhibition and, 208; pastoral relationships and, 213–15; purposes of, 206; 16mm film and, 207, 217, 218, 219–24, 225
Young, Buddy, 282, *283*

Zanuck, Darryl F., 269
Zehrung, George J., 209, 210, 212, 223
Zeiss: planetarium in Jena, 233–34, 235, 236, 250; projectors, 234, 235–36, 242–42, 252, 253, 254; World War II and, 246
Zeiss, Carl, 234
Zenith Portable Motion Picture Projector, 127
Zorns Lemma, 318, 321, 325, 328–31
Zukor, Adolphe, 29–30
Zyrd, Michael, 12–13

CHARLES R. ACLAND is a professor and Concordia University Research Chair in Communication Studies. He is the author of *Youth, Murder, Spectacle: The Cultural Politics of "Youth in Crisis"* (1995) and *Screen Traffic: Movies, Multiplexes, and Global Culture* (2003); the editor of *Residual Media* (2007) and the editor, with William J. Buxton, of *Harold Innis in the New Century: Reflections, Refractions* (1999).

HAIDEE WASSON is an associate professor of cinema studies at Concordia University. She is the author of *Museum Movies: The Museum of Modern Art and the Birth of Art Cinema* (2005) and the editor, with Lee Grieveson, of *Inventing Film Studies* (2008).

Library of Congress Cataloging-in-Publication Data

Useful cinema / edited by Charles R. Acland and Haidee Wasson.
p. cm.
Includes bibliographical references and index.
ISBN 978-0-8223-4997-6 (cloth : alk. paper) — ISBN 978-0-8223-5009-5 (pbk. : alk. paper)
1. Nonfiction films — United States — History and criticism.
2. Documentary films — United States — History and criticism.
I. Acland, Charles R., 1963–
II. Wasson, Haidee, 1970–
PN1995.9.D6U84 2011
070.1′8 — dc22   2011010726